Selling For Dummies®

D0544013

Meeting Prospects for the First Time

When you meet prospective clients – or anyone, for that matter – for the first time, your goal is for them to like and trust you. You can help to accomplish that by completing the following steps, in this order:

1. **Smile sincerely; make your smile real and full.**
2. **Make eye contact.**
3. **Offer a greeting.**
4. **Shake hands.**
5. **Offer your name and get the prospect's name.**

Remember: First impressions last. Long term relationships begin in the first ten seconds.

Qualifying Your Prospective Clients

When you first meet with prospective clients, you need to qualify them, to see whether your product or service meets your client's needs. To help you remember to focus on your client's needs, remember this simple list of five questions:

- What have they got now?
- Why do they have it?
- Why would they change?
- Who would change it?
- What does the solution look like?

Handling Objections from Your Prospects

An important step in the selling cycle is listening to and responding to your prospect's concerns and objections. Here are the steps to take:

1. **Hear the prospect out.**

   Don't be quick to address every phrase your prospect utters. Give him time; encourage him to tell you the whole story behind his concern. If you don't get the whole story, you won't know what to do or say to change his mind.

2. **Feed the objection back.**

   By rephrasing what your prospect's concerns are, you're in effect asking for even more information. You want to be sure that he's aired it all so that no other concerns crop up after you've handled this one.

3. **Question the objection.**

   This step is where subtlety and tact come into play. Be sure to find out what feeling is behind that objection and reassure your prospect that your product or service is right for him.

4. **Answer the objection.**

   When you're confident that you have the whole story behind his concern, you can answer that concern with confidence.

5. **Confirm the answer.**

   You can confirm your answers simply by completing your answer with a statement such as, 'So, does that answer your concerns, James?' If you don't complete this step, the prospect is likely to raise that objection again.

6. **Change gears with 'By the way . . .'**

   By the way are three of the most useful words in any attempt to persuade or convince another person. Use these words to change gears – to move on to the next topic. Don't just keep talking. Take a conscious, purposeful step back into your presentation.

For Dummies: Bestselling Book Series for Beginners

Selling For Dummies®

Getting Referrals

The last step in the selling cycle is to get referrals from your prospective clients – whether they ended up closing the sale with you or not. Here's how to do it:

1. **Time the request – your prospect must be 'sold'.** The prospect must be sold on the concept at least of ownership and be in tune with you and the benefits you offer.
2. **Prepare the client with 'in the zone' thinking.** Set the scene correctly – the prospect needs to be 'in the zone'. A person needs to *feel* the benefits so that she's ready to refer.
3. **Ask 'Who else do you care about who may benefit from what I have to offer?'** Avoid asking 'Who do you know?'. Ask in the correct way.
4. **Look directly at the source of the referral supply.** Yes, it's okay here to stare pointedly at their computer!
5. **Make it personal and get your prospect's permission.** Find out some background about the referrals and get permission to use the current prospect's name. Just a little helps so that you don't go in blind.

Words to Avoid

Here are words to replace in your selling vocabulary. The word on the left has negative connotations for most people, so replace it with the word on the right, which has positive connotations.

Instead of . . .	Use
Commission	Fee for service
Cost or price	Total amount or investment
Monthly payment	Monthly investment
Contract	Agreement or paperwork
Buy	Own
Sell	Help them acquire or get them involved
Sign	Okay, endorse, approve, or authorise

For Dummies: Bestselling Book Series for Beginners

Selling
FOR
DUMMIES®

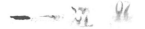

by Tom Hopkins and Ben Kench

John Wiley & Sons, Ltd

Selling For Dummies®

Published by
John Wiley & Sons, Ltd
The Atrium
Southern Gate
Chichester
West Sussex
PO19 8SQ
England

E-mail (for orders and customer service enquires): cs-books@wiley.co.uk

Visit our Home Page on www.wiley.com

Copyright © 2007 John Wiley & Sons, Ltd, Chichester, West Sussex, England

Published by John Wiley & Sons, Ltd, Chichester, West Sussex

Wiley also publishes its books in a variety of electronic formats. Some content that appears in print may not be available in electronic books.

British Library Cataloguing in Publication Data: A catalogue record for this book is available from the British Library.

ISBN: 978-0-470-51259-3

Printed and bound in Great Britain by Bell and Bain Ltd, Glasgow

10 9 8 7 6 5 4 3 2 1

WILEY

About the Authors

Tom Hopkins is the epitome of sales success. A millionaire by the time he reached the age of 27, Hopkins now is Chairman of Tom Hopkins International, one of the largest sales-training organisations in the world.

Thirty years ago, Tom Hopkins considered himself a failure. He had dropped out of college after 90 days, and for the next 18 months he carried steel on construction sites to make a living. Believing that there had to be a better way to earn a living, he went into sales – and ran into the worst period of his life. For six months, Tom earned an average of $42 a month and slid deeper into debt and despair. Pulling together his last few dollars, he invested in a five-day sales training seminar that turned his life around. In the next six months, Tom sold more than $1 million worth of $25,000 homes. At age 21, he won the Los Angeles Sales and Marketing Institute's coveted SAMMY Award and began setting records in sales performance that still stand today.

Because of his unique ability to share his enthusiasm for the profession of selling and the successful selling techniques he developed, Tom began giving seminars in 1974. Training as many as 10,000 salespeople a month, he quickly became known as the world's leading sales trainer. Today, he presents approximately 75 seminars a year to over 100,000 people throughout the world.

Tom was a pioneer in producing high-quality audio and video programmes for those who could not attend the seminars or who wanted further reinforcement after the seminars. Recognised as the most effective sales-training programmes ever produced, they're continually updated and are now being utilised by more than 1 million people.

Tom Hopkins has also written nine other books, including *Sales Prospecting For Dummies* and *Sales Closing For Dummies*, as well as the best-selling *How to Master the Art of Selling*, which has sold over 1.3 million copies in 8 languages and 27 countries.

Tom Hopkins is a member of the National Speakers Association and one of a select few to receive its Council of Peers Award for Excellence. He is often the keynote speaker for annual conventions and is a frequent guest on television and radio talk shows.

Ben Kench, 'The Can Can Man', is Britain's leading small business growth specialist, enjoying a reputation for delivering quite incredible results.

Ben's pedigree and character have been formed over a lifetime of adventure and achievements that culminate in a rich spectrum of knowledge that's life-based with family values and an underpinning of integrity and honesty.

His selling career began with an early foray into double glazing sales as an impressionable 19-year-old, and while his initial success was nationally recognised he also learned hard lessons about life, success, and attitude, eventually falling out with family and loved ones as arrogance overcame the youth. A few months taught lifelong lessons.

Moving on and learning, Ben's first major role in selling was to industry selling air compressors and related tools. Aged 20, he learned to face the 'we've been doing it this way for longer than you've been alive, lad' rejection.

Over the years Ben has enjoyed success in roles selling higher value equipment to corporate clients, selling to the small business market, and selling to the home owner. He's experienced in selling in the consumer marketplace in industries as diverse as unregulated timesharing to heavily regulated financial services. Each have presented their particular challenges and each has added their own unique refinement to the art of selling.

Ben also raised his daughter from the age of 20 months as a single parent and knows well the struggle to balance work and family while also appreciating the real value and meaning of family life. Ben is first and foremost a family man, with old-fashioned values, where truth and integrity are non-negotiable and where business relationships become friendships that last. Those sentiments echo throughout the advice in this book to help you succeed in your selling career.

Ben's programme, 'The Business Booster', is gaining national recognition and his company is often approached by major institutions to assist with their performance objectives. He's approved as a member of The National Consultants Register and is often asked to speak at conventions for The Institute of Sales and Marketing Management (ISMM), and The Federation of Small Businesses (FSB), as well as major business to business exhibitions nationally.

Ben has also written a book on small business growth entitled *How to Grow Your Business and Enjoy More Money, Less Stress!*

Today, Ben's time is spent dedicated to helping individuals improve their performance through a variety of sales and business education programmes.

Dedications

From Tom: This book is dedicated to all my teachers and my students. Some of you have been both to me. Thank you for your loyalty and for sharing your successes with me. You are the reason why my life has been so filled with love, laughter, and abundance.

From Ben: This book is dedicated to the thousands of people who have helped me along my path. Literally every step is remembered with fondness. Lessons learned from teachers mingle with lessons learned from life and the many situations I've been presented with. This book is dedicated to each and every person or situation along the way.

Above all, this book is dedicated to my great friend and sales leader Dave Brazier. Dave you showed me (when I wasn't best disposed to learn!) much of the foundation basics relayed in this book. You showed me the huge value in discipline, order, and record-keeping to become a professional. You showed me the adaptation from direct to consumer sales into selling business to business and all of the variations that entailed. You showed me how to handle prejudice and overcome stacked odds as a young man in an old industry. In short you were a cornerstone and as vital on my journey as snow is to skiing. This then Dave is my way to say Thank You. You probably don't know or dare think about how much you have influenced me but for the record I still bear the scars from those first lessons you taught me!

Authors' Acknowledgements

From Tom: I must acknowledge my wonderful wife, Debbie, who has brought so much joy into my life. I'm grateful for your patience and understanding when my life's work takes me away. I'm also grateful for your valuable input into my teaching, and particularly in this book.

I thank Judy Slack of Tom Hopkins International for writing and managing all my material for so long. I also thank Laura Oien, my company President, and Spence Price, CFO. You all work hard to make my life easy, allowing me to do what I do best – teach.

From Ben: As with any undertaking in life, the singular effort rarely if ever returns the result. Indeed, in my case I recognise the enormous support of many 'background' people.

First and foremost among them must be my wife Stella. You are always there to guide, to share, and to lend a valid thought – nothing I ever do is done alone. Through times of 'word drought' and 'thinking block' you've been the sounding wall and brain agitator while kindly and lovingly also allowing me to work when you'd rather I didn't! To Stella, then, my gratitude and love. Thank you for everything.

To my loyal and long-suffering secretary Alison, who at times has shown remarkable mind-reading skills and is always remembering when I forget! I might ask 'where would I be without you?' but I daren't even contemplate the answer! Thank you.

To manager Marion Cohrs and the truly helpful team at Las Dunas Suites Hotel in Gran Canaria who so kindly allowed me to use their facilities while a holiday doubled as working time even though I'd left my laptop behind! To a superb resort and excellent team of people, I thank you.

To the thousands of people who inspire me when I'm blessed with an audience to share my thoughts with, and to the hundreds of students each year who share their thoughts, their struggles, and their successes with me when they allow me to help them in their business tasks. I am eternally grateful as this task is why God made me. For allowing me to do my life's work, I thank you all.

Publisher's Acknowledgements

We're proud of this book; please send us your comments through our Dummies online registration form located at www.dummies.com/register/.

Some of the people who helped bring this book to market include the following:

Acquisitions, Editorial, and Media Development

Project Editor: Rachael Chilvers

Development Editor: Kathleen Dobie

Content Editor: Steve Edwards

Commissioning Editor: Samantha Clapp

Copy Editor: Kate O'Leary

Proofreader: David Price

Technical Editor: Dr Graham Beaver, Professor of Strategic Management

Executive Editor: Jason Dunne

Executive Project Editor: Martin Tribe

Cover Photo: © Design Pics Inc. / Alamy

Cartoons: Ed McLachlan

Special Help: Jan Sims

Composition Services

Project Coordinator: Jennifer Theriot

Layout and Graphics: Carl Byers, Laura Pence, Alicia B. South, Christine Williams

Proofreaders: Laura Albert, Susan Moritz

Indexer: Cheryl Duksta

Publishing and Editorial for Consumer Dummies

Diane Graves Steele, Vice President and Publisher, Consumer Dummies

Joyce Pepple, Acquisitions Director, Consumer Dummies

Kristin A. Cocks, Product Development Director, Consumer Dummies

Michael Spring, Vice President and Publisher, Travel

Kelly Regan, Editorial Director, Travel

Publishing for Technology Dummies

Andy Cummings, Vice President and Publisher, Dummies Technology/General User

Composition Services

Gerry Fahey, Vice President of Production Services

Debbie Stailey, Director of Composition Services

Contents at a Glance

Table of Contents

Introduction

Welcome to *Selling For Dummies*. In this book, we cover more than selling products and services to businesses and consumers. This book is really about people skills. After all, knowing how to get along well with others is a vital skill – one everyone needs to develop as early as possible in life. Indeed for many years Ben has shared a presentation with his audiences called 'Life's a Pitch . . . and then you Fly', effectively highlighting that everything in life is a sales transaction between two persons. Life is in fact a sales game, and better if you can get people to see things your way. So this book really is for everyone.

However, to play this game well, to be successful in sales, you must also be co-operative, have good listening skills, and be willing to put others' needs before your own. With refined selling skills in your arsenal, you'll have more happiness and contentment in *all* areas of your life, not just in your selling career (although your selling will certainly benefit, too).

About This Book

Selling For Dummies can help you get more happiness and contentment out of your life right now by helping you gain more respect, more money, more recognition for the job you do, more agreement from your friends and family, more control in negotiations, and of course, more sales. Above all, this book is a reference tool – so you don't have to read it from beginning to end. Instead, you can turn to the part of the book that gives you the information you need when you need it. And you can keep coming back to the book over and over again throughout your selling career.

As the original dummies in sales, we're the perfect people to write this book.

Ben's story: I started my selling career in double glazing! For many, this product epitomised the lower end of the selling spectrum. However, it served as a brilliant baptism into the real world of selling and living by your efforts on a commission-only basis. I started out living alone in lodgings and learning fast how to help people see it my way. I remember having a massive need – I literally needed to buy myself something to wear. I owned no suit or suitable footwear for the winter. I got cold because I didn't own a coat and I had a battered Hillman Avenger with no heater. But my need fired me up to get better at this game and fast. So I did. I learned quickly, and climbed my way up the career ladder. Amazingly I soon discovered that, in fact, selling isn't that difficult!

Tom's story: I started my selling career in real estate at age 19. Real estate may have been a great career choice, but at the time I owned neither a suit nor a car. All I had was a band uniform and a motorcycle. And believe me, selling real estate on a motorcycle wasn't easy; I had to tell the prospective buyers to follow me to the properties and hope they didn't get lost along the way. When they finally came to their senses and realised that this kid couldn't possibly be for real, they'd keep going straight on when I'd make a turn. I only averaged $42 a month in my first six months selling real estate.

But I stuck it out, because I knew there was big money to be made in the selling business – if I could just find out what the successful people were doing that I wasn't. I learned it all the hard way, through trial and error.

Needless to say, I've come a long way since then, and it thrills me no end to give you the chance to benefit from the mistakes I made, as well as from the subsequent success I've had. Yes, I've had successes. I achieved my goal of becoming a millionaire by the age of 30, beating my own deadline by nearly three years! At age 27, I was one of the most successful real estate agents in the whole country – a guy who started without a decent suit or a vehicle with four wheels! That just goes to show you that it doesn't matter how much of a dummy you are on this subject when you start – with this book by your side, serving as a reference for all the selling situations you encounter, you'll master the selling, persuasion, and people skills you need to really shine.

Indeed selling isn't a skill that you cannot handle. You too can sell and you'll soon be flying and owning whatever you want.

Conventions Used in This Book

This book is a jargon-free zone. When we introduce a new term, we *italicise* it and then define it. The only other conventions in this book are that Web and email addresses are in `monofont`, and the action part of numbered steps and the key concept in a list are in **bold**. We alternate between using female and male pronouns in even- and odd-numbered chapters to be fair to both!

Foolish Assumptions

We wrote *Selling For Dummies* not only for traditional salespeople who want to discover more about their careers, but also for people who can use selling skills to change or improve their lives. This book is for you

- Whether you're beginning a selling career, or you're just looking to brush up your skills.
- Whether you're unemployed and want a job, or you're employed and want a promotion.
- Whether you're a teen wanting to impress adults, or you're an adult wanting to succeed at negotiation.
- Whether you're a teacher searching for better ways to get through to your students, or you're a parent wanting to communicate more effectively with your children.
- Whether you have an idea that can help others, or you want to improve your personal relationships.

In other words, this book is for *everyone*. People who have listened in our presentations or have been through one of our programmes tell us about how they used a strategy or selling technique outside of business to get agreement from family members on an important decision. They've told us about using a questioning technique to get their spouses or children to agree to do something they previously tried to put off, and some have used the skills to sell themselves into better jobs. Other students have been able to ask for, and to receive, better service simply because their confidence has skyrocketed. As an added bonus, when our students apply the skills and strategies to personal relationships, many find that those relationships became more rewarding too.

How This Book Is Organised

In this book, we lay out the basics of any selling situation in a series of steps. We give an overview of those steps in Chapter 2, and devote Part III of the book to covering them in greater detail. You can go through these steps in sequence or you can skim the Table of Contents and locate a title or heading that strikes you as interesting. Read that section first. Then go on to another area that you think will benefit you the most. Keep a pen or highlighter in hand and make notes if you want. Dog-ear the pages. In fact, use this book in whichever way serves you best. As you get into the material, you'll read about real-life examples of people in various situations where they needed people skills in order to succeed. We tell you the good stories and the bad ones – and you'll remember them when you get into similar situations.

The methods, words, and phrases contained in this book are not put on paper in *Selling For Dummies* just because they sound good to the editors. They've been proven successful by millions of people around the world. If you're truly going to benefit by persuading, cajoling, convincing, or selling someone else on what you have to offer, don't try to re-invent the wheel and do it the hard way. Why not pull out all the stops and master the strategies and tactics that have been proven to work for others (the ones you'll find in this book)?

Selling For Dummies is organised into six parts, and the parts are divided into chapters. In the following sections, we give you a quick preview of what to expect from each part, so you can turn to the part that interests you most.

Part 1: The Art of Selling

In this part, you find out a little about what selling is and what it isn't. We fill you in on what selling skills can do for you in all areas of your life, and give you a quick tour through the seven steps of the selling cycle. We also let you know how important attitude is to the art of selling – showing you how to treat selling like a hobby, and get all the satisfaction and success out of it that you get out of the things you do for fun.

Part 11: Preparation 1s the Key

Just as with virtually any pursuit in life, preparation is the key to success in the world of selling. In this part, we cover the steps to preparation – everything from knowing your clients to knowing your products – that will set you apart from average salespeople and help you hear 'Yes' more often in your life. We also devote a chapter to using technology to your advantage in the preparation stage of the game, steering you to some great resources on the Internet that can make your selling life more successful.

Part 111: The Anatomy of a Sale

In this part, we give each of the seven steps of the selling cycle its very own chapter. We pack in lots of useful information – including ideas or scripts of the right words to say and tips on which words to avoid in each stage of the process. You'll discover how to find the people you can sell to, how to get an appointment with those people and make a good impression, how to make sure they need what you have, how to give fantastic presentations, how to address customer concerns, how to close the sale, and how to get referrals – so you can start the process all over again.

Part IV: Growing Your Business

If your goal is to build a long-term business or to take your career to great heights, this part is for you. Here, you begin to separate yourself from merely average salespeople to become one of the greats. Average salespeople make their presentations, win a few, lose a few, and move on. But the great ones view every presentation as an opportunity to build. So in this part we give you tips for staying in touch with your clients, making more sales with the help of the Internet, and managing your time wisely so that as your business grows you always have time for your clients. Great salespeople build not only businesses but also *relationships*, because relationships take them further and bring them a lot more satisfaction in the long run.

Part V: You Can't Win Them All

Rejection is a part of life. So you need to expect it, accept it, and get over it. The fact that a prospect rejects your product or service doesn't mean that he has rejected you as a person. But when you're in the world of selling, where rejection is just part of the territory, your self-esteem can easily suffer. So in this part we help you imitate a duck by letting things run off your back like water. We also help you understand how best to use your time and stay focused on the big-picture goals, so the little negativities of life won't bring you down.

Part VI: The Part of Tens

These short chapters are packed with quick ideas about selling and persuading that you can read anytime you have a few minutes. They're a great way of psyching yourself up for a presentation or for making calls. They're good for getting you excited – and no one will ever want what you have if you're not excited about it.

Icons Used in This Book

Icons are those little pictures you see in the margins throughout this book, and they're meant to draw your attention to key points that are of help to you along the way. Here's a list of the icons we use and what they signify:

When you see this icon, stories from our years of experience in selling and from our students' experiences are near by. And, oh, what stories we have to share.

This icon highlights phrases to say to go beyond the basics and become a true champion at selling. When you see this icon, you'll find examples of exchanges between you and your prospective client, so you can see exactly how a conversation can develop if you know just what to say.

Prospecting for clients is a lot like prospecting for gold, because clients are what selling is all about. This shovel and map highlight tips for finding the prospects who will make your selling business a success.

Some things are so important that they bear repeating. So this icon – like a string tied around your finger – is a friendly reminder of information you'll want to commit to memory and use over the long haul.

This icon highlights things you want to avoid and common mistakes sales-people make. An important part of achieving success is simply eliminating the mistakes. And the information marked by this icon helps you do just that.

Where to Go from Here

Glance through the Table of Contents and find the part, chapter, or section that flips your switch. That's the best place to begin.

To benefit most from the material in this book, do a little self-analysis to see where you're weakest. Admitting your faults is tough, even to yourself. But reading the material that covers your weaker areas will bring you the greatest amount of success.

For example, studies show that most traditional salespeople lack qualification skills. This means that they waste a lot of time presenting to people who can't truly make decisions on what they're selling or people who aren't likely to purchase the item because it just isn't a match for them. If you're in traditional sales and you aren't sure whether qualification is your weakness, Chapter 9 may be a great place to start.

The most successful people in life are those who continue to grow. The fact that you're reading these words now puts you into that realm – because what counts is not how much you know, but how much you can discover *after* you 'know it all'.

Congratulations for believing in yourself, in your ability to change for the better, in your ability to improve your lifestyle, *and* in your ability to improve the lives of the people you help with this book's many tips on the art of selling. We wish you greatness!

Part I
The Art of Selling

'We're looking for a salesperson who can get his foot in the door – Are you that person, Mr Snartley?'

In this part . . .

Here you find out what the seven steps of selling are and how to put them to work for you. We also fill you in on the importance of attitude in the world of selling – letting you know how you can treat selling with the same joy that you treat your hobbies and pastimes. Whether you're just starting out in sales or you've been at it since the beginning of time, this part offers great information to keep you upbeat and moving forward.

Chapter 1

You Don't Need a Uniform or a Fancy Suit

Selling is everywhere around you, and nearly everybody (even those who aren't in a professional sales role) do it every day, in one form or another. In fact, selling affects every waking moment of your day. So in this chapter, we let you know what exactly this thing called *selling* is, how it's done, and how you can use selling skills to make your life and your career better.

What Selling Is

According to one dictionary definition, *selling* is the 'exchange of goods or services for money' or 'to persuade into accepting an idea'. Selling is the process of reaching an agreement to move goods and services from the hands of those who produce them into the hands of those who will benefit from them. Selling involves persuasive skills on the part of the person doing the talking. The talking's supported by print, audio, and video messages that sell either the particular item or the brand name as being something the customer would want to have.

Nothing ever happens unless someone sells something to someone else. Without selling, manufactured products would sit in warehouses for eternity, people working for those manufacturers would become unemployed, transportation and shipping services wouldn't be needed, and everyone would be

The selling triangle

Whenever we're giving seminars to help people master the fundamentals of selling, we use a triangle with equal sides, like the one here, to illustrate the three main elements of selling. On one side is product knowledge, covered in Chapter 5. On the other side are selling tactics and strategies, covered in Part III, and on the base of the triangle are attitude, enthusiasm, and goals, covered in Part V.

The three sides of the selling triangle are equally important. If product knowledge were all that mattered, then technical designers, manufacturers, or assemblers of products would make the best salespeople – but they don't. Of course, these people often know the product quite literally from the inside out, but until they're trained in selling skills and understand how much of a role attitude plays in sales, their approach is often 99 per cent description of product and 1 per cent relation of the product to the needs of the individual clients – and that doesn't usually result in a sale.

Likewise, great selling skills without product knowledge and enthusiasm won't get you far either. Even if you're comfortable talking with practically anyone, and you've invested a tremendous amount of time mastering language skills in order to create pictures in the minds of your prospects, if you don't have a clear picture in your *own* mind of what your product, service, or idea can do for your customers, how can you paint the right pictures?

Or if your attitude and enthusiasm towards selling is high, but you have little knowledge or experience of selling tactics and strategies, your enthusiasm can open the doors but your lack of knowledge or specific sales skills may amount to no real results.

Remember: A professional who fails to develop any one side of the triangle is failing to reach his full potential and letting down clients who expect to work with a competent person. Do your best to develop all three areas of your selling life, and you'll reap the rewards.

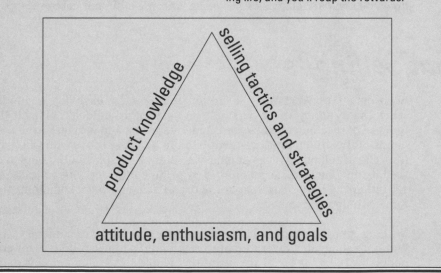

living a simple life, trying to sustain a living from whatever bit of land they owned. Or would they even own the land if no one were there to sell it to them? Think about this scenario.

Look around you right now. You can probably spot hundreds, if not thousands, of things that were sold in order to get where they are right now. Even if you're totally naked, sitting in the woods, you had to be involved in some sort of selling process to have this book with you. If you choose to ignore material possessions, take stock of yourself internally. What do you believe? Why do you believe what you do? Did someone, for example your parents or your peers, sell you a set of values as you were growing up? Odds are, whether you're living in a material world or you've forsaken nearly all possessions, you've been involved in selling, one way or another.

The preceding paragraph should persuade you to at least look at selling a bit differently from how you have in the past. And we did it without pushing facts and figures on you. Good selling isn't pushing; the process involves gently pulling with questions and getting people to revise their opinions.

How Selling Is Done

Although the definition of selling may be fairly straightforward, the approaches to selling are virtually endless. In this section, we cover some of the main ways that products and services are sold today and give you some important tips for using them.

Telemarketing

With a telephone, a salesperson has the potential to reach nearly any other person on the planet; however, what you say when your prospective client answers the phone, if he answers at all, is critical. In some industries, you might actually try to sell the product on the first call (referred to as a *one-call sale*) whilst in others, you're initially only trying to stimulate interest in your offer – enough interest, perhaps, so that the person you're speaking to leaves his home and comes down to your shop, or allows you to visit him in his home or place of business so that you may discuss your offer further. Either way, you're selling what your business is all about, leaving the person on the other end with a very distinct impression of you and your company – whether that be good or bad.

Although telemarketing is still a thriving method for reaching potential clients, many telemarketers are finding reaching a real person when they place their calls increasingly difficult. If you plan to use this method of approach, be prepared to leave curiosity-building messages on voice mail or answering machines in order to make a connection with potential clients. More people are screening their calls with caller ID features and voice mail than ever before. Indeed, especially when calling in a business-to-business sales environment, you're going to come up against the 'gatekeeper' or secretary who may or may not put you through to the person you need to speak with. So your message or introduction must be enticing and skilfully delivered. Whatever the outcome you experience when calling, you need to be properly prepared. (Find more detailed ideas on how best to work with a 'gatekeeper' in Chapter 8.)

Despite the difficulty telemarketers often have in getting through to people willing to listen to them, telemarketing has become widely accepted and recognised as a true sales profession. This approach requires tact, training, and the ability to articulate a message in a very brief amount of time, as well as the skill of helping others recognise you as a warm, caring individual who has their needs at heart. Many companies across many industries are quickly realising that gifted telemarketers can help bring a product or service to market in a much more efficient and cost-effective manner than ever before.

Direct mail

Every piece of direct mail you receive, whether in the form of a letter introducing a company's offer, a money-off voucher, or a catalogue, is devised for the single purpose of selling you something. Companies that do this play the numbers game and hope that enough people will look at or read the offer and actually order their products before the mailing is re-filed in the waste bin.

In recent years the response rate for direct mailing has fallen below 1 per cent, which was considered average for a long time. Even so, direct mail can still be a viable exercise if properly executed. Even though each of those catalogues or mail pieces may cost thousands of pounds to produce and distribute, especially if they contain a lot of full-colour photographs, the justification is simple: when you order from a company, you'll probably re-order something else from that company several more times in the future. You have become a regular customer or client, and good companies work very hard to keep you coming back for more.

E-mail

Many companies are doing less telemarketing and direct-mail selling and are instead sending more e-mail solicitations. Why? Because even though direct mail enables you to get your message to the proper address, that doesn't necessarily mean it will make it into the appropriate hands. Well-intentioned secretaries, receptionists, spouses, or children often throw away what they deem to be 'junk mail' addressed to the recipient before it reaches him. If you send your message via e-mail, however, you're more likely to get it directly to the person you want to reach.

In most cases, business e-mail, when addressed to the correct recipient, appears to be deemed personal territory and is not automatically deleted. Secretaries and receptionists may receive copies of e-mails, but they aren't likely to delete e-mail messages from their bosses' computers. Home e-mail, on the other hand, may not be thought of as so sacred, but it still has a good chance of being seen by the person you want to reach.

In a world in which e-mail inboxes are constantly bombarded with *spam* (unsolicited e-mail), you face ever-increasing barriers of filters and mail-server restrictions, so often the only way to ensure the recipient receives your mailing is if you deliberately ask for permission to send beforehand.

To make sure that your intended recipient receives the message you're sending, put the recipient's name in the subject line (for example, 'Personal Message for John Smith').

If you use e-mail as a way of connecting with prospective clients, you can include your message in the body of the e-mail itself or you can send it in the form of an attachment that looks like one of your ads or printed pieces or that contains a link to your Web site. Another alternative is to include an attached Microsoft PowerPoint slide presentation, customised especially for the potential client you're targeting

However, in a world so painfully aware of computer virus attacks, not only is it difficult to get mail through but it can also sometimes be impossible to send attachments or mail containing graphic images. The recipient may think these attachments contain viruses or they may clog e-mail boxes, because graphic files are large, so seek advice and permission from the recipient before sending.

E-mail, when used properly, is an extraordinary vehicle for getting your message to the ears or eyes of those you want to reach. However, you need to be aware of the laws governing the use of e-mail. Sending follow-up e-mails or proposals and presentation materials is fine, but if you're planning to use

The computer revolution and your role in it

If you plan to have a successful career in sales, you need to have at least a limited understanding of computers. Even if you're still selling something as simple as Wellington boots or woollen socks, you need to track your client contacts in the most efficient manner possible in order to maximise your sales. You also need to have access to the phenomenal volume and quality of information available on the Internet. Not becoming familiar with the basics of computers and what they can do for you is like locking yourself outside your place of business with nothing more than a business card.

Understanding the basics of today's technology is also crucial when conversing with your clients who are also in tune with it. Nothing ruins your credibility faster than pulling out bits of crumpled paper or an obviously old, barely used notebook to jot down a client's contact information when he's using the latest handheld device or Internet-connected phone.

Take advantage of CRM (Customer Relationship Management) software or contact management software, which allows you to maintain customer lists, prospect information, diaries, contact information, and a variety of other sales-related tasks that salespeople used to organise with efficient secretaries and desk diaries. Two superb systems that can help you organise your business are ACT! and Goldmine. They are both excellent programs, operate on recognisable Microsoft Outlook-type systems so that they feel familiar, and are very easy to learn and use. Our personal favourite is Goldmine, which is slightly more expensive than Act!. Both programs only cost about £120 to £160, though – a trifle considering their payback in terms of the relationships they help you develop with clients.

Many companies, such as SalesForce, are also offering online contact management software on a subscription basis. Talk with others in your particular field to determine which software has the features you can benefit from the most. Or see if your company has made arrangements to use a certain program in-house, across the board for everyone.

e-mail as part of a larger sales campaign (similar to the way you would use direct mail), you must first get the permission of the recipient of the message. (You create an *opt-in e-mail list*; we discuss e-mail lists in more depth in Chapter 7.) Failure to get permission before sending repetitive follow-up mail is referred to as *spamming*, which not only creates hugely negative feelings in the recipient but can actually cause your mail service to be terminated by your Internet Service Provider, which of course would not help your business!

The Internet

Imagine that you're a customer, and you really, really want a new jumper to match an outfit you already have. If you want to see it immediately, to be sure the colour matches or complements your other clothes, what's the best solution? You can telephone a clothes shop, hunt all around the town, or wait for a salesperson to contact you and then send you a brochure or catalogue. Or you can visit the manufacturer's Web site and, within a few minutes, see the actual garment accurately portrayed, complete with all relevant information as to size options and so on. As a busy customer, what's the best use of your time? To go online and visit the Web site, of course. This way, you don't waste your time or petrol or get frustrated that what you're looking for isn't there when you want to see it.

Wouldn't your customers want to take advantage of the same opportunity? Yes, and if you don't offer your customers that opportunity, your competitors probably will.

Efficiency is the name of the game when it comes to technology. You need to make it work *for* you; ultimately the technology should make achieving the task easier than it is without the technology. You have to take advantage of every method possible to increase your efficiency while remaining easily accessible to your clients. The focus must remain on the task of selling, not on the technology that assists, so be careful not to invest so much time in mastering the technology that you have no time left to do what you're paid for – sell your products and services.

The Internet resembles a vast library. You can find just about any piece of information you want and so can your potential customers. These days not too many people invest the time required to walk down to their local library to look up information. They do, however, click to the Internet and search for information on your product or service when they want it – and they'll find information on your competition, too.

The people you approach in the course of your business probably have much more knowledge about your product or service and are much better informed in general than they have been at any other time in history, so you'd better know your product or service better than they do (see Chapter 5 for more on this important topic). Look at the same Web sites or brochures that your customers see and if you aren't sure exactly where they might look, add to your fact-finding process a question about where your clients do their research on your product. Find out where your customers are going for information, and if you have any influence on the content, make sure it's positive.

Person-to-person selling

On an average day, most sales are concluded in a face-to-face environment. Meals are purchased in person at restaurants, people physically walk into hotels or check in at airports, a proliferation of goods are purchased in retail

---

I'd like to buy the world a drink . . .

You know that radio and TV adverts sell to you, but you may not realise how deeply their advertising campaigns register in your mind. For example, you may not drink Coca-Cola, but I bet if you hear the music from one of its current adverts you'll recognise it immediately. Indeed, the impact is even better than that. . . you can probably picture the image that a television ad left in your mind after watching it last night. The product manufacturers spent hundreds of thousands of pounds but it was effective. Even if you don't buy Coca-Cola, if someone else asked you to buy some for him on your way home, how long would it take you to find it on the shelf? Not very long. And why is that? Partly because

Coca-Cola has premium shelf space in most supermarkets, but mainly because you know exactly what Coca-Cola's product packaging looks like.

With the use of phenomenal technology and extremely creative art directors, some of today's TV and radio commercials are more fun to watch and listen to than the actual programmes. You may not be interested in the product, but you can probably describe a company's latest commercial, if it caught your attention. Advertising is an important part of selling products and services. For more information, turn to *Advertising For Dummies*, by Gary Dahl (Wiley).

---

stores, and millions of salespeople sit across a desk, conference table, or kitchen table turning prospects into clients. Person-to-person selling is the single largest type of selling conducted worldwide. As a result, much of the content in the balance of this book is aimed at person-to-person selling.

The fun part about person-to-person selling is that you can watch the prospect's body language *and* speak with yours. You can physically pass him information and allow him to handle your product or experience the service first-hand. You can involve all of his senses – entice him to taste, touch, smell, hear, and see just how good your offering is – and generally exercise much greater influence on the prospect's state of mind. (We cover specific methods of influence in Chapter 10.) Selling in the face-to-face environment is fun and a great arena in which to refine your skills.

What Selling Skills Can Do for You

Selling skills can do for you what a way with words did for Casanova and William Shakespeare. They can do for you what sex appeal did for Marilyn Monroe. They can do for you what powerful communication skills did for historical greats such as Sir Winston Churchill, Mahatma Ghandi, and Martin Luther King, Jr. Selling skills can make or break you in whatever endeavour you choose. They can mean the difference between getting the sale, the promotion, the job, the person of your dreams, or having to settle for less.

If you're good at selling, you probably earn an above-average income and have rewarding personal relationships. If you're not completely satisfied with your income level or with the quality of your personal relationships, make the development of selling skills a priority and you'll reap the rewards.

Possessing selling skills is like being given a certain tip from someone on the inside as to the likely winner of the Grand National. All you have to do is invest a bit of your time and effort to understand and apply these tried-and-tested, proven-effective skills to your everyday life. Before you know it, they become such a natural part of your manner that no one, including yourself, even recognises them as selling skills. People around you just see you as a really nice, competent person instead of the stereotypical, cigar-chomping, back-slapping, used-car salesman that most people associate with selling. If you can utilise these skills in all the things that you do, you'll then be in the class of people who make the world go round.

Selling is a profession and can be a rewarding career. Selling is the only career role in which you have such direct influence over your success and can almost write your own pay cheque.

Salespeople are everywhere – even where you least expect them

The person who isn't selling isn't living. Think about that: At some point nearly every day, you're involved in a selling situation of some sort. You may call it by a different name or not even recognise it as an act of selling but selling it is. Whilst we usually only associate 'selling' with a more deliberate situation focused on a business issue, hundreds of 'selling' situations are less blatant. Here's just a short list of the people who sell things, and whose 'products' you buy:

✔ **Actors:** If you've ever watched a TV programme, film, or play and become totally engrossed in the story, you've been part of a selling situation. When the actor gives a wonderful, believable performance, he's 'sold you' on his portrayal of the character.

✔ **Waiters and waitresses:** The experienced waiter offers you cheerful greetings and exchanges pleasantries with a smile whilst he gives you choices of drinks, starters, meals, and desserts. He doesn't just ask to take your order. Why? Because when he employs a bit of salesmanship, he's almost guaranteed to encourage you to purchase perhaps a little more and to leave a bigger tip.

✔ **Doctors:** Doctors get tremendous rewards when they know and use selling skills. Not only is your doctor then better prepared to convince you to follow his professional advice, he's also building his reputation as an efficient and friendly practitioner and very possibly helping you heal better by framing your complaint in a more palatable and less frightening way.

✔ **Solicitors and barristers:** Solicitors need selling skills in every aspect of their profession. When you need to choose legal help they encourage you to choose them over a

(continued)

(continued)

rival. Barristers have to employ effective selling skills to persuade judges and juries that their clients are in the right.

✔ **Politicians:** Everything about the role of a politician is a selling role! How do you as a voting member of the public form opinions and expectations about political candidates? How do politicians get elected? They persuade the most people that, if they're elected, they can and will do the job the voters want done. Indeed they then sell other members of Parliament the idea that their amendment or bill should be progressed through the system.

✔ **Parents:** Whether by words or by example, parents constantly sell their children values and beliefs. They convince or persuade their kids regarding what to wear or eat, how to act, who to have as friends, how to be a friend, and thousands of other things children need to learn in order to grow into happy, well-adjusted adults.

✔ **Children:** Few children can go into a shop and resist the things shopkeepers purposefully place on the lower shelves to tempt the young. (Considerate of those shopkeepers, isn't it?) Get ready, though. You're about to observe master sellers at work. Simply notice what children say and how they act when they try to persuade their parents to get them what they want. They practise selling at its best!

✔ **Spouses-to-be:** If you're planning to get married one day, you'll probably rehearse and deliver one of the most important sales presentations of your life in persuading your significant other of the value of spending the rest of his or her life with you. If you're already married, then you'll be using these skills almost daily, possibly persuading your partner to partake in activities that you wish to do and of course possibly persuading them with your actions and words to stay with you.

✔ **Friends:** If your friends like a film, they'll probably want to tell you about it – and sell you the idea of going to see it yourself. Your friends may also recommend a place to eat or persuade you to go to concerts or sporting events with them. All of these are examples of selling skills in action. As you share experiences, you build a relationship and become closer and this selling is similar to the process of developing relationships in a business selling environment.

You're not immune from selling situations in your daily life, even if you don't come into contact with professional salespeople, and you may not even be aware that selling has occurred. Whether you're watching the process or actively being involved, the truth is that the art of selling is inherent in everything you do. All of life is a sales pitch, so the better you become at selling, the better your life turns out.

Chapter 2

The Seven-Step Selling Cycle

*W*e like to think of selling as a cycle because, if done properly, the last step in the cycle leads you back to the first. Your new, happy client gives you the names of other people she feels would benefit from your product or service, and then you have your next lead or prospect to work with.

Selling breaks down neatly into seven steps. You can remember seven things, can't you? And if you can't or don't want to, you can always come back to this chapter.

The seven steps described here are an overview of what's covered in the chapters in Part III. Each step is equally valuable to you. Rarely can you skip a step and still make the sale. Each step plays a critical role and, if done properly, leads you to the next step in a natural, flowing manner.

Step 1: Prospecting

Prospecting means finding the right potential buyer for what you're selling. When planning where to sell your product or service, ask yourself, 'Who would benefit most from this?' If the end user is a corporation, you need to make contacts within corporations. Larger companies often employ several layers of buying personnel – indeed they sometimes even outsource the process, especially in the earlier stages, so to spend some time researching your chosen target and discovering how best to approach them is critical. If your end user is a family with school-aged children, you need to go where families are (for example, local football groups, school fundraising events, dance classes, the park, and so on). You can also purchase a list of targeted prospects from a list broker (turn to Chapter 7 for more information on how to do this) and start contacting those prospects at home.

To make an informed decision about which prospects to approach, you need to find out some information about the people or companies you've chosen as possibilities. Do some research about any prospective client company at the local library or online. This legwork is sort of a prequalification step in prospecting. You'll do even more qualification when you meet a prospective client, but why waste time on an appointment with a company or person who wouldn't have a need for your offering? *Prequalifying* helps you just like market research helps companies determine their best target markets. In fact, one of the best places to begin your research in finding the most likely candidates for your product or service is your company's marketing department. The marketing department may do research during the product development stage to determine what people want in the product or service you sell. If they have done so, study their results to get a better idea of where to begin.

If your company does advertising to promote your products, you're likely to receive *leads* – names of people who called or otherwise contacted the company for more information about the product. Treat any client-generated contact like gold dust! If this person has taken the trouble to contact you, she's most likely seriously interested. Probably the best person to contact is the one who has called you for information first!

Other valuable assets are your friends, relatives, and business acquaintances. Tell them what type of product or service you're selling. See what suggestions they come up with. Who knows, one of them just may know people at one of your prospect companies who'd be happy to talk with you.

Beware the effect that your new-found enthusiasm for your new position or venture can have. Although you may only be seeking the opinion of your friends and relatives as to where to start prospecting, if you go storming out there to talk about what you're now selling, they may be put off by the feeling that you're trying to sell to them. Be very wary that your friends and family don't interpret your enthusiasm as a disguised sales pitch.

Never begin any selling cycle until you've taken a few moments to put yourself in the shoes of the other person and think about why you might want to buy or not buy if you were in her place. Take yourself out of the picture and look at the entire situation through the eyes of the buyer. Mentally put yourself in her shoes and think about what would motivate *you* to invest your valuable time reading a letter about your product or taking a salesperson's call. If you can't come up with solid answers, you may not have enough information about your product to even be selling it in the first place. Or, you may not know enough about your potential audience to sell to them. If you do lack information, go back to your research task. Study more about both areas until you're comfortable with being in that person's shoes. In other words, don't go out prospecting until you have something of value to share with your prospects – something that's worth their while to investigate and, hopefully, purchase.

We know from all our years of enjoying selling careers that being genuine is a major factor influencing success. If you haven't really found that what you're offering is a huge help to the prospect, then the chances are that she won't be so easily persuaded to purchase and you simply won't enjoy the process so much. Selling's no fun if it's always a battle.

You may need to take a somewhat unusual approach to get noticed by your prospects or to bring about a positive response. Some ideas include:

- **Enclosing a photograph of your warm, smiling, professional self.** If your goal is to arrange to meet these people in their home, they'll need to feel a little trust and liking for you before they invite you in and warmly engage with you. A picture and some contact points will make them feel more at ease.

- **Using humour.** If at all possible use humour to break the ice and have the prospect warm to you and your cause a little more.

  We remember a cartoon of a leader focusing on the job in hand fighting an army with bows and arrows whilst a salesperson is tapping him on the shoulder to sell him a machine gun. The leader shouts, 'Go away, can't you see I'm busy?' without even turning around to see what's on offer! This superbly illustrates the benefits of a time- or labour-saving device!

- **Adding a clever quote or anecdote to the bottom of your cover letter.** You can find books containing quotes for nearly every occasion, along with several Web sites such as Quotations Page (www.quotationspage. com) or U-inspire.com (www.uinspire.com). Taking a few moments to find this kind of attention-grabber can be just enough to make your letter stand out from the rest and get you in the door.

- **Sending a small toy to the target prospect with a note attached.** Here's an example that worked well for a colleague: She discovered that the prospect was extremely keen on classic cars and sent him a vintage model along with a note saying, 'They don't make them like they used to – but some things are actually made better!' She followed up with a telephone call, was remembered, and a meeting and sale followed.

- **Sending a lottery ticket attached to the front of a mailer.** Use a headline: 'Is this your best bet for a brighter future?' or 'If this one doesn't win, what plans do you have for making your fortune?' The headlines in each case indicate the common unspoken thought that winning the lottery is the only way we truly believe we can become wealthy. However, we all want wealth, and so if you attached the ticket to an offer from you involving money-making training or investment, the missive would neatly introduce the thought that maybe, aside from the lottery, your offer should be seriously considered. Without a doubt (whether it's perceived as gimmicky or not), the recipient will remember you and will definitely talk to you when you call.

If you sell a product, merely sending a sample is a blatant pushing of your product and many people won't like that or be impressed by your lack of creativity. Think laterally and send a quirky attachment. You'll be remembered and doors will open.

These ideas may be a bit gimmicky if you're selling very top-end products that have a more serious and longer-term sales cycle, but they've worked well for many colleagues and acquaintances who were marketing everyday products and services to the average consumer. The idea is to open your creative mind to unusual ways of reaching people and capturing their attention.

To ensure that your name gets in front of the prospective client more than once, send a confirmation letter after you speak to her and make an appointment to further your conversation. Use this brief letter to remind her of the subject you were talking about and wish to discuss further and add a human comment, such as wishing her well on her holiday or with another family activity that falls between the time of the letter and the appointment date.

In addition, send a thank-you note after you enjoy your first sales visit. Thank the prospective client for her time and recognise that this is the most precious commodity she could afford you. Thank-you notes always get read, and if the prospect hasn't had the time to review your sales offering when she receives your thank-you note, she'll definitely have another look and remember you on her to-do list. You'll have made a positive first impression that will very likely bring you closer to getting a sale.

Step 2: Meeting and Greeting

You've found the people, and now you actually get to meet them. To persuade another person to give you her valuable time, you need to offer something of value in return. To gain entrance to someone's home or office, a good idea is to offer a free estimate or gift in exchange for her opinion on the demonstration or explanation of your product.

With a business-to-business appointment, you always face the challenge that your prospect is hugely under pressure and thinks she cannot spare the time. Being mindful of your prospect's time constraints and being thoughtful in choosing a more ideal time of the day can and will help the situation. Your goal is to make agreeing to an appointment as easy as possible. We strongly recommend giving your prospect two options – an either/or – with regard to dates and times. Say something like, 'I have an appointment opening on Tuesday at 9.30 a.m., or would Wednesday at 3.00 p.m. be better for you?' This makes the prospect look at her calendar and consider the open blocks of time in her schedule, whereas if you just say, 'When can we get together?' she's likely to look at how busy she is and hesitate to commit. Suggest meeting 'first thing in the day before it all gets too busy' or 'last thing at night when everyone else has gone home', because many people feel they can see you then without creating pressure on their day's schedule.

When you get a commitment, confirm all the details, such as where the meeting will take place, and get directions if you haven't been there before. Also, get a commitment as to who'll be present. You ideally want all decision-makers present so that if you've done your job correctly and your product or service is suitable for them, they're in a position to purchase on the spot. If you sell products to consumers and know you need the agreement of both spouses, for example, you need to confirm that they'll both be present. If you're talking with a young, single person, she may decide to have a parent or other adult there to help her make a decision.

You've passed the first hurdle and been invited to visit a potential client. Be sure to appear at ease so your prospect is comfortable with you. Ensure that the prospect doesn't interpret your nerves as an indication that you have a poor product or service to offer. A key driver in the buying process is the need to feel safe with the purchase, and your nerves may make her feel uncomfortable and at risk; so be very careful as you make arrangements not to put your prospect off.

If nerves are an issue for you, here are some things that you can do to help minimise the negative impact or incorrect perception nerves can give:

- ✔ Do something with your hands that disguises the shaking. Try simply holding your pad and pen showing that you're prepared to take notes on the discussion. This appears professional and you can keep your hands on your knee, which hides or suppresses the trembling.

- ✔ Consciously breathe deeply immediately before going into the call and deliberately relax your muscles by practising going limp – flopping your arms like they're made of jelly! Doing so is good fun and breaks your thoughts, shifting focus away from nervousness.

Often your nerves are a result of your own fear of not saying your spiel right rather than the fear of your clients not receiving it well. Avoid this by constantly reminding yourself that they don't know what you're supposed to say. Even if you 'say it wrong', they won't know! You simply have no need to get nervous!

REMEMBER

Overcoming any tension at this point in the selling cycle takes a bit of doing on both sides. If you don't defuse the tension, you can end up turning a potential win-win into a lose-lose situation. You won't make the sale, and the potential client will miss out on benefiting from your talents and the fantastic product.

First and foremost, you need to consider what you look like to your prospect. You know the old saying, 'You never get a second chance to make a good first impression.' When in doubt about what to wear to an appointment, err on the side of conservatism. Don't be too fashionable or flash. You want to look your best, but also remember to be comfortable. If your new shoes are too tight or they squeak, you'll be conscious of that fact and won't be able to put all your concentration into the visit.

In a prospective client's mind, any untidiness in your appearance translates into untidiness in work habits.

Think twice before you apply your aftershave or perfume too liberally. Subtlety is the motto here. You never know if you'll meet someone who is allergic to your added scents. If the potential client opens the window, goes into a sneezing frenzy, or simply stops talking and falls over, you went a bit heavy on the fragrance – and you probably lost the sale!

Of special concern is the jewellery you wear to an appointment. If your bling could be considered distracting – a glitzy diamond necklace, for example – you may have gone over the top! These days jewellery is no longer solely the domain of women; many men wear earrings, bracelets, and rings. Whilst these may be perfectly acceptable for socialising, consider the reaction if you were to wear these items in your professional role. You don't want to be remembered as 'that woman we talked with who had a stud in her nose' or 'that man who was quite nice but wore an earring'. You want your prospects to remember your competence and professionalism.

Because this is a business situation, be prepared to shake hands, make eye contact, and build rapport. Building rapport is the getting-to-know-you stage that comes with any new contact. You need to immediately begin building trust. People buy from people they like and trust. Your prospect should feel your trustworthiness as early as possible in the contact you make.

Make sure your handshake isn't a wishy-washy limp affair or a bone-crusher one either! Handshakes leave a lasting impression and you'll probably need to shake hands as you leave as well, so don't let a bad one leave a doubly bad impression. Practise hand-shaking with a friend until yours is just right.

Step 3: Fact Finding

When you finally sit down with your prospect, you need to find out if she's qualified to be your client of choice. In selling, *fact finding* with your prospects means finding out who they are, what they do, what they have, and what they need.

You don't have to take on every client who qualifies for your product or service. If one particular client looks like she could become your biggest client, and that in turn makes it likely you'll be spending a large amount of your time with her, then it really isn't very good if you can't stand the person after your first meeting! In the real world you cannot expect to bond absolutely with every potential client. Sometimes you may have to pass a client to a colleague who is better able to deal with her.

If you've done your homework and looked up information about the prospect, you'll know what questions to ask. You'll eventually have to know a lot of information about the prospect, providing you get the account, so if you're truly convinced this is a good match for you, you may as well ask questions now. The more specific your questions, the more impressed your potential client will be with your expertise. Asking pertinent questions now shows that you're interested in more than just a closed sale and that you're looking into the future as a valued business partner of your client.

Your prospects will be assessing you too, so be aware of what you're showing them. Most clients are looking for people who are dependable, loyal, trustworthy, intelligent, competent, and even a little fun. Do your prospects see those characteristics when they look at you? If you need to communicate a character trait of yours that's difficult to see, work out how you can bring appropriate images to mind in the answers you give to their questions and the information you offer in your discussion of their needs. For example, if you're keen to demonstrate your attention to detail in order that your prospect may see how thorough you'll be when dealing with her, you may deliberately display material illustrating how you've taken it upon yourself to research her competitors.

The goal of your fact-finding discussion is to determine how well suited your product or service is to your prospect's situation. Whether you're selling to businesses or individuals, ask questions to get them talking about what they have now, how it's not fulfilling their current needs, and how much of a budget they have for making an improvement.

Step 4: Presentation

Your presentation of your product, service, or idea requires the most preparation. In your preparation, practise your answers to common questions with a family member or close friend. Make a list of the benefits you think are your strongest persuaders in placing your product. Then try to figure out a way to work those points into responses to the common questions.

For example, suppose you're selling a brand-new home-delivery grocery service based upon telephone ordering and a same-day local delivery. Your prospects are busy professional people who are cash-rich but time-poor and to whom the convenience angle outweighs the slightly higher cost of the groceries. Because the service is new, you don't have a track record of success to brag about. So here's where you may start:

> PROSPECT: Well, it sounds like a good idea, but you haven't proven it to be successful. I'd hate to be a guinea pig and end up having to do my shopping anyway because it didn't work out.
>
> SALESPERSON: Because this is a new service, we're paying special attention to the orders that we receive. In fact, we have two people who listen to the recording of each call to confirm that your verbal request is what shows up on our shopping list. One of them will give you a quick call to let you know your list was received in good order and to arrange the best delivery time for you.

The real issue is not that the service is new, but that the client doesn't feel totally confident that the service won't let her down, and perhaps more importantly, she feels if she were let down she wouldn't have the time to shop. By showing that you have backup systems in place to ensure the order is handled properly, you've answered the quality control question that triggered the prospect's 'guinea pig' reference.

To demonstrate personal dependability, tell the prospective client a story of how an issue with a previous client was proved to be the client's fault, but that you personally ensured the satisfactory delivery of the additional items nevertheless.

Your clients buy more than your product – they buy you. Possibly they place more emphasis on how they feel about you personally than on your product or service. They could probably purchase your offering or something very similar from a competitor if they were sold on the item but not you.

Amazing things can happen during the rapport-establishing phase of a meeting. We know of someone who was in a meeting and noticed a small golf figurine on the prospective client's desk. She asked if the prospect liked to play golf – a fairly general and safe question – but the man gave her a brief answer that didn't further the conversation. Then she remembered a new type of golf club that her husband had talked about. She asked her prospect if he'd heard of these new clubs and explained briefly why she was asking: she wanted a set for her husband's birthday. It just so happened that the prospect's son was a co-founder of the company that developed and marketed those particular clubs. Suddenly, this prospective client was very interested in hearing the salesperson's husband's thoughts on the clubs, and a deeper level of rapport was established.

Step 5: Handling Objections

One question that always haunts a person in a selling role is how best to handle any negative comments or qualifications your prospect raises during or after your presentation. To keep the answer simple, handle them with a brief acknowledgement of the prospect's statement and then ask a non-combative qualifying question to discover if the point raised is critical to the potential purchase, or even is worthy of note at all. (Often clients raise objections because they subconsciously feel obliged to make intelligent comments and that they have to appear to at least offer some resistance.) For example, if your product is only available in certain colours, and none of them quite fit the decor of your prospect's office, be prepared to recommend the least offensive colour suggestion. If the comment was to the effect that you don't have the exact colour the client had in mind, you might say, 'I fully appreciate your comment Ms Prospect. Can I just ask, will you be looking to change the blinds or the chairs from time to time over the next few years?' The answer is probably yes, so whatever colour you initially provide for your product, the prospect will eventually have a colour change issue, and she may think, why make an objection to it now?

If you sidestep obstacles during your presentation, a good chance exists that they'll come back to haunt you if you do get the sale. Find a way to bring up and elaborate on any concerns about fulfilling the needs of the buyer as early in the presentation as is appropriate. Don't let unfulfilled expectations bring your long-term relationship with a potential client to a bitter end. Cover all her concerns and make sure that she understands how those concerns will be handled – and that she's comfortable with your methods for doing so.

The most common concern you'll encounter in your entire selling career is the good old standby stall: 'I want to think it over.' When someone says she wants to think it over, that means she's interested. And if she's interested, you need to strike while the iron's hot. Find out exactly what she wants to think over. In the majority of cases, you'll find that her concern is the money involved. Surprise, surprise! Everyone wants a bargain. Unless your product or service is severely underpriced, most of your potential clients will want to bargain or are hesitating just to see if you'll offer to include something else to get them to buy. Chapters 11 and 12 cover how to cope with this situation.

Step 6: Closing the Sale

If you've researched your prospect properly, given yourself enough valuable preparation time, and handled all the previous steps in a professional manner, you'll probably close the sale. Closing should follow naturally and smoothly after you address your prospect's concerns. But if your prospect doesn't automatically pick up a pen to approve your paperwork or write a cheque, don't panic. You don't have to turn into a stereotypical high-pressure salesperson and start leaning on her to get what you want. Getting your prospect's business can be as simple as saying, 'How soon do we start?' At this point, if you're confident about being able to give her what she needs, you should begin taking verbal ownership of your future business relationship with assumptive statements and questions.

You may also want to use analogies, quotes from famous people, or today's news to persuade people to go ahead and do it today. Use similar-situation stories about other clients who got involved with your product or service and are happy they did. Be prepared to show the potential client how she can afford this product or service if cost is her area of hesitation. Often, doing so's just a matter of breaking down the costs and the potential savings to show her how affordable the item is compared to the benefits she'll receive.

By the point of closure, you've hopefully reduced any sales resistance your new client had early on, covered all of the salient points, and reached her level of sales acceptance, so that agreeing on the finer details is all that remains. These may be delivery or pricing issues, but they're not threatening and a sale is the effective outcome. We cover many methods of getting that pen to paper in Chapter 12.

Step 7: Getting Referrals

After you close the sale with your client, take a moment to ask for referrals. Doing so can be as simple as asking, 'Because you're so happy with this decision today, would you mind if I ask you for the names of other people you know who may also be interested in learning about this product?' If the client has mentioned other family members in the area, ask, 'Who in your family would also enjoy the benefits of our fine lawn service?', or, 'Which of your neighbours would you say shares your desire for a hassle-free garden maintenance programme?'

In a larger corporate situation, ask about other departments within the company that may need the same service. In a smaller business environment, ask which other business owners the prospect meets up with.

In today's business environment, a great deal of work is passed via referrals and recommendation, much of it via networking. So ask if your new prospect is an active networker. If she is, then you're in line for a great referral situation.

In conversation, after having established a level of rapport, ask the client what professional organisations she belongs to where networking takes place. However, doing so too early can make the prospect feel that you're using her as a feeder channel and that you care more about who she links you to than about her.

If you get a referral, ask for an introduction to the new prospect. If the client seems uncomfortable with that request, at least get a quick letter of introduction you can use when you contact the person.

If for some reason you and the prospective client find that this isn't the best time to go forward with the sale, instead of just walking out the door and saying goodbye, make the contact a part of your network of people who can help you find *more* people who may benefit from your product or service – if the prospect genuinely likes your offering, you have a good chance of meeting other prospects through her. Don't ever just walk away from an opportunity to network. And immediately upon leaving the premises, post a card to the person thanking her for her time. Doing so guarantees that your discussion will stay fresh in her mind for at least a few days. During that time, the right lead for you may come her way and if you've left a good impression, she'll be more likely to give you the referral.

Chapter 3

Enjoying Selling as a Hobby

- -

In This Chapter

▶ Transferring your passion for your hobbies to the world of selling

▶ Stepping out of your comfort zone and facing new challenges

▶ Becoming a lifelong student

▶ Facing the challenges that are part of any learning process

- -

*T*he main factor that separates the top five per cent of salespeople from those who struggle to accomplish their goals is a basic one: Highly successful salespeople actually *enjoy* selling as an occupation. To truly successful salespeople, selling isn't a job with the connotations that a job usually brings, it is more a pleasurable pursuit that they willingly engage in on a daily basis. They don't feel under the pressures that many feel selling brings. They've discovered how to approach the game mentally and, as a result, find enjoyment where others struggle.

When champion salespeople prospect for new clients, go to appointments, visit people, and ask for sales, they're doing what they love to do. It just so happens that champions get paid very well for their hobbies. If you're struggling with your ability to sell *and* with finding the desire to make it to the top, then you may well be extremely glad you read this chapter, because if you can embrace this process of making your job feel like a hobby or a pleasurable pursuit, you'll have adopted a key to your future success – a success that will spread to all areas of your life.

The more involved you get with selling, the more selling you observe going on around you in all areas of your life. When you truly study selling, you see that selling pervades every communication and interaction between humans. Whenever one person tries to persuade someone else to do anything – to agree with his point of view or to follow him in an action or to obey him in an instruction – the first person 'sells' to the second to get the second person to agree. These sorts of selling situations are constantly enacted around you, and by studying them, you can observe both how to sell well and how not to sell. The best opportunity for discovery often occurs in an informal, non-selling atmosphere. In other words, get used to a new sensation. In situations that you may not usually see as sales situations, a realisation will dawn upon you, and you'll think, 'Hey, there's selling going on here, I should be taking notes.'

This chapter shows you the way people usually approach their hobbies and helps you find a way to approach selling in the same way. You discover how to challenge yourself throughout your lifetime to discover new things and to venture into new areas. We give you an idea of what to expect along the way. Attitude and enthusiasm are a huge part of success in sales – or in life for that matter – and in this chapter we talk about both so that you can put them to work for you.

Taking a Long, Hard Look at Your Job Satisfaction

You've probably heard the advice to 'never mix business with pleasure'. Although we can appreciate that the intention behind the statement is to refrain from bombarding all of your friends with your latest commercial venture, thus eroding your social circle, but whoever wrote that maxim probably derived little pleasure from his business, and he very likely wasn't a champion salesperson. When you make selling your hobby, you blur the distinction between what you do to live and what you live to do. When you get the hang of making your work your hobby, you *always* mix business with pleasure.

When you don't enjoy what you do to earn money, you're in danger of making a terribly sad trade-off – seemingly endless hours of drudgery for seemingly fleeting moments of holiday fun. The question to ask yourself is this: As short as life is, are those fun-filled weeks worth the months of drudgery you have to go through to earn them? Or could you possibly embrace a new challenge and engage in selling as if it were a hobby, and really live? After all, you're on this earth for such a short time that you may as well do something you enjoy.

If you're in sales, you can find ways to enjoy what you're already doing. If you discover and practise the communication skills that are a part of selling, your life is guaranteed to be more interesting. And anything that you're interested in has to include at least a little fun or it won't hold your interest.

Do you ever feel guilty about taking time away from your job when you have fun on holiday? If your answer is 'yes', you need to take a long, hard look at what you do for a living and how much satisfaction you gain from it. You may even want to seek professional career advice. Don't do a job just because it provides for you and your family. Consider what kind of life you're providing if every day you leave the house unhappy to slog at it and you can't even enjoy the little bit of holiday time you take because you're worried about what will lie in wait for you upon your return. Indeed, maybe you're *not* providing properly for your family if you're so fed up with the job that you come

ANECDOTE

Love the one you're with . . .

A merging of passion and profession has occurred in my (Ben's) life with selling. For me, selling began as a job to fulfil a need for cash and transport as a teenager and about which my mum famously said, 'That will do until you get a real job!'. Although it possibly didn't all turn out magnificently in my first sales encounter – commission-only double glazing sales – I did realise very early on the amazing pleasure you get when you actually make a sale. Selling is a truly wonderful high and one I became addicted to.

When I say that selling didn't turn out so brilliantly in my first encounter, that wasn't anything more than a lack of maturity in knowing how to handle the success I enjoyed! The job went pretty well and indeed I knew even as a teenager I was made for the role; I just needed to grow up, perhaps. After a couple of years doing various manual jobs, I once again tried a sales role, this time selling to industry in a business environment, before being encouraged back into a direct-to-consumer sales environment.

Eventually I found myself studying every call I went on, every person I worked with, every phone call I heard, and every style that colleagues used. I avidly applied these techniques in all areas of my life and became addicted to the fun of winning. I loved it! I discovered how to get what I wanted pretty much all of the time – because selling is nothing more than winning people over to your point of view in whatever context.

I made selling fun and it made my life one big pleasure trip – and I earned a few quid too! Money was perhaps the initiator when I was only 19 but it soon became a background issue because the involvement I applied made my skills improve, and I soon just had a great time and stopped worrying about income because I was always making more than enough. By shifting the focus away from the income, I actually created more income than ever.

Today, I live and breathe selling and transforming lives through these skills. I've built my business in such a way that I enjoy what I do for a living. I don't 'work' anymore, if *work* means 'doing some particular thing when you'd rather be doing something else'. Selling now pervades every communication I have with others, and I thoroughly enjoy my life.

home in a bad mood or aren't home often enough to enjoy family life! Consider your family's emotional provision – and yours. Even worse, too many people work twice as hard in the weeks before and after their holiday so that they're not swamped and then in trouble at work for slipping behind! Think about that scenario: if you work extra hard for those weeks away, you really haven't taken a holiday at all. The company has still received 52 weeks of work from you, and you may have effectively worked those extra weeks without compensation!

Wouldn't taking each day and enjoying it to its fullest, looking forward to getting up every morning, bright-eyed and bushy-tailed, vibrant with anticipation for what's ahead be more fun? Wouldn't enjoying your workdays as much as you enjoy your free time be better? What would your life be like if you could enjoy your job as much as you enjoy your hobbies? What kind of life would you be providing for those around you if the central element of your life were no longer drudgery but the joy that comes from self-fulfilment? This job scenario resembles going away on holiday or taking a relaxing day off every day. And if you're willing to spend a little time working out how to make your job into a hobby, you can turn this dream into a reality.

Knowing What Sets Hobbies Apart from Jobs

Think about how you treat your hobbies and how you treat your job. If you're like most people, you gladly talk about your life outside of work. You talk passionately about your children, your sporting interest, or favourite team. You talk for hours about your weekends away or your next or last holiday, your favourite authors, and friends you enjoy. You may display your handicrafts or even proudly invite people to a barbecue so that you can show off your garden. Now imagine feeling the same about your job as your hobbies!

Here's a thought for you: What do you think makes people successful in their hobbies? Have you ever noticed the difference in expression and animation in people when they talk about their hobbies compared to when they talk about their jobs? If you haven't observed this change in emotions, test this theory yourself. Ask a few people this question, 'What do you do with your spare time?', and pay close attention to their answers. The secret to their success in their hobby is the *emotional* attachment they enjoy – as displayed in their answers. They have *fun*!

We contend that if more people looked at selling as a hobby – with energy, enthusiasm, excitement, fervour, anticipation, devotion, and sheer fun – they'd be leaders in all walks of their lives.

The following sections take a closer look at the way people view their hobbies and let you know how you can harness those same traits and apply them to your selling – a path certain to bring you success.

Attitude makes the difference

Studies prove that attitude is one of the traits that separate average salespeople from their highly successful colleagues. And this situation is true of life in general, not just sales. Think about the happiest, most successful people you know. How do you usually find them? Are they depressed, negative, or even apathetic? We doubt it. They're probably upbeat, smiling, and positive about life.

Why not take the same positive, interested attitude you have towards your hobbies and transfer that passion to your ability to sell yourself, your ideas, and your products or services? Challenge yourself to read up on selling strategies. Of course, you're doing so with this book, but what will you do after you've read it? While you're driving, will you listen to the radio, or will you inspire yourself to greater success by listening to CDs about selling skills? Will you continue the journey and attend a selling course or choose deliberately to mix with those who you recognise as 'success models'?

Give yourself permission to explore some creative ways of starting conversations with others who may have a need for your product or service. Observe how the next salesperson you encounter makes you feel. What did he say or do that brought about that feeling? Think of how you can discover what makes some people react or buy and indeed what makes some react negatively and avoid purchasing. Watch, listen, absorb, and apply. Challenge yourself to pay attention and you'll soon find yourself eagerly anticipating the next selling situation as much as you anticipate your next day off. Relish the challenge and love the game, because when you try something and it works you get a real buzz inside. You'll smile to yourself and shout a silent 'Yes!'.

Here's another angle: Instead of turning your selling job into a hobby, why not take the hobby you love so much and design a way you can make it pay the bills? If you're involved in handicrafts, for example making outdoor toys or fitting kitchen or bedroom furniture, you may be able to sell the things you make or sell your skills at doing the task. We're not saying this change will make you a millionaire, but money isn't the only measure of success. If you could support yourself comfortably on the earnings from your hobby, we'd deem you as having a successful life. Think about this scenario. You already have the built-in enthusiasm, excitement, and knowledge of your hobby. Now all you need to do is show others why they need to feel the same way. If you do a little research, you'll find that many very successful businesspeople started out by selling their hobbies. So here's a little challenge for you: Find out for yourself what you really love to do, and then work out a way to get paid for it. What could be better?

Emotional involvement supplies the meaning

Emotional involvement is another key trait possessed by hobby enthusiasts that many people don't feel they have for their work. If your hobby is an outdoor sport, such as mountain biking, nothing is more exciting than cresting mountain peaks at sunrise or soaring downhill so fast that you have a permanent grin on your face. An adrenaline rush surges through your veins!

Success can fit many definitions – including yours

We always enjoy asking seminar audiences and clients for definitions of the term *success*. Rarely have we heard the same answer twice. Success is as individual as a fingerprint. Of course, many answers reflect similar themes – a desire for monetary riches, love, and security – but few people come up with a definition of success that could be understood and agreed upon by all who hear it.

One of my (Ben's) most vivid memories is of meeting a client for a courtesy thank-you drink. As we talked, he asked, 'So are you successful, then?', almost challenging me to declare that I was. I answered, 'I think so, because I'm an extremely happy and somewhat fortunate man able to spend my time doing exactly what I love and consequently am able to enjoy a wonderful life with my daughter.' He was pretty dumbfounded. He certainly hadn't expected such an answer from me, but I like to think I already knew back then what success meant to me and that I had defined it pretty well.

Thus I define success as 'being consciously happy and able to spend your time doing what pleases you'. Success is a state of being.

Many people's success stories relate to commercial, business, entertainment, or sporting success, and thus define success as a temporary condition linked to a specific happening or event. When the event passes or is never repeated, these people are left with an emptiness and unhappiness that doesn't cohabit with a real success story.

In reality, success is a constant feeling of being as opposed to an achievement attained as a milestone. Success is a journey not a destination.

Why not consider using my definition yourself and laying a course for an exciting journey toward success!

This reaction isn't just a physical experience, but also charged with emotional involvement. When you schedule a biking event, it becomes a highlight that gives you a great feeling whenever you think about it. You involve yourself in planning every detail to make the outing the best one yet. You live and breathe for the next opportunity to get out there with your mountain-biking friends. When you think about your biking events, you feel an emotional jolt. Now, mountain biking represents a challenge, both physically and mentally, that could quite easily put you off going. But if the emotional involvement is strong enough, you can hurdle those barriers with no sweat (so to speak). The plain and simple truth is that avid mountain bikers have become 'sold' on their pastime because they want to experience the emotional involvement. They succeed in facing all the challenges and obstacles and they succeed in the pastime because they're emotionally hooked. Doing so doesn't feel like exertion; it feels like fun! People often lack that emotional involvement with their jobs. Too many people are disillusioned with their jobs and are detached from what goes on in their work environment. They become disinterested observers. They don't join in the company's extracurricular activities or interact much with others.

Those who are emotionally involved with their work, however, bring enthusiasm to their jobs. And for those people, life is much more interesting and more fun. Even if you're not thrilled with what you do for a living, you must at least be pleased with living itself. Find a way to bring that pleasure into your work, and your work just may become more fun too.

You must be able to find at least a smidgen of something you like about your job – even just the feeling of importance you get when people hear your title announced or how you enjoy the responsibility of your role and others depending upon you. Whatever it is, there must be *something* you like about what you do for a living.

In a sales career, you can seize upon a vast array of opportunities to make you feel great doing what you do – provided you have an attitude that looks for something to like instead of all of the things that you dislike!

Many salespeople love meeting new people. They are curious, and interested in how other people live their lives. They seek out new ideas and opinions on topics that they previously barely knew existed. Some enjoy the challenge of the selling cycle – meeting a perfect stranger and, before too long, turning that person into a lifelong client. Nearly everyone in sales gets off on the high of satisfying someone's need. Most salespeople have a service attitude. For some, especially in the beginning, the thrill of the job is the knowledge that only they set the limit on how much income they earn. For those sales positions that require travel, many people enjoy meeting other travellers, seeing new sites, and experiencing different climates. Finding out about cultures different from their own inspires many salespeople involved in international business. For some, the flexibility that's often available in certain sales positions allows them to schedule valuable family time or to participate in hobbies or sporting events that occur when the rest of the world is working. In some industries, entertaining clients involves attending sporting events that some salespeople wouldn't otherwise have opportunities to attend.

Focus upon what you like and make it a stronger feeling than the niggles. You can always find people or happenings to taint your rosy view, but it is down to you to see what you want to see and to let nothing else affect your state of mind. Searching for what is good and not dwelling on the bad is a key attribute of making selling a hobby.

Trading Knowledge for a Sense of Wonder

Starting the hobby of selling is pretty simple: you don't need any special tools or equipment, no large financial investment is required, and you don't have to travel far to participate.

Visualising sales success

Develop a picture of the new you who'll take the place of that old, comfortable you and see yourself clearly winning and enjoying the benefits of the new-found success. Then keep that mental image sharp and focused.

At times, developing the 'fake it 'til you make it' approach is extremely valuable. Model yourself on a successful person whom you wish to emulate and then act out the role of that successful person. Think about the person who already has all the traits you desire and then visualise yourself as that person who uses selling skills effectively. When you act like that person, you'll try to say and do what he would say and do. Eventually, you begin having small successes with the material and, before you know it, you *are* that person. You'll wear the suit of success.

And the more you wear it, the more comfortable it will seem.

Professional athletes use this method of visualisation all the time. They cultivate the skill of visualising their success in order to see so clearly their winning performance that they can play it over and over again in their mind, and in doing so make sure their whole body is actually ready for the event and expecting it. When they first begin visualising this scene, their bodies may not be up to speed with the picture, but if they play the picture often enough, the chances are that their bodies will get the hint and soon perform accordingly. And you can do the same with your selling skills if you're willing to move out of your comfort zone long enough to find out something new.

Pay attention to the way your children or parents communicate with you about family matters. Watch how shop assistants treat you, and notice how you feel about the shop as a result. Get into the habit of really *reading* sales notice-boards and newspaper ads, focusing on ones that seem to speak directly to you. Listen carefully to radio adverts; those that hold your attention the longest deserve some analysis, as well as ones that you turn off straight away. Sort out what strikes a chord and why. In general, become a student of the selling presented to you daily by everyone from sales and marketing experts to your friends and family. Become absorbed with the examples all around and get excited that it's soon to be a skill that you can master.

Making learning a lifetime pursuit

Although people allow their children the privilege of ample time to learn, they often don't allow themselves the same luxury. Parents recognise the value of education and how it improves the career and income chances for their children and yet often don't practise what they preach. The large majority of people discontinue their conscious learning experiences in life when they complete their formal education. Hundreds of thousands of mature adults haven't formally learned anything since the day they left school or college.

Working through brain strain

When you begin to learn anything, you can absorb only so much before you experience what we call *brain strain*. You've been there – you literally immerse yourself in a study or reading task and after several hours you're just numb and can't do any more. Well, breaking up your learning into smaller chunks avoids the strain. Approach the material in sections from the outset – learn, practise, learn some more, and then practise some more. You can internalise only so much information at once. If you take on a whole new subject, such as selling, all at once, you'll be overwhelmed and may give it up. Set a goal to find out, one step at a time, what you need to know. Besides, selling isn't all about theory; it is definitely about practice as well, so you must give yourself a chance to have a go before attempting mastery in one fell swoop.

If you're new to sales, concentrate on prospecting and qualifying strategies. That way you'll be spending more of your time with people who could actually want to own your product or service. If you find you're uncomfortable with that first-meeting greeting, work just on that for a while. Write yourself a script and stick to it. Then change one word or phrase and continue to use it, refining it as you go, until you find the one that breaks the ice with more new people faster.

Many novices who choose to consciously develop sales skills want instant success. This instant mindset is fuelled by the Internet-age, on-demand mentality where everything is immediately available. Indeed, one criticism of today's advancement is that much of the old school of life experiences is undervalued and missed out. In selling you won't enjoy immediate success and find that it means lasting success unless you study.

Successful selling is a journey that at times challenges your persistence, so be prepared to see it through. Knowing something and applying it so that it works are two very different things. Don't look at others who are more successful than you are and expect to duplicate their sales techniques overnight. They're successful because they've learned and practised the material over a long period of time. They've already experimented with the nuances of body language, voice intonation, and inflection that you're just introducing yourself to. As with many things in life, when selling is done well it looks easy, but don't think for one moment that it actually *is* easy. Enjoy the process of learning and practising, though, and eventually selling will become easy for you.

Adults make excuses for themselves, saying that they don't have the time to take educational courses. Or they think that they can learn faster on their own. Or they assume that they don't really need to know much more than they already know until they tune into a quiz show on TV or attend a local pub quiz night and are embarrassed by their inability to answer many questions!

Most adults fail to continue the learning process, not because of a lack of desire, but because of a perceived lack of time. They expect youngsters to spend most of their time on education, albeit tempered with some youthful exuberance and fun, but somewhere along the way, as people grow into adults, that focus shifts to the responsibilities they have for financial and family matters. Their desire for achievement overwhelms them, and taking time out for education just doesn't happen. They feel under pressure to perform and that studying or learning is hard work, when in truth lots of fun ways to learn exist.

Here's the good news: Studies show that developing the habit of listening to educational programmes in your car during commuting time can provide you with just as much information as studying for a Master's degree. How hard can it be to carry some tapes or CDs around with you all the time? You probably already do it with music. But when was the last time your favourite group taught you anything that made you more successful in life?

Nowadays, no excuse exists for not learning more. Educational programmes are available on audiocassette, CD, videotapes, and DVD. How often are you in a place where you can't listen to or watch at least one of these forms of education? Indeed a proliferation of material is also available via the Internet, allowing access 24 hours a day, 7 days a week, 365 days a year, so that even the trickiest of time challenges need not prevent your development.

Nightingale-Conant is perhaps one of the most established and comprehensive resources of this type of educational developmental material (see www.nightingale.com). Another recommended company is Craig Beck (www.viralsuccess.com), an excellent online store. Obviously, you can also buy educational books, in any number of formats.

So, in eliminating convenience, what's left is time. Do you recall the old story about the two men cutting wood? One worked hard and steadily all day. The other worked hard, too, but every now and then stopped. At the end of the day the second man had cut more wood, much to the surprise of the first. When asked how he did it, he said, 'Every time I took a break, I sharpened my saw.' Set aside a specific amount of time every week, or at the very least, every month, to sharpen your saw. Go on a course or attend a seminar. Invest a couple of hours a week in the bookshop or library to find out about the latest books published on the field of selling or on your industry in particular. Put your hands on one and read! After taking in that new information, you won't be the same person. You'll see the world just a little bit differently and your hobby of selling will progress even further. One of my favourite quotes is from a Mr Oliver Wendall Holmes who said, 'A mind once stretched by a new idea never regains its original dimension.' If you think for a moment on that thought then maybe you'll realise the true value of any learning experience and push for more.

From now on, challenge yourself to think of training seminars and educational events as professional necessities. Fight the commonly held thought that these events are a cost and view them instead as an investment that will have a positive impact on your future. Take these learning tools out of the realm of things to do when you have the time and put them into the category of things that you *must* do to reach the levels of success you set for yourself. Shift your perspective only that much, and you'll make the time to continue your education – you become a lifelong learner.

No pain, no gain

To get to the level of comfort and success you want from your selling, you need to step outside your comfort zone. Your *comfort zone* is where you are today, and unless you change who and what you are today, you'll never change what you are getting out of life. A phrase Ben shares with students approaching a developmental stage is 'comfort kills'. Staying in your comfort zone kills your ambition and prevents you from reaching new levels. You must not let the desire to be comfortable rule your life. When you open your mind to learning something new, you're not the same old comfortable person you were even a minute before. With that realisation, you make yourself *un*comfortable with the extent of your own ignorance.

The desire for comfort is actually a basic human need, though, so you're not alone if breaking free from it is a challenge for you. But after you've started your quest for growth, set goals, done some research, and invested your time in learning, you soon reach a new level of comfort with the increased knowledge you now have and use in your everyday life. The trick is to find a way to make yourself *keep* growing – to make yourself just uncomfortable enough about today so that you'll better yourself for tomorrow.

This striving for knowledge can become wonderfully habit-forming. You can gain such a kick from learning and benefiting from new concepts and ideas that the highest achievers in life have become addicted to it. They wouldn't think of facing a single day without the anticipation of learning something new. You really do develop a fabulous life when you get hooked on improvement and sharing. You'll experience incredible moments as your new knowledge bears fruit and this feeling in turn fuels your desire for more knowledge. The process becomes a wonderful spiral.

Being accepting of productive mistakes

Giving yourself permission to be a lifelong student can change your life dramatically. However, remember that students don't always do things right the first time round, so also give yourself permission to make mistakes. Acknowledging that you'll sometimes trip up takes some of the pressure off: You don't have to be right all the time just because you're an educated adult. Don't be your own worst enemy and beat yourself up when you aren't perfect straight away!

If you have the attitude and mindset of a student, you won't agonise over your failures and mistakes. Instead, you'll look at your mistakes as learning experiences. As a student, you must admit that you're fallible. Use the Edison approach, named after Thomas Edison, who invented the light bulb only after more than 900 attempts had failed! You're not going to get it right first time but you never fail until you give up trying.

After you admit that you can make mistakes, though, seek out others who can teach you, people who can help you grow into the person you want to become. When you open yourself up to the possibility that you don't know everything and don't have all the answers, you start a quest to discover what you don't know – an important step in the learning process.

One of our favourite reminders about learning is this: You can recognise true professionals by how much they learn *after* they 'know it all'. If you ever assume you know everything about something, or even if you accept that you know enough, you have just doomed yourself to mediocrity.

Being Prepared for the Learning Curve: Passing from Caterpillar to Butterfly

No one masters something new the first time he tries it. Of course, some people have natural talents or skills that apply to the new experience, but mastery cannot occur on initial impact. You didn't learn to walk on your first try, and learning anything takes time and practice. This process is often referred to as a *learning curve* – the time it naturally takes for someone to progress from a complete beginner (or a caterpillar) to an expert (or a butterfly). In any learning curve, you go through four major phases or levels of competency, each covered in the following sections.

Unconscious incompetence

The first level of competency is *unconscious incompetence* – you don't know that you don't know.

In this most elementary phase, you find people who don't even know that they don't know what they're doing. These people are the hardest ones to help because they haven't yet recognised or won't admit they need help. In daily life, these are the people who do the same job year after year, live by a weekly routine, eat certain meals on set days, and follow habits you can set a clock by! They tend to live rather mediocre lives because either they haven't realised there's more to be learned – more to be aware of – or they have simply resigned themselves to be whatever they are at the present moment. They've convinced themselves they're happy and have pretty low aspirations.

In business, this category may include someone who's been in sales for a little while and has achieved a minimal level of success – to the extent that he hasn't lost his job. He knows the product and how to fill out the paperwork and thinks that's the whole story. He thinks that the top performer is so good because of his looks or is given all the best leads because of his friendship with the boss. He doesn't even yet know the finer points in selling that we are about to examine together and he has no drive to learn them. He's unaware and accepting of his station.

Everyone is at the unconscious incompetence level of learning whenever they first try something new. Not convinced? Watch a baby learning to walk. He doesn't know he doesn't know how to walk. He just tries it because everyone else is doing it. When he learns, by falling, that walking isn't as easy as it looks, he reaches for helping hands. The instant he reaches for help, he moves to the next level of competency.

Conscious incompetence

The second level of competency is *conscious incompetence* – you know that you don't know.

People move on from unconscious incompetence when they suddenly realise that they don't know what they're doing. In the wonderful world of sales, you are probably at the conscious incompetence level right now, simply because you're reading this book. You've admitted that you don't have all the answers and that you want to find out more. You've admitted that you have something to learn and taken action to address this situation.

And that's the caveat – don't stop short of taking action. Now that you realise that you need to discover more, take action immediately! Too many potentially great careers stall at this level because people don't know where to turn for help or won't expend the effort to find the right kind of help. Too often people recognise the need for learning but lack a response. Don't be a dreamer. Let awareness of your incompetence spur you on to a course of action to redress the situation quickly. Otherwise, you run the risk of having negative thoughts about sales 'not being for you', killing off your potential. Don't be like the rabbit you see in your headlights at night, frozen to a spot on the road. You must *move* in order to rise to the third level of competency.

Begin by reading this book, of course. Then perhaps move on to *Sales Closing For Dummies* and *Sales Prospecting For Dummies* for starters. Or, if you're a person who learns better in seminars or classrooms, then start reading the ads in the business section of your local newspaper or business magazine to find out what seminars are available (including Ben's) and make a commitment to attend. If you prefer to listen to something while you exercise or drive, borrow tapes from a friend or the library, or invest in some yourself. Then listen to them a minimum of six times to achieve maximum retention of the material.

Once upon a time, a future sales success and professional speaker was totally lost for words

For an example of acutely conscious incompetence in action, think about the first time you had to give a presentation in front of a group. Doing so probably wasn't much fun, was it? If it was anything like Ben's first time, you came off the stage vowing never to repeat the experience. He relates that experience here.

In my early days as a salesperson, I was deputised to take the sales meeting. Now to be fair, I'd been with this sales team for a matter of just nine months. Nonetheless, I was a pretty confident young chap who'd proven over the last few months that my initial weeks of success weren't a fluke and that I could handle selling up against the old-timers despite all of the to-be-expected knock-backs and lousy appointments. The sales manager was called to another arrangement literally at the last minute and he asked me to chair the meeting. Well, I was ambitious, keen, and ignored any doubts, agreeing to the opportunity without thinking about preparation . . . until he left the showroom and it was all down to me.

To say I didn't quite do as well as I might have done was and is an understatement. I faced the team and immediately saw a look of indignation on many senior faces, wondering why this new kid was taking the meeting. I felt their resentment and the attitude that nothing I had to say was of any relevance.

In the face of such hostility, I froze. I mumbled my words, stuttered and stammered my way through an introduction and explanation as to where the manager was, then rushed through my thoughts on last week's sales league tables and this week's performances – all the while conscious of my reddening face and embarrassment. I hated it!

I skipped the bit I'd planned about advising the team on how to handle a challenging sales situation and closed the meeting – promptly rushing to get a cup of tea in the sanctuary of the kitchen. A hideous experience!

When my manager returned, I emptied my anger and frustration upon him. When I'd calmed down, he explained that had he done it any other way, had he given me more notice, I would probably have found an excuse not to do it and avoided the challenge. He went on to explain that I was ambitious and capable and that he believed I would make a great sales leader one day, but that I would have to master the art of holding an audience and that experience couldn't come too soon. A baptism of fire, yes, but with genuine reason – and one I thanked him for several years later.

Although it was true that I didn't do too well, I faced the challenge and realised that it didn't kill me. The audience might have been less than pleased and I had had no time to prepare, and thus it wasn't a 'normal' scenario, but I had managed it and proven that it was a hurdle I could jump. Indeed, I learned that speaking publicly is really no different to simply selling. So I learned to approach public speaking with the same confidence and energy as an everyday sales call. I focused on one person at a time in the audience and 'sold'. Doing so isn't that difficult when you get to see the experience for what it really is and now when I speak to audiences, the bigger the better!

The key is to *do* something. To echo the words of a certain man on the moon, 'One small step for a man, one giant leap for mankind'. One small step now can become a giant leap for your life.

Conscious competence

When you reach the third level, *conscious competence*, you know that you know.

At this level you find new challenges and new victories. By this point, your desire to improve is strong enough to overcome the discomfort of learning something new. You're testing the waters now. You know how to do the thing you're learning, but you have to think about it, be conscious of it, in order to succeed.

You're practising the new material you've learned. You're rehearsing in your bedroom or talking it through to yourself in the car. You're refining the skills with your friends and associates – *before* testing new strategies on qualified clients and potentially losing them due to awkwardness with the material. You're trying new things, making adjustments and moving forwards.

Be careful! Rome wasn't built in a day. Don't place too high a level of expectation on yourself and you'll do better faster. A tendency to demand too much from yourself and to seek immediate perfection creates pressure that can strangle your new performance. Plus, tensing up when you try new things removes your enjoyment from the experience. Relax a little and don't fear failure. Remember, you're never failing so long as you're trying.

Unconscious competence

At the fourth and final level of competence, *unconscious competence*, you're on automatic pilot.

Now you're really flying. It all comes so naturally to you. You apply all your previous knowledge without making a conscious effort to do so.

You're smack in the middle of an example of unconscious competence right now – you're reading this book. Think about this situation consciously for a moment – you probably aren't reading it as would someone who's just learning to read, are you? Instead of uttering each syllable individually as you point and sound it out, hoping for eventual comprehension, you're able to cruise along and seek the content you're looking for, not even thinking about what you're doing. That process is competence without conscious effort.

As an unconscious competent salesperson, the strategies are now a natural part of your presentation. You automatically recall stories and swap anecdotes and ask excellent questions and include all the component parts of a successful sales process smoothly and professionally, without too much strain on the mind. In fact, if you were to tape your presentation, you'd recognise each nuance and recall when and why you added it.

A tremendous advantage of being a lifelong student is that you no longer allow yourself the luxury of seeing yourself as a victim of circumstance. You take responsibility for your successes *and* your failures, and you're more likely to be honest with yourself when it comes to evaluating those successes and failures.

Liking to Sell What Your Customers Like to Buy

As in any area of life, if you have the wrong attitude, you can end up being your own worst enemy. Many people in selling situations have a challenge with their own likes and dislikes – they tend to sell only what they like and mostly to the people they like. You do need to like and believe in what you're selling; however, if you're in a career sales position, you'll probably have to sell other items in the product line that may not be your favourites.

Keep what's right for the customer in the forefront of your mind. If you sell only what you like, you also severely limit your income and you run a huge risk of losing volumes of clients to another supplier who offers them what you don't because you don't like it.

Your job is to enthusiastically sell whatever benefits your customers, whoever they may be. During your selling career, you'll have to work with some people whom you won't particularly like, and sell to customers whom you don't get along with either. (Chapter 7 discusses how to deal with several personality types.) If you refuse to work with some people, both you and the customers lose. You lose opportunities to make sales, and the customers lose opportunities to have their needs satisfied. The people you turn down will just get their needs filled by someone else and that situation doesn't help your finances or your future. The moral of the story is: Keep your mind and your opportunities open.

Someone else's nightmare can be your dream

I (Ben) vividly remember a situation many years ago in which I had the opportunity to learn at first hand this critical lesson in prejudging clients.

I was selling property to holidaying couples possibly looking for a holiday home or investment property. I was a salesperson new to the company and waiting my turn to see a prospect.

A gentleman came into our reception and explained that he'd like to have a look around. Well, frankly he looked decidedly scruffy! His clothing was old and dirty and his general appearance was dishevelled – hardly what I expected of someone who could afford a property worth £200,000 plus.

The reception staff and the more experienced salesperson whose turn it was to see the next client were unwilling to even entertain him, and consequently he was passed over to a less experienced salesperson (yours truly) so that he wouldn't waste anybody else's more valuable time. To cut a long story short, the gentleman was indeed a serious customer, who purchased a property at full price and paid the £10,000 deposit from his carrier bag full of cash!

I will never forget that incredibly valuable lesson. That moment has stayed with me ever since and flashes through my mind whenever I find myself tempted to judge a potential client in a selling situation. It serves as a stark reminder not to prejudge on appearances: the company I worked for had nearly turned him away and another salesperson had lost out on a healthy commission because of this mistake.

Whether you realise it or not, you make some sort of judgement about people the moment you lay your eyes on them. You judge them based on their physical condition, their clothing, their hairstyles, their postures. In selling situations, though, acting on preconceptions is a dangerous habit that you need to control. You cannot predict with any accuracy whether someone will buy or not; that outcome is mainly down to the standard of your performance. We can tell you thousands of stories of sales achieved when the prospect appeared poor and shabby and likewise sales missed to those appearing wealthy and suitable. You simply never can tell what lies behind appearances, so avoid drawing conclusions that influence the effort you make. Always presume that the prospect will buy. If you're committed to becoming a professional, force yourself to look at every customer with clear vision. Eliminate those preconceived notions before they start costing you money!

Treat your prospects with the respect you'd expect to receive were you in their shoes. Extend to them the courtesy and hospitality that you would a friend and you may well then make a friend and in the process make a sale.

Keep in mind the following tips about the kind of attitude you need to have in the world of selling, and your self-control will pay off in the long run:

- ✔ If you want others to agree with you, you must first be agreeable.

- ✔ Don't let people's outward appearances affect the way you react to them.

- ✔ Always act as though each person you contact is the most important person in your life.

With the right attitude your selling career can take you as far as you wish and introduce you to any amount of people and situations. The product, service, or idea you're offering can be a significant link for you to billions of other people who need what you have to offer.

Part II
Preparation Is the Key

'This is a more upmarket product for the brighter child – It contains punctuation.'

In this part . . .

In this part, you'll find information on what to know about your prospective clients and your product before you try to sell. And you'll also gather some great tips for using technology to your advantage when it comes to researching.

Chapter 4

Knowing Your Market

Sometimes the hardest thing in starting something new is accepting an idea that seemingly goes against a firmly held belief that has been with you for years. However, breaking through these ideas is paramount to your new success, particularly when approaching people or situations. In today's sales environment it is most definitely the case that what you don't know can hurt you very much (in lost sales) and the fact that it used not to be like this won't help you make a success in the world you live in now. Times have changed, people have changed, and your habits need to change or you won't survive.

You never see what's gone on behind the scenes when you look at people who make selling look easy and always seem to get the most sales. But the time spent behind the scenes is what selling is all about. When a sales professional makes selling look *natural*, you can bet that she's spent hours of planning and preparation before those few minutes of face-to-face selling began.

This chapter lets you know some specific ways you can prepare, so you can serve your clients better – everything from researching your prospective customers before you even set up an appointment to knowing how to listen to them when you finally do meet. It also gives you some great pointers on selling to people from countries and cultures other than your own. In the world of selling, preparation is key, and this chapter is a great introduction to issues you may not have considered before.

Obviously, knowing everything about everything is impossible – and when you think you know it all, you're only setting yourself up for a gigantic fall. The sign of a true professional is how much she can learn *after* she supposedly knows it all. The enemy of learning is knowing. A defensive mindset of not really listening will hold back your sales progression. Admittedly taking criticism is hard but learning new skills and not getting it right first time is not criticism and not a black mark against you. Don't feel bad about yourself just because you didn't yet get it right. If you can set to one side this fear of not looking good or being wrong then you can open yourself up a lot more to learning. Admitting that you need to find out some things is the first step to achieving anything.

Understanding Why Research Is Important

Why do you need to research your prospective clients and their businesses? Well, meeting someone without knowing anything about her or her situation is never a good idea. Your sales prospect won't take kindly to the fact that you cared so little for her concerns that you didn't even do any research to make sure your offering would fit her potential requirements. Lack of preparation makes you look lousy and sets the wrong tone for any meeting if it's clear you do not know anything or very little about your potential client's operations. Secondly, and probably far more importantly, without some knowledge of the prospect, without some feel for her concerns and situations, you cannot properly communicate and get her talking freely about her challenges. And if she doesn't talk freely and communicate emotionally about her situation you'll find it difficult to bond with her, to create rapport with her, and to get her to expose areas of concern in her business that you can present a solution for – and thus make the sale actually happen more easily.

For example, if you sell air-filtration or purification systems to businesses, and you find out that a particular business must manufacture its products according to exacting standards, that's important information to know. Why? Because that fact means that the business must have a high level of concern for cleanliness and precision and your air cleaner can help it to achieve that.

Research a business, especially by looking at its Web site. The site often shows some of the clients that the company serves, whether it's been awarded a prestigious contract, or is proudly showing the sort of calibre of clients it works for. This information gives you an indication as to how the company sells itself. For example, if the Web site places a huge importance on quality, a solid guarantee, and a long-term history, you can match your selling to suit the company's style. You won't go bowling in there with cheap offers or flash discounts for this racy new gizmo, as doing so will undoubtedly clash with the company culture and alienate you from the buyer.

Adapting your message to what your clients tell you about themselves and their needs

If you doubt the validity of the premise that knowledge is power, take a look at how much information Web sites gather about the people who visit them. For example, Amazon.com doesn't just sell products, it also offers you an opportunity to establish a Wish List of products that you may be interested in buying (or receiving as gifts) at a later date. What does Amazon do with that Wish List? It can use the products you add to that list, along with your purchases and what you look at on its site, to find out where your interests lie. If Amazon.com begins offering a new book that someone with your interests would like, it customises the Web site so that that new book is the first thing you see when you go to the Amazon.com site. Amazon is customising its offers to your particular interests and needs. And you're the one telling Amazon what you're likely to buy.

Perhaps a more striking example of intelligence gathering and usage is that of Tesco. Tesco has seen a tremendous growth in their market share and the range of goods or services they sell over the last few years. How did this situation come about? A key component in their growth is simple – intelligence.

The Tesco Clubcard is brilliant. It allows Tesco to monitor your shopping, see clearly what types of items you purchase, and then offer similar products and tempt you with vouchers to spend next time you are in the store. This intelligence gathering allows them to create customer profiles that indicate likely shopping choices and then they tailor offers to match them. Tesco now offer financial services, insurances, loans, televisions, clothing – everything!

You can take advantage of these strategies for your business, too. If your company is gathering this kind of information and making it accessible to the entire sales force, you're off to a great start. If your company isn't gathering this information for you, you may want to establish a very detailed information sheet on your clients' interests and needs so that you can lead them to purchasing more products and services from you and from others with whom you may share referred leads (with their permission).

Investing time in research prior to going in gives you a definite edge. The more you know about a prospect, the more competent you appear, and the stronger you are when you present your case.

The same principle you use when you sell to businesses applies when you sell to individuals or families: The more you know about their backgrounds, the better. You can warm people up faster when you talk about their hobbies, jobs, and family than if you know nothing other than their address and phone number. For example, if you're selling air-treatment systems and you discover that one of your prospect's children has allergies or asthma, using that key influencing factor can help get you a sale when you present your product.

You may be wondering how you'd find out about that child's asthma. You can do that in one of several ways, including a brief survey-type phone call asking if anyone in the home has or has ever had allergies or other illnesses affected by the quality of the air in the home. Seeking this information wouldn't be seen as intrusive as it is clearly information that is linked to the product you are offering. Indeed, awareness of allergic reactions and asthma is increasing and many homeowners with families would accept this type of question as pretty normal information.

You may also buy from a professional list broker a list of target names specifically related to certain subjects or areas of interest. You may specifically ask for a list of persons known to be interested in the product you're selling or people who already purchase similar offerings and may be interested in a rival supply. List brokers can often sell you names and lists that include a range of information about a potential client. For example, you can find out what types of pets they have, cleaning products they purchase, holidays they enjoy, and whether or not they make a lot of long-distance phone calls. How do they get this information? Think about it. Have you ever filled out a survey about the products you use in order to receive a free offer on a product or a voucher giving you money off? If you do any of these sorts of things, then you probably appreciate that those companies that sponsor the survey don't simply send you your vouchers or allow discounts and then throw away your reply card. They store that valuable purchasing information about you in their databases for future reference.

Starting with the Basics: Knowing Your Clients Inside and Out

To be successful at selling, you must constantly be looking out for and storing all sorts of information. What type of information? Everything and anything about your product, your company, your competition, and (most importantly) your prospect. And with the Internet just a mouse-click away, you really have no excuse for not being informed. An abundance of information is available, quite literally at your fingertips – all you need is the commitment to locate and internalise it. You've heard the phrase 'knowledge is power'. In selling particularly, *applied* knowledge is power – simply knowing it isn't enough; using it is where the magic lies.

The ability to turn a situation around and see it from another person's perspective is the single most beneficial skill you can embrace. The most important thing to keep in mind when you're selling is how the client will benefit from your offering and what exactly she might be looking for and thinking of. You can't be of any help to a prospective client until you truly understand what she needs and where she's coming from.

So where do you begin in your quest to walk in your prospects' shoes? Not at the shoe shop! Instead, you need to do some basic research into your prospective clients, their businesses (or their home lifestyle depending on which market you are addressing), their standards and expectations, and their goals and aspirations. Start by following these tips:

- ✔ **Gather as much literature and other information as possible on a company before approaching it with your offering.** You want to be as prepared as possible before you make that first approach. You need to know what they offer and how they present themselves.

- ✔ **Visit the business's Web site.** Pay particular attention to the business's online product catalogue (if one exists), and look for news items on the site so that you're up to date on the most recent news related to the business. Always look for an 'About Us' link; the information there gives you valuable insight into the management team and their backgrounds. And who knows? You may find out that you know someone who works there or that you know someone who knows someone there.

  In a business-to-business selling environment, the importance of researching the Web site before you even call for an appointment can't be stressed enough.

- ✔ **Get copies of the company's product brochures and/or catalogues.** Take time to telephone the business – you can even pretend to be an enquiring prospect – to find out more about what the company offers. If you're familiar with the products that your prospective client sells, you can better see how your product or service can fit in and thus increase your chances of making a sale.

- ✔ **Visit your local library or research on the Internet to look up past news articles on the business.** If you're familiar with what's been happening in the business in the past few months, you can work that information into your conversations with the people you're meeting. You give the prospect the sense that you've done your homework about the business. This certainly sets you apart and undoubtedly creates a favourable impression.

- ✔ **Check out the business's accounts, if they're available.** If you're selling a fairly sizable investment, you require a financially strong company to avoid a bad debt. Information on prospective clients' accounts may well be useful.

  By law, every limited company must complete a set of accounts for taxation purposes, and you can access them via Companies House for a small fee (see www.companieshouse.gov.uk). You need the correct information so as to identify the specific company but this isn't difficult to obtain. (Be aware that a trading name might not be the actual name of the limited company, so check your information first.)

A story to copy

I (Ben) can tell you a story about a salesperson I had the fortune to do some work and networking with some years ago. Nick was selling for a very dynamic office equipment company – photocopiers, printers, and so on. When I met him to try to help increase his performance, he was already working hard and exhibited a striking commitment to the role, as evidenced by his attention to research and planning before he went out on his calls. Nick showed me his computer records of profiles of target companies with several contact names for each, along with some usage of equipment history in his Microsoft Outlook records. Nick was a thorough sales professional and whilst some of the more flamboyant or flashy salespeople in his team made more noise or went out and enjoyed their success, Nick was a quieter sort and spent the hours doing the boring stuff for work.

Bumping into Nick a couple of years later, I found out he'd been head-hunted by another major equipment provider and landed a senior management role at more than double his previous income. He'd established himself as a top-flight performer, all because he'd applied himself to learning about his territory and waiting for the process to go full circle and pay off. This process didn't happen overnight and it didn't happen easily but Nick made it happen and the result was worth it in the end.

Check out all paperwork and links on a prospect when you do your research. Obviously the larger the sale value, the more vital is this process but always remember that this habit of researching is extremely valuable and can make a world of difference to your results. Knowledge is power when you apply it properly. And you can *always* apply that philosophy to research that can help you sell.

Although doing your research and gathering information about your prospective client is essential, knowing when you have enough information is often difficult. In the end, the limit's up to you, of course. When you think you know enough to get the job done and make the sale, you've probably researched enough. If a question comes up during your presentation that you don't know the answer to, and if what you don't know may hurt your chances of closing the sale, then you don't know enough. Experience will tell you how much you need to prepare, but you're better off erring on the side of preparing too much than not preparing enough.

As you develop and enjoy a level of success and confidence, you may begin to feel that you are good enough to handle any situation and that research isn't that critical. Because of time challenges you may be tempted to skimp on the researching or even leave it out. Doing so is dangerous! You may well make a few sales and not see too much difference initially but over time you will. As a discipline, doing your research makes a difference of thousands of pounds a year to your income. Never get lazy.

Working with Different Types of Buyer

When you work in a business-to-business arena, a key concern is who the true decision-maker really is (this is also true in a domestic business-to-consumer sale, although usually not much of a problem to worry about because many home decisions are made jointly). The decision-maker may be the office manager, a purchasing agent, a department head, or even a director. You can usually find out simply by asking the receptionist who is responsible for making the decisions in the area of business to which your products or services apply, but it may be worth clarifying the information before you end the call. Simply ask again, 'So, just to make sure I'm clear, Mr Jackson looks after this area for your company?'. If more than one person is involved, another name may be mentioned if the receptionist isn't completely sure as to the final decision-making structure. (You need to approach all of the people whose names you gather and you need to make sure all of them get your name.)

The next thing to consider is how to approach any and all of these people and make as favourable an impression as possible in order to win the sale. In devising your strategy, remember that not everyone is the same! You have many different moods and likes and dislikes and the same is true of each prospect you meet. Several different types of character exist and it is worth considering these in a little detail so that you can be prepared for meeting any one of them. (Remember that if the person you are meeting doesn't like you, the chances of making the sale are vastly reduced!)

Your delivery style must be flexible enough to relate to all of the different personality types you meet. Never settle for having just one presentation style. Doing so severely limits the number of people you can serve. We're not advising you to develop multiple personalities; just remember that if you don't like the personality of the decision-maker, you can learn to like the opportunity she's offering you to do business with her.

The next section takes a brief look at some of the distinct character types you may come across as you go about your business. Obviously these are broad types and don't exactly describe every person you're likely to meet, though you probably can identify with some of them immediately.

Buyer 1: Halfway there already

This person is already basically sold on your company or brand. She knows just what to expect from you and likes your company's reliability and reputation. She's easy to work with and, after you convince her of your personal competence, will remain loyal to you and your product. If she's *not* convinced that you're competent, this character won't hesitate to call your company and request another representative.

How do you appeal to this personality type? Essentially it is one of the easiest to sell to but never forget that she can still be sold to by someone else if you don't do your job properly. Never assume that the sale is already in the bag and do a less-than-full sales presentation. Don't short-sell the product or service just because she's already sold on its quality. You need to exhibit great product knowledge to personally win over her trust and belief in your ability to meet her needs. Providing dependable service and follow-up will help you close the sale and gain repeat business.

Buyer 2: The deal-maker

This type isn't too difficult to spot because right up front she'll saying something like 'so what do I get as freebies then?' or 'as long as you can make a special price for me'. This person loves the deal-making process and actually is usually pretty sold on you and the product or service early on. Her love of a deal makes her easily played. We say *played* because deal-making is a game in which one player makes an opening offer and the other counters with a considerably lower one or one that includes too many extras for the price. Sadly today's market is full of these types of buyer because too many poor salespeople have allowed the buyer to think that many offerings are much the same and only price differentiates.

So how do you handle this type? Let her know that she's important and special and that she drives a hard bargain. But although you admire her business savvy, tell her that there really isn't a lot to play with. This approach won't put her off – in fact to this type of character it is such a powerful statement that it sucks her in! She views your statement as a red rag to a bull and then gets excited believing that she can make a deal where others cannot. As long as you make her work for what she ends up with (and *that* of course you have already built into your price and pre-planned strategic negotiation points) you'll come out a winner with an order.

Buyer 3: Cool and clinical

This type of buyer remains remote, cool, and measured so as to not allow emotion to interfere with what she prefers to keep an analytical, logical process. She may well appear to be domineering or controlling, as she perceives her role in making the correct purchasing decision as a primary one. This type appears very official and 'personality-free'. She is often abrupt, giving short answers to your questions as if she dislikes the process and simply wants answers. She wants to keep the topic of conversation strictly business. She expects paperwork and prompt and correct responses to her requests. She believes that simply getting the facts is the best way to honour the responsibility vested in her. The interesting thing is that these buyers are in fact human and do have a life outside of work – you just have to have a special gift for opening them up.

Your job with such a cool customer is to warm her up. This type is especially in need of a human touch. You'll get nowhere unless you have a handle on how she intends to make a decision. You must ease out of her how she perceives her personal role after the purchase has been made, possibly highlighting that after-sales service and trouble-free performance are available only if something is left in the way of monies in the price. Remind her of the longer-term vision beyond immediate facts and figures and gently encourage her to examine how people may feel down the line if something gets missed now. Ask her how a purchase of your product or service would impact on her personally and then gently ask for help in understanding her exact company-specific issues so as to be even more helpful. Above all, appreciate that this person isn't a cold-blooded alien but sincerely believes that she's doing the best for the business.

You win with this type by making your sales approach line up with the client's desire to protect the company. Don't try to win by making her laugh, but help her see that doing the best for the company involves more than cold facts. Gradually you'll warm her to your stance if she feels that you're helping the company, not merely trying to trick her into a false sense of friendship.

Buyer 4: Scarlet Pimpernel

This buyer frustrates you! She's evasive and distant and nearly impossible to tie down. She refuses to return your phone calls, postpones appointments, or reschedules at the last minute. She likes to shop around and keeps you waiting in the meantime, and she tests your patience at every turn. Seemingly this buyer doesn't want to deal with you but still expects you to be ready when she is!

If you find yourself up against this type, enlist the aid of her secretary or support staff because they'll be your best allies in terms of gaining access. Truthfully, the secretary can tell you how best to play this person. Sometimes if you share your honest frustration at missing the buyer, the secretary or assistant can try to be a middle-man.

Ultimately what you must appreciate is that, as with the cool and clinical buyer, this type of person probably believes that she's acting in the company's best interests. (Bear in mind, of course, that she may well be genuinely busy and this state is no reflection upon how she views you or your offering.) Also appreciate that if she's delaying then she feels no sense of urgency regarding your product and your chasing and calling several times may make her feel hounded and could easily go against you.

Your best tack is to maintain a cool approach and leave a clear message that you're trying to help and that you sincerely believe that you can, but that you don't wish to hound her. Often if she's genuinely struggling with her workload, she'll tell you that it is just a temporary phase but can you please keep on at her. An open approach stating how you feel often draws out the true picture and either kills or cures your future success.

Buyer 5: The bully

For this personality type, you see it her way or not at all. She's a self-proclaimed expert but also poor at delegating authority and insists upon everyone and everything reporting to her. A bully may also be rude and interrupt your presentation while she takes calls or gives directions to her secretary.

The symptoms of a bully are frequent interruptions, a demanding tone, and refusal to alter specifications when you suggest that something very close if not exact will do the job. This type of buyer craves strength and importance and feeds that need by being dominant and abrupt. She's likely to be intolerant of poor timekeeping, for example, and will list the failings of those who've passed before and didn't make the grade. She of course has pity for mere mortals and is loudly strong, not quiet and cool. She is confident in her strength and bullishness.

When dealing with a bully, be extremely polite, prepared, and concise. Don't make any assumptions and don't bite at her attempts to strong-arm you. Let her know that you value her time and her business, but you absolutely must maintain integrity and politely offer your perspective if she is dismissive of your needs. You simply must *not* confront her and enter into battle because all parties lose if you do. Rather, maintain your dignity and clearly state that you value your offering to the extent that if she wishes to do business then you are willing, but that your success isn't dependent upon her and that if it doesn't work for *both* parties you don't want to do business.

Being Aware of Unique Cultural Needs

If you're planning to do business in another country, expect to invest as much time understanding the culture as you do understanding the needs for your products and services. The same rule holds true even if you do business within cultural groups different from your own in the country in which you live. Even if you're not actively doing business in another country or within another cultural group, but you're building a Web site that may be viewed by people from many different countries or cultures, you need to be aware of words and phrases that just don't translate or may be offensive when a translation is made.

To help you avoid some mistakes, we take a look at some cultural traditions you need to be aware of when dealing with clients. But first, here are a few general pointers:

- **Dress to impress.** Because your appearance is the first cue others get about how you feel about yourself and your business, take extra care in dressing for business meetings and events. When in doubt, dress conservatively and more formally than usual. In many cultures, such as Asian or Arab, wearing short skirts or shorts is considered inappropriate for a woman.

- **Meet and greet appropriately.** Some cultures, particularly Arab ones, include embraces or handshakes when meeting and departing and many of our European neighbours kiss on the cheeks one or more times as a natural greeting or departure. Determine in advance what greeting style is correct for your potential client – remember, doing so is considerate and may be financially beneficial.

- **Be patient when building trust and establishing relationships.** People whose origins are from countries other than the UK generally need more time to build trust. Observing a greater degree of formality when becoming acquainted is important.

- **Speak more slowly than you normally do, but don't raise your voice because you think the other person can't understand you.** Volume doesn't usually increase comprehension.

A word of caution, though, against speaking too slowly – you may suggest that the prospect's inability to understand you is the result of ignorance. Very often, the ability to understand a foreign language is greater than the ability to speak it fluently. Avoid slang, idioms, and jargon.

- **If you're using an interpreter, make sure the interpreter meets ahead of time with the people for whom she is interpreting.** This allows the interpreter to learn the language patterns, special terminology, and numbers used by the people she's translating for, such as product identifiers or other codes specific to a company or industry. All of these details can change the whole dimension of what's being said.

- **Pay attention to non-verbal interaction cues.** The word *yes* or an affirmative nod often means, 'Yes, I hear you', in Asian cultures, not, 'Yes, I agree'. Remember that not all body language is universal (take a look at *Body Language For Dummies* by Elizabeth Kuhnke for more).

- **Get your client's name right.** If you forget a client's name or mispronounce it you'll have to work that much harder to remedy the situation and earn her respect in the future. Introduce yourself first and listen to how she introduces herself in response. For example, you may say, 'Hello, my name is Ben Kench. How are you?' If she replies, 'Good morning, I'm Mrs Johnson and I'm very well thank you,' then she's clearly issued an instruction to maintain formality until she tells you otherwise. If however she introduces herself by saying, 'Good morning, I'm Caroline Johnson,' then the ruling is simple – first names will do.

> ✔ **Respect personal space.** If you want to be sure that people feel comfortable around you (a necessity in the world of selling), don't invade another person's space. If you're working with people from cultures where less personal space is required than you're used to, be sure not to back away when they step into your larger personal space. Doing so can be construed as a sign that you are fearful or hesitant about the other person. Neither are good feelings to have about potential business clients.

Culture is as much an influence on people as their personal experiences, so knowing about your clients' customs and traditions makes sense. That way, neither you nor your client will be made to feel uncomfortable. Remember: Knowledge is power.

Making appointments

The modern world is changing to the extent that virtually wherever you live and do business a mixed culture exists and you come across many languages and customs even within a short drive of your home. If you're going to do business within a non-native culture, consider a couple of points.

Decide which environment is most conducive to doing business with the prospect. Although many business people prefer formal, corporate, conference-room settings, others prefer more relaxed locations (such as restaurants or clubs) for business discussions. Ensure that all parties feel comfortable with the place chosen.

In the UK it is common practice to meet and do business in a neutral environment such as a hotel lobby. But be prepared: realising that people no longer book meeting rooms, hotels can make up for lost room revenue by charging you £5 for a cup of coffee and charging for parking too!

When you have an appointment, confirm all the details and do your homework on what to wear, what to bring with you, and how to give your presentation. Always be punctual, but don't expect the other person to be. In many cultures, relationships are much more important than time clocks. Value the time your client gives you, but don't count the minutes.

Presenting your business card

If you really are serious about doing consistent business within another language or culture, have some business cards printed with your contact information in the language of the recipient. If your card is two-sided, with your language on one side and another language on the other, always present your card with the client's language face up so that she sees this information immediately. If you are considering a multi-language print, use a professional to ensure the language and format are absolutely correct or you risk giving even greater offence than by merely presenting your usual home-based card.

Whatever language or format you have your card printed in, allow the client a moment to read the card before talking or moving on to the next aspect of your presentation. Some cultures have specific etiquette surrounding the use of business cards, so find out what rules apply in the culture you're dealing with.

In any culture, take the time to read the card of each person who gives you one before accepting another card. Don't set the cards aside quickly because doing so can appear to be dismissing the person to move on to someone else. Instead, keep the cards in your hand until the introductions are complete. As a good habit pronounce the name carefully as soon as you get the card if the name is unfamiliar or not easy to pronounce. At this first instance, your new contacts won't mind helping you say their names correctly. If you miss this chance to pronounce a name correctly or later on you use the wrong name, it will appear awkward and won't assist your cause.

Making presentations

In some cultures, getting down to the bottom line as soon as possible is critical. In others, you need to spend more time telling your clients about the history of your company and helping them feel comfortable with you and your product. In yet other cultures, underscoring the personal and emotional benefits of your proposal is important. In some cultures, people prefer to touch and feel samples of your product, whereas in others they may prefer just to read analyses, complete with graphs and testimonials. In some cultures, the negotiation is the best part of the game. Negotiation may include shouting orders, banging fists on tables, or simply silence. Alternatively, you may present and the clients either accept or decline and then move on with little or no chance for you to reiterate important points or give a benefit summary.

Remember, when you give a presentation, *especially* when dealing with other cultures, always be organised. Have professional-looking paperwork to explain all the details of your proposal, and bring a copy for everyone in the room. Leaving anyone out or asking for additional copies to be made is a big mistake.

You simply *cannot* prepare too much for a meeting with someone from another culture. Expect to be asked for any and every little detail about your company, product, service, and location, as well as about yourself. That way, no matter what comes up, you'll be ready.

Giving gifts

The decision-makers at most companies understand the value of appropriate gift giving and often establish certain parameters for gift giving by their staff. If your company doesn't have specific guidelines for you to follow, ask what they prefer. Or, better yet, suggest some appropriate parameters based on the potential value of each client to the company. If you're the sales representative who is the main source of contact with the client, you need to ensure that the client thinks well of you when she receives the gift. So, don't be afraid to jump in with some solid suggestions.

The stronger your relationship with your client, the more personalised your gift should be. You wouldn't send a long-standing client whose business represents 20 per cent of your sales volume a cheap-looking plastic-covered diary! If you've done business with the client for a while, you should know what that person likes and gear your gift to her highest level of enjoyment.

Beware that some cultures find the giving and receiving of gifts a personal matter, not a business matter, and that in other cultures gifts that would be considered very appropriate where you're from may be completely offensive to the people you're visiting. For example, in France, business gifts aren't generally given and someone from India would not appreciate a gift made of leather, because the cow is considered sacred in her country.

Also be sure that the recipient doesn't construe the gift as being inappropriate. In any scenario the giving of gifts must relate to the size of account you have developed. (Giving a Rolex watch to a client who only purchased £500 worth of product from you is probably not a wise move either financially or for the business.) If the client is uncomfortable at all with the gift, she may wonder whether you're offering a bribe for future business. In an opposite sex scenario, the giving of a gift may be misconstrued as suggesting another angle to the relationship.

Indeed, before you give a gift to a client, determine whether the recipient's company has a policy on receiving gifts. Many companies don't allow their employees to accept gifts; if you offer one, your client may be in the uncomfortable position of having to decline or return it. (This point is particularly pertinent at Christmas: Various taxation rules on benefits and past histories of jealous wrangling and accusations of discrimination have caused companies to simply say no to gifts.) If the company doesn't allow employees to receive gifts, ask the person with whom you have the best relationship in the company what you can do. Maybe you *can* send a box of chocolates or a basket of fruit for the department to share, but not a pen-and-pencil set for the individual.

Eating out with ease

Eating with prospects can be an issue. As an example, if you're working with an Asian client, you may be expected to wine and dine as part of the meeting, as this is more in keeping with her longer-hours culture.

In some cultures, slurping, burping, and even drinking from another person's glass during dinner are perfectly acceptable; in others, they're absolutely not. When you're dealing with another culture, you don't necessarily have to join in with behaviours you have trouble with, but at least be aware of them so you don't seem inappropriately shocked if your guest does so. And at the very least, know what's considered rude, and avoid those behaviours during your meals.

Be sure to understand your potential client's needs with regard to specific foods or preparation of such foods. When dining with a client, make certain you're not taking her to a restaurant whose menu will not provide appropriate foods for her. Also, consider customs the client may have, whether cultural or religious, with regard to taking a meal. You may need to allow a few moments for prayer or indulge the client in eating very slowly and consuming many courses.

Etiquette, in any environment, is all about behaving in such a way that everyone feels comfortable: 'When in Rome, do as the Romans do.' And when you are the one doing the entertaining, do everything you can to make your client feel at home.

Responding to Your Clients' Fears

In all its forms, fear is the greatest enemy you'll ever encounter in persuading your clients. The toughest part of your job is helping other people admit to and overcome their fears so you can earn the opportunity to do business with them. Fear is what builds those walls of resistance that salespeople so often run into. You need to know how to climb over or break through those walls if you're going to travel the road to sales success.

We identify some common fears you need to help your prospects overcome. When you recognise these fears you're ready to discover how to dismantle the walls, one brick at a time, thus gaining your prospect's confidence and trust.

Your goal is to get your prospects to like and trust you. They do that when you serve them with warmth and empathy.

Fear of salespeople

At first, every prospect is afraid of you. Why? Because you're a salesperson, and you want something from them. In addition, what you want involves some kind of a change on the prospect's part, and most people are afraid of change, at least to some degree. Even if you're selling to someone you already know, when you meet that person in the role of a sales professional, certain fears inevitably arise.

As a salesperson, when you meet someone who tries very hard to hang on to her hard-earned cash (or at least not to part with it too easily), you can safely assume a certain amount of fear is involved. Not many people over the age of 21 walk around looking for places to spend their money. They separate themselves from their money only for products and services they *believe* they *need*. Your job is to help them feel the need, and build the value of your product's ability to serve that need to a point where their fear now becomes a fear of what happens if they *don't* allow you to help them.

A wise tactic is to warmly invite them to stand or sit beside you while you show them all the good stuff your product does or has. This way, you're looking at your product together. You encourage them to touch your product so that they can imagine owning it.

Get potential customers to place their hands on the product, push buttons, turn dials, make things light up, heat up, or move. If you're offering a service or an item they cannot actually have at that moment, have them handle pictures or documents. When they get *involved* with the product, their fear of you lessens. After all, you're the one who introduced the prospects to the product, and look what great fun they're having now!

Fear of failure

The fear of failure is one you're likely to encounter in your clients, because virtually everyone has this fear to some degree. Why? Because everyone has made mistakes, and everyone has regrets. At some stage everyone has made a poor purchasing decision. Whether your failure was in choosing the wrong hair colour or purchasing a vehicle that wasn't right for you, you know the frustration of making a mistake. Somewhere in your psyche, you have a fear, not necessarily because of your bad decision, but because you remember that mistake as being associated with a salesperson – after all it was her fault you bought it (the hairdresser who told you that you'd look great with green hair or the car salesperson who convinced you that your five kids could happily pile into a two-seater convertible).

No one wants to handle a transaction in which the customer may be dissatisfied with the result. Trust us, the grief you get from a dissatisfied customer isn't worth the commission you earn on the sale. Although dissatisfied customers aren't (and shouldn't be) the norm, you must go into every presentation with a sharp interest in the who, what, when, where, and why of your client's needs. When you've satisfied yourself that buying your product or service is in your client's best interest, then your duty as the expert is to convince her that this decision is truly good for her. Take the time to carefully talk your prospect through every aspect of her decision, giving her the time she needs to make a choice she'll be comfortable with.

Sell to your client's needs, not to your wants.

Fear of owing money

Prospects are also tremendously afraid of spending too much money. Many people have an attitude of scarcity – that there isn't enough to go round. Thus, they have a huge reluctance to spend money, fearing that it won't be replaced very quickly. Your fee for your service is almost always a point of contention with prospective customers and not because they're being stubborn, but because they're legitimately afraid of not being able to find the money, replace what they spend, or indeed get in more debt.

Most people won't attempt to negotiate with a company about its fees, but as a salesperson your clients don't see you as an institution. You're not cold, forbidding concrete walls and corridors. Instead, you're a warm, flesh-and-blood fellow human being and because of this, your clients often try to negotiate with you. You're human and they're less afraid and more confident of scoring negotiation points. Depending on your clients' negotiation skills, they may do any or all of the following:

- ✔ **Put off making a decision, forcing you to draw them out.** We cover what to do in this situation in Chapter 11.

- ✔ **Tell you point-blank that they're concerned about the cost.** In this situation, you need to sell them on the value of the product or service you provide.

- ✔ **Voice their concerns in a roundabout way.** For example, a client may say something like, 'Another company I talked with will charge a lot less.'

If your client has reservations about the cost of your product or service, we recommend saying something like this:

You know, I've learned something over the years. People look for three things when they spend money. They look for the finest quality, the best service, and, of course, the lowest investment. I've also found that no company can offer all three. They can't offer the finest quality and the best service for the lowest investment. So, for your long-term happiness, which of the three would you be most willing to give up? Fine quality? Excellent service? Or the lowest fee?

In response, most people say that quality and service are of the utmost concern, which overcomes their concern about the fee. Your next move is to reiterate everything you will do for them. Again, sell the *value* of the product you and your company provide.

If you run into a client who is concerned only with getting the lowest investment and you can't provide it, you may have to bow out of the picture. Do it gracefully and stay in touch. Chances are good that she'll get what she pays for and will eventually see the wisdom in spending more for the quality product or service that you can provide.

Fear of being lied to

Another common fear in buyers is that of being lied to. As a general rule, clients who are afraid of being lied to doubt everything you're saying about how much they'll benefit from your product, service, or idea.

When you face a client with this fear, a strong past track record comes into play. Having a long list of happy clients should help you calm this anxiety because these buyers *will* believe others who have no reason to lie. Also try showing more written detail because they might doubt what you say but generally believe what they read, especially corporate literature or product supplier material. Also involve the other people you work with and bring their personal integrity and credentials into play – it's very hard for them to believe *everyone* is a liar! Use endorsements and provide referees that can vouch for your integrity – preferably well-known names or at least names known to the prospect. Try using recorded video testimonials from the clients who have purchased; you only need one or two. You can hand a CD to a prospect or refer her to your Web site. Video testimonials are incredibly powerful as they almost prove that you aren't faking your story.

You *never* have any reason to lie to a customer. If you're honest with your customers and always share the truth with them, even bad news, they will respect you and give you the benefit of the doubt. Honesty and integrity in every selling situation will make you a winner each and every time.

Fear of embarrassment

Many people fear being embarrassed by people knowing about a bad decision they've made. Have you ever made a poor decision that was big enough that most of your friends and family members knew about it (and then kept reminding you about it)? They may have only been teasing you, but you probably felt demeaned and embarrassed. Bad decisions make you feel like a child again – insecure and powerless. Because many potential clients have this fear of being embarrassed by a bad decision, they put off making any decision at all.

If you're selling to more than one decision-maker (such as a married couple or business partners), neither person is likely to want to risk being embarrassed in front of the other. The chances are they've disagreed about something in the past and they don't want to have that uncomfortable situation arise again.

Your primary goal is to help them feel secure with you. Focus upon removing the doubt that things could ever go wrong and so eliminate the potential for embarrassment.

Fear of the unknown

Fear of the unknown is another common emotion in buyers. A lack of understanding of your product or service, or of its value to the prospect's company, is a reasonable cause for delaying any transaction. Name recognition dispels some of it, but if you work for a local or small new company that doesn't have a huge reputation, getting past this fear is harder.

You need to ask the prospect more about her hesitancy and see if you can alleviate some fear by exploring more deeply where it comes from. Undoubtedly she has had some bad experiences that are pretty much unrelated to your offer and finding a way around her fear isn't difficult. You may be able to calm her nerves with creative negotiation, a staged payment plan, and an absolute guarantee of satisfaction or her money back.

Always spend a little extra time on what your product actually does and the benefits it brings when you're working with a customer who is a new purchaser of the service or product, as she has a natural fear of the unknown but one that can be readily overcome.

Fear of repeating past mistakes

Having a bad past experience generates fear in the hearts of some potential customers. If they've used a product or service like yours before, find out what kind of experience it was for them. If they hesitate to tell you, you may assume that their past experience was bad and that you have to overcome a lot more fear than if they've never used a product or service like yours before.

Try offering the product or service on a sample or trial basis. Give the prospect the names of your satisfied customers who will give unbiased testimony as to the value of your offering. (Check with those customers first to make sure they don't mind if prospects contact them.)

Fear generated by others

A prospect's fear may also come from third-party information. Someone she admires or respects may have told her something negative about your company, about your type of product, or even about another representative of your company. Either way, that third party stands between you and your prospect like a brick wall until you convince or persuade the prospect that you can help her more than the third party can, because *you* are the expert on your product or service. You'll have to work hard to earn the prospect's trust. Enlist the aid of some of your past happy clients as references, if necessary.

In essence this situation is a battle between loyalties. Initially, the prospect has more respect for the person giving her the negative comment than for you with the positive sales one. Try asking more about the person who told her the bad story – helping the prospect see that the other person isn't always as reliable as first thoughts suggest.

Choosing Your Words Wisely

When you're getting to know your clients, you need to think about the effective power of language. Every word you utter has a learned meaning attached and memories stored in the mind of the listener. Do you use that power to your greatest advantage?

Every word has a meaning attached to it in your mind. When you hear a word, you draw from a memory bank a picture of what that word represents. Each memory record of that meaning often has emotions attached to it as well and these are often very different from person to person. Words such as *spring*, *summer*, *autumn*, and *winter* for example can generate positive or negative emotions in you. If you love gardening, the warm spring air brings to mind beautiful blossoms, the opportunity to get your fingers in the dirt, preparing your soil for a summer crop. If you are a hay fever sufferer, the picture painted by the word *spring* is totally different.

The same rule applies to the words you use in your contacts with customers. You don't know in advance which words about you, your product, and your company will generate positive feelings in your clients. If you want to have a successful sales career, you need to become extra-sensitive to the way you use words.

Knowing the best words to use

Many words common to sales and selling situations can generate fearful or negative images in your clients' minds. The experience of hundreds of thousands of salespeople confirms that replacing such words with more positive, pacifying words and phrases (such as the ones in Table 4-1) is crucial.

Table 4-1	Words to Eliminate from Your Sales Vocabulary
Instead of . . .	*Use . . .*
Sell	Help to use
Contract	Paperwork, agreement, or form
Cost or price	Investment or amount
Deposit	Initial investment or initial amount
Monthly payment	Monthly investment or monthly amount
Buy	Own
Deal	Opportunity or transaction
Objection	Area of concern
Problem	Challenge
Pitch	Present/presentation or demonstrate/demonstration
Commission	Fee for service
Appointment	Visit, as in 'pop by and visit'
Sign	Approve, authorise, endorse, or okay

The first terms we recommend that you remove from your vocabulary are *sell* and *sold*. Many salespeople tell prospects how many units of their product they have *sold*. Or they brag about having *sold* the same product to another customer. What are the mental images these words create? No one likes the idea of being *sold* anything. The word reminds people of high-pressure sales tactics and usually turns them off. It makes the transaction sound one-sided, as if the customer really had little say in the matter. So what can you use in place of these common words? Replace *sell* or *sold* with *helped them acquire* or *got them involved* – phrases that create softer images of a helpful salesperson and a receptive customer becoming involved together in the same process.

Contract is another commonly used word in sales. For most people, *contract* evokes negative images – legal connotations and 'trapped' scenarios. Contracts bring with them fine print, legalities, and being locked into something. So stop using the word *contract*, unless your particular line of business requires it. Instead, use *paperwork*, *agreement*, or *form*.

What about *cost* and *price*? Those words evoke images of hard-earned cash going up in smoke. Substitute the words *investment* or *amount* for *cost* or *price*. When most people hear the word *investment*, they envision the positive image of getting a return on their money. For products for which the word *investment* just doesn't fit, use *amount* – this word's been proven to be less threatening to most consumers than *cost* or *price*.

The same idea applies to the terms *deposit* and *monthly payment*, so replace those phrases with *initial investment* and *initial amount* or *monthly investment* and *monthly amount*.

What about the word *buy*? When people hear the word *buy*, they see money leaving their pockets again. Use the term *own* instead. *Own* conjures up images of what they'll get for their money, where they'll put the product in their home, showing it with pride to friends or relatives, and many other positive thoughts.

Deal is another term overused by salespeople. This word brings to mind something people have always wanted but never found. Images of used-car salespeople are only too closely associated with the word *deal*. Top salespeople never give their clients *deals*. They offer *opportunities* or get them involved in a *transaction*.

Customers don't raise *objections* about your products or services. Instead, they express *areas of concern*. You never have *problems* with your sales. Every now and then you may, however, face some *challenges* with your transactions. You never *pitch* your product or service to your customer. Instead, you *present* or *demonstrate* your product or service.

And as an authority or expert on your product or service, you don't earn *commissions*, either. You do, however, receive *fees for service*:

Mrs Johnson, I'm fortunate that my company has included a fee for service in every transaction. In that way, they compensate me for the high level of service I give to each and every client, and that's what you really want, isn't it?

Another word that can potentially raise concerns in the mind of a consumer is *appointment*. Now, in the business-to-business world, this word may not be as strong. However, consumers will view the appointment as interfering with their regular schedule even if the schedule shows that time as free time. Rather than equate meeting with you to an appointment with a doctor or dentist, use the softer term *visit*:

> I'd love to have the opportunity to visit you; would Wednesday evening or Thursday afternoon be better?

Better yet, offer to 'pop by and visit'. What mental image does that phrase create? That you're going to pop in and pop out – that you'll only be there a short time. In the business world, a 'pop by' can conjure the image of a brief handshake and exchange of information in the lobby with no sit-down, conference room involvement at all.

However, don't make the call sound too casual or you could very well arrive and not meet the correct atmosphere for business or have the relevant parties present. You may upset the prospect if you try to turn the conversation towards a more business-like approach because she may be under the impression that it isn't a sales call.

Like many things in life, striking a perfect balance isn't easy and getting the tone and pitch of your voice right so that your meaning is totally clear may take a bit of practice.

The last but definitely not the least important term to replace is *sign*. If you replace nothing else in your selling vocabulary after reading this book, never again ask a customer to *sign* an agreement, form, or paperwork. What happens emotionally when people are asked to *sign* something? In most cases, a warning goes off in their heads. They become hesitant and cautious. They want to review whatever it is they're signing, scanning the page for the infamous fine print. Instead of asking your clients to *sign*, ask them to *approve*, *authorise*, *endorse*, or *okay* your *paperwork*, *agreement*, or *form*. Each of those word pictures carries the positive associations that you want to inspire in your clients.

Concentrating on what appears to be such minor details may seem foolish, but some of those details pack a hefty punch. You may consider these words minor and think that fussing over them is misplaced. But if you really think about the situation, you'll see that language is a salesperson's *only* tool. The salesperson who uses language well, for the genuine benefit of other people, is a salesperson who sells, and sells, and sells. The words you use aren't minor details at all – they are the very centre of your profession. So, when you write down and practise your own product presentation, go through it and make sure that your words stress comfort, convenience, and ownership from your prospects' perspective. After all, satisfying your prospects' needs is what this business of selling is all about and the words you send out to them are the only way that you, and not your competition, can earn the opportunity to satisfy those needs.

Don't ask 'em to sign when you can ask for an autograph. As a way of softening the moment of 'signing the contract', try making a comment we overheard: 'Just in case you ever become famous, can I have your autograph on this please?' While you say these words, smile and hand the customer a pen. Nice picture, isn't it?

Using only the jargon your clients know

Today, more than ever, your selling vocabulary matters because of the phenomenon of *trade talk*, or jargon. *Jargon* is defined as words and phrases particular to a given field of work. It creeps into everything and anything these days and acronyms and fancy abbreviations are everywhere. For example, if you sell medical supplies to doctors, you need to know the jargon medical professionals use and use it yourself liberally. But if you sell medical supplies to the general public, limit your use of technical terms to the bare minimum until you can determine your client's level of knowledge about the product. Don't alienate your customers by using acronyms or words they're not familiar with. Your goal is to make your customers feel important and feeling important when you don't feel very clever is tough.

When your product or service has anything to do with the Internet, knowing when to use jargon and when to steer clear of it is especially important. Although by now you may feel like the whole world knows about the Internet, seeking out the lowest common denominator with potential clients is always wise. That way, you won't overwhelm or confuse them with terms or acronyms specific to your field. Your client may not know what you mean by RAM, be clueless about operating systems and browsers, and expect to be able to munch on cookies!

The human mind can assimilate information rapidly only if it understands what is being said. If you're talking to an average consumer about bits and bytes and she doesn't understand those terms, her mind stops at those terms and tries in vain to find an image that fits them. Many people won't stop to ask you for explanations, because they're afraid of showing their lack of knowledge and being embarrassed in the process. Others may get the gist of what you're talking about but struggle to keep up. While they're trying to keep up, they miss the next few valuable points you relay to them. In other words, you've lost them. If your subject sounds more complicated than your customer can comprehend, you risk squelching her desire to ever own or use your product or service *and* you risk losing the sale. More often than not, you lose such customers to a competitor's salesperson who uses lay terms and simple definitions.

Good things come to salespeople who take the time to find out how to speak their clients' language.

Developing your vocabulary to excel in sales

Words are readily available to anyone who wants to use them. The dictionary doesn't reserve certain words and their meanings for the rich. Everyone has access to the same dictionary, and everyone has the same opportunity to choose the words that make her speech outstanding and memorable. Every time you need to convey a concept to someone, you have a choice of any one of thousands of words to establish your meaning. You have no excuse *not* to choose your words carefully. Because you know that your words reflect the person you are, investigate the word choices you make and the reasons you make them.

Developing your selling vocabulary isn't about mastering the words you were tested on at school or college. This process is about taking the time to make a list of powerful but easy-to-understand words and phrases specific to your product or service. With new or prospective clients, be prepared to give them the definition in lay terms if it refers to something vital to the transaction or if the term will recur frequently in your discussion with these customers.

Describing your offering without using some jargon or terms that sound like jargon may be impossible, but if this is the case, explain the jargon very simply so that a child could understand.

You need to strike a balance between speaking the language of your clients and educating them about the terms they need to know if they're going to use your product or service. The key is to not make any assumptions about the terminology your clients are familiar with and to be ready to explain any terms they don't know.

Anyone who wants to persuade others (and if you're in the selling business, that's you) should recognise and choose appropriate language. Take a look at the two following examples. Be aware of the differences in language between the two situations. Even though you can't *see* these two salespeople, pay attention to the mental picture you get of each of them and their selling styles.

The manager of Continual Care Hair (CCH) has been courting an account with a major chain of salons, owned by Mr Dunn. Mr Dunn's salons now carry the products of one of CCH's competitors, but he's agreed to hear a presentation by a CCH representative. The CCH manager needs to choose the salesperson who can consummate all of the manager's hard work and make the sale to land the account. The manager calls a meeting with each salesperson she's considering. The one who succeeds in representing the company receives a sizable increase in earnings. First example:

> MANAGER: Now that you understand what will be expected of you, how would you give this presentation?
>
> DAWN: I'd just love the chance to tell Mr Dunn how much better our products are than what he's using. I'd go and see Mr Dunn as soon as possible. I know I could convince him to dump what he uses now and replace his stock with ours.
>
> MANAGER: What's your next step?
>
> DAWN: Well, after I got all the information, I'd tell Mr Dunn what we can do for him and I'd try to get him on my side before the presentation to his staff so he can help me sell his stylists on the products.
>
> MANAGER: I'm interested to hear how you would do this, Dawn.
>
> DAWN: Well, I guess I'd tell him how much money he would save and how much more he'll make by selling our products.

Now, here's the same situation – a hopeful salesperson talking to CCH's manager – except now the salesperson is Sue:

> MANAGER: Now that you understand what will be expected of you, how will you handle this presentation?
>
> SUE: I believe the first step would be to contact Mr Dunn and request a meeting at his convenience. Then, with your approval, I'd examine your files on the salons, so I'm prepared for the presentation.
>
> MANAGER: What's your next step?
>
> SUE: I will ask Mr Dunn to show me his salons. I'll familiarise myself with Mr Dunn's needs, his stylists' needs, and those of the salons' clientele. Then I'll offer Mr Dunn the opportunity to use Continual Care Hair products and ask his permission to present the products to his stylists.
>
> MANAGER: I'm interested to hear how you would do this, Sue.
>
> SUE: Although considering his financial benefits is important, I'll encourage Mr Dunn to examine the improved condition of hair that has been treated with Continual Care Hair products. Making hair more beautiful will give Mr Dunn happier customers as well as increased profits. Would it be possible to take a few company models with me on the presentation?

These two conversations create two pictures in the mind of the manager. Who will represent her company with the most success? The answer is Sue.

Why? Because Sue radiated calm enthusiasm and a thoughtful manner. But the turning point in Sue's interview is her choice of the phrase *I will* instead of the indefinite terms like *I guess* or even *I would* that Dawn uses. Sue speaks as if she's already been chosen, whereas Dawn uses iffier, less confident language. This difference is subtle but very effective. And it isn't long before the manager agrees to send models out with Sue for her presentation.

Sue is an *above average* salesperson with a powerful command of language. She creates positive word pictures with every word she utters. Here are some words you may hear an *average* salesperson deliver. Think about the pictures they create in your mind.

> SALESPERSON: All the local kids will love playing in your new pool.
>
> PROSPECT: I'm probably going to have trouble getting my kids out of it.
>
> SALESPERSON: When should we start digging? Would this Saturday or next Monday be better?

What image comes to your mind from the salesperson's statement that 'all the local kids will love playing in your new pool'? The thought of loads of noisy children jumping, splashing, running, and yelling at the tops of their lungs comes to most people's minds – not a peaceful scene, is it? What's wrong with this dialogue between the salesperson and the prospect?

Think about the word pictures you paint. Just a few careless words can destroy hours of hard work. In this case, the salesperson would do better to say, 'Most of our customers tell us they enjoy spending quality time with their families in their new pools.' This image is much more pleasant and it leaves the picture more open to interpretation. So if the client would *enjoy* a bunch of noisy children playing in the pool, that's what she can see, but if she'd prefer a more laid-back atmosphere, she can see that as well.

The salesperson's next words – 'When should we start digging? Would this Saturday or next Monday be better?' – also carry their own negative images. The word *digging* may conjure up pictures of a huge tractor ripping through her garden, digging up plants and leaving huge piles of dirt everywhere – and on a weekend to boot.

The salesperson would do better to say this:

> Some people prefer to be present when we begin the first phase of their new swimming pool. Others prefer to just tell us when, and then have us tell them when the pool is ready to swim in. We can begin Phase 1 Saturday or next Monday. Which would you prefer?

We can't emphasise enough how important your choice of words is to your selling career. Your words can make or break the sale without you even knowing it. In many cases, if you ask a customer why she *didn't* buy from you, she may not be able to put her finger on any one deciding moment. She 'just didn't feel right' about going ahead.

Words have meanings attached to enable comprehension. Often images are linked to the word or meaning, which in turn evoke emotions, and emotions drive or trigger action. So, start paying careful attention not only to your prospects, but also to the effects your words have on them.

Knowing How to Listen to Your Clients

The old and overused cliché says you have two ears and one mouth. To be good at persuading or selling, you must find out how to use those natural devices in proportion: Listen twice as much as you talk, and you'll succeed in persuading others nearly every time.

Contrary to popular thought, selling is not about having the gift of the gab or having kissed the Blarney Stone. These sayings imply that sales success comes when you do the talking. Truthfully, a far more productive attribute is that of listening. When you do most of the talking:

- You aren't finding out about either your customer or her needs.
- You aren't hearing buying clues or concerns.
- You may be raising concerns the prospect may not have had in the first place.
- You're shifting your prospect's attention from your offering.
- You're giving your prospect more opportunity to disagree with you, to distrust one of your statements, or both.
- You aren't able to guide the conversation.
- You aren't able to convince the other person of the best decision for her.

Most people don't think they talk too much, but in our years of selling, sales management, and teaching, we developed a keen ear for how much talking is done compared to how much is needed – and the answer all too often is: too much.

To develop your ear, try these two simple exercises:

✔ **Listen to a salesperson selling to others or trying to sell to you.** Pay attention to what her words are doing. While you're listening, ask yourself these questions:

- Do her words paint positive or negative mental pictures?

- Do her words say anything that may raise a new objection to her product or service?

- Are all her words necessary?

- Does she ask questions and then carefully listen to the prospect's answers?

- Does she move forward with questions, or does she drift off course by talking about features and benefits the customer has not expressed a need for?

✔ **Record yourself when you're talking with a customer.** You may be shocked at how much chatter you can cut out. To detect what you need to cut, ask yourself these questions:

- What is the quality of the questions I ask?

- Am I asking information-gathering questions to help myself move forward with my sale, or am I just asking questions to fill a sound void?

Watch and listen to others and to yourself more carefully than you're used to listening in everyday conversation. As you discover more and more about selling well, the phrase 'putting your foot in your mouth' will gain new meaning for you. After all, you can't put your foot in your mouth if it's closed. So close it, and listen more.

Chapter 5

Knowing What You Sell

· ·

· ·

*O*ne of the best advantages of a career in selling is that good selling skills are portable. By that we mean that after you master the skills, you'll have the education you need to sell any product that interests you when you complete your product knowledge. Product knowledge is one whole side of the selling triangle discussed in Chapter 1 – that is, one-third of what you need to know to be successful.

This chapter covers some specific suggestions for ways you can develop your product knowledge and be prepared for nearly any question that comes your way when you're with potential clients. Investing time in product research upfront will pay off when you're ready to put your selling strategies to work.

What You Need to Know

What must you absolutely, positively, truly *know* about your product in order to sell it? Always begin with the obvious:

✔ **What the product is called.** Know the specific product name and model, as well as the product/part number so that if your customers refer to it by a number, you'll know exactly what they're talking about. You also need a clear understanding of what it does, as you're bound to run into potential clients who'll refer to it as, 'that type of machine that cuts metal and things like that! At least I think that's what it said in the ad.'

✔ **Whether the product is the latest model or release.** Many of the potential clients you'll encounter will want the latest version of your product.

✔ **How it improves on a previous model or version.** Be able to list the new features or options and what they can do for your customers.

✔ **How fast, powerful, or accurate it is.** Be able to offer up a comparison of the product to its competition so you can tell your customers how your product performs when compared to others. If the comparison was done by an independent study group, so much the better – with just your word against that of the competition, you may not have much of a leg to stand on and the listener may not believe you. If no independent study is available, at least get testimonials from your satisfied clients who are already using the product, stating why this model's better than what they had before.

✔ **How to operate it during demonstrations.** Nothing is worse than trying to demonstrate a product to a prospective customer, only to find out that you're not sure how to make it do what he's asked. Be able to operate the product as well as you operate the car you drive every day.

✔ **What colours the product comes in.** Being able to tell your customers immediately whether you have a specific colour available will come in handy when they want to know whether it meets their needs. And if colour is an issue with a buyer, find out early what his desired colour is and steer him away if you cannot supply it.

✔ **What your current inventory levels are when setting delivery dates.** Your client may have seen a review of your product in a magazine, even though it won't be available for another two months. You need to know what he's talking about, inform him of delivery delays, and see if he needs the benefits of the product sooner. If the product is currently in production, but on back-order, brag about its popularity and know the projected delivery dates.

Scarcity is a very strong buying incentive because it denotes demand and exclusivity – both important decision influencers.

✔ **How much of an investment the product would be.** Be sure to phrase the price of the product in terms of an _investment_ as opposed to a _cost_. Also be prepared to reduce the total cost to a monthly amount if your product is something that requires financing. Many buyers and company decision-makers will consider how much something will add to monthly overheads and how soon they can recover their investment and, of course, how great their Return On Investment (ROI) will be. Return On Investment is simply an equation comparing the amount paid and the amount that you can gain with the new product/service purchased. For example a new printing machine might cost £60,000 but will enable you to embrace and capitalise upon new work to the tune of over £220,000 annually. With a lifespan of five years the machine represents an excellent investment return. Very often ROI is a prime driver.

> ✔ **What terms and financing are available.** If your company offers financing, regard it as another product and know how it works as well as you know the product itself. Don't risk losing a sale because you cannot answer the key questions on financial issues at the end of the presentation.

> ✔ **If you work for a manufacturer, whether other distributors may offer the product for less.** If this is the case, know who these distributors are and what price they're selling the product for.

Even companies with the most basic product training should cover these topics with new salespeople before sending them out to talk to customers. Unfortunately, some companies provide only the bare minimum of information, and you have to develop the rest on your own. If you do all of the preparation described in this section, you'll be sitting pretty.

However, be prepared to encounter a potential client asking an odd question – something out of the ordinary that you can't discern the answer to with your current knowledge. Never make up an answer! Indeed, congratulate the client on asking such a thought-provoking question and assure him that you're happy to find out the answer. You must then go and find the answer quickly – before he considers the competition's product over yours. In this circumstance, you may have to do a lot of additional information gathering in the course of researching the answer to your customer's question, but that's okay, because you build your product knowledge and credibility with the prospect as you do so.

Keep in mind that if a potential client ever comes to you with valid information about your product or service that surprises you, your credibility with that client will be on shaky ground if he discovers that you were not aware of it. After all, you're supposed to be the expert clients come to for information or advice. If they know more than you do, why do they need *you*?

How to Get the Information You Need

How can you be sure you're armed with the product knowledge you need before you head out to make a sale? Take advantage of as many different resources as you can. If your company offers training sessions on the product, attend. If they hand out brochures and leaflets, know them backwards and forwards. Talk to your customers about the product so you know what questions they have, and discuss the product with your fellow salespeople to get suggestions. And be sure to know your competition's product so you can tell your customers how your product measures up. We cover each of these resources in the following sections.

Attending training sessions and reading product literature

In reality, after your initial enrolment with your employer, you may not have much new material or product development to learn, and you can focus on knowing thoroughly the current offering so as to handle client queries. However, if you work for a developing company or a company at a period of change then of paramount importance is that your knowledge is current and accurate.

For example, your company or the manufacturer of the products you represent may hold regularly scheduled training sessions about the product. If they do, then by all means go to these training sessions. They're your best opportunity for learning thoroughly and correctly about your product from reliable sources. And *always* attend these sessions with a list of questions and a notepad for writing down the answers. If the speaker doesn't answer your questions during the presentation, approach him politely before he leaves and ask him any questions you may have. He'll usually be very pleased to see someone as keen about the subject matter as he is!

Many salespeople view these training days as either a 'jolly', and don't take them very seriously, or as a boring day wasted instead of being productive in the field. Whilst it may be that these days aren't all as constructive and entertaining as they could be, always attend them with an attitude that, 'if I learn just *one* thing today that might be useful with just *one* client then it has been worth it'.

In between training sessions, watch for e-mail or memo updates of product information from the company. If you work for a fast-moving, dynamic company and new stuff is happening all the time, then it may be worth visiting your own company's Web site every morning and checking for product revisions, if those are posted on the site. If something has changed in the past 24 hours, you need to read it and be familiar with it as soon as possible. After all, your best new prospect may have read that information already, and you want to be able to show that your information is current.

Your company will probably provide you with brochures containing technical information on your product or service, even if they don't offer specific product-training sessions. Set aside a specific amount of time in your schedule to sit and read such literature – but don't just read through it the way a customer would. Study it. Read it every day for at least three weeks. You need to know the terminology and how it applies in the field. By the end of that time, you'll have memorised the information and know exactly what your customers are referring to when they ask questions. Nothing's worse than having to look to a higher source when your customer asks a question that you should know the answer to.

If training sessions and product literature aren't available to you, and what you sell is a tangible product, get your hands on a product sample immediately. Be like a kid with a new toy: Play with it, experiment, read through suggested demonstrations, and try it out as if *you're* the customer. Make notes on things you find hard to understand. The chances are that at least one of your prospects will have the same questions or concerns that you come up with. Resolve those concerns now, and you'll be well prepared for your demonstrations.

Try sending the questions you come up with to your customer support department online. See how long it takes them to provide an answer and how detailed the answer is. What you receive from them is what a customer is likely to receive when using that service after a sale. If the return time is unacceptable for the type of question you asked, see if you can do anything within the company to help speed things up. Or if you know the response time is slow, you may recommend, during your presentation, that your clients contact you directly with questions. This strategy shows that you provide added services *and* that you're knowledgeable about the product.

Make sure that taking care of customer support questions and concerns doesn't occupy so much of your time that it interferes with your selling time. After all, you're paid primarily to find and serve new customers for your business, in addition to keeping those you've already gained.

Talking to customers

Get as much feedback as you can from the people who already use and benefit from what you sell. Ask what their experiences have been with your product. If it isn't already common practice with your employer, initiate surveys asking existing clients for feedback on the products used and the service provided. Your surveys can be simple printed questionnaires mailed to your clients, or conducted via e-mails or the Internet so that they can be quickly completed and returned with a minimum of fuss. If you prefer the personal touch and feel the time is valuable, handle those surveys in a personal phone call. The advantage of talking to people personally is that you can get the client talking and, hopefully, discover something new that will help you serve all your clients better. Very often a long-standing user will have a deeper and more 'prospect-friendly' view that will be more useful than official sales-speak! Get to know him and speak his language.

Your current customers are an extremely valuable resource *if* you keep in contact with them.

Picking your colleagues' brains

Long-standing senior salespeople have all kinds of information about products that they may never document. Talk to them as much as you can in order to put their knowledge to work for you. They've learned all the tricks for how to present for maximum effect and what angle is best to point out to the prospect. Time spent watching and listening to old hands is massively valuable.

If your sole purpose in meeting senior salespeople is to gain product knowledge, then remember to keep your meetings focused on product knowledge and information; otherwise, your time could drift. If, however, you're talking about how they mastered the role and survived for years at the top, and they're sharing examples of techniques, then stay as long as you can – that sort of valuable information is never available in company training manuals. Beware though that conversation could just as easily descend into old war stories or other unrelated matters, and as sociable as it may appear, this isn't a good use of your time. If you want product knowledge, focus the conversation there. Now is not the time for gossip.

Ask your sales manager for permission to shadow the top salesperson in your territory. You'll almost always get a positive response, because the request shows your manager that you're sincere in wanting to become the best salesperson you can be. The more senior salesperson will usually be proud to show off his skills to a rookie . . . after all, we sensitive salespeople have huge egos! If you do tag along, watch extremely closely how the salesperson handles everything: the client, the use of brochures, discussing proposals, using visual aids, and the product itself. Listen to the word pictures he uses in describing the product (see Chapter 4 for more on these). Notice the mood he sets.

The how of handling products and information is as important as the what and why.

Going directly to the source

Whatever type of product you sell, try to create an opportunity to tour the facility where your product or service was created. Try to discover the original reason for the start of the company. What was the motive of the originator to set out on your company's journey? Did he subscribe to an ethos or vision that is still powerfully resonant with prospects and clients? This knowledge can be hugely valuable in the art of persuasion, as most people look for and are triggered by noble intentions.

Being a student of selling

When you're in learning mode, you need to set the stage for learning. That means you're prepared and properly equipped. You need to keep a notebook and pen to hand to record anything you learn, or private thoughts you may have if you're studying alone. Many ideas and questions will spring to mind when you're studying on your own and if you don't write these down, believing that you'll remember them in the morning, you'll be sadly mistaken. In practice, if you don't jot something down, you'll forget it. Be prepared for note taking even when studying alone.

Studying may also mean asking questions of a training director, company owner, or top salesperson. It may involve watching hours of product-training videos or attending classes on the products. Your learning may also involve interviewing current customers.

Regardless of the type of education on offer, you must begin every session with a clear respect for the information to come. Treat the sessions like gold dust. Show up on time, if not early. Be courteous to those who are sharing their knowledge with you. And never forget that what these people are imparting will make you money.

Treat them and their messages with the utmost respect. The better you treat the people who are helping you, the more they'll relax. You'll be making them like you and trust you, which will lead them to offer you even more valuable information. Hmm, sounds a lot like selling, doesn't it?

You cannot know too much about your product or service. Customers love to feel that you have the inside knowledge on the latest and greatest products and services; they want to believe that you are the most competent person in your industry. Face it: no one wants to be represented by an incompetent, poorly informed salesperson.

Keeping an eye on the competition

Most large companies designate a person or department to gather information on the competition and to prepare analyses of that information for the sales staff. If your company has this situation under control, sing their praises and encourage them to keep up the good work because such research can be a voraciously time-consuming feat. Unfortunately, many people don't use this research and don't value it highly enough, but when used correctly, such research is highly usable.

If your company *doesn't* provide this service, you need to take it on yourself. Don't become obsessed with information on what the competitors are doing, but keeping tabs so that you aren't caught by surprise when pitching against them is worthwhile. Take advantage of online searches that will seek out any information for you that includes the keywords you give it, such as your competitor's company name, product name, and so on, and visit competitors' Web sites as these often contain new releases that keep you as well informed as many of their own staff.

In today's fast-moving society and close-knit business communities, you often hear about any new, relevant topics on the grapevine. Earth shattering, ground-breaking advancements are not so common! Smaller minor advantages are pretty frequent but these are never that difficult to combat, so don't sweat over knowing everything you can about competitors' offerings. Concentrate instead on what you can do and how good you can be.

Talking to customers who've had past experiences with your competitors works well and can become part of your rapport-building and selling process. Ask customers if they wouldn't mind sharing their thoughts on the competi-tor's product and service with you. Ask what they liked about the product – particular features and benefits, how their customer service needs were han-dled, what they'd like to see improved upon, and so on. Asking in a sincere, caring manner sends the message that you want to do better, be better, and help them have a better experience than ever before and won't be inter-preted as merely dirt digging. When they tell their tales, take comprehensive mental notes and keep them stored for future reference.

In particular, if a new customer has just switched from the competition to your product, find out exactly what the deciding factor was and work it into any presentations you make in the future.

Product information doesn't just come from the technical booklet that's pro-vided with the product. This information is everywhere the product has been. In seeking out as much information as possible, you'll earn and keep your expert status, and more people will want to take your advice. Ultimately, gathering and using information may seem laborious and definitely unglam-orous but it pays handsomely in the end – and you won't be complaining when you win large commissions and possibly awards!

Chapter 6

Using Technology to Your Advantage

. . . .

. . . .

A few years ago an organised sales professional may have kept organised and up to date with a card index file on her desk that simply had a hand-written note on each client card – if she was a true sales professional. Other salespeople had a more restricted view of the need for notes and organisation and regarded the challenge of becoming organised as too troublesome to bother with. Sales for many was 'on the go', with success based upon flair and good fortune, not so much order and precision planning. Well, those days are gone.

Computers have come along and have taken over . . . even simple telephones have more computing power in them now than the first office computers did. And frankly if you haven't embraced computers in this modern world, then you're pretty much left for dead in the business world. However, you still have an opportunity to make the leap forward and harness the technology to help your career explode. By applying just a little attention to getting to know these applications, you can leverage a huge return on the investment through to seeing pounds in your pocket.

In this chapter, we start by lessening some of your fears and motivate you to get up to speed. Then we share some great resources that can help you sell better – everything from tools to use when making presentations to online map services to help you get where you're going. We don't even come close to describing all the technological resources at your fingertips, but we do highlight the best of the best, letting you know which ones to check out first. Consider this overview a jumping-off point to the wide range of innovations at your disposal.

Fitting into the New Economy

If you've listened to the news in the past few years, you've heard the term *new economy* bandied about. This term refers to the Internet businesses that have exploded onto the scene in the last decade, as opposed to the *old economy*, made up of the bricks-and-mortar businesses you grew up with. Whether you were comfortable selling in the old economy, or are a new younger sales starter, the following sections help you overcome your fears about technology and show you how to use it to your advantage. So even if hearing about computers and the Internet gives you a chill down your spine, please read on!

Considering your attitude towards technology

If you've been in the sales profession for decades, the Internet Revolution and the accompanying technology may have left you reeling. Many veteran salespeople – and by veteran we mean those who've been selling for 20 or more years – are afraid of the new technology and even scorn it as not having any bearing on the selling process. They fear that consumers may become more aware and educated about the offerings available than they are themselves and that customers may end up getting all the information they need from the Internet. Many people who consider themselves sales professionals are afraid the Internet may take over their jobs, just as the Industrial Revolution took much of the manual labour away from workers. These salespeople fear that if consumers can order online, they won't have any need for a salesperson, and the role of salesperson may become obsolete.

On the other hand, newcomers may have an apprehension towards learning a specific new software system, while also holding the view that newer technology actually makes it easier to get more done with less effort because the prospect is already half-aware of what you sell because of the Internet and information availability. Whatever the mindset, your attitude towards technology determines the success achieved.

We firmly believe that the Internet can't possibly bring about the demise of the sales profession any more than automation eliminated the need for living, breathing people in the industrialised world. Sales aren't made to machines; sales are made to people. 'People buy from people', as the saying goes, and even though your computer may be able to talk to you and your clients, it hasn't yet mastered people skills. As a salesperson, you still have the upper hand in developing those skills to serve your customers better.

Being able to persuade potential future clients to like you, trust you, and want to listen to you when making buying decisions is still critical. Real people with real challenges always want to talk with other real people – that's where the fun is. Technology can't empathise with clients. It can't understand their needs and calm their fears the way a living, breathing sales professional can. It can't build a caring, mutually respectful, long-term relationship either.

Technology *can* do some of the work for you though. It *can* speed up processes, allowing you to get more successful, and it *can* help you involve other people and resources that are crucial to your selling. Having a healthy respect for technology that you haven't used before is a good thing.

Motivating yourself to change

Whatever the age, background, or circumstances of people, many hesitate to discover something new, even if you're assured it will make your job easier or make you more effective – even if the new knowledge or behaviour is guaranteed to extend your life (like exercise) or help you earn more money (like sales training). An in-built fear warns you that attempting to try something new may cause you to feel embarrassed or stupid when you get it wrong. Or you fear that the new task is not as revolutionary as you're led to believe and that the time spent figuring it out may be better spent doing other tasks. You may also suspect that the guarantee that practising the new task is going to be beneficial is just a sales pitch! (We salespeople *are* a funny bunch at times.) Or you may be genuinely worried about the new task adding to the already almost overwhelming time pressures. Whatever the underlying thought, you need to try to alleviate it and push ahead with discovering how much technology can transform your sales habits for the better.

Instead of thinking of the change or learning process, focus upon the post-learning period and mentally live in the future – where you *are* equipped with the skill and enjoy all of the benefits it brings you. If you're like most people, when you're motivated by your belief in how much better you'll be *after* the change is complete, you'll quickly find the time and be energised to put in the effort.

Flexibility and adaptability are the keys to success in today's ever-changing business world. Computer literacy is no longer just a business skill, it's a *life* skill – just like adding, subtracting, or knowing how to drive a car were for essential living 20 years ago. In today's world we all need to keep up with the usage of technology or we'll surely get left behind. Comfortably using the Internet, wireless phones, handheld or palmtop devices, and certain common computer software programs such as the Microsoft Office suite all fall under this umbrella. The more you know, the more indispensable you are to your company – or the more valuable you appear to a new company if you decide to change jobs.

Using Technology to Make Your Life Less Complicated Instead of More

If you're new to some of the technological tools that are available for you to use, you may think of all those gadgets as time-consuming things you have to spend hours struggling with before you get to use them. To some degree, you're right. When you use a new product or program, you have to spend a little time upfront learning how to use it – but if the tool is right for the job you have in mind, the time is well spent.

The techno-salesperson you talk to about any new tool should do a good job of understanding your specific needs before recommending any device. If she doesn't invest that time, she may not have your best interest at heart, so be clear about what exactly you want to use the gadget or program for and explain your needs to any salesperson before you buy.

The following sections highlight some key tools that you can use in your selling career to make your life simpler. If you do your homework and get up to speed with these tools, you can put them to use – and be more profitable in the process. How can these tools make you more profitable? Because, when used properly, they can free you up to focus on your clients' needs more completely – both by releasing physical time and by relieving you mentally (because you will know the job is done and you'll worry less).

Your attitude towards adopting new technology and software impacts on your success. If you look at new technology positively, with the motivation to learn how to use it for your benefit, then you'll see the advantages. What's covered in these sections is just the tip of the iceberg in terms of what current and developing technology can do for you in your sales career. We recommend allowing yourself at least 30 minutes a week to investigate new sites, improved sites, and up-and-coming technology. Keep an eye out for those truly wonderful developments that may help you save time in tracking all the details of your career and give you more time to do what you're paid to do – acquire new clients.

Using PowerPoint in your presentations

Microsoft PowerPoint is a software program that allows you to create simple or intricate slide-show presentations using your computer. When you're ready to give the presentation, you can use the PowerPoint slides you've created in a couple of different ways:

- ✔ You can print the slides and give them as handouts to your audience.
- ✔ You can display the slides, either on your computer – especially a laptop – or on a wall or screen with a projector.

Giving presentations is one of several key elements in selling, and PowerPoint makes it easy for you to tell your prospective clients about yourself, your product, or your service in a more absorbing and interesting way. You can also customise the slide presentation for each prospect and in much less time than it would take you if you were doing it all by hand, the old-fashioned way. Plus, you can get quite fancy with your presentations by including music or spoken messages, still pictures from another source, or even video clips if any or all of these make the presentation a better selling tool!

People include all sorts of useful and creative additions in their presentations, including humorous video clips or weird and wonderful images gathered from global news items. All these extras are designed to hook in and entertain the audience and thus get them to invite the speaker back – a sales presentation, in effect, about the speaker herself.

PowerPoint is often bundled together with other Microsoft software programs (such as Word and Excel) in Microsoft Office and you probably already have it on your computer as most recent computers come pre-loaded with Microsoft products. If you don't have PowerPoint, you can easily purchase it for less than £200 from any local computer shop.

For more information on how to use PowerPoint or any of the other programs, see *PowerPoint 2000 For Windows For Dummies* by Doug Lowe (or titles matching the other programs required) (Wiley).

Keeping track of clients with contact management software

If your business is a simple one and requires only name, address, and telephone contact information on each client, you can get by with nearly any simple address book, such as the ones found in Microsoft Outlook or Lotus Notes. But if you need to track each contact with your clients and co-ordinate those contacts with your daily, weekly, or monthly calendar, using contact management software makes more sense. *Contact management software* is a database of information – as much information as you'd like to include – about your future clients and long-term clients. You include contact details such as:

- Names (make sure the spellings are correct)
- Company names
- Addresses
- Various phone numbers
- E-mail addresses
- Assistants' or secretaries' names

✔ Best times of day to reach the clients

✔ Dates, locations, and times of appointments

✔ Notes on each conversation with the clients

✔ Copies of letters or documents sent

✔ A history of products or services ordered

✔ Delivery dates

✔ Challenges that arise and how you overcame them

✔ Future growth plans for the company or division

✔ Birth dates

✔ How long they've been with their companies

✔ Hobbies (to establish common ground)

✔ Holiday tastes and information on places and preferences

✔ Just about anything you can possibly learn about the people

The best thing about contact management software is that it keeps *all* information quickly and easily accessible and in one place and lets you alter information as your relationship with each client evolves. Some better contact management programs also allow you to link to other programs, for example Microsoft Word, and generate letters or process orders for a client. The name and address information can be automatically placed in the letter so you don't have to worry about misspelling anything after you've entered the details correctly into the database.

The whole sales team for your company may use a certain software program. Many of these programs provide reporting information or sales analysis information for management so they can see how efficient their staff are being and where clients may be dropping off. So, your software decision may be made for you by someone higher up. If that's the case, you simply need to take advantage of whatever training is available – even if you're only offered a manual to read through – so that you master this system as best you can.

Thorough use of a contact management system gives you a huge edge and can be more responsible for cash in your pocket than any other area of your sales career.

If your company doesn't offer or suggest a software program to use, spend some time researching your options and choose the one that's right for you. Although different requirements arise from different business types, some contact management systems are more refined and adaptable than others. As with many things in life, the adage of 'getting what you pay for' is often true, although you may not need some of the benefits listed for more expensive options and thus can select a cheaper version. Here are a few systems to research:

✔ **GoldMine** is our personal favourite and worth the extra few pounds in our opinion. It retails for about £170, but as with any software, you can find better deals if you shop around – although you may well find that buying cheaper – say from an Internet supplier – then leaves a support issue unaddressed.

GoldMine includes a Web data capture tool, a document management centre (for those great sales letters you send), and a literature fulfilment centre for information you send out regularly. You can purchase multiple licences at discounted rates and loads of really useful bolt-ons, such as a link with quotation software or accounting packages, are available. GoldMine has many great features that allow you to import data from programs such as Outlook or Excel and then send bulk mail or e-mail to prospects and clients. It has a wide network of distributors that can support you if you have a problem. Check out *GoldMine For Dummies* by Joel Scott (Wiley) for more information on what this software offers.

✔ **ACT! 2000** is an economical investment. It retails for about £100, but you can find it for less at numerous computer stores. As with GoldMine, you can also purchase licences for five or more users and many bolt-on products are available. The account software company Sage purchased the brand and have developed it further and all in all it offers excellent value for money. Importing of data is easy from most sources. If you want to find out more about this software, check out *ACT! 2000 For Windows For Dummies* by Jeffrey J. Mayer (Wiley).

✔ **Sage CRM** from the accountancy software giant Sage is a brilliant system (in our opinion). Certainly for multiple-user groups and some quite specific project type sales such as Web site development and support it's difficult to beat. This is a more expensive option (up to £10,000 for a complete set up involving up to 10 users) and is aimed at operations with this amount of users or more. This system is only really workable when clearly set up for your specific use (as opposed to the two previously mentioned that work well in a more 'out of the box' state) and thus requires expense in setup and support. Definitely a worthy investment when larger groups of users all record different information after liaising with clients.

✔ **Sage SalesLogix** helps mid-market companies manage their customer relationships. This service is subscriber-based and offers access to the contact management database as well as many other linked services, including travel information, motivational and training tips, and so on. Licences offer varying levels of usage and thus costs range from an affordable leased arrangement to a sizable investment depending on your user level. Again this is a company purchase rather than individual. Visit the SalesLogix Web site at www.saleslogix.com for more information.

> ✔ **SugarCRM** is a *free* Internet resource that works extremely well. We certainly recommend it as a budget approach to adopting a much-needed business skill. It allows you to track your clients, manage your enquiries, note your past histories, and diarise future projects. One drawback is that you need to be logged on to the Web to use SugarCRM, though that may not be an issue in today's 'always on' Internet age. In fact, it may be a bonus if you travel a lot; you can access your info anywhere you can tap the Internet – no need to be tied to your desk. Check out www. sugarcrm.com.

Getting the most from gadgets

If you can think of a task that needs to be handled, very likely a bit of technology has been invented to handle it. The trick to not owning so much technology that you can't carry it all around with you is to concentrate on your own priorities. Which tasks take so much of your time that it would be worth having them mechanised or, at the very least, simplified? In the following sections we review some of the more common tools that sales professionals are using to get organised, plan their time, and communicate – or at the very least, get from Point A to Point B with clients, both physically and verbally.

Personal digital assistants

A *personal digital assistant* (*PDA*) is an electronic device that is smaller than a videocassette tape yet works like a computer. It has a screen display and works on a touchpad system using a stylus. Companies such as Palm, Casio, and Hewlett-Packard make the most popular ones. You can purchase one at most computer or office-supply stores for as little as £130 up to £350 or more, depending, of course, on how much you want your PDA to handle.

PDAs are wonderful for keeping track of your contact lists, merging your personal and business calendars into one organised program, and getting connected to the Internet for current information. In essence a PDA allows you to 'be in when you're out' by giving you Internet access and synchronisation with your office computer, so that diary activity, client contact details, and e-mail functionality are all bundled together. The advantages are huge. This type of mobile functionality means that you can always keep vital communication with clients and prospects seamless and even allows you to remember client events and send them good luck messages. Most PDAs are compatible with software you're likely to have on your computer (such as Microsoft Outlook, for example).

Some PDAs have keyboards as accessories, where the PDA plugs into a standard keyboard for easy data entry, and some of the latest ones actually have a slide-out qwerty keyboard. If you're constantly on the road, the PDA can become your best (lightweight) friend.

Wireless phones and smart phones

How times have changed! A few years ago having total phone connectivity when you were out and about was simply amazing – so to have complete computing power in your hands whilst you roam is truly mind-blowing. However, such is the modern world. Everybody has a mobile phone, and newer phones are ever more packed with functions. Indeed often the focus is less on phone aspects and more on added gizmos. A modern phone holds more computer power than was used in the lunar expeditions!

With the newer *smart phones*, you can also receive e-mail, dial up the Internet, listen to and record voice notes, meetings, and important business phone calls. Most have a camera function – particularly useful if your sales role involves selling property or office interiors where a picture or three of the layout might hugely help the sale. The phones all have a calendar function so that you can store your appointments and many also allow sat nav software so you can be sure of not only remembering the appointment but finding your way there too! They even enable you to have office functions such as a complete database and spreadsheets so you really can be in the office when you're out.

In truth, the smart phone PDAs on the market are a must-have for most salespeople. Although, like most new technologies, they may take a few hours to learn before getting the best from them, they really are invaluable tools for a professional salesperson.

Business card scanners

If you're like most salespeople, you collect a lot of business cards. Then you have to enter the information from those cards into some sort of program in order to keep the information accessible. Luckily for you, some wonderful people decided that entering that information by hand wasn't a wise use of their time, so they invented business card scanners. These nifty little devices allow you to insert a business card and have the information magically transported in electronic format into your contact management software or other software program. They really are superb.

When you start out in the sales business, you collect a massive amount of contact data – especially if you're a good networker – and you could easily end up with hundreds of cards that never get entered or followed up. If you don't have a secretary, a card scanner is the next best thing.

All types of card scanner come complete with their own software and installation is really simple. Once installed they scan several cards a minute and are another must-have if you're an individual operating without a secretary (indeed, even if you have a secretary often the time/cost equation makes using the machine a more cost-effective method). The software accurately organises information into your chosen data storage program and reads international and two-sided cards. It also synchronises with PDAs and most digital mobile phones.

Helping your clients locate you

You probably have a lot of information on your business card – your company name, your company address, your direct phone number (or at the very least your extension number), your fax number, your mobile phone number, your company's Web site address, and your business e-mail address. So, what's the best way for a client to reach you when she has a problem? If the problem is causing her grief or a slowdown in her own business, you can bet she'll use every number and address she has in order to track you down. In order to prevent this hassle factor for clients, you can subscribe to an answering service that's always available to handle your calls and can locate you wherever you are. We personally use and heartily recommend MoneyPenny (www. moneypenny.biz; 08000 199944); look for local equivalents in your area.

Of course, at times you'll be out of reach, such as when you're actually on a sales call. However even at these times a virtual secretary can reach you, provided that you maintain a communication link that includes diary information. If you use this type of service fully, an answering service can literally be your secretary and can even interrupt meetings, because the operators are in control of your diary and have the number where you're visiting. For many new and start-up sales roles or own-business situations this type of service is excellent and extremely cost-effective – after all, what price a lost client?

Making travel plans and getting maps online

A live person at a travel agency can be a great help when you're planning a business trip but if you find out at 9.00 p.m., after checking your e-mails, that you're needed in a city miles away for a client meeting within the next day or two, you'll want to check the best route to take and possibly search for the latest traffic information.

Whilst many newer cars have satellite navigation, planning to arrive the night before and book into a hotel so as to arrive fresh and relaxed for your meeting is sensible. Being able to book a hotel with a few clicks on the device in your hand is incredibly useful and so for many business travellers the use of a PDA or palmtop computer is invaluable.

If you'll be travelling by car, you can find maps online at several different Web sites. Two of the best are Google Maps (www.google.co.uk/map) and Yell.com (go to www.yell.com and select Maps). Both sites give you estimated travel times, all the turns you need to take, and the total mileage of your trip. You can print out the information or download it onto your computer or PDA. The directions are provided in step-by-step text form, along with maps of the area. You can also find the nearest hotels and restaurants along your route.

Part III
The Anatomy of a Sale

'What sort of sales training did you go through before you joined us, Thomas?'

In this part . . .

The chapters in this part cover the seven steps of the selling cycle in more detail. Here you'll discover exactly how to find the people who need what you have and how to get appointments with them. You'll find out how to make sure your product is right for your prospects and give a presentation with ease. And you'll discover how to address your prospect's concerns, close the sale, and get referrals so that you can start the cycle all over again.

Chapter 7

Finding the People Who Want What You Sell

The first step in the selling cycle is what salespeople call prospecting. *Prospecting*, essentially, is searching for people to sell your products and services to. In many ways the process is similar to simply digging for treasure as in a treasure hunt, except that the prospecting you do as a salesperson uses telephones, e-mail, and word of mouth instead.

If you already know the people you'll be selling to, you probably don't need this chapter right now (although the tips and suggestions you'll find here may help you find even *more* prospects, which is always a good thing). On the other hand, if you have a great opportunity, service, product, or idea, but you don't know where to find other people who'd be interested in getting involved with it, this is exactly the place to start.

Over the years, literally hundreds of people have enthusiastically relayed their ideas and ventures that are going to make them millions. Unfortunately, rarely are these moments of elation grounded in sufficient planning or thought, especially when it comes to defining where the customers are going to come from. Who exactly is going to buy this offer and where can he be found? Prospecting and marketing are fuzzy issues that these potential millionaires overlook and thus their ideas soon die in a romantic haze.

If you don't know whom to contact to help you get from Point A to Point B, you doom your product, service, or idea right from the start. You soon lose your enthusiasm or invest too much of your own time and money with little or no payoff at all. You run out of energy before you even get on that road to success. This chapter is vital in helping you avoid that situation. You can master everything else in this book and technically become a great salesperson, but if you never get the opportunity to get in front of the right people, all your selling techniques add up to nothing. You won't even make enough profit to feed yourself.

Finding the Gold: Knowing Where to Start

When you're finally prepared enough with knowledge about your product, service, or concept, and when you feel comfortable with your selling skills, you need to begin finding the people to sell to. Because you won't have a lot of qualifying, presenting, closing, or follow-up to do when you're new, your primary focus is on prospecting. In fact, in the beginning, make it your daily plan to invest about 75 per cent of your time in prospecting. Use the other 25 per cent to develop your product knowledge and presentation skills.

Many successful sales veterans can tell you how important prospecting is even after they've built a large customer base. Successful sales professionals – those with a strong desire not only to reach the top but to stay there – make prospecting a part of their everyday selling strategy. They understand that achieving success doesn't mean they can stop looking for new business opportunities. Successful sales professionals explore every avenue in search of new customers, no matter how long they've been in the business.

The best place to start prospecting is with people who already have paid money for products and services similar to yours. If you're selling home exercise equipment, begin with people who jog, belong to health clubs, or join local recreational sports teams. Why? Because you *know* they're already health-conscious. The convenience of being able to exercise at home may be just what they're looking for. If you're selling graphic design, start with the people responsible for advertising in local companies. If you've already worked for people in a certain type of business, such as gift shops, you may want to concentrate on other gift shops in the area. The items in your portfolio will then be very appropriate displays of your work.

To some degree at least, where you find your prospects depends on what you represent. If you sell products or services for a company, you probably found out during your product-knowledge training where the likeliest places are to find your products or services in use (if you didn't, ask). Those places are, obviously, the best places to begin prospecting. After you have some sales under your belt, you'll have time to get more creative with finding other fresh sources of enquiry.

Prospecting on your own

If you're running your own business (as opposed to being employed), you need to have a very clear idea as to where to find new people to talk with and sell to. You won't have had the benefit of having this drummed into you during your initial training so prospecting may seem a daunting task – but it isn't that difficult.

Start with your local Chamber of Commerce, local library, or the local networking groups where business owners similar to yourself meet regularly. Business Network International (BNI, www.bni-europe.com), Business Referral Exchange (BRE, www.brenet.co.uk), and many other excellent networking groups can help you.

Selling something that isn't of interest to the audience is useless, so make sure that you clearly identify where your product or service is best suited and then where these people to whom it is suited might go.

Depending on your budget, you can use a variety of angles to put yourself in front of prospects. For example, if you were selling a will-writing service you might want to simply write to all home-owners in a certain property type or area where inheritance and estate values might be an issue. You might equally decide that many of those with valuable estates may also be business owners and thus meeting them via business networks is also a great strategy. If you're selling software for a manufacturing process, you need to source a list of relevant manufacturers; send them an interesting software summary; then phone to arrange to visit and discuss further.

Whatever the angle, prospecting and finding people to sit in front of and sell to are absolute necessities if you want to make any money selling your wares. Get good at prospecting and never stop doing it and you can have a glowing sales career.

The simplest place to start prospecting is with the people you already know, such as the groups covered in the following sections. Talking with these people first helps you find easy leads and gives you an opportunity to practise your prospecting presentation with people who are less likely than complete strangers to rudely tell you to go away.

Prospecting your way to riches

When you're just getting started, split your time between finding out about your product, improving your message delivery skills, and finding people who need that product. The key to success in a people-orientated business such as selling lies in how many people you can see in the time you have available. Initially, you'll probably find yourself working very hard just to find a few prospects. But with every experience, you'll discover a little more, refine your strategies and techniques, and eventually find yourself working more cleverly. The biggest factors in all of the successes and failures we've witnessed are work rate and targeting of clients. Low work rates and poor attention to prospecting inevitably lead to failure, whereas the opposite – consistent hard efforts and clearly identified targeted prospecting – are pretty much certain to bring the desired results.

If, as a result of this reference to prospecting, you're asking yourself, 'Am I a miner or a salesperson?', bear in mind that the two jobs share many similarities. In each, you stake a claim; you bring with you the necessary tools to help dig out your own little niche of success; you have high expectations of success; you persistently and consistently work towards your goals; you have a firm belief in your ability to achieve those goals; and, finally, you refuse to let others' negative reactions to your work inhibit your behaviour and beliefs.

Searching for prospects among your friends and family

When you're new in the world of selling, honing your selling skills may help to draw you out of your comfort zone. So prospecting among those people with whom you're most comfortable can take away a little of the stress of this thing called *selling*. A salesperson's friends and family are his *warm* or *natural market*. Friends and relatives are less likely to reject you (which means you're less likely to fail), and rejection and failure are the two biggest fears of those who are trying anything new. Your friends and family like you, they trust you, and they want to see you succeed.

However, do not bombard your friends and family with your new enthusiasm for what you are selling! The quickest way to lose friends is to create the impression that all they are to you is the next meal ticket. Your friends want you to succeed, and they want to be kind, but they definitely do not want to feel exploited.

Perfect an approach that allows you to subtly introduce what you're doing so that your family and friends enquire more and thus feel as though they got you to divulge the information, not that you downloaded it. If you truly care about these people, you'll only offer them your product if it is genuinely suitable for them. If it does meet their needs and they see that it does, your family and friends will respond in kind and possibly become some of your best clients.

Be selective when you prospect among your family and friends, though. If you're selling exercise equipment, don't get discouraged if 90-year-old Aunt Annie doesn't buy two of everything.

You must be considerate and careful when contacting your friends and family and telling them that you're in a new business or you're starting a new career and that you want to share the news with them. Speak to them first about loves, life, and trivia if you haven't spoken to them for a while and certainly convey the impression that you didn't ring just to tell them about what you're now doing. Better still, plan to 'bump into' them at an event and then talk casually as if you're just catching up.

Try using this key phrase when getting your friends' permission to share with them your new product, service, or idea: 'Because I value your judgement, I was hoping you'd give me your opinion.' This statement is bound to make them feel important and willing to help you – if they weren't already. You can then outline the new venture and let them ask questions to draw information out of you rather than you going into a long sell on it.

After you've contacted all your family members and close friends, move on to acquaintances. Consider talking to other parents, your accountant, the group you play football or go walking with, and the sales assistant you always see at the local shop – of course, making sure that you never stop them doing their work. If approached properly, most people are more than willing to give you advice or opinions. Ask the right question, and they can advise you right into a great connection with a big client.

If your friends and relatives aren't good candidates for your offering, contact them anyway. The first rule in prospecting is never to assume that someone can't help you build your business. Indeed it may even be better for you in as much as the friendship is likely to remain less threatened if he's clearly out of the ball park when it comes to purchasing . . . and because of his friendship he'll probably want to help more with introducing you to others.

Looking electronically

Unless you represent a unique product or service, the opportunities you have for making contact with prospective clients are practically unlimited. You simply need to test a variety of methods to narrow down those that bring you the best people.

If what you sell is good for businesses, begin with your local *Yellow Pages* and simply plan a strategy to contact those who you feel will be more willing to listen or more aligned to the offering you have. If your product or service can bring a business even more business or make that business more efficient, you owe it to them to contact them.

In today's world the Internet has a massive influence on the buying decision, and you need to make use of this medium to at least research your market. A proliferation of bulletin boards, chat rooms, and forums exist for sharing information and if you're serious about finding out something on a service or product, it will be out there somewhere! (If you're new to the Internet, refer to *Internet For Dummies*, 10th edition (Wiley) to get a clearer idea of how you can use this phenomenal tool to your greatest advantage.)

Bear in mind the old adage that 'you can't believe everything you hear' and understand that some of what you discover is opinion and speculation and not always accurate. Verify information through a reputable source before relying on it yourself or passing it on to your clients.

Using the help of professionals

Getting advice from others who have already been where you're going and are willing to share their knowledge is always a wise move – no matter how long you've been in the selling business.

A *mentor* is someone who has more experience than you, an interest in what you're doing, and a willingness to take you under his wing to guide your actions. Mentors want to help others overcome obstacles they faced, to help others learn from their experience.

If you're new to sales, the company you work for may partner you with one of its more senior salespeople for a brief training period. This type of company-sponsored mentoring programme is working wonders around the world. It gives recognition to the established professional for his knowledge and expertise and at the same time helps to train the new people in proven and successful methods of conducting business. Take advantage of a programme like this, if offered. And if your company doesn't have an organised mentoring programme, talk to your manager to see if you can be paired with someone anyway. Your interest in learning and becoming the best salesperson you can be will most certainly be viewed favourably.

If this idea of a mentor appeals to you, then you may find such services available from your local *Business Link* – a government-funded business service often run in conjunction with your local Chamber of Commerce. Very often the staff can provide mentors, or guidance in a friendly one-to-one format. Take a look at www.businesslink.gov.uk.

Employing someone else to prospect for you

You can always get someone else to do prospecting for you. The prospecting part is perhaps a less glamorous side of the selling role and often is seen as a dirty job. If this is how you feel about prospecting and you have enough money to pass this task on, you may find a tele-marketing agency useful. They can be hired to source clients for you and often at a very reasonable cost – although a trade-off always exists. If you choose this route, do some checking first as to the pedigree of the agency and the promises it offers. You can very soon be parted from your money and see nothing in return. Look for an agreement that requires you to pay only if the agency actually gets you an appointment. You don't want to pay on a daily or hourly rate.

Especially if you've only been in the game for a short while, we do *not* recommend this option. Experience really has no substitute and even though at times the gathering of that experience is monotonous and even unpleasant, it is still valuable and teaches you many lessons.

If you do hire an agency or agent to find prospective customers for you, never, never stop prospecting for yourself. If you ignore this valuable step in the selling cycle, you may walk by your best potential client without even a glance.

Taking advantage of lists generated by your company

When you work for someone else's company, the company usually handles the details of advertising and marketing to generate leads for you and the other salespeople. But in order to become a great salesperson, keep prospecting on your own, too. That way, if the company lead programme hits a lull, you'll be prepared.

Don't do what most people do and only turn to self-prospecting when leads start slowing down. Bear in mind a gestation period always exists between first contact of the enquiry and the prospect being warm and ready and becoming a sale. Thus if you wait until the lead flow slows down you won't be able to turn it on again quickly. You need to have some prospects already in the pipeline that you can then turn on and trickle in so that a slow-down period doesn't present a problem.

You may be in a position to help answer questions that are e-mailed to your company by customers or prospective clients. If that's the case, don't just reply; make the enquirer curious for more information. Do your best to capture more than the person's return e-mail address: Get the person's name, address, and phone number, if at all possible. Add him to your contact list and follow up with him to ensure he's satisfied with your reply. Offer to provide him with additional service as well. This strategy is just one more way to add to your list of prospective clients.

Putting phone, mail, e-mail, and face-to-face interactions to work for you

You can contact your prospects in four major ways: By post, e-mail, phone, or face to face (each of these methods is covered in the following sections). Bear in mind that when you use any of these four methods, you're asking busy professionals to give up time that they may think can be spent more productively. So before you have a chance to convince your prospects otherwise, they'll try to shut you out – and shutting you out is easy for them to do. They can just make a paper plane out of your letter, delete your e-mail with a simple click of the mouse, leave you on terminal hold, ignore your incoming phone call, or cancel your appointment.

Most professional salespeople integrate all four methods into an effective prospecting strategy. For some, one method works better than others. Different situations call for different strategies, so be well versed in how to handle each. As you gain experience in prospecting, you can work out which methods work best for you and at which times.

Telemarketing

Telemarketers' phone calls are easy to hate – especially when you can hear the pages of their script turning as they read it at lightning speed, hardly taking a moment to breathe. You may feel that telemarketing calls are intrusions or interruptions in your daily life and say, 'No, thanks', and quickly hang up in common with a lot of people. If that's your response to most telemarketers, you probably wonder why businesses keep using telemarketing. The answer is simple: Telemarketers can reach more potential users of a company's product or service in one hour than most salespeople working face to face can meet in a week. Plus, telemarketers don't have to travel from one location to the next; they just dial the next few digits.

Telemarketing comes with its share of pitfalls. Salespeople who use telemarketing need the skin of a rhinoceros, though the pain of the process is eased when you do it with a little finesse and consideration.

Telemarketing, whilst being effective, can also do a lot of damage to your reputation if it isn't done well, and it can burn out your enthusiasm for prospecting in no time if you do it badly. Our suggestion is to be considerate of your prospects' thoughts and approach from a perspective of helping them, not selling to them.

Times have changed considerably. In the last 20 years, sales communication has swung from the face-to-face approach to mass telemarketing to mass e-mail and now to a 'bit of each' approach. To make telemarketing effective, combine the phone call with a flyer or an e-mail and possibly a visit as well. Prospecting is harder than ever in some ways, but skilled prospectors can still enjoy tremendous results by adopting a tweaked approach.

A few core tips we strongly recommend are

- Make sure that it's convenient for your prospect to talk. Don't just flick the switch and start downloading your message. Ask if now is a convenient time to talk and offer to call back when it might be more so – making sure to find out when that is.

  If your prospect says it's a bad time, acknowledge the bad timing, apologise, and make an appointment for a better time to call, qualifying that your call is only going to last a moment or two.

  Unless the person appears very interested in what you're saying, each call should take no more than two minutes.

- Be honest about what it is you're doing. *Don't* say that you're merely doing a survey unless you're genuinely only carrying out a survey. The survey gambit was very effective and thoroughly used in the 1980s and early 1990s but sadly was abused and callers turned 'surveys' into a sales call after the listener had answered a couple of questions. By all means ask a couple of questions to assess the listener's suitability but be honest with the prospect about your intentions and say, 'Do you mind if I ask you just a couple of questions to see if I can actually be of service to you?'.

- Ask questions. Asking questions involves the prospect and starts conversation. Hardly anyone wants to listen to a one-minute dissertation. People want to be involved in the phone calls they receive. Script your call so that it's courteous and filled with brief questions that your prospect can answer easily. People have to decide whether they like you before they'll consider doing business with you. Make the questions you ask light and brief and limited to just a couple related to your subject.

  Ask a question about what your prospect might experience as a problem relating to your offering. For example, if you're selling a service that offers advice in employment law and personnel, ask to speak to whomever deals with the employment issues and would be the one called upon to answer a tribunal case should one arise. Simply asking this question ensures that the person on the other end of the phone cannot just say 'No' – he'll probably either tell you a name or ask a little more about what you're offering. Either way, he at least has a clear impression as to what you're calling about and selling and this sets up a much higher chance that you'll be listened to when you do get through.

  Your questions should generate answers that tell you whether the person you've called may potentially qualify as a good client. For example, if your product is IT support and service, then your first questions might ask how many computers are in use (in either the home or the business that you've called) and when they were purchased. From the answers to these questions, you can gauge the odds of the prospect wanting and needing your service.

If your product is family portraits, you want to know when the prospect last commissioned one. If it was some time ago, ask how often that photo is looked at and how family members have changed since then. You'd then encourage your prospect to consider having a new photo taken to enjoy as much as the last one.

You have two possible goals for a telemarketing call:

✔ To arrange a time for a face-to-face meeting

✔ To get permission to send information via mail and e-mail and make another brief follow-up call

Mail

If you choose to use mail as your primary method of prospecting, choose your target recipients carefully. Mailing is a great way to prospect, but mail sent to the wrong list of people is a tremendous waste of your time, money, and effort. Nothing is easier to get rid of than the 'junk mail' that we all love to bundle up and throw away without so much as a cursory glance, and this is especially true if your prospecting piece of paper winds up on the doormat of someone who wouldn't care about your product or service in a hundred years.

Instead of sending a piece of mail that talks about your product or service, send a single-page introductory letter to the people you know who are most likely to want to get involved with what you're doing, indicating that you'll be calling on a certain date and time. Including something in the mailing that helps your letter stand out or be remembered is also useful. For example, small quirky magnets are great: Every time your prospect goes to the fridge, he sees your badge and thinks of you, thus building familiarity. He isn't as likely, however, to buy from some anonymous voice on the phone. Prospecting is all about establishing rapport, remember.

Whatever you send in the post, be absolutely certain that it includes your Web site address and your e-mail address, as well as your telephone number. As much as people love talking on phones, they're still more likely to check you out first by visiting your Web site to see if you have anything interesting that may make it worth their while to talk to you in person. In fact, before a purchase of any value, many people usually visit a Web site, so make sure you point them there. Your Web site can encourage visitors to download a free article establishing the benefits of buying from you.

E-mail

You can handle e-mail prospecting in two ways. One is to purchase an opt-in e-mail list from a list broker and send an e-mail message to the group of people who've expressed an interest in your type of product or service. The other is to search out the e-mail address of a consumer or purchasing agent whom you may have met or know through a third-party contact and mail a very specific, customised e-mail.

In either case, you want to use your e-mail like the introductory letter mentioned in the preceding section. Introduce yourself, your company, and the benefits your product would provide to the recipient. For the opt-in list, you may wrap up your message with a call to action: 'Reply to this e-mail within 24 hours and we'll have a specific proposal to you by Friday of this week.' Or, in a custom e-mail you may tell the recipient that you'll be calling within 48 hours to ask him two quick questions.

Sending an e-mail that looks like an advertisement is not effective. Your goal with e-mail is to make a personal connection, stimulate the recipient's interest, and tell him how to learn more.

Face-to-face interactions

Face-to-face prospecting is almost always the best method, but it's also the most time-intensive. If you prospect in person, one of four things can happen:

- You can be asked to leave literature and be told that the person you want to talk to will contact you if he's interested.
- You can be allowed to book an appointment for a future date.
- You can uncover valuable information about the company and who the real decision-maker is.
- You can actually get the opportunity to present your product or service to the decision-maker himself.

Walking from office to office or house to house trying to find someone to talk to is physically exhausting, but even worse is the sad fact that you may not get many appointments out of all your legwork.

What you will get, though, is a load of information from receptionists. Very often this 'gatekeeper' is the perceived barrier to getting through to the person who signs the cheques and yet when dealt with correctly is in fact the key to the unlocking process. They can be powerhouses who help you either eliminate a company as a prospect or advance your chances of obtaining an appointment for making your presentation with the decision-maker. Working with receptionists, not around them, is an absolute must. One of the best places to prospect is probably a meeting of secretaries rather than the one where all the executives meet. Receptionists, secretaries, and assistants hold the keys to opening the doors you want to get through.

Treat receptionists or secretaries with the respect they deserve. Their time is valuable, too. If you try to rush past a receptionist or quickly ask to see his boss without first showing concern or interest in him, you may as well not have gone in at all. Introduce yourself, ask the receptionist's name, and then try to have a friendly dialogue with him before asking to see the boss. He'll be more inclined to introduce a friend to his boss than he will a pushy salesperson, so try to get him to see you as the former rather than the latter.

When you engage in face-to-face prospecting, remember how lucky you are to be able to get some of the precious time out of the busy schedules of important people. Your prospects are offering something to you, too: an opportunity to show them how they can benefit from your product or service. In today's society, suspicion and distrust are rampant. When you professionally prospect (with the right attitude about your prospects), your contacts will come to trust you and welcome you into their homes and offices.

The face-to-face system can be the most effective over the long term but it is slower to reach numbers; thus if you sell a low price, high-volume offer, this approach doesn't really work. For higher-price purchases, though, the relationship between the buyer and seller is much more important and the chance of a sale is stronger. Thus a thorough, but slow, face-to-face approach probably proves a better option, especially if some thought and planning are added before the legwork begins.

Finding the Right People: Proven Prospecting Strategies

The following sections cover ten of the most effective methods you can use to find those people who are the best candidates for what you have to offer. When you apply yourself to finding these people, and if you continue to prospect on a regularly scheduled basis, you can be up and running on a successful selling career.

Mining the people you already know

You don't conduct your normal daily activities in isolation, do you? That means that you already know a horde of people who may be potential prospects for your product, service, or idea.

Think beyond your closest circle of friends and relatives (which we talk about in 'Searching for prospects among your friends and family' in this chapter) and consider people you interact with in more casual environments – you have neighbours, you may go to church or school functions on a regular basis, you may have a partner who works or is involved in other activities through hobbies, you encounter the same shop assistants every week. When you think about it, you touch literally hundreds of people in your usual routines.

The chances are good that several people in this wider circle of acquaintances may be able to benefit from your product or service in some way or they may know others who do. In prospecting with the people you come into contact with on a daily basis, your job is simply to communicate. If they don't know what it is you do, they cannot ever buy or recommend your offering; if they understand and appreciate the benefits of your product, you may be pleasantly surprised at how much value exists in the contacts you already have. Letting others know what you do opens many doors of opportunity for you. All you need to do is start a conversation.

Make a list of all the people you know, and begin there. Here's a list to get you started:

- ✔ Your parents
- ✔ Your grandparents
- ✔ Your siblings
- ✔ Your aunts, uncles, and cousins
- ✔ Your colleagues
- ✔ Members of your sports team
- ✔ People at your house of worship
- ✔ Parents of your children's friends
- ✔ Your neighbours
- ✔ Your hairdresser
- ✔ Your friends
- ✔ Members of business or civic groups you belong to
- ✔ Your mechanic
- ✔ Supermarket shop assistants
- ✔ Your drycleaner
- ✔ Your pet's vet
- ✔ Your doctor
- ✔ Your dentist
- ✔ Your solicitor
- ✔ Your accountant
- ✔ Your kids' teachers
- ✔ Your teachers
- ✔ Your kids' coaches
- ✔ Your bank cashiers
- ✔ Your kids' babysitters
- ✔ Your spouse's friends

Dressing for success . . . of a different colour

It is often the case that the more imaginative you can be to create a reason to open a conversation, the better the prospecting task feels. Many people assume that you need to wear clothes conforming to the standard dress code and that the only way to open conversation is by saying something. But thinking outside the conventional can pay big dividends.

A business colleague deliberately wears his hair in a ponytail and dresses in bright yellow and orange clothing, appearing almost hippie-like. He then asks people if they'd notice him in a crowd of other business people. When they admit that he quite obviously stands out in the crowd, he asks if they'd like their businesses to stand out too.

His service as a marketer and his potential to develop their businesses is easily introduced and this approach never fails to generate business for him. Simple, different, and very effective.

Tapping your business contacts

Whether or not you're new to selling, you've probably been involved in some sort of business. Even if you've only recently left full-time education, you've probably held part-time jobs throughout your school and college career. Surprisingly, business contacts can be easier to talk to than some social contacts because business contacts prospect all the time, too. Besides, they probably are very impressed with how you're making efforts to advance yourself and your career. You can probably be more direct with business contacts than you can with your personal contacts.

Visit the Web sites of the companies where your business contacts work. Look for the names of other companies they may have affiliations with so you know before contacting them whether they may have another good contact for you. If the affiliates they have posted on their Web site aren't good candidates for your product or service, or if they could be considered part of your competition, don't waste their time or yours in asking for these particular contacts.

Pay attention to the e-mails you get from your business associates. You may have received that e-mail as part of a group of recipients and one of the other people in that group may be a prospective client for you. If you want to try prospecting with them, call the person who sent the e-mail and see whether the people you want to contact would mind if you did so (as opposed to just sending e-mails without checking first). That way, you can contact the person and say, 'John Smith asked me to contact you,' which is much more professional and courteous to all parties involved.

When you're sending out your own e-mails to more than one person, put your recipients' e-mail addresses in the *blind carbon copy* (BCC) field instead of the *To* or *cc* field. That way, you're not sharing your personal or business lists with others.

When you're prospecting, think not only of the people you know in your business life, but also get involved in clubs or organisations for business professionals and prospect there. Excellent opportunities exist at functions held by Chambers of Commerce and similar business network groups.

We can't recommend highly enough organisations such as BNI, BRE, and many organised networking groups that allow you to prospect over breakfast, lunch, or evening functions. Simply use the Internet to search under 'business networking *your town*'.

Many industries also have their own associations through which you can discover valuable new strategies for approaching people in your specific industry. Staking your claim in these groups can be highly beneficial. Ask your business contacts if they have a back issue of an industry publication available. Studying it will give you a good feel for the type of potential business you may find within that organisation.

You'll also do well to research your industry's exhibition profile to find out where and when the industry exhibits, and then make a point of being there. You don't need to spend any money exhibiting but as a visitor you spend a day talking to and starting relationships with all those who *are* exhibiting.

When you find a prospective company, do further research with reputable resources. Dun & Bradstreet (www.dnb.co.uk) provide an excellent research service, as do Credit Safe (www.creditsafeuk.com). Credit information pertaining to the prospective client is invaluable when selling any high-value order with possible payment terms involved and both of these companies provide accounting and stability reports to allow you to assess whether the proposed sale is actually worth the risk. This information is good to have before you prospect heavily – when you may discover that the new client has a reputation for not paying and you lose out!

Talking to salespeople you currently buy from

Talking to salespeople you buy from is one of the most overlooked strategies of prospecting. Other companies send you highly knowledgeable, professional salespeople who already know loads of other people. They wouldn't be coming to you if you were in a similar business, right? So, because you're in a non-competing business, why not talk to them about any leads they may have? At the very least, ask them to keep you in mind the next time they call on their customers. Any extra sets of eyes out there looking for prospects on your behalf are of tremendous value, especially when most likely your only investment will be returning the favour sometime down the road.

Looking out for each other and sharing reciprocal arrangements or joint venture partnerships are simply the best way to develop your business, in our opinion. So look at every person selling something non-competitive as an ally not a threat and cultivate these relationships whenever possible.

Maximising your opportunities as a consumer

Imagine that you're at a restaurant and your waiter does an especially excellent job. If you're looking for someone to join with you in business, not work for you, and if this person already has great people skills and is competent at performing his duties, he may be a good candidate. You probably run into these kinds of people every day, everywhere you go, so take advantage of the situation and talk to them about the opportunities (or products or services) you have to offer.

Be careful not to approach people while they're working. Professional etiquette dictates that you don't interfere with other professionals while they're conducting business. What you can do is drop a hint that you'd like to talk more and that the conversation would be beneficial to them; usually they'll make an effort to get back to you or arrange for you to contact them at another time.

So what do you say to such people when you have the opportunity to talk? Here are some approaches that have proven to work in this particular situation:

> I can't help but notice that you have a nice way with people. I'm curious, are you achieving all your goals working here? The reason I ask is that the firm I represent is expanding and we're looking for quality people to take advantage of the opportunity. Do you have an interest in knowing more?

If the person asks, 'What's this about?' say:

> Ethically, because you're working now, I'm not at liberty to discuss it. However, if you'd like to jot down a number and a convenient time when I can reach you when you're not working, I can visit and we can discuss whether we can both benefit from my proposal.

You can then either arrange a time to call or, at the very least, leave your card and a time to contact you. This strategy's simple, but it still gets the person's attention.

Another way to prospect through other businesses is to send the business a letter or thank-you note for providing you with excellent service. Many businesspeople publish or display these letters in their places of business or on their marketing literature. If they have your permission to use your name in promoting their business, they're also pretty likely to list your profession or business name. When other people read your words, they'll see how professional you are and, hopefully, remember your name when they need services such as the ones you offer.

If you market a consumer item, chat with the people you meet when doing your own shopping to see whether they're good potential candidates for your product or service as well.

The key to successful prospecting is to acquire the mindset that *every* person you meet is either a potential client or knows someone else who may be.

Benefiting from the itch cycle

Face it – nearly every tangible product brought to market has a limited lifespan. At one end of the spectrum are computer software and hardware, which can have a lifespan as short as six months. At the other end, are things such as refrigerators and freezers, which can last 20 years. No matter how long a product's lifespan is, every product has one.

The precise lifespan of your product doesn't matter. What matters is that you know what its lifespan is. When you know that information, you have a goldmine of opportunity waiting for you to strike. If you're new to the product, ask people already in the business about your product's lifespan.

When you review your past customer files (see the following section for more information), you'll see that Mr Brown's microwave oven will need to be replaced in the near future. So don't wait for his microwave to break down and then quietly hope he'll come to see you again. Get in touch with Mr Brown *before* his microwave breaks down, and let him know you have some great new products with greater energy efficiency, space-saving designs, and other all-around better features. Put a reminder on your calendar or tag his file for follow-up in your contact management software. Your call may just help Mr Brown move a little quicker in replacing that old microwave!

The chances are good that Mr Brown knows that his microwave is on its last legs and that he's been putting off making the decision to shop. Maybe he's been waiting for a great offer or sale to catch his eye. What matters is that he hasn't acted *yet*. And these facts matter, too: Mr Brown already knows you and/or your product personally and he knows that you're the expert he turns to when the time for decision-making arrives.

Always make sure strategies such as this one are approved by your manager or are acceptable according to company policy before you implement them yourself.

If your company allows it, take advantage of a strategy we call the Puppy Dog scenario. Imagine you're considering getting a dog, but images of the hassle involved in training a puppy make you uncertain. Now, swap places and imagine you're a pet-shop owner trying to sell the puppy. If you were in the pet-shop owner's shoes, what would you do? You'd let the potential buyer take the puppy home for a few days to see how things go. Almost every time, the person – that is, the *prospect* – becomes so attached to the new puppy, that he can't bear to part with it. He starts out thinking that a puppy is messy, noisy, and so on, but after a few days he gets used to it, starts to really enjoy having it as company, and laughs at its antics. The upshot is he becomes attached to the puppy, enjoys having it around, and believes life is better with it.

If you're a car salesperson, you let a potential client try out the latest model of the car you think he'd like, preferably for several days or at least long enough to get attached to it and before a few days are up, the prospect loves the new car and wants to keep it. You've guaranteed yourself an itchy customer to serve. Such thoughtful and personalised service is guaranteed to keep customers coming back for more. Some salespeople might even drop off a DVD of the latest model of the car their prospects drive, so that they can fantasise about owning it, all in the comfort of their own home. Now that's nice!

You can also try e-mailing your client with an attached URL of a Web site where he can see photos and detailed information about the vehicle you think is best for him. Offer to bring one by for him to test-drive. All he needs to do is reply with the word 'Yes' and you have permission to confirm an appointment with him.

A little creative thought as to the best angle and a varied approach to the prospect so that he isn't just hearing from you when you do an impersonal mass mailer can really help your success rate. (For more ideas on how to prospect, try *Marketing For Dummies* by Craig Smith and Alexander Hiam (Wiley).)

If you don't already know the replacement cycle for your line of products, do some research to find out what it is. When do people begin getting that itch for something new? To find out this sort of information just make a few phone calls to people who currently use your products or services. You can treat this approach like a survey or market study and simply ask for their help. If they know it won't take long, most people love to help you. Begin by verifying that they're still using the product your records show them owning. Then ask what they used prior to the product or service they bought from you. The only time such research will fail is if the product or service that you sold to your customer is your customer's first foray into your market. If the customer is on his second, third, or later product or service of this type, ask how many years, overall, he's used such products or services before replacing them.

You can also look at your own records to determine the lifespan of your product or service. For example, if you sell copiers and your customer has used your copiers for 17 years, trading in only four times during your association, you know he'll need a new copier after he's owned his present model for about four years. When that fourth year rolls around, you may want to ask the client a few questions about his current needs and get permission to send him information about the latest and greatest models. If he won't need another machine for two more years, thank him for his help and make a commitment to stay in touch.

With replacement products, the salesperson who gets to the customer at the right time is often the one who wins. Plan to be that person and you'll be doing a lot of the winning. The early bird makes the sale.

Using your customer list

Any business that's been around for at least three years should have a pretty good customer list. It may be that former salespeople are now in other positions in the company so it may be possible to talk with some of them and get background information on clients and prospects if the systems that your company use aren't recording it. If those customers weren't reassigned to another salesperson, you may want to ask to be given the authority to contact those clients yourself. If nothing else comes of your contacts, you still leave a positive impression of the type of follow-up your company provides. And, hopefully, you can update your database along the way. Be sure to get e-mail and Web site addresses (for business contacts), too.

With the many changes that occur in business these days, managers don't always take the time to complete the basic task of transferring clients to new salespeople when the former salespeople move on. If the company is growing rapidly, some customers may get left in the dust. These *orphan clients* have no one looking after them. Why not be the one to pick them up and take care of them? They've already bought your brand or service before, so they're likely to again.

If your company has lived up to its promises, your customers should want to continue to work with such a fine organisation. However, very little loyalty exists these days and an ever more competitive market may leave the client open to poaching by a competitor. If he hasn't made any purchases lately, it may be simply because no one has asked or it may be that he's considering going elsewhere. Don't leave the door open for a competitor to come in and snatch up valuable customers. Prospect your list of past customers, and you may not only solidify their future business but also the business that they'll refer to you.

Riding the wave of technical advancement

Why do you suppose people itch to get something new? In some cases, the answer's simply because the product wears out. In others, though, the itch is created by something more personal, such as status. They want to have the latest, greatest, shiniest, top-of-the-range products with all the bells and whistles you can provide. When people have the best and latest products, they appear to be doing well. We live in an image-conscious world where business can be won or lost on impressions.

Think about this situation. If you see someone with a hand-held computer taking a few moments to type in what looks like an e-mail message, your impression is of a person who's upwardly mobile, highly connected, and probably a busy executive. Fifteen years ago if you'd seen someone talking apparently to no one, you'd have assumed he had an imaginary friend. Today, you realise that he must have an earpiece, and you're left with the impression that he's on the cutting edge of technology, which means he must be successful, a real go-getter.

Few people, except the older and more stubborn personality types, really want to have the old model of anything unless they're collectors and the old model is a true antique or classic. In today's world, everyone is accustomed to new models, greater benefits, and updated versions and is used to people offering the 'upgraded' version. Thus you have a perfect excuse to call your former clients with any of these types of reasons. The key to success with this strategy is in how you contact them. Take a look at the following examples to see how you can put this strategy to work for you (and how it can backfire if you're not careful).

Bill invested in a top-of-the-range home entertainment system a couple of years ago, but now some improvement has been made in the product that wasn't available when he bought it. Don't just ring Bill and say, 'I've got something even better for you.' Doing so would be both pushy and presumptuous and may very likely have the opposite effect to what you want – you may turn Bill off to even hearing what you have to say, because you've just, in effect, criticised his system.

Instead, call Bill and ask him how he's enjoying listening to his favourite music on his home entertainment system. Being sure that he's still happy with what he's got before bringing up anything else is critical. If he has a complaint you didn't know about and you start talking about new products, you could lose Bill as a customer forever.

When you've determined that he's happy, say the following:

> Bill, I know how diligent you were in your research before investing in your system. Because I value your opinion, would you mind evaluating something else our company is launching?

See the difference? You've complimented Bill, acknowledged his intelligence, *and* asked for his opinion. You've made him feel important. Of course he'll be happy to look at your new toy now. And if the product's truly better than the one he has, he'll probably want to upgrade his system.

If you take the time to know what's going on with your current customers, you'll know exactly when and how to contact them with new products or innovations and increase the volume and number of sales you make to each one. Now that's a clever sales technique.

Reading the newspaper

Here's another idea for prospecting: sifting through your local newspaper. You can even use an electronic version of most newspapers these days, but whichever way you do it, realise that the 'news items' are often stories of promotions, new business successes, new births or family happenings, and so on, and along with each of these stories is a potential business opportunity. We say local newspaper for pretty obvious reasons, and unless you do business internationally, this is all that you need. A local paper provides a more intimate basis for prospecting to the person who appears in the news item.

Knowing how to read your newspaper for leads only takes a few days of practice. When you get started, you'll be amazed at the number of leads you used to glance over. Behind every story you read is an angle to say 'hello' and offer a product or service. Here's just a brief list of some of the things people need and want when they go through life changes (all of which you can find in your local newspaper):

- ✔ People having babies need more insurance, bigger homes, different cars, delivery services, nannies, and nappies and baby products.

- ✔ Families who are moving into new homes need decorating services, security systems, maybe new curtains, carpets, or furniture, and possibly also handyman and gardening services to make the new home the vision they dreamed of.

> ✔ New or expanding businesses may well require recruitment services, office furniture and supplies, and many other items.
>
> ✔ A fundraising venture picturing the business owner and the sponsored cyclist offers a clear opportunity to talk about promotional goods and name awareness schemes.

One enterprising salesperson saw a picture of a prospect in a newspaper article relating to a business expansion and then posted him a beautifully wrapped 'new car' – a small model Ferrari with a card that said, 'I see the company is growing well. I hope you enjoy your new car!' This approach was quirky, got attention, and was remembered. When the salesperson called for an appointment a week later, he was granted a meeting and eventually secured a lucrative client account.

Take today's local newspaper and read every headline. Circle those with stories that may hold some business prospects for you. Then do what any top salesperson who's striving for excellence would do and *contact* those people. Cut out the article, make a copy for your records, and then send a brief note, saying, 'I saw you in the news. I'm in business in the community and hope to meet you someday in person. I thought you might enjoy having an extra copy of the article to share with friends or relatives.' Make sure you include your business card. People love seeing that they were in the news. And they love having extra copies of the articles to send to friends and relatives who aren't in the area. By providing this little service in a non-threatening way, you can gain a lot of business.

Knowing your service and support people

If you're in touch with the people in other departments of your company, you may be able to discover valuable information that may help you keep the clients you already have (and get more down the road). For example, someone who works in accounting for your company may know that one of your clients has made several late payments for your product or service. That's a valuable piece of information for anyone in sales. By reconnecting with that client, you may be able to make other arrangements for him. Perhaps his growth rate isn't as high as he anticipated and your equipment or service just costs too much for him. He may be experiencing problems in cash flow and you can ease this by offering different payment terms or restructuring the product or service sales format. He'll never forget you because your actions are truly perceived as helping him, not merely helping yourself to commissions. He may become a loyal, long-term customer, referring his friends and business associates to you when they need the product or service you provide. If you let such information go without addressing it, you may lose that person as a customer just because he was too embarrassed to approach your company about his situation.

Also get in the habit of periodically checking your company's service and repair records. Even better, see if your company can set up a system so that when a service call comes in, the salesperson is automatically notified of this fact by e-mail. Amazingly, although many garages and car sales outlets have both a sales department and a service department, they rarely swap valued information! If only they did so, they'd hear about the mum who delivered the car for servicing full of the residue of kids, moaning that it just wasn't big enough to carry everybody! A perfect excuse to invite a sales call!

So, consider asking the people in your customer service department how many times your clients call with questions about the product or service you've sold them. If your clients are calling frequently, you need to get back in touch with them. Maybe they're in a growth phase and you can help them acquire new services. Or maybe they're having some problems with particular equipment. If they're less than perfectly happy, the situation may well be rectifiable if you get in there early enough with a genuine solution. Leave rectifying the problem to the service team and it may be dealt with by the book, which isn't really written from the client's perspective. The result may be a disgruntled client who'll move when the opportunity arises.

Always strive to provide service above and beyond what the average salesperson would give. You'll build long-term relationships, trust, and referral business in the process. Go the extra mile.

Practising the three-foot rule

Many businesspeople subscribe to the *three-foot rule* when it comes to prospecting: Anyone who comes within three feet of them is worth talking to about their product, service, or business.

When you're comfortable with what you're selling and with talking to people about it, we highly recommend applying this strategy. All you need to do is say, 'Hello, it's nice to meet you.' Pay attention to the people you talk to. Notice something about them you can compliment. For example, if you're a woman and you're talking to another woman, you can say, 'That's a nice necklace (or dress, or coat). Where did you find it?' After she answers, go on with another question about her response or bring up something else you have in common, such as why you're standing in the queue at the post office on a Friday morning when you have a million other things to do. After you establish a little bit of rapport, exchanging names is considered the polite thing to do. And at that point you can bring up the subject of your idea, product, or service. Ask a question such as, 'Have you ever found a product to get red wine stains out of blouses?' (if what you sell gets stains out of blouses). Or use a question such as, 'Have you been to the new restaurant on the high street called Tarantinos?' (if the new restaurant is yours). If you market financial services or loans, you could say, 'I see you're wearing a wedding ring. Do you have a personal family protection provider that can help you make certain your family's financial needs will be met? Lots of wives I meet mention that they aren't sure if their children will be properly provided for if anything should happen.' When she answers that it is something that sometimes concerns her, talk about the great family protector policy that you found (and sell). Personal testimony moves more products than any other method.

Many business contacts have been made while standing in queues in places such as coffee shops, take-aways, and even toilets! Be ready to talk about your product or service wherever you go and don't pass up any opportunity to talk with a prospective client. Such forwardness is often uncomfortable for many people; however. we all live in a cold and impersonal world at times and very often a friendly chat and a smile from a stranger is extremely well received and does not come across as a sales approach. So try this tactic – you may soon find you enjoy the process and the results.

So how do you handle these brief encounters with people and get leads to build your business? This method doesn't bring you great leads *every* time, but even if it only produces a gem now and then, it is still worth using.

As an idea, grab a few of your business cards and across the front of each card, in very neat handwriting, write, 'Thank You'. Then, when you meet a new person – someone who's entered your three-foot space – be warm and friendly and introduce yourself as you hand him a card and ask him what his business is or why he's at that place. Such banter almost obliges him to do the same. When the prospect gives you the courtesy of looking at the card, he'll probably ask about that 'Thank You'. (Curiosity gets the better of most people and they blurt out their questions almost as a matter of reflex.) That's the moment you've been waiting for. At that point, you simply smile and say these words:

> I guess I'm thanking you in advance for what, hopefully, will be the opportunity someday to serve your [whatever your business is] needs.

Make sure you use those words exactly. *I guess* makes it sound spontaneous. *Thanking you in advance* shows that you're a nice person. *Hopefully* shows humility. *Someday* places your offer way out into the limbo of the future; it's a very passive, non-threatening word. *Serve your needs* elevates your prospect to a place of importance in your life – and *everyone* needs to feel important. When your prospect feels like he's important to you, he's more likely to make a move that can help you.

He'll probably do one of four things, any one of which is a move in the right direction for you:

✔ He'll give you a chance to discuss it further.

✔ He'll give you a time to call him to discuss it further.

✔ He'll ask you to send something, either by e-mail or post.

✔ He won't be interested, but he'll possibly refer you to someone who may be interested in what you have to offer.

What have you got now? Maybe not a lot yet, but you potentially have a lot more than you had a moment ago. Instead of merely standing there waiting for your cup of tea and cake, you've now got a prospect . . . and possibly some icing for the cake!

Some of the ideas and strategies may look scary and you may say, 'I couldn't do that' or you may not believe that people will be receptive to your conversation when in a queue with strangers, but we wouldn't recommend you try it if we didn't know from lots of experience that it actually works really well. Go on, try it – you'll be pleasantly surprised and better off financially when it becomes a habit.

Chapter 8

Making Appointments the Easy Way

*I*n virtually every situation in which you can use selling skills, if you don't get directly in contact with the right person, all your hard work developing your selling skills goes for naught. If you cannot present directly to your clients, you'll never be able to discover their needs in order to figure out how you can satisfy them.

So how do you get directly involved with the people you want to persuade? In order to get face to face with people, you first must sell them on scheduling an appointment with you or, at the very least, agreeing to allow you to visit without a pre-set time when you're in the area. And you must schedule an appointed time to discuss your offering properly before you can ever persuade your prospect to own your product, start using your service, or consider your idea.

Of course, to begin with, you have to find the right people to contact, and you do this by prospecting, a topic we cover in Chapter 7. But you also have to be firmly convinced that what you have is right for the people you're selling to. If you're not convinced of that match, you can't deliver your presentation with enough conviction to persuade them to give you the time of day, let alone consider your product or service.

In this chapter, we let you know exactly how to get an appointment with your prospective clients. Then we take the selling process a step further and give you some great pointers for putting them at ease when you finally do come face to face.

In this chapter, 'face to face' refers to direct contact with the correct person whether over the phone, via e-mail, Web conference, or in an actual meeting.

Knowing the Basics of Contacting Prospects

Your first line of approach when you're contacting a prospective client may differ depending on how you received the person's contact information, for example:

- ✔ **If the prospective client contacted you by phone, mail, e-mail, or any other in-bound contact method then a polite telephone approach is right and proper.** If she contacted you, she effectively solicited your call and invited you to make contact. The telephone with a light and friendly approach is always best . . . she'll soon tell you if the time isn't convenient or if she wants anything in writing.

- ✔ **If you got the person's name from a referral (another client or business associate recommended you call her), ask the person doing the referring to introduce you to the new prospect.** If she doesn't make time or chooses not to get involved, a brief polite telephone call to the introduced prospect is perfectly natural: in your first sentence mention that you're calling because of a conversation you had with her friend and yours, Mrs Blythe. Mentioning the introducer's name almost immediately softens any hesitance your prospect feels at receiving a sales call. The prospect often goes with the 'any friend of hers is a friend of mine' philosophy.

  If you can't get through on the phone, then sending a quick e-mail (if you were also given her e-mail address) or an introductory letter in the post is next choice.

- ✔ **If the person left her name and e-mail address on your Web site, it may well be that she prefers electronic communication.** Indeed, it may be that this is the only way you can contact her if you don't have any other contact details. However, if she left complete contact details including phone numbers, she is inviting you to call – working on the generally accepted premise that if she didn't want you to call, she wouldn't have left a number.

Your goal when you contact a prospective client (whether by phone, mail, or e-mail) is to have direct, live contact with her, so you must approach the sale of the appointment very carefully. You first have to sell to the prospect the fact that she'd be better off speaking to you than not speaking to you. And to deliver that message you must offer benefits to her in your very first contact.

Bear in mind these tips when you're trying to get an appointment or secure an opportunity to pop by and visit:

- ✔ **Always be courteous.** Say 'please' and 'thank you'. Refer to the person in a similar style to that in which she's been passed to you. For example, if you get a referral from a client saying 'call Jenny Smith, she's a good friend', then asking for Jenny Smith when calling is appropriate. When speaking to her, calling her Jenny carries across the friendship of the referral and will be accepted as a continuation of that friendship. Creating a sense of friendship is more conducive to sales. If the prospect was passed on as Mrs J. Smith, then initially refer to her as Mrs Smith until she says 'call me Jenny'.

- ✔ **Do anything to meet the prospect.** Even if you have to drive miles out of your way to be where she is and all you get is an introduction, those miles can turn into smiles when you later close the sale. Besides, being prepared to put yourself out for her makes it apparent that you're respectful and considerate in that you didn't suggest to her that she drive to you.

- ✔ **Hit the high notes early.** That means you must stimulate her interest immediately. Tell her about a benefit that she'd be likely to enjoy – saving money, making money, and improving lifestyles are big ones for most people.

- ✔ **Confirm all the details about where and when you'll meet.** Verbal confirmation is a must. Written confirmation is even better. Whenever possible take all address details thoroughly (it helps you find the place when making your visit) and mention that you'll send a confirmation letter. You can include in your confirmation note that you'll invest plenty of time in researching just the right information for the meeting to make it worth your prospect's while.

These instructions may seem too simplified at first glance, but many a novice salesperson has become so excited about getting an appointment that she's let her professionalism slip and said, 'Damn right, I'll be there!' (And although a little swear word among friends may be acceptable, avoid swearing at all costs when you're dealing with new prospective clients.) Likewise when you first start making appointments you may easily 'forget' to reconfirm details about when and where to meet – and not knowing accurately the place and time can potentially mean you miss a big opportunity. If you do your best to be courteous, to secure an appointment no matter how busy the prospect is, and to confirm the details of when you'll meet, you're well on your way to a great appointment.

Reaching Your Prospects by Telephone First

The important thing to keep in mind when you've come up with a list of prospective clients is that not all of those clients need your product or service. You may have to contact 20, 30, or more people to find one who wants just what you have to offer. But every one of those other calls brings you one call closer to the right person. So you just need to stay focused on your ultimate goal; don't let a little bit of rejection send you scurrying to the nearest hidey-hole. Salespeople cope with rejection every day in a variety of ways; try reminding yourself often of that old saying, 'there are plenty of fish in the sea'. Remember, sales is probably the only job in the world where even at the top you still only get it right approximately 30 per cent of the time!

So what do you do when you're ready to approach those prospects? What strategies work best? You go through seven steps in that introductory phone call, all of which we cover in the following sections:

1. **Offer a greeting.**

2. **Introduce yourself and your business.**

3. **Check that the time is convenient for the call.**

   If 'Yes', then express your gratitude for the person's willingness to talk to you. If 'No', then ask when would be convenient and call back. Don't push for more time now if she says it isn't convenient.

4. **Tell the person the purpose of your call and verify that she is the right person to talk to.**

5. **Get an appointment to talk to the person face to face.**

6. **Thank the person while you're on the phone.**

7. **Send a written confirmation letter clearly stating what was agreed as to time, date, and place of meeting.**

The rest, as they say, is selling.

When you're about to contact your prospective clients, keep three things at the forefront of your mind: your belief in what you're offering, the happiness of your current clients, and your desire to serve others. This advice remains the same whether you're selling yourself as an employee, selling your services as a part-time copywriter, or pitching in for a multi-million pound high-level contract.

Step 1: Going with a great greeting

When you call a prospective client for the first time, begin by using the most important thing for anyone to hear: her name. Using a formal approach, such as 'Good morning, Ms James' or 'Good morning. I'm calling for Ms James', is best because it conveys respect. (But be sure to check your watch before you call . . . you don't want to look a complete idiot by saying 'good morning' when it's actually the afternoon!)

We recommend the use of *Good morning*, *Good afternoon*, or *Good evening*, especially if you make it a cheery greeting emphasising with your tone of voice that it *is* in fact good. The more formal greeting also sounds more professional and businesslike than just saying, 'Hello'. This phrasing distinguishes you from all those other people who call your prospective client – and the difference definitely favours you.

Be very careful about use of names: Only call the prospect Bob or Liz instead of Robert or Elizabeth, or indeed Mr or Mrs Smith, when he or she invites you to do so. Too often, new salespeople are tempted to use a person's first name over the phone and try to be too casual too quickly; this approach can sour first impressions.

Common courtesy goes a long, long way in making initial contacts. If you aren't confident in your skill level in this area, then quietly ask a colleague or seasoned professional to guide you along. In essence, simple open human honesty shines through brightest. Admitting your nervousness to a client or prospect and asking for her consideration is usually a benefit, not a drawback. She'll view you as less threatening and thus be more attentive and more easily involved in the selling process.

Ben once trained a very young salesperson to overcome her nerves and use them to her advantage. She literally told every client in the first sentence or two, 'I apologise if I sound a little nervous, this is my first call and we're just so busy that I've been called upon to help out. I'm not usually in sales, so please bear with me.' The effect was dramatic: every client then felt a little sorry for this young woman, became more receptive, and gave her a little time. Of course, she then did just what she was trained to do and sold loads! We promise that nerves and lack of experience don't need to hold you back!

Step 2: Introducing yourself

After offering your greeting, introduce yourself and give your company name. If your company name doesn't explain what you do – as it would if your name were, say, Jensen Portrait Studios – then you must also mention briefly what type of business you're in. The key word here is *briefly*. Ben once asked a salesperson what she sold, and got 45 minutes on the features and benefits of owning his very own electronic high-sensitivity weighing device! And no, he didn't buy one!

To keep your prospect on the line and awake, you may not want to say that you're in carpet cleaning, for example. Instead, describe your business in terms of benefits to the prospect. For example, you may say:

> We're a local business that helps companies like yours enhance their image with customers and reduce employee sick time.

Clean carpets create a good impression. Dirty carpets spread germs. Is Ms James ready to hang up? Not yet, probably. Your description is creating all kinds of pictures in her mind because you haven't been so specific as to mention carpet cleaning. Your business could be anything from fancy plasma screens showing constant images on the office wall to high-tech air-filtration systems. Because she probably doesn't have a clear picture yet of what you're selling, she's probably curious to know more. After all, no one likes to end a conversation with all the blanks not yet filled in.

Paint a tantalising picture with the words you use, but keep it simple. This creation of an image all happens in a matter of seconds. If you hear snoring on the other end of the line, you've gone on too long. You're trying to get Ms James to give you anything with which you can extend the conversation.

Step 3: Expressing gratitude

After you've introduced yourself and your business, you need to acknowledge that your prospect's time is valuable and thank her for taking your call. Doing so lets her know you consider her to be an important person.

Say something like the following:

- ✓ I appreciate your giving me a moment of your valuable time this morning. I promise to be brief.
- ✓ Thank you for talking to me. I'll only be a moment, and then let you get back to the important work you do.

It doesn't matter if she was just walking into the room with nothing in particular planned for the moment. Acting as if you've called her when she's just finished a meeting with the Prime Minister never hurts the impression you make.

You don't need to gush at your prospects with gratitude, though. Just be professional and businesslike in your manner.

Step 4: Stating your purpose and qualifying your prospect

When you've expressed your gratitude for your prospect's time, you need to get right to the heart of the matter by letting her know why you're calling. Here we recommend either of two effective approach styles:

Firstly, a direct question relating to the specific offer that you intend talking about. Try:

> If I were to show you how to reduce employee sick time, while improving the image your company presents to its customers, would you be interested?

If she says 'Yes', ask permission to ask her a few brief questions. When you have her permission, go ahead with your questions.

If she says 'No', be prepared with one more question that may stir her interest, such as:

> Do you believe an improvement in the image of your business would have the effect of increasing sales?

If she still says 'No', you may want to be more direct and ask:

> When was the last time you had the carpets in your office steam cleaned to eliminate germs and improve your company's appearance to your clients?

If she says the carpets were cleaned only last week, you may just need to remain polite and ask for permission to contact her when she needs the service again. (Ask how long ago she had her carpets cleaned before that and you'll find out when she'll need them cleaned again, or simply ask how frequently they have them cleaned.) Thank her for her time. Put a note in your calendar to contact her a couple of weeks before she needs the carpets cleaned again, and move on to your next potential client call.

A second extremely effective method to use is that of the *market research approach*. In place of the questioning about improving the image of your prospect's business, you ask five or six questions related to your offering, including 'Would you mind if someone called another day to discuss your needs in more detail?' and questions that give you some 'meat' to discuss in the follow-up call. You then thank the prospect for her information and leave it to follow up another day. A market research approach definitely works if you keep it sounding like genuine research – not a sales call in disguise.

To ask for the time to answer a few survey questions try saying:

> The company I represent has given me an assignment to conduct a quick five- or six-question survey of just ten businesses in your field. You're the sixth person I've contacted. We would greatly value your opinion. Would you help me by answering these few brief questions?

When you ask for the prospect's help and show that you value her opinion, she's likely to comply. After all, who among us doesn't have an opinion? Also, by informing her that your company is having you do this, you're likely to gain her empathy and co-operation.

Be careful not to just go from one question to the next without really listening to your prospect's answers. If she thinks you're not listening and don't care about her issues as reflected in her answers, she'll quickly hang up and send you packing.

So how can you show that you're really listening to what your prospect is saying? Paraphrase her responses before moving on to the next question. When she hears that you cared enough to listen, she'll be more inclined to continue – and you get the chance to call again another day and pursue a sales visit.

The purpose of conducting this brief survey is to get the information you need in order to reach the right prospect. This is a critical stage of the prospecting and selling process because you cannot afford to be making appointments with the wrong people or with people who are never going to be qualified to buy your offering. This questioning process will save you thousands of pounds and hours and could well be the difference between making it or dying of starvation before the flood gates of cash open up. Hopefully, what your prospect tells you can give you the information you need and then you can make the call back another time to discuss her 'challenges' with her current situation and offer your 'solution' in the form of a personal visit.

You cannot afford to be sitting with non-qualified prospects, so you must ask relevant questions. Making a sales appointment with someone only to find out that a key factor for making a sale happen is missing is pointless. For example, if you're selling financial services, mortgages, life insurances, investments, or something similar, then it might well be a prerequisite that the prospect is in employment or at least can verify an income; so you need to ask a question about the prospect's income and employment status pretty early on in the call. Or say you sell a service that saves a load of money on telephone calls and other business utilities. It might be useful to establish usage levels before making a visit because if the business only has nominal usage, the savings you can offer will be virtually pence and such a small saving is unlikely to make them move services. Better to save time and focus upon larger-volume users such as companies with hundreds of staff and lots of telephone lines.

So, when using the telephone to make an appointment, you need to introduce yourself and show gratitude for the prospect's time but you must also do some digging before you blindly make the appointment. Whether you choose a 'one call' direct questioning approach or the market research 'two call' style, you ultimately need to proceed with making an appointment for a sales visit.

Step 5: Making the appointment

If you've used a market research approach then this stage is in fact a second call. You make pleasantries and greetings again with the person who answered the call and then ask for the relevant decision-maker. If you've chosen a direct 'one call' approach, you'll have determined by now that you're talking to a qualified prospect and someone who has a need for your offering and whom you can genuinely help out. Either way you can reasonably proceed with a direct request for a meeting to take the potential enquiry further.

So, if, after sharing with your prospect the purpose of your call and asking the questions you've prepared, Ms James seems inclined to set a time for a visit, you need to use an 'either/or' type of question to help her decide when the appointment should be.

> Would tomorrow at 10.20 a.m. be good for you, or is Wednesday at 2.40 p.m. better?

This question lets your prospect choose yet keeps you in control. What's she doing if she chooses either option you've given her? Committing to the appointment, which is exactly what you want.

Notice that the example mentions off times, as opposed to 10.00 a.m. or 2.00 p.m., for example. Using off times differentiates you from all the other salespeople who call. It also shows that you must know the importance of punctuality if you can keep a schedule using those times. If your visit will last only 40 or 50 minutes, it also lets your prospect schedule other appointments around you in the more standard time slots. You may find also that your prospect asks how long the appointment will take. Our advice is to say something like, 'Well Ms James, that depends a lot upon you. If I can learn a little more about how you operate your business then I may not need very long at all but obviously you'll want to ask some questions and it would be good to allow time to do a thorough job for you. I would suggest 40 to 50 minutes.'

The client will probably have a mental picture of one hour – an average allotted time for a social and business call – so won't feel this will be an issue. Frankly, she'll either be inclined to see you because your offering sounds interesting to her or she won't. Rarely will time be a real issue.

Making sure you don't set yourself up for disappointment

When you are in the sales business and making lots of appointments, give yourself a reality check. You'll always have a percentage of 'blow outs', where the prospect just doesn't turn up or isn't there when you visit her. Expect a 20 to 30 per cent blow-out rate – but keep trying to make them all stick.

Watch what you say during the appointment-making call so that what *you* call an appointment is also what she calls one – not just you talking your head off and she not even having a chance to say no! Even when appointments are made properly, however, some prospects fall by the wayside and some are postponed for a legitimate reason – she may decide to sleep in that day, an important call may come in, she may just be running late, or she may just plain forget.

Step 6: Thanking and confirming by phone

When you've secured an appointment, you move on to thanking your prospect again, reiterating the time that has been agreed to and verifying the location of her office (or the place where you'll be meeting). Nothing is worse than showing up late and presenting the excuse of getting lost. If the location is difficult to get to, *now* is the time to ask for explicit directions. If this is 'The Big Sale' you've dreamed about for years and you finally have the appointment, drive to the office the day before and familiarise yourself with the area. Know at least one alternative route in case traffic presents a problem or there are roadworks that cause disruption or diversion.

If an appointment is important enough, schedule at least the earlier part of that day in the prospect's part of town so that you're already in the area when the time for the appointment arrives. If you still end up with appointments later in the day, then allow yourself to take some clear time to get there without stress and spend some productive time researching the prospect or preparing properly for the call. Never, ever risk being late for a first appointment because you don't know where you're going or because of circumstances beyond your control.

Make the appointment as early in the day as possible – even around 8 a.m. or 8.30 a.m. for business-to-business calls. Doing so not only conveys the impression that you're a solid, committed professional who is serious about business but it also lends itself to showing consideration for the other party by saying, 'Shall we meet early on so that you can still have a fairly clear day without me stealing your time?' or 'Shall we meet early and that way we won't get snarled up in rush-hour traffic?'

Step 7: Sending a written confirmation letter

If your appointment is more than two days away, immediately send your prospect a written confirmation letter confirming the details of when you spoke and what was agreed to. A professional-looking piece of correspondence can solidify any doubts a prospect may have about this commitment and provides an excellent reference piece should she need to re-schedule the meeting for any reason.

Making sure you don't come up cold when cold calling your prospects

Most appointments are made over the phone, but that seemingly harmless invention of Mr Bell's can be both a godsend by allowing you to make volumes of calls *and* a threat to your sanity when you make outgoing calls to people you've never met in an attempt to get appointments. Making calls under such conditions is often called *cold calling*, partly because it can send shivers down your spine and partly because you're calling someone cold, with no prior contact. But cold calling doesn't have to be that scary; after all, it's only 'a numbers game'. Instead of thinking ill of the task and hating every call, try to just think of it as a slot machine and every call as a penny going in the slot; eventually, the tactic's going to pay off. And if you use cold calling right, it can land the jackpot!

Your success at cold calling depends on your perspective. The best way to sell or persuade anyone is in a face-to-face situation, and the phone is the most effective way to achieve that position. If you focus on that simple point, you'll overcome those sweaty palms, the trembling sensation on your upper lip, and the churning in the pit of your stomach when the time to make the call arrives. With practice, you can easily overcome those emotional reactions to your fear of saying the wrong thing or of being rejected. Even when you feel scared to death, realise that it isn't so scary when she doesn't know who you are and you'll probably never see her anyway.

If you doubt that you'll ever become comfortable with making cold calls, think back to a similar feeling that you used to have and now don't experience, for example, when you first started talking with members of the opposite sex somewhere in your pre-teen or teen years. Your physical reactions then probably resemble those you experience now if you're not used to cold calling, don't they? Your reactions were pretty much the same then because you wanted to impress someone and were afraid you'd look like a fool. Your fear arises partly because you have a lack of experience and partly because you don't know the person. However, you now know as an adult that the fear is less of a barrier because if the person says no, there's always another, and anyway you won't see her again. You'll get over this fear just as you have overcome others . . . who knows, you may even enjoy cold calling when you get going!

Bear in mind that if your prospect has given you a home e-mail address as opposed to a work one, she may not check that e-mail account on a daily basis, which means it may not be the best method of reaching her. Again, in a business-to-business situation a written letter is a better idea even if it duplicates the e-mail confirmation. In many businesses the 'spam' problem, irregular connectivity issues, and the likelihood of technology glitches all mean that 'snail mail' is often a winner, so always send a hard copy.

Also remember that unless you're already known by the prospect, she more than likely wants to do some research on you before you get there (she won't tell you this but expect it). The letterhead on your stationery steers her in the right direction. Give her some pointers too – invite her to look at a Web address, because the more familiar you feel to a prospect, the better your chances of a sale when you actually meet.

Getting to the Elusive Decision-Maker

When you're seeking an appointment with a prospective client, what you really want is to get in with the person who has the ability to make decisions about the products and services the company uses, otherwise known as the *decision-maker*. Unfortunately, in addition to facing the challenge of that initial phone call with a prospect, you may find yourself not even able to get through to the person you want to reach. In fact, that person may have so many people contacting her that she's established a hierarchy of people around her who screen calls quite heavily on her behalf, widely known as *gatekeepers*. This situation may cause you to wonder exactly where your prospective client is and what she's doing and feel frustration with her for 'avoiding your calls'. Paranoia can easily set in! But what she's doing doesn't matter, as long as you can eventually get to her.

When you have trouble getting through to the decision-maker, you get the opportunity to be a little creative. Yes, this situation requires more work, but bear in mind that those people who are hardest to get to are likely to be tough on your competition as well. So if you stick it out, get in to see them, and win their business, you'll be on the inside of that same protective wall. And those same support people will keep not you, but your *competition*, at bay.

Going head-to-head with the receptionist

If you're having trouble getting through to a decision-maker, begin with the receptionist who answers the phone when you call. If at all possible, get the name of the decision-maker on your first contact. Tell the receptionist that you need her help and ask, 'Who would be in charge of the decision-making process if your company were to consider getting involved in a [whatever your product or service is].' The receptionist is the person who has to know what each employee's area of responsibility is in order to direct calls properly, so she should be a great help. Then, whenever you make follow-up calls, use the decision-maker's name.

Make sure you ask for the correct pronunciation and spelling of any names the receptionist gives you. Never guess about names or take the chance of writing them down incorrectly; business practices like that are likely to haunt you later. Getting the receptionist's name can be useful as well.

The receptionist may well be a key 'influencer' and as gatekeeper may even take it upon herself to screen callers. Use the person's name and keep her sweet. Take a moment to send a thank-you note to her along with your business card. Businesspeople often tout the value of a good receptionist when they need to hire one, but only smart businesspeople reward other people's receptionists as well. A little bit of recognition now can prove valuable later on. When you've built a solid relationship with the receptionist, she'll always look forward to seeing you and future visits will be much warmer. She may also help guard your account against infiltration attempts by your competitors.

Working with the decision-maker's assistant

If the decision-maker has an assistant, the receptionist will probably put you through to that person first. Expect this situation, and don't be put out by it. Treat this person with the same respect and courtesy you would use with the decision-maker herself. As with a receptionist, the assistant can make or break your chances of ever getting an appointment, so ask for the assistant's help as well. Get all of the people who stand (or sit) between you and your prospect on your side. Schmooze them, flirt with them, and involve them. If the prospect holds great potential, make every effort to succeed where others fail – make the gatekeepers into door openers.

As for help in actually trying to make an appointment, give the middle person some idea as to what to say you are calling with. First tell the assistant that you have a way of increasing efficiency while decreasing the costs of a service the company is already using. Give her a little hint as to the benefits of your offering and the idea that the boss is likely to be pleased to find out about these. Then tell her you need her help, and simply ask how to get an appointment with Ms Decision-Maker.

Most businesses have an established procedure for setting up appointments. By asking what that procedure is, you show that you're not trying to beat the system; you just want to find out how to work with it. Showing respect for the company's system moves you up a notch on the respect scale.

Unless the procedure for meeting the decision-maker is too complicated or your offering has a stringent time deadline, try to book an appointment her way first. If the system doesn't work, consider how much effort the company's business is worth. If the prospect's a once-in-a-lifetime proposition, then you need to get creative (see the following section for tips on how to do that).

Getting creative in your efforts to meet the decision-maker

Whatever unusual method you choose for getting in touch with the decision-maker, always consider how the other person may receive it. Your goal is to find an inoffensive method for getting a person's attention. You want to appear on her radar so you need to know what already appears in her view. You need to find out what the hot buttons are and build your contact method around that. Receptionists, secretaries, and assistants can come to your rescue here.

We heard of a salesperson who sent a loaf of bread and a bottle of wine in a basket to a hard-to-reach decision-maker. She included a note that said, 'I hate to w(h)ine, but I know I can save you a lot of dough if you'll just meet me for ten minutes.' This tactic broke through the barrier in a creative way and she did get a confirmed appointment.

Consider what you send to ensure that it never gives the wrong impression. For example a gift that seems expensive or romantic may offend – trinkets or flowers may appear to be either bribery or a show of desire for the wrong sort of attention, even if the gift actually only cost a few pounds!

Another creative way to make a good impression on the decision-maker is to ask her receptionist or assistant about the decision-maker's tastes in reading and music, or what hobbies or leisure activities the decision-maker enjoys. A straightforward gift of an invitation to an event that you know the person would enjoy, such as a football match featuring a favourite team, shows that you care about the person as well as the account.

If you're working your business correctly, you're bound to find some way that your circle of contacts connects with the prospect. The real skill in meeting people is turning those points of contact into strong links.

If the decision-maker's schedule really is strict and all else fails, try to arrange for a telephone meeting instead of a face-to-face one. You'll have to adjust your presentation to give it impact over the telephone, but this approach may be worthwhile.

Making a Good First Impression

Your prospective clients make many decisions about you in the first ten seconds after they meet you for the first time. That's right. Within *ten seconds* you're either potentially welcome to share the family home or viewed as a pariah. Just quickly check the second hand on your watch right now and find out what ten seconds feels like. When you're watching your clock, it seems like a long time but when you're walking into a room and meeting someone for the first time, it passes by in an instant. Your job is to have some impact in those few seconds that your prospect can internalise and so that she *feels* she's made a wise move. Your clients must *immediately* see some benefit from investing their time in you. Knowing how to maximise those first ten seconds enables you to make the impression you really want to make, so that you can comfortably move forward in your selling.

If you're new to the sales profession or just plain nervous, be careful not to cram everything you know (or think you know) into the first ten seconds. Instead, that time needs to be natural and comfortable. That way, you'll help your prospective client to relax, which always makes a good impression. Probably a huge smile, a warm handshake, and sincere 'Hello' are all that's required. Practise doing this slowly!

Dressing for success

Before you arrive for your appointment with a potential client, you need to give some thought to the way you dress. Your goal is to ensure that your prospects like you and feel that you're like them. So how do you dress to accomplish this? Dress like your clients dress and fit into their surroundings so that they feel comfortable with you there. Or, you may choose to dress like the people your prospects turn to for advice.

Much of your clothing decision depends on where you're meeting and with whom. If you're going into a home environment with the family including young children and grandparents, you probably dress differently than you do for a business meeting with two senior board directors.

Use good judgement and common sense when it comes to the way you dress, and you can't go wrong. If you sell farm equipment and show up at a client meeting dressed like a banker, the farmer you're selling to isn't likely to feel very comfortable around you – after all, in the past, bankers have foreclosed on farmers. So you want to dress less like the banker and more like the farmer. Doing so doesn't mean you have to show up at your client's farm in a pair of wellies, but more relaxed clothing is probably in order. On the other hand, if you sell to a board director-level buyer and you show up in casual trousers and a T-shirt, you won't make the impression you want to make either. Know your clients, and you'll know what to wear.

Walking into a 'Yes'

In a well-documented study measuring initial impressions prior to a 'Yes' to a sales pitch, the amount of influence attributed to non-verbal communication was a staggering 93 per cent! So the actual words used accounted for only 7 per cent. The single largest factor of influence was the way a person walked, her posture, smile, and 'air of confidence', which accounted for 55 per cent of the decision to say 'Yes'. If you doubt the power of projecting positive body language, think again.

If you're new in sales or new to a particular group of clients, a good rule of thumb is to find a successful salesperson you want to emulate and model what she does. If your company has a dress code, a good reason probably exists for it – they've probably done some research or determined the hard way through trial and error the correct clothing to get results and are more attuned to what customers expect to see. Be sure to abide by this dress code.

If you show up at a meeting with your prospective client wearing something considerably different from what the prospect is wearing, then you must work during the first few minutes of your meeting to find a way to get yourself on even footing with her. After that, it's too late.

Paying attention to your body language

In addition to the message you communicate to your clients with what you wear, the body language you use also expresses something. Your posture, your facial expression, the placement of your hands, the tone of your voice, the frequency with which you have to pry your tongue away from the roof of your mouth as you talk – all of these govern first impressions just as much as what you wear.

Being aware of your body language may require some time in front of a mirror or video camera, or you may need to spend time with someone who truly cares about your success and is willing to give you an honest opinion. But dress for work and walk your normal walk when you're doing this. If you feel that your normal body language doesn't present an image of success and confidence, then watch someone whose body language does and emulate her. Basically, you want to walk with your shoulders comfortably back and your arms should be freely at your sides (no hands in pockets or held down rigidly and stiffly). Make good eye contact with the people you meet – don't stare them down or eye them as if you're assessing their clothing or glare as if you're afraid to blink and miss something. Smile warmly with both your mouth and your eyes and maintain a confident tone of voice. When you rehearse, if your voice sounds shaky, keep practising until you have it smooth and natural every time. If you're truly nervous when meeting new people, take a few slow, deep breaths to calm yourself before entering the room.

If you're sincere about your pleasure in meeting people, this behaviour becomes automatic.

Establishing Rapport with Your Clients

Your clients feel comfortable around you when you know how to establish rapport with them, which is what selling situations are all about – establishing common ground. 'People like people like themselves', as the saying goes. Bringing out the similarities you share with your prospects proves that, contrary to folklore, this particular salesperson is not an alien from another planet. You're just like they are: you have a family, you have a job, you have similar values, and when you're seeking any product other than the one you represent, you work with salespeople, too, just like your prospects. You just happen to be more of an expert on the particular product line or service you represent than your prospects are – and you're happy to use your knowledge to their advantage.

If you sense that your prospect doubts that what you're saying is valid or thinks that you're a con artist, say something like this:

Ms James, when I'm not helping people get involved with my product, I'm a consumer, just like you, looking for quality products at the best price. What I hope for when I'm shopping is to find someone who can help me understand all the facts about the item I'm interested in so that I can make a wise decision. Today, I'd like to earn your confidence in me as an expert on my offering. So feel free to ask any questions you may have.

Don't squirm at the thought of using these words – they've been proven to work successfully in lowering barriers people put up when dealing with salespeople. We appreciate that you may not like using or learning scripted words but they are only going to sound scripted if you don't learn them and practise delivering them well. If you do your part, these words work excellently.

Ben wins over the headmaster from hell

I distinctly remember many years ago visiting a local company and meeting a man who at first glance to my mind was the exact opposite of the person I would have preferred to meet.

I had driven there in my 'pre-sale warm me up' mode and was prepared to bounce in, full of enthusiasm and energy and simply wow the call into a sale. I was dressed as a successful young salesperson might dress – fashionable trousers, large tie, and long hair (yes, okay, it was a long time ago!) – and brimming with cheery confidence as I knocked on the door.

To my immediate horror I was greeted by a sour-faced older woman and ushered into a dark austere room where I was introduced to my client. In the first few seconds it was blatantly evident that we were at opposite ends of many spectrums – age, style, energy, modernity, everything! Talk about potential for mismatch!

However I mentally immediately set myself the challenge that 'no way was I coming along for nothing' and I needed to get a deal. I was not going to be beaten. I asked myself what I could do . . . and then I thought about common ground and rapport and where I could find some.

It wasn't glaringly obvious but within three minutes I had cause to ask about a photograph on the desk of his daughter at her graduation. I steered the conversation to the pleasure of being a father and how special daughters were, in my eyes at least. He eyed me with suspicion but allowed me to continue.

I explained that I was a proud father to a wonderful eight-year-old daughter, and as a single parent I was especially privileged to bring her up on my own and to thoroughly enjoy the role.

Well I struck a chord and instantly he seemed to view me in a different light. Instead of seeing me as a flash young nuisance salesman with probably little morality and discipline, he now saw me as akin to himself with a strong sense of morality and regard for discipline.

He mellowed and even positively warmed . . . we got along like friends and I walked away three hours later not only with a sale but with two friends and a welcome anytime I was passing – especially if I brought my daughter.

The process hadn't been easy, it hadn't been obvious, and it had taken a concentrated effort to mentally think of and design a route to rapport – but it worked and served to endorse always in my mind that nothing is necessarily what it seems. With a lot of practice and applied thought you can win in most situations – even with a stereotypical headmaster from hell!

In order to build rapport with your clients, you have to be truly interested in them. You need to be sincere in wanting to get to know them well enough so that you can help them have more, do more, and be more. Even if you're selling to a loved one, she needs to feel that high level of personal concern as well. If your clients believe you're being real – talking from your heart – they'll put their confidence in you much more quickly.

Getting Your Clients to Like and Trust You

When you meet people, your main goal is to help them relax with you. No one gets involved in a decision-making process when they're uptight. You want your prospective clients to like you and trust you because, if they don't, they won't do business with you. Always remember that your goal is this: To be a person whom other people like, trust, and want to listen to.

So how can you help your prospective clients like and trust you? Well, first impressions last, so concentrate on these simple, immediate things:

1. **Smile widely.**

2. **Make eye contact.**

3. **Offer a greeting.**

4. **Shake hands.**

5. **Offer your name and get the prospect's name.**

Even before you have a chance to open your mouth, signals pass between you and your prospect and impressions are formed. Your first task is to ensure that you're clean, tidy, and well groomed. Then you need to show by your facial expression that you're looking forward to a friendly and productive meting. If you handle these steps properly, you'll earn the opportunity to continue building rapport and lead into the next phase of selling, which is fact finding (covered in Chapter 9). Fact finding is where you determine whether you can help your prospective client and set the stage for a matching of the client's needs and your offering, but if you can't get to that stage by making a good first impression, all your previous efforts will be worthless.

Most of the time, people will be the kind of people you expect them to be. That's because your *demeanour* – what you say and how you say it – sends others a distinct message about what sort of mood you are in or what sort of person you might be or indeed what you think of them. People are, for the most part, reactive and respond according to what's given to them. So if you expect them to be cordial, open, and friendly, they will be. When your body language and opening statements are pleasant, people are very likely to respond in kind. If you're uptight, feeling pressured and frustrated, they'll probably pick up on this and you could be in for a very unproductive call.

The next sections go through each of the key elements that go into making a good first impression.

Step 1: Smiling widely

When you first come into contact with a prospective client, smile until you're almost grinning. A smile radiates warmth. If you're not smiling, or if it looks like it hurts when you do, your prospect will want to avoid you and will put up a wall of doubt and fear in just a few seconds. Think about it: Don't you just know when someone is smiling for the sake of it and doesn't mean it? You hate fake smiles and so do your prospects, so be genuine. If something is really troubling you, then either stay at home or share the troubles so that you may at least get a sympathy vote.

Long-term relationships begin in the first ten seconds. So smile! But keep it natural – avoid looking like a grinning hyena.

Some people forget how to smile because they don't do it much. If you ever feel that you don't smile often enough, then take a step back and look again at your life to find something to smile about, perhaps the children in your life or the crazy way your partner cooks. We even recommend being nice to yourself on a regular basis – actually smile at yourself in the mirror. Tell yourself you're a lovely person and that actually you have a lot in your life to be proud of. Do this every day until it becomes natural. 'When you're smiling, the whole world smiles with you', so they sing.

If you're contacting people over the phone, smiling still counts. Believe it or not, people can hear a smile (or a lack of one) in your voice. A well-worn cliché in telesales rooms says 'smile when you dial' because any experienced person can tell you it makes a serious difference even when it cannot physically be seen. Smiling is infectious and helps you win.

Step 2: Making eye contact

When you meet a prospect, look in her eyes. This aspect of body language builds trust. People tend not to trust those who can't look them in the eye. Actually, people usually glance away when they're lying to you. So when you don't look your clients in the eye, they may doubt what you're saying. Developing the ability to look someone in the eye and lie to her takes a good bit of intentional practice, which is what con artists do – but we're not saying you should do that! Merely make a point of developing eye contact.

Making eye contact is probably what you do anyway in a usual way with people you mix with, so don't feel overwhelmed or daunted by having to remember to do it.

Try to match your prospect's eye contact. For example, a client may easily hold your gaze for 20 seconds and then glance away, which shows you her subconscious pattern. If you then hold her gaze for approximately 20 seconds then deliberately glance away before she does, you communicate to her subconsciously that you are the same and she immediately feels less threatened and more comfortable. Try this technique – it really is amazing how it helps the prospect relax and tune into you.

Although looking your clients in the eye is very important, be sure not to go to the extreme and lock onto their eyes. Getting into a staring contest is dangerous in any selling situation. Give your prospect a couple of seconds of solid eye contact while smiling, and she'll probably be the first to glance away.

Step 3: Saying 'Hi' (or something like it)

The style of the greeting you offer depends on several factors, such as whether you're calling a long-time friend, a new acquaintance, a total stranger, or the Pope. Your greeting is also affected by the particular circumstance of how you're meeting your prospect. If you have any doubt at all about what kind of greeting is best, err on the side of formality.

Depending on the situation, any one of the following greetings may be appropriate:

- Hi.
- Hello.
- How do you do?
- How are you?
- Good morning, good afternoon, or good evening.
- Thank you for coming in.
- Thank you for seeing me.

If you already know your prospect's name, use it with your greeting (for example, 'Good morning, Bob'). If you don't know your prospect's name, don't rush to get it. Pressing strangers for their names so that they're no longer strangers is fine in many parts of the world and in many situations. But in others, this approach is seen as being pushy. If you're in a situation where you're obviously a salesperson, be atypical and establish a bit of rapport *before* asking for your prospect's name.

You probably do fine when meeting new acquaintances in any usual social situation, so don't worry when you meet clients for the first time. Just be yourself and say whatever you feel comfortable with as long as you're polite. (If, on the other hand, you resemble a trembling mess and crumble into a heap at contact with new people, then it may be that selling isn't the best choice of career!)

Step 4: Shaking hands

The greeting in a sales call almost always includes a handshake. With more established friendships, the handshake may become a hug (hugs are great but probably not best suited to the first meeting with a senior board director!), or with a foreign client, it might even be a greeting kiss, but mostly in the UK you're expected to shake hands.

Not everybody is comfortable with handshaking, however, and you may want to hesitate slightly until you see how your prospect is proceeding instead of forging ahead with this move. You can keep your right arm slightly bent and held by your side. If you see the other person reach towards you, you're ready. If she doesn't reach towards you, then you haven't committed the grand faux pas of reaching out too eagerly.

You may well be selling to people who are just plain nervous and whilst they're not rushing to shake they're actually crying out silently for some help in this scenario. So, if you can be relaxed and natural about shaking hands it helps them relax and go with the flow. By taking the lead, you are truly helping them – and yourself in the process. We strongly recommend always using a relaxed and friendly handshake.

The handshake is appropriate in most instances, but only if you do it properly. If you're sceptical about the value of spending time practising a good handshake, take some time to notice how others shake your hand. If you've ever shaken a hand that feels like a dead fish, you'll understand what we mean. Or, if you've experienced a bone-crushing handshake, you'll also see the importance of using just the right pressure.

To convey the highest level of trust, confidence, and competence, you need to grasp the whole hand of the other individual and give it a brief but solid squeeze – not too tight, but definitely not limp and wet either. Keep it brief. Nothing's more uncomfortable than to have someone keep holding your hand when you're ready to have it back.

What's in a name?

If you're being introduced to a group of people, be careful to use the same level of formality with each member. Don't call one person Mrs Johnson and call Mrs Johnson's associate by her first name, Sarah, just because you can't remember Sarah's last name. Doing so's more offensive than having to ask again what Sarah's name is.

At times you'll ask for a name and don't quite grasp it and maybe even ask again and don't quite grasp it. In those situations, you can always do what many experienced salespeople do – reach for a notepad and become the ultimate professional who records notes and ensures correct service, and simply ask, 'How do you spell your name?'

If you're meeting a married couple, shaking the hands of both the husband and the wife is appropriate. If they have children with them, shaking the kids' hands is a nice gesture too. After all, if the product you're selling involves the children, you want to earn their trust as well. If you can tell a child would be uncomfortable with having her hand shaken, simply give her a moment of eye contact as well. Don't do any cheek tweaking or hair tussling of the kids. Remember how you hated it when your mum's friends did it to you? Besides, the parents may well feel that you're over-friendly way too soon with their kids, and because parents are naturally highly protective, this approach could easily backfire.

Step 5: Exchanging names

The handshake is the most natural time to exchange names. Depending on the situation, you may want to use the formal greeting of, 'Good morning. My name is Rebecca Smith and I'm with Jones and Company.' If the setting is more casual, you may want to give your name as Becky or Becca or whatever you want your prospects to call you. Make sure they get your name right, though. Nothing is more difficult than correcting a potential prospect who calls you Becca when your name is Becky. Besides, when you've won her over and she's begun sending you referral business, you don't want the referrals asking for the wrong person and letting someone else earn your sales.

If a woman says her name is Judith Carter, don't regard her greeting necessarily as your permission to use her Christian name. Our advice is very simply to ask, 'Do you prefer that I call you Ms Carter?' You're quickly saved any embarrassment as she lets you know how familiar you should be. Again as a rule, don't shorten someone's name (from Judith to Judy, for example) unless she tells you to. Some people prefer their given names to the more common nicknames.

When you're involved more deeply in the qualification or presentation stages of selling and you feel some warmth building, most people generally become more comfortable with using first names. Asking politely though, rather than assuming, is a wonderful small way of showing respect and giving the impression of not being pushy. Although this may seem like an old-fashioned approach, it's what sells. People yearn to be treated with respect and courtesy.

Knowing How to Respond to Prospects in a Retail Setting

Selling in a retail environment is really no different to selling in any other environment in that you need to get each customer to like you and trust you enough to ask for help. All too often you've experienced an assistant immediately pouncing on you with a reflexive 'May I help you?'

As a customer, you may have heard variations of the 'May I help you?' greeting, including something like: 'Hi, my name is Julia. What can I do for you today?' What kind of response does Julia hear 99.9 per cent of the time when she says those words? 'Oh, nothing. I'm just looking.' That's what you say, isn't it? You don't want to be pounced on or bothered when you're just having a quick look around, and when you want assistance, you'll ask for it! If something doesn't work 99.9 per cent of the time, doesn't it make sense to try to come up with a better initial greeting?

If you work in retail sales, two important suggestions can increase your sales and the sales of anyone else in your company you share these suggestions with:

- ✔ When people enter your establishment, never walk directly towards them.
- ✔ When you do approach customers, don't rush.

Think about a time when you've been approached by a quick-moving, over-zealous salesperson, and you had to step back away from her. You don't want that scenario to happen to you. Let your customers know you're there in case they have questions. Then get out of the way and let them look around.

Figuring out what to say instead of 'May I help you?'

So what can you say instead of 'May I help you?' Try either of the following:

✔ 'Hello, thanks for coming in. I work here. If you have any questions, please let me know.'

What does this greeting do? It projects a warm, welcome feeling rather than an overwhelmed feeling. You've just invited your customer to relax, and, when people relax, they're more open to making decisions.

✔ 'Hello, welcome to Jacksons. I'm very pleased that you had a chance to pop in today. Feel free to look around. My name is Karen, and I'll be right over here if you have any questions.'

Pause momentarily in case the customer does have questions. Then step away. When you step away from the customer, instead of towards her, you distinguish yourself from all the typical salespeople she's ever encountered – and for most customers that's a very good thing. When you leave customers alone, they walk towards what they want. By observing them from a discreet distance, you know exactly what they came in for.

If you apply just a touch of intelligence, you can observe from the customer's body language what you can do to make a sale. If for example she seems rushed or flustered, you can be supportive and help her find things; if she's mooching around at a leisurely pace, you can drift past a couple of times, possibly even steering her towards a new range or a similar item to the one she was just viewing. When she finally stops in front of something for a moment, that's when you want to move closer to be ready to answer questions. Don't hang over her like a vulture, though. Just be where she can find you when she looks around for help.

Recognising the signals your customers project

If a customer doesn't look around but remains by one item for a while, then you may walk up and ask a question. Use an involvement question as your opening line so that your customer has to answer it with more than a 'Yes' or a 'No'. You'll discover something that will help you keep the conversation going.

If the customer is looking at a piece of furniture, for example, ask, 'Will this chair replace an old one, or is it going to be an addition to your furnishings?' When she answers, you know why she's interested and you can then begin guiding her to a good decision.

In any place of business where you have a display area or showroom, let your customers look around before you approach them. Being relaxed and gentle is much less threatening and far more professional than barging past your fellow staff members and dashing to the customer. Be cool and your approach will pay off.

Some places of business, such as car supermarkets or some furniture stores, are so large that people usually *do* need a guide (or at least a map) in order to find their way around. If you work in such a setting, you have to take your customers to the type of product they want. But, again, step away from them when you get them where they want to be, and let them relax. When they're ready to talk to you, they can still find you quickly, but you haven't invaded their space and taken control of their shopping experience. Every person shops in a different way and you need to learn to read signs and ask great questions, perhaps as to the time requirements or budget constraints, so that you steer your prospect to the correct area. Retail selling is still a sales process where the client needs to feel relaxed and also liked, and you want to build a friendly rapport in order to progress the sale.

Building Common Ground

When the introductions have been made and you're out of those first ten seconds of a meeting with a prospect, you need to smoothly transition into establishing common ground. How do you do that? By being observant.

If you just walked into Mrs Johnson's office, and you noticed that she has family photos all over the place, ask about her family. You don't need to know details now. Just say, 'Great looking family', and let her decide how much to tell you. If you see trophies, comment on them. If you can see that she plays netball and you do too, bring up the subject of netball.

The power of observation is incredibly important to develop as you work on your overall selling skills. If you only have time to really focus on learning one thing, learn to see what people are telling you rather than learning a script. Signals and clues are everywhere, and when you correctly spot and interpret them you have a key to unlocking most situations and people.

By allowing your prospect to first see the human side of you rather than the sales professional side, you help her break through the natural wall of fear that encloses her when typical salespeople walk through her door.

Someone may have referred Mrs Johnson to you. If that's the case, mention the mutual acquaintance, as doing so's usually a great starting point. 'Good old Molly' may have an excellent talent, great family, or wonderful sense of humour. Those are all nice, non-controversial topics to cover, so mentioning Molly straight away is a great way to break the ice and establish common ground.

If Ms Smith has an accent, you may ask where she's from. Perhaps you've travelled there or know people in that part of the country. Be careful here, though: Ms Smith may be self-conscious about the accent or tired of people always asking about it, so don't dwell on it too long, especially if she seems uncomfortable.

In the following sections, we cover ways to reach common ground with prospects or existing customers with whom you may not yet feel entirely comfortable.

Keep the conversation light, but move ahead

Don't let the conversation part of rapport building become too hard for you. Most of the time you can spot clues in the surroundings you meet in – and if this is an aid then avoid meetings in sterile or open places such as hotels until you've improved your rapport-building conversation skills. Conversation topics can be something in the local news or breaking news or some controversy in your industry. Just make sure that you don't get into a heated debate over a controversial subject if you have opposing views. However, discussing something a little controversial or emotive encourages the prospect to 'warm up' on her emotional scale and thus is actually extremely conducive to bonding and selling.

Try your best not to bring up the weather other than literally for 20 seconds as you take off your soaking wet coat and mention that 'the garden needs it even if you don't'. If you start off talking about how hot or cold it is today, your prospect will know you're struggling for something to talk about or that you're nervous.

Another good tactic is to give your prospect a sincere compliment. *Sincere* is the key word here. Sincerity takes you everywhere; blatant, insincere flattery gets you nowhere. A stale line like 'Mrs Fletcher, you look absolutely terrific; that dress makes you look just like royalty' does not qualify as sincere.

To keep the conversation moving forward, try an approach we call *tacking* – in much the same way as a sailing boat makes forward progress by going side to side and back and forth, your conversation goes back and forth with angles determined by your prospect's responses. In this technique, you simply ask a question, and when your prospect gives you an answer, acknowledge it with a nod or an 'I see', and then ask another question based on the prospect's response. For example, the tacking may go like this:

> YOU: Good afternoon, Mrs Johnson. I appreciate your time. Nice-looking family you have there.
>
> PROSPECT: Thank you.
>
> YOU: What school years are your children in?
>
> PROSPECT: The oldest is just starting college. The middle one is in the sixth form and the youngest is just taking her GCSEs.
>
> YOU: You must be very proud of them. What's your oldest studying at college?
>
> PROSPECT: Business. She wants to work for me when she graduates. But I've told her that she needs to see a little of other businesses and some of the wider aspects of business before she comes to join me.

Or:

> YOU: Good afternoon, Ms Thompson. I appreciate your time. I was wondering how long the company has been in this location? I know I've seen your sign on the building for many years.
>
> PROSPECT: We've been here for 25 years.
>
> YOU: That's great. And how long have you been with the company?
>
> PROSPECT: I started ten years ago in the area of stock control. For the past five years, I've handled all the purchasing.

When you tack, don't make a hog out of yourself by asking too many questions unless you think that the other person is agreeable to answering more.

Acknowledge their pride

If you happen to be working in a business where you give a lot of in-home presentations, and the people you're presenting to have a nice home, say this:

> I want to tell you that I spend a lot of time in the evening in other people's homes, and you should be proud of what you've done here. Your home is lovely.

But only ever say this if you can genuinely point to one or two things that make you believe they have made their home lovely – otherwise it sounds like a false compliment and can do more harm than good.

Look for signs of hobbies or crafts that you can comment on. If a woman is an artist and has her paintings on display, you can say, 'You did that? What a great talent to have.' If you like the painting and art is an interest or pastime of yours, you can then talk freely about it. If not, you can move on after allowing her time to reflect in the glory of your genuine compliment for her work. If your prospect has any hobby she's obviously proud of, give her a sincere compliment about it.

As a golden rule, ask about any obvious pastime or interest. If the hobby's enough of a person's life to be on display then she must have a whole evening full of stories to pass on that she's probably just dying to share. If she feels that you're interested, this will be interpreted as your being like her, which is over half of the battle in encouraging her to buy from you.

Avoid controversy

Be cautious of the prospect tempting you into a conversation about a controversial subject. Some people do that just to test you. Specifically, avoid discussing politics and religion at all costs. Only ever do this if you have very good conversation skills and can solicit their feelings about a subject and can agree with or at least make them feel like you agree with them. If you haven't mastered this skill yet, then best avoid subjects that could become divisive.

Here's how to get around any topic that may lead you down the wrong path:

> I'm so busy serving clients, I haven't had time to keep up to date on that topic. What do you think?

By throwing the ball back at the prospect, you've deflected what may have been a killer comment, and you also got a chance to let her know how committed you are professionally to your chosen vocation. If the prospect comes back at you with a very strong opinion, you'll know to avoid that subject in future meetings. Or you may feel the need to brush up on it if she's deeply involved, so you have a better understanding of this person before you build a long-term working relationship with her.

In a consumer sales environment it may well be that you have no need to really spend much time with such people again and so it matters little if they have radical views that in the long term would create conflict with you. Over the course of one evening that you spend with them to close a deal, you can avoid or agree with anything. In a business-to-business relationship, obviously this is more important, but if you are clear as to the limits of what you wish to discuss then you can steer a business conversation around to business issues and avoid damaging conflict.

In any business contact, be certain to never, *ever* use any profanity or slang until you absolutely know that it is within the language patterns of your prospect or client. Be sensitive to the values, beliefs, and morals of the person sitting or standing across from you and make every effort to match them. If your client swears like a trouper it may cause her discomfort if you maintain a grip on your language standards, so you may try to relax your code a little to prevent her being embarrassed – it could be that you appear 'posh' and this might put her off you if she views herself as more 'down to earth'. Always try to resemble the client but let her identify where she stands first.

Keep pace with your prospect

Taking time to become aware of your normal speed of talking is extremely valuable. And notice the rate of talking of everyone else you encounter. When you become tuned in to it, this awareness happens naturally.

When you're aware of your speaking rate, you need to know what to do about it. If the person you're trying to persuade talks faster than you do, you need to increase your rate of talking in order to keep her attention. If she speaks much more slowly than you do, slow down or pause more often in your side of the conversation. Any distortion in your rate of speaking can be deadly. You may lose her if you talk at the rate of a professional auctioneer, or her mind may wander if you're too slow. Try to talk at the same rate as your prospect.

Chapter 9

Finding the Best Way
to Proceed with the Client

● ●

In This Chapter

▶ Thinking like an ace detective

▶ Leaving your preconceptions about your prospects at home

▶ Discovering your prospects' needs by asking the right questions

● ●

*B*y the time you get to the fact-finding stage in the selling cycle, you've found your prospect, made an initial contact, and succeeded in getting an appointment with a qualified prospect. The prospect has shown a certain level of interest in your product, service, or offering and in theory you are well on your way to making a sale.

At this stage you need to determine exactly what will turn your client on and get him hot to buy. And you need to determine who actually is going to sign the cheque and reward your efforts.

This step in the selling cycle is particularly important in situations in which you don't have a close enough relationship with your prospect to know from the outset (your telephone appointment-making process) whether he needs your product or service or who else might be involved in the buying process.

One of the biggest mistakes people make when they try to convince or persuade others is going into a full-blown presentation before they know whether the listener is a qualified decision-maker or needs what they have to sell. Neither of the people involved wants to be caught up in something that's a total waste of their valuable time. So, when you see the word 'receptionist' on a desk, don't give the person behind the sign your whole presentation.

Using this step in the selling sequence correctly is the single greatest factor separating those who win most often in their selling presentations from those who don't. Salespeople may offer excuses that they don't have enough time or aren't getting warm leads or whatever the gripe, and yet when analysed, most of the time the prospecting or qualification was poor and the rep in question was simply trying too hard with the wrong people. A salesperson's skill in qualifying whether or not to proceed is vital – and all it takes is asking the right questions.

Taking a Few Sales Pointers from a Famous Detective

So how exactly do you go about fact finding in order to know which way to present your offering with greatest effect? You need to ask the right questions. In some cases, you wait and watch for the perfect opportunity to ask. In other situations, you have to create the opportunity to ask. Think of yourself as a detective, a gatherer of information to solve the mystery of your prospect's buying needs. If coming up with a couple of questions that would always be answered completely and honestly were all you had to do, your life would be simple. But the process isn't always that easy. Being able to discover your prospect's needs and concerns, as well as successfully incorporate such information into the opening of your presentation, takes a lot of time and practice before you even walk through the door for each appointment.

Taking a lead from one of the world's most famous detectives, Dame Agatha Christie's fictional sleuth Hercule Poirot, you can see that the art of detecting is similar to the art of selling and that the smooth efficient manner of Monsieur Poirot is a perfect example of the job done properly.

We love using the example of Hercule Poirot when we cover fact-finding tactics and strategies, because he does a wonderful job of adjusting his questioning techniques to fit every situation. He also acts as if the person he's questioning is better, more important, or smarter than he is. Poirot's demeanour throws his 'prospects' off guard, and they often drop their defences. Often he asks seemingly irrelevant questions or talks about a subject that seems to be completely different, only for the reader to find that he is following his own path, which ultimately leads to the correct conclusion in an intricate and perfect way.

Poirot asks the same sort of question many times to solicit different answers to verify the correct one and to catch off guard those who attempt to lie and mislead. As a sales detective you too want to verify answers to see if they match up by asking similar questions over the course of the sales call. You want to steer your prospect towards a sale yet also allow him to feel he's in control and safe.

Warming prospects up and cleverly soliciting information so that you have all the ammunition with which to sell to them is a critical skill. Only those who practise and perfect this area of selling really make the top grade in both income and achievement. Of course, these successful salespeople are the ones who are reportedly lucky, get all of the best leads, and are looked after by the boss! If you believe that nonsense, then you're in the wrong job. You get out what you put in and if you want a lot more out than the average, make sure you put a lot more in. Don't aim to be good; aim to be outstanding. Don't settle for selling to some; push for selling to them all.

In the following sections, we highlight some of the key strategies detectives use to solve every case. And they're strategies you can put to work for you when you're trying to get information from your prospects.

Play the lead

Poirot never presumes to be the top dog or the smartest person in the world; he just goes about his work in an unassuming manner. And yet he is always the star performer. The other players in the story look to him for the answer and have faith that he will prevail, even at the moment in each story when the situation looks to be slipping away from even the great Hercule Poirot.

Your task when selling is to be the lead role. You don't need to flaunt your position with flash, noise, and exuberance, but prospects do expect you to know your stuff, and they rely upon you to solve their problems.

In essence, as we mention throughout this book, *people buy people*, and if you don't sell yourself then you won't sell the product. Your prospect can buy any product with very similar appeal from anywhere. You may argue that your offering is unique, but very rarely are those unique differences in demand from a prospective purchaser, so, ultimately, you're the one who makes your offering unique. You need to sell you.

Always take notes

Taking notes is vital, but Poirot doesn't rush to get every word of vital information written down verbatim. Instead, he seems to jot things down casually. His notepad isn't large and threatening, but small enough to fit in his pocket and rather nondescript. And he refers back to this information again and again during his investigation. The information he turns up helps direct his future efforts with each suspect (who, in selling, is called the *prospect* or, more optimistically, the *future client*). Use the same tactic or at least use a simple A4 notepad where you can easily refer back to comments and clearly record any relevant points.

When you state a fact back to the prospect, glance or point to where you have it in your notes. Doing so shows that you have the correct information and that you're on top of the details.

Make the people you're questioning feel important

Ever the humble searcher for truth, Poirot always reminds his suspects of how accommodating they are to let him impose on their busy schedules. He thanks them profusely for their time and the vital information they provide. No matter what the reason for his presence, he makes each person feel as though his information is the single most important key to solving the case.

Don't just jot down the notes. Make comments on the facts and figures provided by each prospect. Compliment them on being on top of things enough to know these details without looking them up. If they did look up some of the figures, compliment them on their dedication to accuracy by not calling out numbers from memory.

Mix the questions and focus on background

As a detective, Poirot asks a multitude of questions in various ways. He asks questions in a police style and yet asks unexpected Poirot-style questions as well to ascertain background information. Your job is much the same. Ask many questions – especially about the background information.

When selling you need to know a lot about a client's situation and indeed about the client – background information.

Background information might be about his children, his hobbies, his holidays, his car, but is always more focused on his personality than his business and gives you a strong opportunity to bond with him. The bonding process isn't necessarily to get to a thigh-slapping, back-clapping matey status in one visit but to reach a level of rapport where the prospect likes you.

So get good at asking questions and be a detective in search of your prospect's hot buttons – the topics that turn him on and make him want to like you enough to say what exactly it is that you need to do in order to get the order. For example, if you spend 40 minutes chatting about his favourite motorbike or his passion for hill walking and he can tell that you obviously share the passion, then when he really is on your wavelength he might just say to you, 'So, John, I need this coffee machine to serve up to 50 cups an hour and be easy to operate but above all cost only £28 a week – if you can do that, then why don't we do business?'

Listen to both verbal and non-verbal responses

A great detective also notices *how* people tell him what they have to say, not just noting the words they use but paying attention to their body language as well. He knows and evaluates not only their postures, but also what they're wearing, the surroundings they spend their time in, and even the cars they drive. It is vitally important to include in the background information the clues that you pick up in a non-verbal exchange or from what's left unspoken in conversation.

If someone lives in a £500,000 home and drives the latest Mercedes, he'll probably be interested in owning the top-of-the-line model of your product as well. In other cases, if someone is looking at the top-of-the-line model and then steps away when you approach him, he's probably hesitant about whether he can afford it.

Build on the answers you get

Rarely do Poirot's suspects realise they *are* suspects until they've let their guard down a bit and said something that doesn't fit with a previous answer. They often find themselves in the uncomfortable position of having to explain the difference in the two answers. They try to give credence to their errors and to maintain their innocent attitudes.

Someone may tell you he invested £10,000 in his last series of widgets. You would then assume he'd be comfortable investing in that price range again. If, when you get to your presentation, your bottom line is that same amount and he says he can't afford it, something was missing in the information you were given. Don't call the client a liar there and then – or ever! – but instead ask a few more questions to see whether you weren't told all of the facts or you misinterpreted them slightly. It may be that he did spend £10,000 on his last widgets but either it was a gift and not his own money or he spent the last of his inheritance and was unusually flush but is now back to watching the pennies.

Try asking, 'Mike, I thought you told me you invested this much the last time. Was I wrong in my understanding that it was an acceptable amount?' Doing so gives Mike an opportunity to explain further without you coming out and saying, 'Hey, you gave me bad information!'

If a potential client initially says he has to have a new mobile phone that has a camera, an MP3 player, voice-activated dialling, and also does e-mail, and then says actually just a simple phone is all he really needs, possibly the climb-down is financial and he's potentially embarrassing himself with that discrepancy and may be uncomfortable if you bring it up.

Relieve any tension your questions create

Many people naturally feel slightly uncomfortable when asked several questions (as indeed a 'suspect' feels in a detective scenario – you have to appreciate the difference between asking questions and interrogation and practise your style!). If you sense the prospect feels uneasy when you're questioning him to discover the facts, you need to gently defuse the situation.

A good tactic is to make a comment such as, 'I'm so sorry if it sounds like I'm interrogating you! Please forgive me for asking a lot of questions. It's just that I've seen some clients end up with something that wasn't exactly as they wanted because the salesperson didn't ask all of the relevant questions. I promised you I'd help you out and I really don't want you to have something that isn't perfect for you. If I can just get all of the information then I know you'll be happy with the finished outcome.'

Another tactic to defuse an uneasy moment is to pretend that you've finished with questioning. Say something like, 'That's all then, I think I've asked all of the questions I need to for now.' The prospect almost visibly sighs with relief, and after he's relaxed you can always ask other questions later if you add, 'Oh, I'm sorry, I forgot to ask . . .' and he'll hardly notice it in his relaxed state. The prospect may even come out with a more helpful answer than his more measured previous responses.

Use non-threatening language and a sympathetic tone

Imagine the effect if every suspect was confronted by the image of a police cell and constantly reminded that 'everything you say will be taken down and used later in evidence against you'! Would this image help in the early stages of gathering information? Most definitely not. Thus a definite need exists to measure the language in accordance with the situation, the person, and the urgency. When selling you need to be a chameleon in your approach and use language and questioning styles in a varied way to maximise impact.

Meeting potential clients in their environment makes them more comfortable. Many business negotiators tell you that you need to meet on home ground to hold the power – the home fixture scenario so often assumed as an advantage in sport. In sales, you're not in a win or lose situation. The goal is to reach a win-win agreement. Making people feel comfortable with you is the first step you take in coming together to determine what the best solution will be.

Let them know you'll be in touch

Any good salesperson who doesn't make a sale on the first contact will do whatever he can to leave the door open for further discussion with a prospect. Poirot thanks the person for helping him by answering a few questions, and he introduces the possibility of a future meeting by saying, 'I look forward to meeting you again.' You too need to suggest that goodbye doesn't have to be the end by mentioning that you'll call him again a few days later.

Mr Smythe, I appreciate your time today and I'm confident that what we've discussed will prove to be the best offer for your company. However, I will contact you again in a couple of weeks' time to clarify the situation regarding delivery times, as we discussed earlier. Is that okay?

The Basic Facts When Qualifying Prospects

The average salesperson lets the consumer have total control over the decision as to what he wants and whether he'll buy it now or later.

A professional salesperson takes full responsibility for steering the prospect into a knowledge-based choice that's best for all parties. Making that choice must always be an ethical process and be a win-win scenario, but you must take responsibility for making the sale happen and not let the customer take control.

A customer cannot buy until you guide him – and he needs guiding. Aside from perhaps a retail store where some shoppers have looked around and do actually have an accurate idea about what they want to purchase, in most other areas of selling, prospects don't simply come out with a statement such as 'That's what I want and that's what I'll buy'– and if they ever do say this, you're in a tough situation, as they'll probably be buying on price alone, which is rarely in the client's best interest or yours.

Take control and steer the prospect into the best choice. Use lots of guiding language to help him subconsciously go with the flow:

✔ I know just what you're looking for.

✔ This is my favourite.

✔ I have the best thing for you.

✔ The advanced option is probably better for you.

✔ This one looks so good in red.

The sale process is about you creating rapport with the customer, finding out what makes him tick, what problems he currently has, and then giving him a solution to the problem. A sale is, essentially, a solution and to ensure that you have the right situation to sell into, you must be good at uncovering your prospect's problems. The following sections offer a simple, five-question strategy to do so.

The success ratio for your entire company would rise if you could get all the salespeople to concentrate just a little more on simple steps leading to the goal and focus on the prospect instead of themselves. All too often the salesperson is so consumed with what *he* is going to say, what *he* wants to sell, what *he* needs to talk about, how *he* will react in a given situation, and he makes the situation all about him. *Wrong!* Make your focus the client's needs and desires and remember just these few simple steps, and you really will enjoy a fabulous career in selling.

What has he got now?

Why should you ask what the customer has now? Because average consumers don't make drastic changes in their buying habits. If you know what your prospect has now, you have a good idea of the type of person he is and of what he'll want to have in the future.

WII-FM: What's in it for me?

An old sales training lesson goes like this: What's everyone's favourite radio station? The answer is always WII-FM. The call letters in this case stand for 'What's In It For Me?'

People have a WII-FM mentality, whether they admit it to themselves or not. Human beings are selfish creatures whose natural tendency is to make themselves as comfortable as possible. Be painfully honest: when was the last time you did something for someone else with absolutely *no* expectations of getting anything in return? Now before you tell us what a self-sacrificing person you really are, think about that answer for a second. We're asking you to remember a time when you did something for someone else without expecting *anything* in return for what you did – no thank you, no undying loyalty, no unspoken thought that one day it might rebound with good effect.

If you're like most people (including us), you'll have difficulty thinking of such a time – especially in a business environment. This knowledge doesn't make us hideous selfish creatures who care not for our fellow humans – it just makes us normal. We have our own lives, our own concerns, and our number-one prerequisite is that we have to be okay first. So, most people are motivated to do things for others only if they themselves expect to receive compensation that they value in return *and* the compensation may not always be monetary. The sought-after rewards may be intangible and emotional – hugs, kisses, a warm smile – but something is still sought after.

And your prospect or client thinks in this way: What is this going to do for me and why should I buy it? Or conversely, he may be asking himself the opposite, but very similar, questions: What will it give me in terms of pain if I buy? Why should I purchase this and upset the apple cart?

One person may be looking to the gains and one may be looking to the losses. One may be thinking that you present a chance to gain benefits, whilst another may be thinking that you represent a need to not lose cash. Your job is to solicit answers that guide you to understanding the ideal way to move them across to your way of thinking. But never forget that they'll be thinking of themselves first – and you need to tune into that and not into you before you win.

Ensure that the customer actually purchased what he has now! Possibly he inherited the situation or item. So once you establish what he currently has, then you must ask how he came to own it. The history will uncover lots of incredibly useful information. For example, if you ask how he came to own a current computer and software setup, he may tell you that it was all that he could afford at the time but definitely not what he wanted; now he's in a better financial position and is going to get what he ideally wants. Imagine how powerful this information is! You could get him to tell you exactly what he's after, match it up to your offering, and then walk into a relatively easy sale. You may not even have to 'sell' him on the features of your offering but just say, 'Okay, so if I can give you a package that includes all of the items you just said you wanted, then can we look forward to arranging a delivery date and booking your training?' Ask more about the current situation and you'll uncover gold.

It may be that the current ownership *is* something that he chose and indeed has been using quite successfully for some time and so he isn't even completely 'sold' on the need to upgrade or change. Indeed in many business situations this scenario is often the case and your job is slightly harder if you try to assume that he can see immediately the advantages of moving upwards. As a broad rule of thumb, most people choose to buy in a similar style and show a pattern to purchases that can give you clues as to how they may interpret your offering – but never assume this information.

Most people don't like change and prefer to stay with a known entity. So uncover as much as you can about how they feel and what they think of the existing scenario before making assumptions as to what they want to buy.

Why does he have it?

Why does your prospect own the existing item? What features of it does he enjoy? Does it represent a chosen item or service and if so what made him choose it? Are circumstances the same and is this still a chosen requirement?

You can ask lots of great questions, but essentially you must always dig to uncover the enjoyment factors and what he likes about the current offering. If he's actually a pretty big fan of the existing item, rubbishing it as old merely because the new one is bigger, louder, and faster is foolhardy. He might like slow, dependable, and trusted!

Don't assume anything: Every chance exists that what a customer *enjoyed* about the product or service in the past, or what he *enjoys* about what he already has, is exactly what he'll want again unless circumstances are now very different.

What would he change?

One of the wonderful paradoxes of life is that whilst many people are uncomfortable with change they also love it. People mostly desire new and better if they have an option. If the new or better represents 'more' then they're sorely tempted. Simply asking what your prospect would like to change can help a lot. When you know your customer's answer to that question, you can structure your presentations to show how your company can provide those changes.

Often a potential client won't see the reasons why he should change, and thus you could easily get the answer, 'I wouldn't change anything'. Now, this isn't in fact true; your prospect just doesn't appreciate what could change. To assist him, simply ask what he would like to go faster or do more tasks or similar. For example, if you ask a user of a current mortgage broker what he'd like to change you might hear the answer that nothing springs to mind. However far from being a dead-end enquiry, you can follow up with questions such as, 'Would you like it if you got a free buyers' guide to mortgage updates whenever the rates changed?' or 'Would you like a personal rate tracker service that can guarantee to save you money when rates change?' or 'Would you like a reduced premium insurance that covers the mortgage debt?' The answer will probably then be 'Yes'.

You have to prompt the prospect's ideas for areas to be changed by mentioning the differences your product has in the form of added value. His answer might be that he wouldn't want any extra cost, but usually he wouldn't mind having added value if no extra cost is involved.

Who decides to change it?

You need to know who'll be making the final decision on the sale.

Now you should already have at least tried to confirm the identity of the decision-maker when you make the appointment (Chapter 8 has tips), but it's worth checking again that the person you're talking to is able to make the changes or new purchase or whether someone else needs to be involved in that choice.

Often salespeople meet a customer who is looking for a car, a home entertainment system, maybe some furniture, and they meet only that one person. Is it wise for the salesperson to assume that the person he's met will be the decision-maker? No. Never assume anything about your customers. The customer may be scouting or researching, or planning to bring in a spouse or parent later before he makes the final decision.

You need to ask qualifying questions to discover whether the person you're talking to is the decision-maker. Here are some examples:

- Will you be the only person driving the car?
- Who, other than yourself, will be involved in making the final decision?
- Do you usually consult anyone else when making decisions of this type?

You've probably heard the standard response to a decision-qualifying question: 'I'll have to talk it over with my husband/wife/parents/best friend.' Maybe this *is* the case – and you cannot afford to habitually find this detail out when you are already making a sales presentation. You'll never get the correct ratio of sales to calls if you are presenting to an 'information gatherer' – you must have the decision-maker present or you will lose impact. Rarely will the information gatherer relay your offering to the decision-maker's ears as competently as you can. On the other hand, the 'talk it over' plea may be a smokescreen and the person you are talking to isn't yet ready to buy or is unsure of some detail and is stalling for time and trying to be polite.

You need to find out who makes the decision to change and then talk directly to that person if possible.

You need to be just as enthusiastic to everyone you meet. Even though the person is not the decision-maker, he might be an influencer or a champion of your cause. Presenting well and then arranging to go back again to meet with the actual decision-maker should mean that you have an ally when you need it most. Don't give a lacklustre performance just because you find out your current contact isn't really all that powerful.

What does a solution look like?

As a salesperson, you're in the business of creating and presenting solutions. You find out what your prospects need, and then you come up with a solution. In most cases, the solution is that your customer owns the benefits of your products or services.

To be effective, therefore, you absolutely need to know what a solution looks like and why your offering represents that solution. You need to introduce the reasoning behind the solution, and to get your potential customer to agree with you. You then get him to state clearly that he recognises and agrees with the issues or challenges raised and also that he recognises that your new offering represents a possible solution.

Boldly stating that you have the solution is useless if the prospect is merely nodding but not actually agreeing. He may be choosing the path of least resistance and allowing you to carry on because he knows he can turn round when you are finishing off and say that he needs to think about it and thus get rid of you without having to cope with a confrontation. So be very careful not to present a solution as if that's the obvious answer and you won't hear anything against it. You must engage the prospect in the process of finding a solution. Questions like the following can help:

As a representative of [name of your company], it's my job to analyse your needs and do my best to come up with a solution to satisfy those needs so you can enjoy the benefits you're looking for. How do you feel about this solution that we have looked at together, Mr Client?

What do you feel would be the perfect solution to the problems we talked about earlier, Mr Prospect?

You serve customers by finding out what they need and then creating the right solution. When you do so, you create a win-win relationship where people want to do business with your company and they get the products or services they need. They give you business and, in turn, you both grow and prosper.

Questioning Your Way to Success

Part of fact-finding and indeed the overall sales process is the skill of knowing the right questions to ask. But questioning is a technique you use throughout the selling cycle, so don't be afraid to use these strategies when you're presenting, addressing customer concerns, or closing.

So why do you need to ask questions of your prospects? You can use questions to acknowledge or confirm a statement your prospect made that is important to the decision you want him to make. For example, if your prospect tells you that fuel consumption is very important to him when buying a new car, when you're getting ready to ask him for a final decision, you need to include a question relating to this in your summary of the reasons he should go ahead with the close, such as: 'Didn't you say that fuel economy was your primary concern?'

Such a question starts the 'Yes' momentum you need in order to encourage him to go ahead and agree with you. The 'Yes' momentum is what every persuader strives for. After you get your prospect agreeing to things, if you simply keep asking the right questions – rather like following a flowchart – he'll follow where you want to lead him. And he'll have enough information at the end to make a wise decision, which you hope is that he can't live without your product or service.

Questions also create emotional involvement. If you're marketing home security devices, you can ask: 'Wouldn't you feel more confident about sleeping safely in your home knowing you'd be warned beforehand if danger was present?'

Avoiding déjà vu when you ask questions

To save yourself from needlessly repeating questions, make written notes on your prospective client's responses during the fact-finding process. Referring to your notes to remind yourself what questions you already asked and what the client said his needs are is perfectly okay. Inadvertently asking the same question twice (or more) doesn't inspire confidence in the customer about you or your product. In fact, it smacks of amateur unprepared sales activity and very few prospects wish to part with their hard-earned cash to someone who is apparently unprofessional, fearing that it might backfire on them with poor product, poor service, or both. Plus, written notes not only aid you during the presentation, they also help you to remember what you've already covered when you follow up with the prospect after he's become a regular, happy client. In fact, that's part of how you keep him happy.

Seeking permission to take notes before you start taking them can be a good idea. Some people get nervous when you start writing down

what they tell you. For all you know, they may visualise themselves being grilled in a court of law on what they say to you. This reaction is rare however as everyone appreciates that being professional and accurate improves service and fulfilment, and note-taking is simply interpreted as professional and thorough. (If you think you're with someone who is nervous about what you might record in your notes, give him a piece of paper and a pen – preferably with your company name on it – so that he can take notes, too.)

Getting permission to take notes is easy; just say: 'I don't have the best memory in the world, and I do want to do a good job for you. So would you be offended if, while we chat, I make a few notes?' Putting the request that way gives you an opportunity to admit that you're human and that you're also smart enough to have learned how to overcome the human failing of a poor memory. And even if you happen to have a photographic memory, these little sentences will help put your clients at ease and build their confidence in you.

What does that question do? It raises a prickle of alarm on the back of your prospect's neck about the unknown possibilities of a burglar or dangerous criminal entering his home. That question engenders a sense of emotional involvement in the prospect – a requirement in any selling situation.

Tying down the details

A superb method of closing a question so that it has a more powerful impact and is more likely to lead the prospect your way is using what is called a 'tie-down' at the end of a sentence. A tie-down doesn't involve tying clients into their chairs until they say yes. Instead, a *tie-down* involves making a statement, and then asking for agreement by adding a question to the end of it. Here are some of the most effective tie-downs:

- **Isn't it?** For example, 'It's a great day for golf, *isn't it?*' When your prospect agrees, you whip out the latest clubs.

- **Doesn't it?** For example, 'Getting out for a party this weekend sounds like fun, *doesn't it?*' When your customer agrees, you show him your latest taxi rates.

- **Hasn't he?** For example, 'The previous owner has done a great job with the landscaping, *hasn't he?*' When the prospective new home-owner agrees that he likes the landscape, he's just moved one step closer to liking the whole package – house included.

- **Haven't they?** For example, 'The manufacturers have included every detail about the questions you asked in this proposal, *haven't they?*' Having all the details covered and having the buyer agree he's covered helps reduce the possibility of stalling when it's time to close.

- **Don't you?** For example, 'Cleaning up the area where our children play is important, *don't you* think?' When the person agrees, sign him up for one hour of cleaning at the local recreation ground.

- **Didn't you?** For example, 'You had a great time the last time you went hiking, *didn't you?*' Then sell the prospect a new pair of hiking boots, socks, and matching weatherproofs.

- **Shouldn't we?** For example, 'We should make that one of the bonus requests when negotiating the final price then, *shouldn't we?*' Thus teasing the prospect into a negotiation mindset, which assumes a purchase is on the cards.

- **Couldn't we?** For example, 'We could book the installation date to suit your family holiday in the last week of August then, *couldn't we?*' Especially if you're selling home improvements and don't want the holiday season to be a quiet season.

Use tie-downs to influence your prospect to agree with you. Professional salespeople often use tie-down questions such as: 'A reputation for prompt, professional service is important, isn't it?'

Who can say no to that question? The salesperson asking such a question has begun a cycle of agreement with the prospect, who, hopefully, will continue to agree all the way through the selling sequence.

Giving an alternative

You've certainly seen or heard the *alternative choice* questioning technique used before, but you probably didn't recognise it as a sales strategy. This tactic involves giving your prospect two acceptable suggestions to choose from, and is mostly used for calendar events such as appointments, delivery dates, and so on. Here are some simple examples:

- ✔ **'I can arrange my diary so I can visit on Thursday at 3.00 p.m. or would Friday at 11.00 a.m. be better?'** Either answer confirms that you have an appointment.

- ✔ **'This product comes in one- or five-litre bottles. Which would you prefer?'** No matter which bottle size your prospect chooses, he's still chosen to take one of them.

- ✔ **'We'll have our delivery available for Monday at 9.00 a.m. or would 2.00 p.m. be more convenient?'** Whichever option your prospect chooses, you've agreed upon the delivery.

You can also use the alternative choice technique when you want to focus or limit the conversation to certain points. For example, if you're on a committee to refurbish the facilities in the local school, you may want to find a way to gather information without getting into a debate about other aspects of the project. Perhaps some of the parents want the gym updated or others want more classroom equipment purchased. Your total involvement may be just to manage the access to the school during closure so that builders can complete the task. You might ask: 'Shall we be giving a key to the builders or shall we attend each day to ensure access?' Offering just two solutions helps you get right to the point of the matter.

Alternative choice questions are particularly effective in surveys. The market researchers are seeking particular information, not general answers, so they build the questions in such a way that the prospect is limited in his responses.

Getting them involved

Another questioning technique is the involvement question, in which you use questions to help your listeners envision themselves *after* they've made a decision to agree with you. If you're marketing office equipment, you can involve your prospect with a question like: 'Who will be the key contact for us to train on the use of the machine?'

Now you've got him thinking about implementing training *after* he owns the product, not about whether or not he'll own it.

Similarly, if you want to involve someone in business with you, use a question such as: 'What will you and Janet do with the extra income that our business plan says we'll generate in the next year?'

ANECDOTE

Asking the right questions kept Ben out of serious trouble

I remember early on in my life the power of questions being a saviour to me. I was a bit of a rebel as a schoolboy. I caused mischief, stirred up trouble, and acted as the ringleader – but I was usually clever enough to avoid real punishment. We were having a school photograph taken, with all the pupils lined up on desks and chairs and standing and kneeling in a semi-circle on the tennis court, when I really learned how questions can keep you out of trouble. Do you remember those school photos taken by a slowly revolving camera so that when finished the semi-circle of pupils looks like a long line in a really wide photograph? Well, I was looking for a prank and decided to get into the photo at both ends!

As soon as the camera started sweeping round the line up, I slipped out and ran all round the line of pupils stood facing the camera and appeared quietly at the other end. I thought I'd got away with it – after all everybody had been watching the camera to make sure they looked good in the photo so I figured I was safe – safe, that is, except I'd forgotten the photographer who was watching eagerly to make sure he had a perfect shot. He saw me appear. He saw me and identified me. And he made sure he took another photo.

Later in the day I was summoned to the headmaster's office and was presented with a scenario in which the photographer reported seeing a boy run round the line and appear twice – and he could describe. The headmaster could only think of one boy who both fitted the description and was likely to carry out this 'irresponsible' act.

I suppose I was shocked to be discovered and flattered that I should be so memorable, but Mr Green didn't seem impressed. He proceeded to question why I was prepared to disrupt everyone's afternoon and cost the photographer time and money. My panicked 11-year-old mind went into overtime. I didn't want to be punished, so I thought fast. I asked if he could be really sure it was me. I asked if he could possibly question the visual recall of a photographer who was concentrating not on me but on a line-up for a treasured shot. I asked if Mr Green was aware that several boys had mentioned doing a prank and if he was willing to balance these doubts with a slight feeling that the act was actually harmless. I asked if he was prepared to punish a boy who had promised since our last encounter to be good and had kept to his word. I thought I'd at least cast a shadow of doubt and possibly also appeal to his conscience. Young Ben Kench was fighting here!

To make a long story short, I *did* manage to get him to have just enough doubt to avoid action – although he promised me when the photo came back he would know! Actually, although I got away with it at the time through excellent questioning in the pressure of the moment, I also got caught two weeks later when evidence showed me twice on the photo! But at least I'd earned a little respect in the way I handled the situation the first time around; indeed, many years later Mr Green remarked at a school reunion that whilst I'd been 'trouble' at school it had been evident from how I acted that day that I would probably 'charm my way through life'.

Great questioning had avoided a severe punishment and got me out of a sticky situation. Great questions do that. And you can develop great questioning skills at any age. Start asking smart questions now.

Ask what they know

In some selling environments you may find yourself spouting technical jargon to a non-technical person. You may think that you are both using the same language, but can come unstuck very quickly if you assume that your prospect is on your wavelength and start asking questions he doesn't know the answer to.

Sometimes rather than appear ignorant and unqualified, a person will clam up and briskly try to complete the call (because he's feeling uncomfortable). This scenario isn't helping you sell. You need to ask him questions that he's comfortable answering or at least help him identify gaps in his knowledge. Reassure him that gaps always exist and you can help fill them.

Often an opposite approach can be equally effective. Whereas with one person you want to make sure he feels really good and can answer all of the questions you ask, with another you might want him to *not* know the answer and thus expose a need for you to fill. For example, if you're selling computers you want him to know the answers to questions such as: 'What will you be using it for – homework and study or music recording and video work?' Different specifications will obviously be necessary for these uses and so the prospect's answer provides critical information that you can use to shape his requirements. Follow up this question with one about what the prospect will do *after* he owns your new computer.

Another questioning technique can be demonstrated by an example of selling life insurance cover. You ask the prospect how much his current policy provides for him in the case of an accident and if this is really enough when considering the children's education, their clothing demands, the transport needs of a modern family, and everything else. Hopefully he'll feel like he does *not* know the answer – which in turn is interpreted by him as probably not enough insurance cover, in which case you can steer him into a sale.

The answers you want to hear lie in the questions you ask. Always ask great questions.

Is your listener thinking about whether to go into business with you? Nope. He's just envisioning spending the money he'll earn *after* he goes into business with you. If what he plans to spend the money on is something he wants badly enough, a good chance exists that he'll find himself *having* to go into business with you to satisfy a need he's been feeling without knowing how to fulfil it. Aren't you the good little fairy bringing him just the right solution?

Chapter 10

The Pitch: Presenting Yourself and Your Offering Properly

*T*he presentation stage of the selling process is the show – your chance to get your prospective client's senses involved. Most salespeople regard this step as the most important part of the whole process, insomuch as the prospect needs all the details in order to make an informed decision and the pitch is your opportunity to put these across in a cohesive and understandable manner. You need to prepare fully.

Major companies often prepare for the presentation stage by investing hundreds of thousands of pounds and a great deal of time in creating graphics, models, and samples for their teams to use.

A presentation can be as simple as distributing a brochure and giving a quick explanation as to its content or as complex as an exhibition complete with a grand display, bright and attractive stand designs, and attractions within the stand such as video, sound, food, drinks, and a show of some sort to lure in potential prospects. How you present your show depends on what product or service you represent and the potential investment of the prospect.

The presentation is part of the selling process, but not the whole selling process. You don't have to make sure your prospects understand everything nor that they learn everything about how your offering would fit into their scenario. The presentation is simply where you explain what you can do in a little more technical detail, fitting your offering into their scenario using the information you gleaned from your fact-finding time.

In this chapter, we steer you through the often-frightening territory of the sales presentation – covering everything from finding the power players in the room to giving a presentation over the Internet. We also give you some great tips for avoiding common presentation pitfalls. So before you give a presentation, read on.

Getting More Than a Foot in the Door

Earning the right to give a prospective client a presentation of your idea, concept, product, or service doesn't mean that you virtually have her cash in your bank. In reality, the show hasn't even started, let alone become a done deal. The more likely truth is that your prospect is considering a purchase from you, but probably also has invited or intends to invite at least two other companies in for the same purpose. Possibly your prospect isn't even close to purchasing, and her time frames and internal issues are going to be huge influencers in the way your game plays out. This stage in the selling process isn't just down to how well you do, so understand that whilst presenting is a critical factor, the outcome from your superb presentation is not 100 per cent in your control.

In any selling situation, understanding the perspective of your contact person is vital. (We cover this point at length in Chapter 7.)

Every day, salespeople just like you probably bombard your prospect with overtures for their business. Your contact person may be a real decision-maker or someone designated to narrow the field to two or three potential suppliers for the real decision-maker to talk to. Often, the person responsible for buying will bring in several competing companies to give presentations to a committee.

If you've already established a decent relationship with your prospect, it may be possible for you to find out who else is in the frame; indeed, if you have a superb relationship, you may also get her to tell you what it takes to win her custom, but truthfully these are rare occasions. Probably you're going in a little blind and the only thing you can focus upon is what *you* do, not the other players.

Find the power players

So, how do you optimise the presentation situation? When you begin an in-person presentation, thank and acknowledge the person who invited you, make eye contact with each person in the room, and see if you can tell which member of your audience is the power player – which one really has the most input into the final decision-making process. One power player exists in every group, and it may or may not be the person you've already been talking to. Just watching how the other members of the group treat each other helps you feel how the land lies. You may well see people looking to one figure in the room consistently before they answer a question, for example, or one person may fire questions towards you. Dominant workplace power players are often evident – and even when selling to the home market you often see a power play between husband and wife!

Often this power behaviour is pretty obvious and indeed when selling in a business-to-business environment to a group, you'll probably be told the job role and rank as you're introduced to each member of the committee. So the key decision-maker is identifiable and you can focus on him or her, though definitely not at the expense of ignoring the other people present. Assuming that just one key person makes the decision alone is foolish; indeed, if that were the case why on earth are you seeing several? Obviously everyone present is important to the decision or they wouldn't be there, so identify the major strength but don't lose the others.

Sometimes the key decision-maker is non-conformist and sits unobtrusively in the back of the room. By watching everyone else's body language, though, you should still be able to recognise that person.

Be quick or be sorry

Broadly speaking, in today's world of the ten-second TV advert and the instant Internet, few people bother to develop their ability to concentrate. In fact, the average person has a limited attention span, which means that you must compress the heart of your presentation down to a matter of only a few minutes. Droning on about how wonderful your offering is and showing 36 Microsoft PowerPoint slides and endless spreadsheets with loads of variables will just send your prospect to sleep. Be brief and to the point and make your presentation snappy whenever you can so their brain stays engaged. Spend your time involving your prospects directly in the presentation through questions, visual aids, or a hands-on demonstration and keep it clearly on a particular topic.

To help your prospect focus during your presentation and to help yourself stay on track, good practice is to create and introduce an agenda to each and every sales meeting. Try to get agreement beforehand so that all parties can make sure their points are covered, but even if you hand the agenda to the prospect at the beginning of your presentation, having it helps keep her and you on track. In your agenda, you can clearly state your objectives prior to beginning your presentation. Limit your objectives to three. For example, you might say the following:

> Bob and Linda, today I would like to cover three things. First, I'd like to understand your business better. Second, I'd like to demonstrate a product I think you'll find beneficial to your company. And finally, if you see the value in what I'm presenting to you today, I'd like to discuss the action steps required to help you benefit from it as soon as possible.

As a rule of thumb, make your presentation last 15 to 20 minutes. Longer than that means that your prospects are less involved for too long a period and may lose interest. Better to be short and sweet and allow your potential customers to ask lots of questions if you didn't cover the points they were looking for.

The 15 to 20 minutes don't begin the moment you enter the room or while you're building rapport. The presentation period begins when you get down to the business in hand and cover the finer points of your product's features and how those features can benefit your client.

Beware of two-stage presentations

Sometimes you may be forced to make your presentation happen on more than one occasion or indeed you may be interrupted as new parties arrive or others leave. Whenever you're interrupted or have to go back to a person and pick up the sales process again, always do a brief recap before starting back into your presentation.

In some industries – for example, financial services – the authorities have deemed that as a salesperson you cannot be giving 'best advice' if you haven't been away and thoroughly researched all of the market options before coming back to the prospect to recommend that she take out a relevant policy. Thus you're forced to make a sales process happen over a minimum of two visits. How does this situation change things? Well obviously the flow of rapport and ideas and connection as you talked freely in the first meeting will cool down by the time you meet again. This cooling doesn't mean that suddenly you'll have fallen out – you'll still feel friendliness – but you'll have a distance when compared directly with the last few moments of the previous meeting. This distance needs crossing and you need to rebuild the warmth. Once the client has warmed up, the meeting can reconvene with a brief recap of where you were, what you were discussing, and what you had agreed to look at for this meeting. A *brief recap* is just a restatement of the major points that you've covered so far, a quick way to bring everyone back to where you were before the break.

Indeed, remember that any break allows your listener's mind to wander and allows other people and happenings to impact on the scenario. You must find out if anything has happened before you steam straight into what you were last talking about. The prospect may possibly have been served with a redundancy notice or the company could have been told via internal memo to cut back or hold all spending. Any number of events could have occurred in a domestic situation, for example an accident or a family fall-out, which may interrupt the flow of your presentation.

If you have a two-stage presentation, re-establish rapport first, then ask about any changes since you last met, and then resume your presentation.

Knowing the ABCs of Presenting

The general guidelines for giving effective presentations are simple. You need your prospect to remember both what you are offering (especially if other people are in the frame) and the specific points that make your offer the one she should purchase. Use repetition to help your prospect remember. Tell her what you're going to tell her, tell her, and finish by telling her what you've told her.

This method serves the same purpose in oral presentations as it does in written ones. Repetition helps the person on the receiving end understand and remember the story you've told her. Repeating the message doesn't bore the client and won't cause her to think ill of you because you've already said that; it merely confirms in her mind the message you are conveying and makes your points stand out.

To help you achieve the desired level of attention and retention, you need to master the four basics of presentations: talking on your customer's level, pacing your speech, using the right words to create ownership, and interpreting body language. Use these techniques well and you're on your way to winning because your prospects will like and understand you and *feel* that you are right for them.

Being all things to all people

Research is important because you really want to know as much as possible about your prospect before your presentation so that you can address it to her level.

Consider this example: Suppose you're in your 30s, and you're trying to sell a refrigerator to an older couple who want to replace a 20-year-old appliance. What do you say to them? Well, you need to reflect a moment and think about what they may be like as buyers and as people. Are they 'newest, latest, loudest' type people or might they be 'safe, proven, reliable' type people? Question why you think they're the type they are. Because they've used something for 20 years, they've obviously resisted and ignored 'newer better, louder, faster' in the past. They resisted sales speak and stuck with an old, reliable model. To present to these people, you probably need to talk about dependability and service back-up, along with the fact that although the fridge is new to them that doesn't mean risky new technology. Show the new features as being easy and simple to use, with clear benefits in terms of both time and saving money – lower utility bills with the increased efficiency of new appliances, longer food storage time (which means less waste and greater convenience of getting at things), for example – as frugality is obviously their mindset.

Now cut to a different scene: You're trying to sell the same refrigerator to a newly married couple for their first home. Do you talk to them in the same way you do to the older couple replacing an old appliance? No, with the younger couple you accent the features and benefits that apply to their situation and satisfy their present needs. The features are the same, but the benefits are seen in a different light when viewed from their perspective. They may want something less expensive because that's all they can afford. But if you can show them the overall savings of getting a bigger or better fridge now, as opposed to the replacement costs down the road, they'll be more comfortable making the investment when the decision is rationalised for them.

Tweak your presentation to suit the prospect's style – or, another way of putting it, speak their language.

This versatility of message can be considered as being *multilingual*. You speak senior citizen. You speak yuppie. You speak single parent. You speak high-end business director. You speak economy or small-business owner. You simply become all things to all people. Being able to converse with someone at her level, whatever that level is, pays dividends. If you want to test this theory, try talking at your normal business level to a 5-year-old child and see how long you keep her attention. Then talk to her on her level and watch the animation in her face as she realises that you've just entered her world.

Appreciating how fast to proceed

When you give a presentation to a prospect, you need to be sensitive enough to recognise the proper demeanour to adopt with each client. You have to identify how to act with a certain type of person to best perform the task in hand. This part of your presentation resembles what stage actors do: they mirror the attitude and enthusiasm of the audience. If you're too energetic for your audience and speak at them too fast, they'll be turned off. Likewise, if you're too mild-mannered for them and speak too slowly, you may lose them.

Paying attention to the rate and pitch of your prospect's speech and then closely matching it is the ideal approach. Listen carefully to the speed of reply to a question – for example, is it immediate or does the prospect pause and deliberate before responding? Watch what happens when you offer a greeting: Does the prospect hurriedly rush to shake your hand and shower you with a flurry of words? Or does she slowly and laboriously tell you her name, job title, and previous work history? Adjust your presentation to match each prospect – whether she's animated and passionate or fairly static and talks in more of a monotone.

You really can see lots of clues – and if you copy an action or speed or style of voice, you create a connection and subconscious bond with the prospect. When this happens, your prospect understands on a subconscious level that you're like she is. Also, she'll understand you better and be willing to share more of her thoughts. Be careful, though, if the other person has a different accent to yours. If you adopt her accent, she may think you're mocking her or that you're insincere. Also, if her pacing is slow, you can speak at a level slightly above hers but slower than you might normally.

Forcing yourself to get down to her level can have an adverse effect on your entire presentation. You may have practised your presentation and got quite excited, animated, and even passionate when accentuating your key points; when you then adjust this presentation for the slower, quieter prospect, you may feel very weird and awkward. Don't worry – with a little practice, you'll develop an intuition for what each situation requires. Actually a little animation and passion for your offering is well received even if your client's style is less demonstrative. She receives and interprets your animation as sincere belief, and reasons that if you're that excited about your product, there must be something in it. So your passion usually sways your prospect in your favour instead of putting her off.

The first part of your sales meeting when you do your fact finding and rapport building is the more critical time to focus on matching the prospect's style. Once you gell with your client, the presentation style is accepted as you are.

Using words that assume your prospect will buy from you

A very powerful and subtle form of persuasion is to use language that directly involves the prospect with ownership. Speak as though your prospect already owns what it is you're selling. Don't say, 'If you join our insurance scheme . . .'; instead, say, 'When you participate in our insurance scheme . . . '. Giving your prospect the ownership of your idea, product, or service helps to move her closer to making a decision. This tactic is called *assumptive selling*.

Assumptive selling isn't the same as *suggestive selling*. With suggestive selling you offer something the prospect hasn't yet asked for or about – for example, asking a customer in a take-away restaurant if they'd like a side order. Assumptive selling is operating as if the prospect has made the decision to own a product or service and you talk in the future tense – for example, 'When you have . . .', 'you will get . . .', and 'you will enjoy the benefits of . . .', and so on.

Deciphering the human body's vocabulary

You don't necessarily need to learn to speak Spanish, French, or Russian to conduct business (though in the global marketplace, it wouldn't hurt to do so), but an awareness of another language – body language – definitely helps.

Most people are aware of body language, but they don't consciously read it and benefit from it. Investing in a book on body language is worthwhile (*The Definitive Book of Body Language* by Alan and Barbara Pease, published by Orion, is one Ben wholeheartedly recommends, along with *Body Language For Dummies* by Elizabeth Kuhnke, published by Wiley.) A knowledge of body language helps you see that even simple displays can have a profound impact on how your messages are received. When you find out a little bit about body language and start studying the body language of others (as part of your full-time hobby of selling), you'll quickly see how to benefit from it.

Here are just a few examples of the kinds of messages your body language communicates to those around you:

✔ **Leaning forward:** Doing so when you're talking to someone shows that you're interested and paying attention. When you recognise that positive sign in other people, keep moving forward, too. In fact, you may be able to pick up the pace of your presentation a bit if your audience is leaning forward.

✔ **Leaning back or glancing away:** These gestures mean that you're losing interest in what the other person's saying. What do you do if you recognise this body language in your audience? Pause if you're in the middle of a long monologue, summarise the last couple of points, and maybe ask a question if you feel it won't embarrass the person in question and do even more damage. Or, if you're giving a group presentation and you see several people displaying this body language, suggest a short break or a question-and-answer session, and change your presentation for next time!

✔ **Crossed arms:** This action indicates that you doubt what the other person is saying. When you receive this sign from your audience, move to a point-proving demonstration, chart, graph, or diagram.

Just as important as knowing how to read body language is knowing how to speak it. When you understand positive body language cues, practise them as part of your presentation. Your gestures can be as critical as the words you say. If you want to successfully persuade your prospects, you need to use positive, warm, honesty-projecting gestures, such as the following:

✔ **Sit beside the person you're trying to persuade instead of opposite her.** You're not on an opposing side. You're on your prospect's side.

✔ **Use a pen or pointer to draw attention, at the appropriate times, to your visual aids.** Some people hesitate when they use a pen or pointer, and that hesitation says that they're uncomfortable. If you wonder about the effectiveness of this technique, watch magicians. They sustain their 'magic' by their ability to draw your attention to (or away from) what they want.

✔ **Use open-hand gestures and eye contact.** These actions say that you have nothing to hide. Don't use the palm out (or pushing) gesture unless you're trying to eliminate a prospect's negative concern. Even then, push to the side, not towards the prospect.

We cover here just the basics of body language, but the whole field of study on this subject can help you so much more. When you begin paying attention, you'll find that many other body language cues will become obvious to you. We highly recommend that you research this subject and master the basics so that you know what you're seeing and then know how to respond or direct in return.

Being comfortable with remote presentations

When you can't possibly meet in person with your prospective client and you have to conduct business over the telephone, you need to apply certain strategies. First, because you can't see your clients, you may have trouble knowing whether they're being distracted or interrupted. Even though you can't read body language over the phone, you can definitely listen to their voice inflections (just as they'll be listening to yours). You can tell fairly easily whether someone is paying attention by counting the length of pauses between their comments, and the number of *uh-huh*s or *hmm*s you hear. If you're in doubt as to whether your prospects are on the same page as you, ask a question of them. Don't, of course, ask if they're paying attention. Instead, ask how something you just covered relates to their business or what they think of it. Restate that point or benefit clearly so they're not embarrassed if they really weren't paying attention.

Another strategy to use when you're giving presentations from a distance is the *pregnant pause*. If you briefly pause during your presentation, the pause will make your prospects wonder what happened and draw their attention to what you'll say next, thus drawing them back to the point in hand.

Don't be put off. Selling and presenting over the telephone is perfectly possible. Remember, you could probably engage with several clients or prospects in the time it takes to physically drive to visit only one, so you may be able to leverage up your selling time considerably if you develop the skill of remote selling.

If at all possible, send a sample product or, at the very least, an attractive visual of it to the client so she'll be seeing what you want her to see during your presentation. And refer to your Web site so that your conversation is interactive.

You may also be asked by a prospective client to join her for a presentation via videoconference or through an online service. If you're not used to these types of communication tools, ask someone who is to show you how to use them effectively. These tools aren't too difficult to work with, but the logistics of setting the stage just right can be tricky. For example, when videoconferencing, you'll probably use an 'eyeball'-type camera attached to your computer, so you need to be aware of what the camera is picking up and of what else is in the picture with you. Check your camera and make sure that it doesn't allow your next potential major client to see a torn poster hanging on the wall behind you, or a neglected plant. (Trust us, these kinds of objects can harm your credibility.) Be certain you have an attractive background even if you have to borrow something to put up behind you. If you decide to place a plant behind you, beware of putting it (or any other object) in a position in which it may look like it's coming out of your head. Be aware of the lighting level – people and places look less than inviting when in darkness or shadows and you really don't want prospects thinking of you as some shady character because you didn't have a nice bright light illuminating your videoconference moment.

Take note of how your television news reporters appear and act on camera. They're in the talking-head type of shot, which is how you'll be appearing – your head and shoulders will be in the frame, but not much else. News reporters make great eye contact with the camera – they 'smile' into it with their eyes.

If your presentation online requires you to show slides or other visuals, maintain as much control of their flow as possible. For example, you can control a PowerPoint presentation from your computer while it's being viewed online from someone else's computer. Indeed, many computer software programs allow you to share the viewing experience with others who are online with you and looking at your computer monitor. Many options in software such as PowerPoint help you create presentations, so if this is to be a factor in your new selling career, learn the basics of the program and how best to adopt the technology. Seek professional help to set up any specific functionality requirement you might have.

Remembering That People Buy People, Not Products

Rarely does a prospect have no other option except to purchase from you, and she can always choose one of your competitors. And, unfortunately, little difference exists between the more serious players in any competitive market. inasmuch as the key competitors have similar offerings with similar benefits and similar prices. Thus it follows that a prospect of yours won't have a lot to lose by shopping elsewhere, even though your company's sales lines try to convince you and her that she will miss out!

The only thing that a client definitely cannot get from a competitor is you. Your determination to ensure her satisfaction and to personally sort when mishaps happen is the key difference and you must play upon that.

For example, consider your tour operator when you go on holiday. You booked with a well-known travel company and you arrive in a resort. Who is the person there to greet you? Your rep. During your holiday you're encouraged to socialise with your rep and she encourages you even harder to go on trips with her to make the most of your holiday. But when the room is full of flies or the hot water won't get hot and the hotel staff don't help, who do you turn to? You know these problems aren't the rep's fault, but you still expect her to sort them out. Why? Because she's the representative, and in your eyes she is responsible for your holiday. You, too, are seen as totally responsible for your product. The client will buy from *you* in the end and you must therefore remember to put the ability to create rapport and a bond with people at the top of your learning list.

Whilst you develop a strong bond with your product, ultimately the prospect is another human being with feelings about what is best for her. So your offering alone isn't enough and actually accounts for only half of the selling process. The other half is the service and back-up you can provide for your prospect; she knows she can call on you to sort out her problems, should they arise.

In a confusing, fast-paced world, everyone likes the anchor of a familiar face. The after-sale offering is as important to the whole selling process as the product – and *you* are the key element. You need to build and enhance that connection with the client and allow her to see how personally involved you will be in ensuring her satisfaction.

Feeling safe is a primary need of all people. The buyer must feel that your offering contains no hidden snares or untold truths. As a seller, whatever you focus on when selling to or gelling with a prospect, you must first ensure that she's comfortable before you can hope for a sale. If your prospect isn't comfortable with what you're offering, she'll never part with her money for it. So your principal goal when presenting is to make your prospect feel safe, with both you and your product.

Getting out of the picture

A slight contradiction exists post-sale because inasmuch as you want to be the familiar face your clients are happy to buy from, ideally you need to slightly sidestep the client after the sale so that your company's service department professionals can do their job. You have neither the time nor the ability to handle all of the post-sale issues and must take a backseat.

During the presentation you need to explain the role other people in your organisation may play. You make clear that you won't back off and let the client feel dumped, merely that you are not equipped to give her the best service she deserves. Stress that you will take an interest and monitor the situation but that the service team or accounts department or whatever can best resolve after-sale issues. You get out of the picture to a degree.

Whatever the case might be for involving other scenarios or for talking in your presentation about post-sales support, always remember that the objective is to sell – and initially the prospect thinks that the only thing that is relevant is the product or service you represent. Thus you must maintain her interest and keep it focused on the product also. Your potential client absolutely must be sold on the offering you represent and must clearly see and feel the benefits and what they really mean to her. If she cannot see these benefits, she won't buy – even if she likes you.

Staying in control

Don't let your prospects see what you want them to see until you're ready for them to see it. If your demonstration involves the use of a piece of equipment, don't let your prospective client come in and begin punching buttons or demanding answers to a lot of questions – effectively taking control of the presentation away from you. Just tell the prospect that she's asking great questions and that you'll answer them in your presentation, then ask that she holds them until after the demonstration. When she recognises that you've planned something special for her, and she can see that you maintain control politely but firmly, your prospect will respect you and probably settle down to let you do your thing.

Keeping control can become a challenge when you have several things to display. If your demonstration falls into this category, bring something (like a cloth) to cover your display items, uncovering only those items you're prepared to discuss. If you're using a video or computer screen, have an attractive screensaver that you can go to when you need your prospect's attention focused back on your planned presentation. Otherwise, your prospect will probably be trying to read ahead on the screen instead of listening to what you're saying.

Mastering the Art of Visuals

The majority of people learn and understand best when they involve as many of their senses as possible; however, each person usually has one dominant sense. Some people learn best by closing their eyes and listening. Others have a strong need to touch and feel things. Most people, however, gain the best understanding by seeing things. Except for the visually impaired, sight produces the strongest sensory input and carries the most weight.

You've heard the phrase 'seeing is believing', which comes from the desire of most people to be shown proof that what they're being told is real, or at least that it can come true – they rely upon their sight to give them the proof they are looking for. Take a moment to see the difference between *telling* someone about a new product and letting her *see* it, either in picture form or through a product demonstration.

Visual aids need to show three things to new clients:

➤ **Who you (and your company) are.** Visual aids – a PowerPoint presentation, for example – should identify your company and the industry to which it belongs. If you are worldwide suppliers of your particular type of product, put that information in your presentation. The story of your company builds credibility.

✔ **What you've done.** If, for example, you've managed to attain a credible status as preferred supplier to a household-name company or have been awarded recognition by your industry associations, prominently outline this information in your visual aids and your status is elevated accordingly. Be careful not to labour the point, though; being proud of your company is one thing; being a bore is another thing altogether.

✔ **What you do for your clients.** Your prospective client will be most interested in this part. Here, you tune in to her favourite radio station, WII-FM, where they ask the pressing question, 'What's In It For Me?'

The best visual presentations include all of these key points so try to incorporate them.

Although the presentation includes several images of all that these three points cover, you also want to encourage the use of other senses such as sound, smell, taste, and touch. You can ask creative questions about how it might *feel* to use the product or how the product fits when being worn, or how sweet the *taste* of success will be when your prospective customer uses this offering to become a winner. Being creative with conversation that stimulates the other senses as well as sight is difficult but not impossible, and when you master the involvement of other senses you pull your prospects into the experience and it becomes more real to them. When you make the scenario seem real, they begin to take ownership and a sale is easier to make.

Using the visuals your company supplies

If you represent a company's products or services, you've probably been shown the current sales material they work with. Often, especially in larger corporations, these are slick, high-quality sheets and brochures with graphs, charts, diagrams, and photos. Such material often contains quotes from various respected authorities about your product or service, and even testimonials from satisfied clients, probably all neatly packed in a presentation-ready format such as a hard folder or zip wallet.

Often presentation materials also include a selection of electronic format images and messages and all leaflets, flyers, brochures, and PowerPoint-type presentations are visible and downloadable from the company Internet site. For computer presentations, you'll probably have a laptop computer and multimedia projector if you're often called upon to present in a group scenario. When you prepare for one of these high-tech presentations, be sure that your prospective client has a whiteboard or screen for you to project your images onto. Presenting your product professionally is tough when all you have to work with for a background is wood panelling or flowered wallpaper.

You may also find yourself working with videos for your presentations, although these are rarely, if ever, actually on tape format but again streamed as Web files or stored multimedia. Videos often include recorded testimonials from actual customers your prospect can relate to. When your prospect sees someone just like herself who is benefiting from your product or service, the relationship between the prospect and your product grows a little stronger.

Whatever your specific visual aids depict, the important thing to remember is this: your company invested in the creation of your visual aids for a reason. And that reason was not to make your life more complicated by having to carry all this stuff around and keep it updated. Instead, they did it because many, many years' experience has proven that visual aids are very effective when they are used properly.

So what's the best way to use visual aids? Probably the way your company recommends. Few companies succeed in business by putting out poor presentation materials and then leaving the sales process to chance as they encourage their salespeople to use them as they see fit! Often these materials are the result of years of trial and error and many intelligent minds accumulating resources that have worked brilliantly, and disposing of those which have not. The material has been processed and subsequently approved and can be relied upon to do the job – moving product into the hands of consumers.

If for some reason you don't like or have trouble using the company's presentation materials, talk to the people who trained you on how to use them. If their suggestions don't satisfy you, talk to a top salesperson, someone who uses them effectively. You may even want to go on a customer call with that salesperson to watch how she handles things. After you master her suggestions for using the materials as well as possible, if you still think you have room for improvement, ask to meet the people who put them together. They'll probably be glad to offer you constructive suggestions and, hopefully, listen to yours.

Developing your own visual aids

If you aren't involved in formal selling or you have no visual aids to work with, put some thought into what you can develop on your own. Involvement of the senses in attempting to persuade others is critical, so make sure your materials appeal to as many as possible.

For example: say you want to sell your family on the idea of taking activity holidays in the mountains and forests when you know they'd rather go to the beach. You may consider showing a video on all the outdoor adventures available to them in the countryside. Doing so can involve them and help them see and experience the feelings of freedom, fresh air, and nature; a brief film may very well stimulate enough desire to see for themselves and try an outdoor adventure holiday. Because many people are swayed from their usual habits in exactly this way, many holiday locations now offer free videos as promotional items in information packages. Or you can get a video on nature in general, with flowing waterfalls, gentle breezes blowing in the trees, canoeing, horseriding, whatever appeals to your audience (in this case, your family). Such a video immediately involves two senses – sight and hearing – but you can easily involve other senses with techniques mentioned in the preceding section by asking questions such as, 'What's that I smell cooking on the open fire?' and 'Can you hear that cuckoo through the trees?' If changing your family's holiday destination really means a lot to you, you can go the whole hog and pitch your presentation in a tent!

The point is that the more real you make the experience, the more chance that you'll persuade them to switch. Emotional involvement is stimulated with sensory input, so involve more senses and move more people across to your way of thinking.

The same strategy applies to formal business sales presentations: The more senses you can involve, the better. If your sales materials limit you to sight and hearing, find ways to get additional sensual involvement. You can involve your prospects' sense of touch just by handing them things. Smell and taste are a little harder to arouse, especially if you're selling an intangible object such as a service. But think about language for a moment: We talk about 'the taste of success' and the 'smell of fear' amongst others, and you can find creative ways to use the full range of senses to illustrate a sales point. With intangibles, you can paint visual pictures that bring those senses into play by encouraging the client to 'imagine . . . ' as you describe a scene that allows her mind to paint a picture and put her in it.

For example, say you're selling a cleaning service to a working mother. You may not necessarily want to have her smell the cleaning agents you use but you can talk about how fresh the home will smell after your professional cleaner has completed her duties. You can say, 'Imagine how you'll feel to walk into your home after a hard day at the office and immediately notice that the air smells fresh and fragrant and see that the carpet's been vacuumed and the cushions straightened and you just know that your home is perfectly ready for you to settle into and unwind.' Always refer to the residence as your prospect's *home* and not her *house* – a house is made up of lifeless bricks and boards; a home is made up of the people who live there and the events of those people's lives. The word *home* evokes a much warmer feeling and immediately softens your prospect's mood.

Demonstrating Products to Your Prospective Clients

When you demonstrate a tangible product, you have to resemble a magician who intrigues and entertains whilst simultaneously talking and engaging the audience. You need to show your prospect all the features that you know are relevant to her from your earlier fact finding and rapport building, but you must also allow her to hold and use the article, too.

Selling isn't a spectator sport; it's an involvement sport.

If you sell office machinery such as photocopiers and you don't get the people you're trying to sell to push the buttons, change the paper, and open and close the machine, you're not selling – you're showing. Selling needs to involve the customer and allow her to get excited and imagine ownership. You absolutely *must* let your prospective clients try out the various functions of the photocopier to make them feel linked to your product.

The prospective office manager won't care that you've won all the time trials at your office for making the most complicated copying challenges come out perfect. Your mastery of this machine and your badge stating that you understand it better than anyone else aren't relevant; the client's involvement is what will make her purchase. Indeed, instead of showing that you can handle a complicated machine, simply demonstrating how easy it is for everyone on your prospect's staff to use the machine without hiccup is more effective. Build into your demonstration the proof that they can do so by letting them. During your demonstration, your prospect and her staff members should be able to make normal copies simply and to find out something about a new feature that will make their job easier. Your key contact person should find out about all the warning lights on the machine and what to do about each one and feel confident that she can not only work it but that it isn't going to let her down as soon as she takes delivery and cannot get hold of you.

If you're selling computers or software, stand or sit at the client's shoulder, giving her instructions on how she can do whatever it is she just asked about. Make sure the client's hands are on that keyboard and mouse thus creating a positive experience with the product and building her confidence in the capabilities of the machine. What's really happening is that the client is learning something new and building her confidence in her own *ability to use* the machine. She may even be overcoming a fear of computers altogether – and if she overcomes that fear and becomes comfortable using the product, she'll be much more likely to want to own it.

One of the greatest fears all clients experience in selling situations is that they'll trust what the salesperson tells them, buy the product or service, and then, after they own it, find out that it doesn't meet their expectations or their needs. The best demonstration, the most thorough, and the most involving, gives people the opportunity to prove to themselves that what the salesperson is telling them is true.

Avoiding the 'Shock, Horror, Disaster' Scenario of Amateur Sales Presentations

If we were to tell you all the horror stories we've heard about failed sales presentations, we'd need a week without interruptions! The unfortunate thing is that those same salespeople could have avoided the problems they came across if they'd taken a few simple precautions. Fortunately for you, hearing so many of these horror stories has helped us develop effective suggestions for avoiding your own sales presentation nightmares. In the following sections, we cover just a few things you may not think of, but all of them must become a vital part of your pre-presentation preparation checklist.

Find the electrical outlets and know how to reach them

When presenting in an office or hotel lobby-type environment, always make sure that you can locate the plug sockets. This may sound like obvious advice but we often see people arriving to present and being unable to sit near a power supply as all of the seats in those positions are taken – they needed to arrive first, not just in time for their meeting! Always make sure your laptop has a fully charged battery just in case you cannot plug it in. If your laptop runs out of power, you'll rightly carry the can.

A businesswoman Ben knows well invested hours in preparing her computer-generated demonstration with high-quality graphics, customised charts, graphs, and diagrams ready for a group presentation of some importance the next day. Her only problem: the power cord she brought to her presentation was too short. Assuming that the company would allow her use of their equipment she hadn't taken an extension cable with her. When ushered into a special meeting room that was much larger than her expectations, she found that the power points were all on an outside wall and the tables centrally located. She had to place all her equipment right next to a wall, which was about 20 feet from her audience. As a result, she lost vital eye contact and rapport-building closeness with her audience, and probably the sale too – all because she'd assumed they'd have what she required and wasn't prepared for other eventualities.

ANECDOTE

Being prepared for the worst . . . and hoping for the best

For many years now Ben has been presenting to groups of prospects and speaking to audiences all around the country but he remembers well a particular incident in the early days when he was involved in sales recruitment. His specific role was that of recruitment and training director and as such he was responsible for the gathering of new troops and their initial training.

The company employed salespeople of all nationalities as it operated an international salesforce based in southern Spain, and Ben was on a trip back to the UK for new recruits. The standard format had been proven to work – several localised adverts in the recruitment sections of newspapers and then a day in a hotel where all potential applicants were grouped together and given a presentation; essentially Ben sold them on the idea of the company before the applicants sold themselves to him. Well, Ben duly arrived at the hotel, checked out the room ready for the next day, and did some rudimentary checks on the technical equipment.

Ben was fairly new to his recruitment role but knew that he was using a proven formula and that the results were always very good for the company. He was determined to head back to

Spain with the largest, brightest group of salespeople the company had ever seen. As the room filled the next morning and expectations were raised, he was filled with nervous anticipation.

Then it happened: Ben turned on the projector and the laptop only to find that the two were incompatible. The video was meant to show off the luxury resort the salespeople would be based in when working for him. But Ben now faced a room full of people looking to work for a professional company and judging it on his performance. . . and the video that wowed applicants into a new life and consequently gave the company a chance to recover its recruitment costs didn't play!

Finally, a member of the hotel staff made the equipment work and Ben made the rest of the day probably better than it might have been to try and make up; he introduced a 'stay for a drink and get to know us session' in a blatant attempt to win them over!

Check your equipment and all presentation materials in advance – every time you present. You only get one chance to win people over, so don't be remembered for getting it wrong.

Be sure your visual aids are in order

If you use printed materials such as brochures and pamphlets to show off your offering, make sure they're not tatty! You'd be amazed at how many salespeople get used to using the same items from their portfolio without noticing them becoming gradually battered. Simple things such as food stains and bent corners on your presentation materials give the impression that you don't care about details – and small details can be of crucial importance to prospective clients.

And don't forget the potential for pranks, especially if you work in a vibrant and competitive team. Team members have been known to reorganise presentation materials or even delete some much needed slides for a laugh, which isn't so funny if you're the target and don't find out until you´re in front of an audience! Review each and every piece of equipment or presentation material that your audience will see. You'll sleep better knowing things are in order.

Always check your materials after someone else has been through them. Misplacement is rarely intentional, but it does happen.

Test everything in advance

You may have a very dependable demonstration model of your computer software, for example. In fact, it could be one you've used for several weeks or months without problem. But on the day of your big presentation, Murphy's Law may strike – if anything can go wrong, it will. Having a bad cable for your equipment or your computer can wreak havoc with the best-laid plans. So always arrive early enough to test your equipment on site. And test it early enough, so that if you find something isn't working, you can replace it.

Customise as much as you can

Don't you love it when someone gives you a generic presentation that you just know she's given, word-for-word, to at least 40 other people before? Where even the humorous touches are no longer funny because she's used them hundreds of times already and the whole thintg just looks and feels like a second-hand show. Of course you don't; no one does. By making the extra effort to personalise your materials, and especially your presentation, you appear competent and knowledgeable about your customer's specific needs. And that's just the kind of person she's looking for.

Remember that humans are naturally interested mostly in themselves. Whenever you're presenting, the more often you use the person's name or the company name in your presentation and support material, the more your client will feel that you're giving her the attention she believes she is worth – and the more she will naturally respond to become involved with you. Personalising your material is hugely conducive to increased sales conversion, so do so whenever you get a chance.

Don't customise by skipping over materials in your generic, full-blown presentation. People will feel slighted by the absence of this information. Instead, remove pages or slides you don't need. If you can't skip them, go ahead and show them but make sure you offer a brief explanation about why those particular slides don't apply to your present audience's needs and that you won't waste their valuable time going over them in detail.

Bring a protective cover sheet

If you're scheduled to make a presentation in someone else's office, don't take a chance that any of your equipment will mark her furniture. To prevent damages, always check the bottoms of your equipment before placing anything on a potential customer's furniture. Rough edges can easily leave scratch marks.

To prevent causing damage, carry a loose sheet that you can place under the equipment. That way, you'll always be safe. Also, writing with a hard pen and a heavy hand whilst pressing firmly onto a sheet of paper or order form can leave marks on a table top, especially a softwood desk. So, just place a block pad or a clipboard under your order form and don't leave a permanent mark that you were there.

Chapter 11

Addressing Customer Concerns

• •

• •

*U*nless you sell balloons at a fairground, you won't often have clients or prospects simply walking up to you, purchasing, and walking away again without any questions. In reality, customers have concerns. They have needs for a better understanding and a desire to ensure that they're doing the right thing.

Little fears creep up on customers when they feel the urge to invest in your product or service or to commit to your idea. The concerns that arise when a customer makes any commitment that involves his time or money are completely natural. In this chapter, we show you how to address these concerns and make the sale.

Seeing Hesitation as Encouragement

Most people new or inexperienced at selling think that a sign of hesitation means: 'Not going to buy, thank you anyway'. The seasoned sales professional, however, knows that customers can have good reasons to hesitate.

The best reason of all is that they feel themselves leaning towards 'Yes'. So your client's hesitation can simply be a sign that he wants to slow down the selling process so he can absorb all the information you're giving him. Whilst you have been explaining your offering in terms and at a pace you believe is comfortable, the client may need more time to process the information. The desire to slow down and feel comfortable drives questions.

Or hesitation can mean that the customer needs *more* information. In such a case, the customer objects in order to show you that you need to back up and resell him on a certain point. When a potential client hesitates or raises an objection, just think, 'He needs more information'.

Amongst the concerns will be questions such as

- ✔ Will the product or service do what you say it will?
- ✔ Will you really be able to make his required delivery date?
- ✔ Is he getting the best price or at least a fair price?
- ✔ Is he making a good decision?
- ✔ Is it something he needs right now?

Be prepared to address all these basic questions before you walk into any sales opportunity.

Remember this sentence and you'll always come out with more sales: 'No means not yet, tell me more, and/or give me another reason to say yes.'

'No' does not mean that the customer cannot buy or will not buy, it merely means that, based upon the information that you've passed on to him, thus far he cannot say 'Yes'. Add a new factor such as timing of delivery, price reduction, or scarcity of supply and you'll often see buying decisions speeded up and sales happen where only minutes earlier the prospect had said he wasn't going to buy.

Try to overcome the client's objections. In the worst case, your prospect doesn't like the way you handle his reservations and you're heading for the door anyway – thus you're no worse off! So why not experiment with ways to address your client's concerns or handle his objections? The worst that can happen is that you don't get what you want and you move on to the next likely candidate. The best that can happen is that your customer sees how competently you handled his concern and that his concern wasn't strong enough to keep him from going ahead with your offering.

If you get nervous or afraid when you hear an objection and start packing up your briefcase and beating a hasty retreat for the door, then you're making a choice to leave empty-handed.

Until you come to expect customer concerns, you won't know how to handle them. And until you know how to handle them, you won't come close to reaching your highest earning potential in sales. Go into every presentation anticipating objections, and you'll come out ahead.

Reading Your Prospect's Signals

Prospective clients tell you three important things when they voice objections or raise concerns during your presentation:

✔ **They're interested, but they don't want to be thought of as an easy sale.**

If you've properly qualified the prospect (see Chapter 9 for more on how to do this), you know what he has now, what he enjoys most about it, what he would alter, and that he's the decision-maker. Armed with that knowledge, if you're confident the prospect would benefit from your offering, the chances are he's interested, but he doesn't want you to think of him as a pushover. In that case, slow down the pace, encourage questions, and generally get him relaxed and chatting before you ask him to make a decision.

✔ **They may be interested, but they aren't clear about what's in it for them.**

If your prospect is already asking lots of questions and looks somewhat perplexed or doubtful, he's interested – he just doesn't have a clear picture of what he can gain from your offering. This situation is especially common when the prospect doesn't have previous experience with a similar product. To respond to this kind of prospect, you have to cover the features and benefits in a bit more detail, develop more of a relationship with him, and concentrate a little more on asking the right questions along the way so that you can draw him into a more involved and sale-friendly position.

✔ **They may not be interested, but they could be if you educate them properly.**

If you face this kind of questioning client (the one who's disinterested because of a lack of information), you must first earn his trust so he'll give you the time you need to educate him on your product. You also have to build the prospect's curiosity about the product, service, or idea so he wants to know more.

All three situations tell you one thing: The prospect needs more information.

How often have you purchased something that at first glance didn't appeal but later, as you realised how useful it was, you changed your mind and became a 'must have' owner. Very often in a selling situation all that is required is a better understanding and more involvement.

By backing up and clarifying exactly what the prospect is objecting to, you find out just which direction to take for your next step.

Using Some Simple Strategies to Address Your Prospect's Concerns

Objections from prospects are just part of the business of selling. You just need to know how to handle them. Fortunately, you can use some key strategies to address your prospects' objections so that they come away with more information *and* more respect for you and your product. In the following sections, we show you how.

When the fish aren't biting, change your bait

Most salespeople find influencing people who voice no objections and raise no questions very hard. In other words, the most difficult people to persuade are those who seem to be non-responsive: They reply to a question every now and then, but they don't really get involved.

In selling and negotiating situations, you carry the presentation forward by directing and redirecting your course of questions and information based on what your prospect tells you. If you get nothing in response, the communication often stalls. When that situation happens, you have to guess which direction to follow next – and guessing is very bad because you're no longer in control. Guessing is like casting your line with no bait – hardly the best way to catch a fish!

When you're in this scenario you must stop and ask a direct question, along the lines of: 'Excuse me Mr Prospect, when I spoke to you on the phone to arrange this meeting you mentioned that you were interested but I feel that today things may have changed slightly. Might I ask, is your intention still to purchase some new widgets this year?' A chance always exists that something is distracting him that is not your fault or indeed even relative to your efforts. Or the problem could just be a timing issue that is best addressed by simple acknowledgement and a revised visit another day.

Salespeople are possibly the most paranoid in the world because we always think that the apparent change in interest level of the prospect must be our fault or a cooling in his desire, when the fact is it could be anything from a death in the family to a leaked memo about a company take-over that is distracting the prospect – nothing to do with the sales call at all. Always ask and find out *exactly* because it will help you and be a relief for those in the situation if they need to stall but don't want to pour water on your bonfire. Of course possibly the person isn't in fact interested but it's better that you know now and save your time for someone who is.

In today's world your sales prospects, whether in a domestic or a commercial environment, have too many other things to do with their time than deliberately waste it. So provided you have qualified your scheduled meeting correctly then any lack of interest or involvement is either an indication of a very poor performance by you or totally a side issue playing on their mind. Most people though will bring up reservations and be involved to a degree in your presentation.

Those who *do* bring up issues for you to address are, at the very least, interested. If they're really tough to convince, they'll probably become your best customers when you finally do convince them. So the next time you hear an objection, be glad. Getting objections and getting past them is a necessary step in the selling cycle.

Condition versus objection

If your prospect's objection is 'I can't afford it', and you're selling a luxury item, the chances are that you've just heard a condition, not an objection. And a big difference exists between the two.

A *condition* is not an excuse or a stall, but is a valid reason for the prospect not to agree with what you're proposing. If you're trying to exchange your offering for your potential customer's money, and the customer has no money and has no credit, then this may be a condition. A condition is something that you cannot get around. If he genuinely does not have any money then you cannot give him the money to buy from you. For example, if you find out that the prospect you're trying to sell to doesn't own his property and has several county court judgements against him for non-payment of debts, you know you're going to be stuck if you're selling anything of higher value that usually requires a credit arrangement to balance the sale price. Just thank him for his time and move on. With so many potential customers out there without conditions, don't beat your head against the wall with those who *do*.

Always leave people who voice valid conditions on a positive note, though. You never know how that person's situation may change down the road. He may win the lottery in the next 24 hours. An elderly relative might suddenly die and leave him a sizable inheritance. Or he may borrow the money from his rich grandpa or get grandpa to buy it for him. You never know – though you need to play the right odds, so move on when you think you're pitching to a poor chance.

An objection of 'I can't afford it' is different. An *objection* is where the prospect says he has no money but you can pretty much tell from other things he's said and from his surroundings that this is actually not true. This objection is a stall because the customer isn't sure whether buying is the right move. Affordability is a smoke screen to buy time. When you recognise this situation and skilfully continue educating the prospect you often find that the money issue isn't raised again. Indeed, if you're honest with yourself, you've probably bought something that you couldn't really afford, and so have we, and so has everyone we know! You just got involved and carried away and ended up buying! So, never stop when you hear an objection about 'cannot afford it' – unless you can clearly see and ascertain that it is a real condition regarding the money.

Bypassing your prospects' objections completely

If you know that your prospect wants and needs the product or service you're offering, but feels a natural inclination to object, you may be able to bypass the objection altogether. Simply say, 'That's a good point, Mr Smith. I believe it will be addressed to your satisfaction by the end of my presentation. May I make a note of it and come back to it later?' If he gives you permission, he'll be watching the rest of your presentation for a satisfactory answer. Or, he may see enough benefit during the balance of the presentation that the value outweighs his concern and it becomes a moot point.

Many different psychologies are at play in the buying process. Often the buying party feels the need to 'defend' his position and justify his stance by asking questions and throwing objections at you. He doesn't want to be an easy sale or doesn't want to give in because he fears he'll get ripped off. This type of customer feels an inherent need to throw something at you to 'prove' to himself he wasn't easy. Once you appreciate that this is his game plan and that these reflexes indicate a level of discomfort, then you can comfortably continue to handle him.

If you're new to persuading, don't ignore any objection completely – especially if it's raised more than once – without testing the waters to see how big a concern it truly is.

Sometimes just acknowledging the concern is enough. Your prospect is satisfied that you're really listening, and then he'll move ahead. Always acknowledge any objections or questions, otherwise you could put your prospect's back up and create a resistance that will kill the sale. Acknowledge his concern but if possible don't address it immediately – it may just be a reflex and not need dealing with.

Your prospect raising a concern doesn't necessarily mean, 'No way'. It may simply be a way for the prospect to say, 'Not *this* way'. The concern doesn't mean 'No' but 'Not yet' – and you simply need to take another path to the same destination.

Helping your prospects to see that they're trading up

If your prospective client has money, credit, or both, but he just doesn't want to part with it now, you haven't convinced him that he'd be better off having the product than having his money.

Trusting your instincts

Selling instincts (expressed by that little voice inside your head telling you what's right and what's not in a selling situation) develop through practice and experience. Everyone has these instincts, but some people's selling instincts are more developed than others.

To start developing and using your selling instincts, carefully listen to your customers' concerns and genuinely put their needs before your own. Then, and only then, can you trust your own instincts. If you can't honestly say that your customers' needs come before your own, then you place your own desires before what you instinctively know is right for the customer – and your self-centredness will show. Your customers will see the pound signs in your eyes and won't trust you. And why should they trust someone who only thinks of himself?

If, for example, an investment you're offering requires the person's time, 'no time' is not a valid condition – it's an objection. Everyone has the same 86,400 seconds in every day. How people use them is their choice. If you want someone to invest his time with you, you have to show him enough benefits for him to *want* to spend his time on your offering instead of on what he's already planned. His choice will come down to priorities and everyone is in control of that priority list. You just need to make the prospect feel that your offering is worthy of climbing up the list a little.

Beating your prospects to their own objections

Too often salespeople handle objections so badly that all that results is a confrontational situation and a stand-off where no sale is made. Avoid this situation if you want to become a top salesperson! Handling objections needs some skill.

The 'flushing out' technique enables you to handle all objections seamlessly and walk away with literally twice the volume of sales as your competitors. *Flushing out* requires that you tell a story about the anticipated objection prior to the prospect raising the objection. Your story illustrates the example of someone who was in a similar position to that of your immediate prospect, how the supposed barrier to the sale was present, and how you managed to overcome this barrier so that all parties were happy. The immediate prospect listens to the story, mentally engages with the illustrated client, and appreciates that his challenge might be similar – and when he sees that you dealt with the issue on the previous occasion, he doesn't raise it as an objection again. Flushing out is immensely powerful.

You need to list all of the objections that you frequently hear – cost and pricing issues, delivery and timeframe issues, style, colour choice, and supply issues, and of course timing of purchase and attention to the decision issues. You must plan a couple of stories and practise relaying them effectively.

For example, if you know that your product costs more than others on the market, you can be fairly certain that your prospect will be concerned about that cost. But you can beat the prospect to that objection by explaining upfront that your product requires a higher investment because it contains only the highest-quality ingredients. And those high-quality ingredients make people feel better, last longer, or perform in a superior manner. Those benefits are worth bragging about *before* your prospect gets busy laying bricks for that wall of defence against the investment. Using specific illustrations about the car he drives, the area of the town he lives in, or the style of clothing he wears are all opportunities to illustrate the 'get what you pay for' analogy and thus set up your sale along the 'quality not price' angle and defuse the objection about the cost being too high.

And, you can always simply employ a little of the human factor and ask a question! Just ask the prospect how critical costs are when compared to the other factors involved in the purchase. You may well have the very best kitchen on sale, with the highest attention to craftsmanship and quality fixtures, but if the client is planning to move home within a year he's more likely to want something that looks good in the short term and will be planning to spend less. You can get this information if you just ask a simple question – a better approach than lots of slick talking about your craftsmanship. You can save that spiel for someone who says he's looking to refurbish a kitchen and enjoy a lengthy retirement in the same property.

So, whenever you feel you're going to hear a frequently voiced objection, raise the point before the prospect does, wrap an illustrative story around it, and let him listen. If he radically disagrees he'll voice his concerns. In the kitchen illustration, for example, you might cover the price issue with a story about how a former prospect had gone for a cheaper kitchen and then turned up two years later to order a new one from you because the cheap one fell to pieces. As you say this, the person listening may say he's planning to move anyway and so your story has flushed out the real issue – potential mismatch of client and offering.

Whatever the potential objection, come up with a story that covers it. For example, if you potentially have a delivery issue – you cannot deliver for a period of, say, 12 weeks and many purchasers feel that they want a shorter supply time – you can cover this by telling a story. For example, explain how one of your former colleagues moved to a competitor to make his fortune but now says he regrets the move because, although he can now deliver within six weeks, he gets constant complaints because the customer service is dismal or the machine itself is inferior. You, on the other hand, recognise that a long wait when you've agreed to buy something isn't ideal but the demand in itself is the testimony to the better choice of machine . . . everybody's after one.

Using this story tells the client that trying for a quick solution is foolish when everybody else has learned the lesson the hard way and is now voting with their wallet and waiting for your product.

Take advantage of this tactic with objections that you know are most often heard about your product or service. If people object to the cost, have a testimonial at hand from a happy client who had the same objection and now feels his return on investment was well worth it. Many companies post such testimonials on their Web sites. You can easily impress your prospect by calling up the Web site on your laptop right then and there to address the prospect's concern. Let him read it rather than telling him about it. In fact, asking your prospective client to take a look at your company's Web site prior to your presentation is always a good idea. Send the prospect an e-mail with your Web address and a few suggestions of areas within your site he may find helpful.

This method of 'flushing out' or beating prospects to their concerns – bringing it up, bragging about it, and then telling a story to elaborate upon it – has proven successful for many salespeople who used to see common challenges as stumbling blocks. Now they see them as springboards to success, and you can, too.

Understanding the Do's and Don'ts of Addressing Concerns

Before you get too deep into dealing with your prospect's concerns, you need to be aware of some basic do's and don'ts of this important step in selling. In this section, we fill you in on a couple of each that will guide you through any selling situation.

Do acknowledge the legitimacy of the concern

Dismissing your prospect's concerns as unimportant can cause those objections to get completely blown out of proportion. Often a simple 'I see' or 'I understand' is acknowledgement enough. Sometimes, you may do well to say, 'Let me make a note of that so we can discuss it in depth after we've covered everything,' – and then jot it down. Making a note of it validates the concern and shows professionalism on your part. Whatever you do, though, acknowledge the prospect's reservation.

Do get the prospect to answer his own objection

The most important 'do' of addressing concerns is: Get the prospect to answer his own objection.

That advice may sound tricky to follow, but here's why this tactic's so important. You are in the act of trying to persuade your prospect to part with his cash, so obviously he'll have reservations about anything you do or say. Why? Because anything you say is going to be interpreted as biased. While you're saying that your offering is good for him, he's hearing that it must be good for you, too. Until the prospect fully realises that you're acting in his best interest, he'll doubt you.

So, when *you* say the offering is perfect for your prospect, he tends to doubt it. When *he* says it, he tends to think regard it as true. For that reason you need to get your prospect to answer his own objections – because he's much more likely to believe *himself* than he is to believe *you*. All you need to do is provide the information that answers his concern and let him draw his own conclusions. You let him persuade himself.

This technique often works well when you're selling in a domestic environment and have both partners present. When one partner objects to something, don't respond immediately. Average salespeople are quick to defend their offering, jumping in on the comment and addressing it there and then – but those are *average* performers. Top-flight performers sit tight and wait. Often, the other partner jumps in with the next comment and you have a 50/50 chance that the originally silent partner answers the objection for you. If the second partner agrees with his partner's objection, you know you'll have to work a little harder to overcome it. The point is that these two people already have a positive relationship (you hope) and trust each other's judgement. Be quiet while they think it through – often these types of situations involve the prospect thinking out loud, and doing so often causes the objection to evaporate into thin air right before your eyes.

When something important to you is hanging in the balance, being patient is difficult. During such moments, seconds feel like hours and you can quickly become very uncomfortable. However, your strength at keeping shtoom may pay off to the tune of hundreds of extra sales, as very often the two people in front of you will help each other through the handling of the objection – especially if you have done a half-decent job upfront with the creating of a relationship and building rapport with at least one of them. Say nothing and let them answer their own objection.

Never look at your watch or at a clock in the room while you're waiting for a response. Even a slight glance at a timepiece can distract the prospects, because they're already looking at you, waiting for your next move.

Don't argue with your prospect

Although not arguing with your prospect may seem obvious, when you're negotiating with someone, emotions can take over and things can get out of hand. Arguing or fighting against an objection or concern raises a barrier between you and the person you're trying to persuade. You're trying to persuade your prospect to purchase something that should be beneficial for him, not go ten rounds with him. If you keep the perspective that objections are simply requests for further information, you shouldn't find it difficult to stay calm, slow down, and backtrack. Possibly the prospect misunderstood or misinterpreted something you said; whatever – never confront and argue!

Don't minimise a concern

To the person you're persuading, every point he raises is valid. Remember to put yourself in his shoes. How would you react to someone who acts as though your concerns are stupid or unimportant? Treat the comment with respect. Calmly state that you can see why he said that but then apologise for not having made yourself as clear as you should have and tell him that actually the concern is not a real issue, pointing to the features in your offering that resolve it.

Handling Objections in Six Easy Steps

The following sections give you six steps for handling objections or addressing concerns that will almost always work in your favour. They also work pretty well in defusing any unusually tense situations, so heed them well.

Sometimes you'll hear more than one objection or concern from a prospect. If you start running through all six steps with each objection you hear, you can spend a lifetime trying to overcome every objection. Experience helps you tell which concerns you need to address and which you may be able to bypass (see the section 'Bypassing your prospects' objections completely' in this chapter).

If a concern or objection is raised during a group presentation and you have to do a bit of research and get back to them, be certain you have the contact information (specifically, an e-mail address) for each person in the group. You may sometimes struggle with this request but always try. Collecting e-mail addresses takes just a bit longer and a smidgen of extra courage but they'll admire your professional strength and usually you'll get what you ask for. If you don't follow up, then you have to deal through the 'lead' character and just hope that he relays information with a little passion for your offering. If you get the group contact details, send an identical message to each person, and let them all see that they're part of the group e-mail. If each person receives it individually, they could all wonder what else you may have shared with the others.

Outsmart your prospect's last objection

People can voice objections or concerns regarding many things in life. Even when selling yourself, reservations can arise. Ben remembers applying for a job selling industrial air compressor equipment and then being ill on the day of the interview and not being able to make it. He did of course ring in to apologise but felt the company thought it was an excuse. Not to be outdone, he waited until he had recovered and then rang the company to arrange a new interview date. He was passed from a secretary to the sales manager who basically said that he had missed his chance and that the manager was on the verge of hiring someone else. Immediately Ben challenged his statement and said to him that if he was on the verge of hiring someone else it meant he actually hadn't yet done so. He was surprised by this rather bold challenge to a senior sales manager from a 20-year-old kid, but he couldn't lie – and Ben said that he would give the manager the chance to make a better decision by meeting him that afternoon, so that he could hire the best instead of a second choice! He laughed at Ben's cheeky confidence, arranged the interview, and Ben got the job.

Ben merely challenged his objection and cleverly used a loophole in his argument. It worked for him then and it'll work for you now. Try a smarter approach, not a confrontational approach, and win every time.

Identifying and outsmarting the prospect's last objection to what he was selling was a turning point in Ben's life. It can be in yours, too.

Include the link to your company's Web site for each member of the group to peruse. Often in a committee decision-making situation, only one or two members get the whole package of information. They then break the information down for the rest of the decision-makers. This may be the way the *company* wants the process handled, but what *you* want is to get as much information as possible equally distributed.

Step 1: Hear him out

When someone trusts you enough to tell you what's bothering him, do him the courtesy of listening. Don't be quick to address every phrase he utters. Give him time; encourage him to tell you the whole story behind his concern. If you don't get the whole story, you won't know what to do or say to change his feelings. Don't interrupt either; you may jump in and answer the wrong concern.

Step 2: Feed it back

By rephrasing what his concerns are, you're in effect asking for even more information. You want to be certain that he's aired it all so that no other concerns crop up after you've handled this one. You're saying to him, 'Go ahead. Lay it all on me. Get it off your chest.' In doing this, you're asking him to trust you.

Step 3: Question it

Subtlety and tact come into play at this step. If the person objects to the fact that you're asking his team to dress in workwear with logos all over it while operating your machine, don't say, 'What's wrong with it?' Instead, gently ask, 'Does wearing this clothing make you uncomfortable?' If it does, he'll tell you why – maybe he's shy. If so, you have to build his confidence in the respect the uniform generates and in the authority it lends to him as a participant.

Step 4: Answer it

When you're sure that you have the whole story behind someone's concern, you can answer that concern with confidence. As an example, if the prospect's concern is cost, you can engage in the following dialogue:

> SALESPERSON: I can certainly appreciate your feelings. At first glance it might indeed seem like a lot of money; however I can promise you that, as with many of my other clients, you will probably still be using this equipment for another five or six years.
>
> Do you see that as a real possibility?
>
> PROSPECT: Yes, I do.
>
> SALESPERSON: Thus in fact the £1,000 equates to only £200 per year and actually to only £40 a week or just a little over £5 a day. Truthfully, Mr Prospect, do you really feel that you would wish to miss out on these superior benefits for just the price of a newspaper and a cup of coffee?

Reduce the cost difference to a ridiculous amount and the client will probably agree with you. The sum isn't worth fighting about and you've just got the prospect to answer his own concern.

The prospect doth protest too much

If prospects bombard you with objections, you may want to ask a few questions to get them to express their *real* objection. If people protest too much, they're either not interested and don't have the guts to tell you so, or they're hiding the real reason for not going ahead. For some people, liking your offering but being unable to afford it is hard to admit. So instead of admitting that they're strapped, they come up with a hundred other reasons why your product, service, or idea isn't right for them. Indeed you will often get this type of almost aggressive, attacking, objection-ridden meeting when a prospect has heard something bad about your company or offering and is inclined to believe it. He'll constantly throw objections at you based upon his hearsay. Whenever this situation occurs and for whatever reason, you may need to say something like this:

Mr Johnson, obviously you have quite a few concerns about our product. May I ask, what will you base your final decision on: the overall benefits to your family or the financial aspects of this transaction?

Mr Johnson, you obviously have a great many concerns – can I ask you, have you used this offering before and found it to have been a bad choice or has somebody else given you some incorrect information?

Using this approach, you're asking, as is your right, for the real objection to your product or service while still being nice, warm, and friendly. Always bear in mind that you can't move beyond this step in the selling cycle until you identify and handle that real final objection.

Step 5: Confirm your answer

When you've answered the objection, confirming that your prospect heard and accepted your answer is important. If you don't complete this step, the prospect will probably raise that objection again.

You can confirm your answers simply by finishing off with a statement such as, 'So does that answer your concern, James?' If James agrees with you that your comment answered his concern, then you're one step closer to persuading him. If he isn't satisfied with your answer, now is the time to know, not later when you try to get his final decision to go ahead.

Step 6: By the way . . .

By the way are three of the most useful words in any attempt to persuade or convince another person. You use the phrase to change gears and to move on to the next topic. Don't just keep talking. Take a conscious, purposeful step back into your presentation. Pause and then deliberately say something like 'By the way, James, did I show you our optional paper-shredding attachment that comes with our new range of office copier machines?' If doing so's appropriate, turn the page in your presentation binder or booklet, point to something other than whatever generated the objection, and steer ahead. Take some sort of action that signals to the other person that you're forging on and assuming he's happy.

These six steps, if you practise and apply them properly, will take you a long way towards achieving your goal of selling to others even when they raise objections or concerns.

Chapter 12

Easing the Sale to a Close

In This Chapter

▶ Asking for what you want

▶ Finding out whether your prospects are ready to buy

▶ Using skill and empathy to help your prospects overcome their hesitation

*C*losing is the name originally given to the final part of the sales process, whereupon a salesperson succeeds in getting the prospect to agree to the purchase and sign along the dotted line. While closing is still a separate part of the process and you still are required to get the agreement before you've earned any money, in this chapter we run through a few techniques that you can and should use to ease the prospect gently and gradually towards agreeing. You can use any of these at the end of the process – however, we're not suggesting that you use all of them in a frenzied attempt at closure!

And in this chapter, we share several techniques that help you ease the final choice and assist the prospect to say yes without any ruffle of feathers or friction. Use these techniques only as an integral part of the process; don't throw them out at the end as some sort of outdated pressure close. By using these techniques with skill as part of the whole conversational process, you'll elicit the correct information and steer the prospect's brain along the correct path without her feeling pushed.

Closing as a Step in the Process

Closing was seen by slick 1980s-era salespeople as a polished trapping process that they turned on at the end of the sales call. Indeed, heavy-handed closes earned salespeople a reputation for 'hard closing' and 'pressure selling' and gave the whole industry a tainted image. Thankfully these days we've all grown up a little – or a lot in some cases – and if you use these outdated techniques the result is most likely to be no sale. You'll also create a very bad impression and damage your reputation. The objective of the game is still the same, but the techniques have evolved.

Closing is an actual stage of the process in which the mini-agreements you attained all the way through the meeting are formalised and the prospect actually says, 'Yes, let's go ahead', and agrees the terms of payment. The close is the moment in the sales process when you tie it all together. It is the moment when what your client's needs and what you're selling become the same thing and she says 'Yes'.

Closing is also the fun part of the sales process if you view it as a sort of challenge with yourself to see how smoothly you can make the agreement process happen. In an ideal world, the sales process is so smooth that the client feels as if she purchased, instead of being sold to, and that the purchase was the most natural thing in the world.

Closing – defined as succeeding in getting an agreement – is an ongoing part of the whole and is integral from the first moment of the selling process. You must work on closing the sale from the moment you first contact any prospect, when you first meet her or engage her directly on the telephone. That's just a given in the world of selling.

But unless you specifically guide the process, you will be sitting there hoping for a yes, and waiting a long time. Sadly, most prospects, even when they've said they love everything about you and your offering, don't lean forward and eagerly ask to pay you large sums of money! You still need to *ask*, and that means you need to know exactly *how* best to ask, and to read the signs that tell you *when* is best to ask.

In closing, the end is in the beginning

As we mention on several occasions, closing the sale starts at the beginning of the transaction, when you *first* make contact with your prospect. If you're weak on making that initial contact, on qualifying, on handling objections, on presentations, or on any other area of the sales process, or if you're generally poor at asking pertinent questions, no matter how great a salesperson you think you are, you're costing your prospect, yourself, and your company a lot of money, time, and aggravation.

First impressions last, unfortunately, and from the moment you approach or talk to a prospect, the selling begins. If the relationship starts off badly, turning it around at the end in a 'closing' style will be hard if not impossible. Effort and practice are needed to improve the sequence of your selling process and your success rate. No one closes every sale, but just think how much better you can become when you put your best effort into it.

A perfect ending needs a perfect beginning.

The bottom line with selling and actually getting the agreement is very simple – if you don't ask, you don't get!

After you get past being nervous and you've done it a few times, we assure you that you won't have any fears about the end going wrong and losing the sale. You'll know way before the end whether you are in tune or not, and the chances are high that if you don't have the sale by the time you're wrapping up your presentation, you won't win it with a few slick words at the end.

Recognising That Sometimes Asking Is Enough

Salespeople are often uncomfortable if they have to go beyond simply presenting the offering. If a prospect doesn't quickly see the value and jump right in to own it or to participate in some way, a salesperson may start to lose confidence. Very often the salesperson doesn't feel able to proceed with strength unless she receives hugely positive feedback – possibly coupled with ooohs and aahs or other such utterings of delight! These salespeople lack confidence if the offering isn't endorsed and embraced fairly quickly. And this wavering of confidence weakens the salesperson's desire to close the sale. In other words, the salesperson doesn't ask for the order, call for a decision, or otherwise try to get a commitment from the prospect. Indeed unless the client or prospect says outright, 'Can I have one, then?', a lot of potential sales go by the wayside.

Numerous surveys have asked people who weren't persuaded to buy during a sales visit why they didn't go ahead with whatever it was they were offered. Interestingly enough, the most common answer was that (drum roll, please) *they were never asked*. The prospects were contacted, a product or service was demonstrated to them, and their questions (or objections or concerns) were answered. In some cases, they were convinced of the value of the offering and probably would have gone ahead, but nothing happened – the salespeople didn't ask the prospects to make a commitment or to part with their money, so they didn't.

Don't ever let the fact that you didn't ask someone to make a buying decision be the reason a prospect doesn't go along with you.

In the following sections, we give you several ways to confirm your prospect's level of interest.

Try a trial close

Knowing when to ask is just as important as doing it in the first place. Often salespeople are trained to ask at a specific time – after they've run through everything else in their scripted procedure – which means they feel they should explain *all* of the benefits, examples, variations, and features. In covering everything, they go way past the point of interest when the prospect was 'hot' and they actually lose a sale. The right time to ask passes them by. To get past this timing challenge, you need to learn how to gauge a prospect's buying temperature.

One way of checking your prospect's readiness to buy is by asking an ownership question such as the following:

> As a matter of interest, if everything we've discussed here makes sense and we can see that your company would benefit from the Whizzbang Software approach, when would be an ideal delivery time frame for you?

Because you're asking an ownership question, soften it by beginning with 'As a matter of interest'. This opening is much easier for the prospect to hear than a more in-your-face question such as 'When do you want this, then?'. However, it does convey the impression that you are serious about asking for the order if you're able to show her the benefits she's looking for. This approach uses the wonderful formula, 'If I could . . . would you . . . ?'. Using these words is a brilliant way to tweak pressure but also to let her know that you're making the process a two-way street: you're trading a giving of something that matters to her for a taking of something – her money.

If the prospect answers such a question enthusiastically in the affirmative, she's probably ready to go ahead. For example if she replies, 'Well, yes, actually I have already given this some thought and wondered if you could have a delivery set up for the end of this month,' you are almost certain of an order and in fact if you don't close that sale something is seriously wrong. She was asking to buy! She's thought about it and even come up with a date. Although this example isn't the most common response – more often a customer tries to avoid directly committing to a date as she's aware that doing so indirectly gives consent to purchase. However, the direct question will probably unearth another indirect excuse from the prospect as to why she should give the purchase decision some thought – and stall. If such a question brings up another concern or hesitation, then she's probably not ripe yet to make a commitment and you've got some work still to do. This strategy is commonly referred to as the *trial close*.

When you gently ask your prospect for the order in this way, you are in fact using an indirect question to line up a direct question. You are confirming your suspicion that she is in agreement and allowing her to gently slide into a yes rather than making a bold admission of her intention to buy. Most people like to be eased in rather than forced to shout out, 'Yes!'

Give your prospect alternatives

Using the *alternative choice strategy* involves giving your prospect two choices, both of which advance the sale. No matter which option your prospect chooses, the sale moves forward, because you haven't given her the option of saying no. Giving your prospect positive choices helps her focus better on what would be best for her – and that's what you really want, isn't it? For example:

> SALESPERSON: Mrs Hall, which delivery date would be best for you: the 8th or the 13th?
>
> MRS HALL: I'd need to have it in my warehouse by the 10th.

What happened in this exchange? As long as the salesperson can meet that delivery date, she closed the sale. If Mrs Hall is uncertain, she'll raise an objection here or try to change the subject.

Another example of the alternative choice:

> SALESPERSON: Julia, would you be the one trained on the use of the new system, or would you want someone else to be involved?

When Julia tells the salesperson whom to train, she knows that she's going ahead with the sale.

You need to make these types of questions a part of your everyday language. You always want to ask angled questions that close down your customer's escape routes when you are in the process of persuading her to own or endorse what you are offering.

Alternative choices, where either way you win, are also key components because they subtly advance your message without a potentially offensive direct push. Posing such a question tells the other party that you want her to own, that you believe ownership is good for her, and that you need to be directly told to stop before you will. The prospect hears and gets the message that you want the order without feeling that you are pushing. She usually comes out with a sentence or avoidance gambit that tries to lead you away, but of course you gently ignore that comment and leave the semi-commitment that 'Yes, next Wednesday would be fine for an initial site visit' in her mind.

Ideal topics to use in the alternative choice strategy include questions about delivery variables, package options, payment terms, people-matching scenarios, or even colours, sizes, and model variations. Wherever a choice exists, offer one and the answer either way is a mini-agreement to own.

Whatever happens in any given scenario, using the alternative choices style well is a very powerful technique throughout the meeting process. Consider each alternative carefully so as to gently take the prospect with you rather than force her along. You are offering a choice, remember, an alternative, not an ultimatum!

Make a deliberate mistake

A *deliberate mistake* is an intentional error you make to test how serious the prospect is about going ahead with the sale. If the prospect doesn't correct you, you may have missed some information along the way that would have told you she wasn't serious. If she does correct you, her buying temperature is heating up. In this kind of test, all you want to do is take your prospect's buying temperature to see if it's warm enough to go ahead.

For example, Greta is trying to sell a conservatory to John and Cathy in their home, and during her demonstration Cathy tells John, 'Darling, my mother is coming in July, so if we decide to do anything, it makes sense to have it finished by then.' Many salespeople would ignore that remark or regard it as an interruption. But the champion salesperson hears that comment and remembers it. Later, at the close, Greta may smile at Cathy and have the following exchange, deliberately using an apparently accidental mistake:

GRETA: I can see that you're excited about this new conservatory. Now, your mother is coming in August, isn't she?

CATHY: No, in July.

GRETA: So if a two-week installation process is necessary, the first week in June would be the best time to get started?

CATHY: Yes.

GRETA: Okay then, let me make a note of that on the order form.

Greta *knew* that Cathy's mother was coming in July, but she asked whether her mother was coming in August because she knew Cathy would correct her. Then, when Cathy offered the correct answer, Greta could lead smoothly into the best time to begin with the conservatory installation, getting one step nearer to that final close.

You can use the erroneous conclusion test on almost anything. For example, Cathy may have said to John during the presentation, 'I think I'd like sliding patio doors leading into the garden.' Later, Greta can use that line for a deliberate mistake test:

> GRETA: Let's see. You said you wanted double French doors to lead onto the garden.
>
> CATHY: No! I want sliding patio doors.
>
> GRETA: Oh, yes, that's right. Let me make a note of that.

This technique allows the prospect to talk herself into buying by using her own pressures – Mother's visit – to speed the process, or the correct details – sliding doors – to move her forward.

The purpose of this method isn't to tell a lie or trick the customer and we never recommend using it in that way. The deliberate accidental mistake is simply a test for you to determine whether the prospect is sincere in moving ahead. After all, the prospect wouldn't correct you if she weren't interested. If you're at all uncomfortable with this method, however, don't use it.

And, getting the customer involved through a deliberate mistake isn't fool-proof – some customers will see your errors as proof that you weren't listening. Such questions can actually put off some detail-minded individuals who are proud of their attention skills and the fact that they never get it wrong!

Like many things, a deliberate mistake can be useful when used in the right way at the right time, but don't overdo it. Using it just once or twice can give the prospect sufficient time to indicate her degree of intent without destroying your reputation and credibility.

Try a porcupine or a rebound shot

Porcupines are small animals covered in spines to prevent prey eating them. Thus, if someone tossed a prickly porcupine at you, what would you do? Instinctively, you'd probably either jump out of its way or catch it and quickly toss it back. You can use a method of questioning in much the same way. When your prospect asks you a question, you throw it straight back in the form of another question about that question.

The real power in selling is in pulling with questions.

Here's an example of the rebound or porcupine method in action at a car dealership. A young woman walks into a car showroom possibly looking to purchase a convertible. Suddenly she stops, points at a car, and says, 'This is the convertible I'm interested in. Do you have it in red?' The average salesperson would answer her by saying, 'If we don't have it in red, I can call around and get one for you in a hurry.' Nearly everybody in a selling role believes that answering the person when you can truthfully give an answer is the best way to give her what she wants and that only by giving the person what she wants can you sell. Not so. This approach is not in fact the best way to handle such a direct question. Actually, this answer merely allows the prospect to say, 'Oh, great, thank you', and carry on walking – quite possibly to another car showroom where they do in fact have one in red!

Unlike the average salesperson, the champion salesperson answers the customer's question in one of two ways:

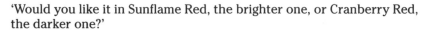

> 'Would you like it in Sunflame Red, the brighter one, or Cranberry Red, the darker one?'
>
> Or
>
> 'I'll have to take a look at the stock sheet. Can I just ask, is it a red car with a black roof or do you want the roof to be red too?'

How is the customer going to respond to the salesperson's question? She's already said that she's interested in the convertible and she wants it in red, so she'll probably choose one colour or the other or say 'a black roof is fine'. Either way, she has taken a little more ownership and the possibility of her buying that car is narrowed provided you can give her what she wants. The salesperson is now one step closer to getting the customer's autograph on that dotted line and having her drive away happily in her new Sunflame Red convertible.

Notice that while her question rebounded back to her, it also involved an alternative choice so that she was eased into a statement that said, 'I want a Sunflame Red car with a black roof', without her actually saying those exact words.

You can then also add in an 'If I could . . . would you . . . ?' question such as, 'If I could get you a Sunflame Red model with a black roof, would you be looking to take immediate delivery?'. (See the section 'Using Closing Questions and Statements'.) This question very quickly gets to the point and the client will either say when she is looking for delivery, in which case you have a serious and ready prospect, or start pouring out objections, in which case you may well have a dreamer walking through your lunchtime! Selling a car would be nice, but even nicer is knowing where you stand, and direct but skilful questions sift out the wheat from the chaff and leave you handling a genuine enquiry.

CHAMPION STRATEGY #1

Knowing when to go for the close

The crucial question in any selling situation is, 'When should you close the sale?' A certain electricity is in the air when the prospect is ready to go ahead with the close. *You* will feel it and actually she will too if you've done the job right. Nearly everyone *likes* to buy when they have their heart set on something; they love to have something new. When they're on the edge of the right purchase, their excitement creates a buzz in the air. At this exact moment, the sale is ripe for closing and sealing. Here are some positive buying signs to watch for:

- **The prospect has been moving along smoothly, and suddenly she slows the pace down and says something like 'let me just get this straight'.** She's making her final analysis or rationalising the decision and organising the money in her head so that she knows everything's fine before she says anything.

- **The prospect speeds up the pace.** She's excited to move ahead.

- **The prospect suddenly starts asking lots of questions.** Like anyone else, she asks questions only about things that interest her. These questions are telling you she's working out the reasons why she should have your offer, so keep her flowing your way.

- **The prospect asks questions about general terms of purchase before settling on one particular model.** Some people immediately start asking questions about initial investment, delivery, and so on. They feel safe doing this because they know you can't sell them everything. But if they ask these questions after you know exactly what they want, take it as a good sign.

If you notice any of these positive signs, test the waters. If you think that your prospect is ready to close the sale, ask a test question to make sure you're reading her correctly. Use a question that suggests involvement or ownership to see whether she's leaning one way or the other. Knowing early, when you have time to still make an impact, is better than right at the end, when you probably don't have the time to do anything about it. When you ask this question (from which you expect an answer confirming that the prospect wants to go ahead with the purchase), one of two things will happen:

- The prospect will give you a yes or an answer that indirectly confirms her desire to go ahead with the sale.

- The prospect will give you an objection or ask for more information to enable her to make a decision.

Don't start talking before she answers. You want to be sure to get either a confirmation to go ahead or an objection. If you get the former, you can go ahead with the close. If you get the latter, you need to answer the prospect's questions and address her concerns (see Chapter 11 for more information).

Using Closing Questions and Statements

The closing process goes on throughout your presentation, but the actual final agreement needs to be verbalised and payment terms chosen. So an actual closing stage does exist when you need to be more direct. And, as you might expect, your prospects aren't simply going to say yes all the time, no matter how well you follow our guidance and use all of the techniques we suggest.

Unless what you're selling is the latest and greatest and everyone has to have it, you're likely to hear the word 'No' quite frequently. In fact, the average consumer will say 'No' or 'Never' to a new product or service approximately five times before she'll give it serious consideration (which means she says 'Yes'). If you, as a salesperson, only know one or two ways to ask for her business, you'll run out of reasons to ask for a yes before she runs out of reasons to say no.

Take and keep proper notes! You'll never accurately remember everything she's said or that you asked if you don't help yourself with notes. Don't be shy about using a notepad to record pretty comprehensive notes. Take as many notes as possible to make sure you remember all of the facts when you get back to the office. Your desire to take good notes shows the prospect that you're a professional salesperson who knows how to get things done.

You have to be very astute at discerning the right moment and saying the right thing and be equipped and prepared to handle some objections that only come out when you are more direct. The following sections offer some techniques you can use.

The straightforward approach

When you're talking with your prospects in person, you have the perfect opportunity to close the sale through your conversation. We are great believers in simply stating a direct question. By this point you've been with the prospect some time and developed a rapport with her, and she's feeling warm towards you. So even if her answer is no, it won't hurt and will probably be qualified with a reason as to why the answer is no, which is wonderful news when selling because then you know exactly what you need to work on to get the sale.

Following are two examples of simple closing statements:

'Mary, I'm excited to help you take a major step towards financial independence. Shall we go ahead with the policy as we've discussed?'

Or

'Paula, as you can see we have included in the package all the additional items that you requested, which strictly speaking as you recall are non-standard. And we have arranged it to be paid for as a one-off over six months. Is this the package that you are happy with? [You get a nod of the head and a yes while pointing at the piece of paper signifying the package.] So, shall we do it like that, then? [still pointing at the package]'

If you know everything is right and that all the cards are on the table, go ahead and ask for the order. Don't keep selling – that's one of the biggest mistakes novice salespeople make. They don't always recognise when they can close; they simply continue to talk, or re-demonstrate the product, or even change the subject while flapping around and waiting for the client to say, 'Can I buy one, then?'

When you've built up a rapport and have used several trial closing scenarios to get to the stage where you genuinely believe from her actions and words that she's interested, you can never do better than to just come right out with a direct, 'Do you want to buy it as we've discussed, then?' This statement demonstrates a natural confidence, and unlike many who are slightly afraid and wish to skirt around an issue, it shows your strength and commitment. Clients like that show of strength and respond with an agreement.

The sharp-angle close

A sharp angle, as the name suggests, is a little more direct in its delivery, as it leads more directly to the yes you are seeking. As with any sharp item, though, be careful how you use it or it could cut you. You don't want blood on the sales floor!

Essentially a sharp angle is a very direct response. It doesn't skirt gently around to asking for an order but cuts straight to the point.

This technique is very powerful when the moment is right, and can be damaging when it's not. Indeed a strong buyer who challenges you on some delivery or payment terms, for example, sometimes creates the opportunity to use the sharp-angle close. It is entirely possible that your prospect will, in essence, throw down the gauntlet and challenge you to give her exactly what she wants. The key here is to accept the challenge – but with the understanding that if you can come through, you win by getting the sale, and she wins by owning the product or service just the way she wants it. You throw back a response that isn't a yes, it is an 'If I could . . . would you . . . ?', which is a more direct or sharper-angled approach.

For example, your prospect may ask you an assumptive question, a question that assumes that she'll buy your product or service. What do you say in response? Answer with a question that shows that, in her own mind, she has bought your product or service:

> MRS STEWART: If I decide I want this boat, can you handle delivery by May Day?
>
> SALESPERSON: I'm not 100 per cent sure at present. Please let me go and find out. If I can guarantee delivery by May Day, are you saying to me that you'd like to order it immediately and plan delivery arrangements?

The salesperson is still guiding the prospect towards what she wants to do: buy a boat.

The average salesperson would be tempted to jump in and say yes, whether or not she could 'handle that' and probably get very excited because she's in front of a seemingly serious buyer. However, 'Yes' is *not* the best response from a salesperson at this point. Asking a sharper-angled closing question in return tests the client's validity. After all, why ask about delivery if she isn't serious and, if delivery is possible, then why shouldn't she buy as she mentioned it as the only criteria needing clarification.

If you are not sure as to delivery schedules or whatever else has been raised, then phrase your answer to allow you to check. Do not say it is okay if you haven't checked, but combine the option for you to check with a question that says to the customer that she's ready to buy subject to that one criterion.

Then you remain silent until Mrs Stewart answers. Remaining silent is important here. Generally you want to keep the focus upon the customer and as she asked the first question, she is the one who needs to answer first. Do *not* butt in if she's quiet – you'll lose the sale. Keep your lips sealed until she responds and then deal with her response. If her response is a simple 'Yes', all you need to do is offer congratulations on her excellent choice and a cup of tea while you go and check exact delivery schedules.

You must play this game even if you know the exact answer to the customer's question. Whether you know or not, the question isn't about the point the customer raises, it is about whether the customer is ready and serious enough to buy.

Many apparently serious buyers will come your way and will ask similar questions, and you may be deadly sure that a sale is about to happen. Then if you break the rules and answer yes to the enquiry, the buyer walks away! You must use this technique if a customer asks about specific criteria, so that you can determine if she's a serious buyer. Sadly, many aren't!

To use the sharp-angle method, your prospect must first express a demand or desire that you can meet. (Although the example here uses delivery, you can sharp angle many other demands or needs besides delivery.) For you to use your prospect's own demand as your way to get to a yes, always remember that sharp angling involves two pivotal points:

- ✔ You must be able to clarify the uncertain criteria there and then in order to get the sale.
- ✔ You must not speak first after throwing back the sharper-angled response.

Be aware that sharp angling can be hazardous to your selling health: A dangerous part of the sharp angle is that you may be tempted to apply it before you've gathered enough qualification information or before you've built enough rapport. Do *not* use the sharp angle too early in the selling process. If you sharp angle too soon, you may offend some people, because the method can be interpreted as overly aggressive. However, if the prospect's thinking and the rapport you have with her are in good shape, the sharp angle is a wonderful way to get agreement as soon as you feel that you have gelled and can gauge the customer's level of intent.

You can also use a softer response to determine the level of intent and set up a sharper-angled approach by using something like the following dialogue:

PROSPECT: Can you get it for me in red?

SALESPERSON: I may be able to. I'll have to check, but before I do can I ask, is everything else to your liking?

PROSPECT: Yes.

If the prospect answers yes, you can use a sharp angle such as:

SALESPERSON: Okay, well let me go and check if we can get a red one for you. Can I also just clarify that if I can get red, then you'd like to take one with you today?

If the prospect responds that she may buy but still needs more information, you have more work to do and the challenge isn't a colour choice, it is whether she actually wants the item or not. If this is the answer you hear, then get back into rapport building and understanding how best to suit your offering to the prospect's needs and wants.

Before you ask, 'If I could . . . would you . . . ?' you must be absolutely sure that you can deliver your product or match the criteria that has the sale hanging upon it. Creating a 'subject to me being able to do that' type of criterion is excellent if you know you can deliver, but disaster if you cannot, so check before committing.

The higher authority close

This scenario is a very effective tool to keep in your selling toolbox. It isn't highly technical and doesn't demand lengthy debates or reams of paperwork, it merely does what it says on the tin – uses a higher authority to create an environment conducive to attaining a yes.

The *higher authority* must be exactly that – someone who's respected by and known to the prospect or at least perceived to be known, such as your boss. (The prospect will assume the existence of your boss even though they probably have not yet met or spoken.) The prospect doesn't have to know the higher authority personally, but she must know of the higher authority's existence and position.

The method essentially relies upon you using the sharp angle as in the preceding section, then checking with the higher authority about the criteria the customer is questioning.

The way in which you use this situation is the key to its effectiveness. Many people older than, say, 25 years of age have seen and heard of numerous sales scams. One that was highly prominent in the 1980s was using the telephone to ring a manager. Thus if you were to say, 'I just have to call my manager', nearly every buyer older than 35 would smell a rat and assume that you don't in fact have a genuine need to call the manager. You may well lose a sale in that instance because of fear of a perceived scam. Thus you need to exercise care with this scenario.

A very real danger also exists that you'll expose yourself to the prospect saying, 'You can go away and check with the manager and call me another day,' which is disastrous because it effectively elbows you out of the hot moment when she's almost ready to buy.

To use a higher authority effectively you need to have some confidence that in fact you can obtain what you're about to ask permission for. Perhaps you're about to ask permission for a sizable sales discount, but you know that when you asked in the past your request was granted. Or you may be asking for a special delivery concession or non-standard payment terms. Provided that you're sure you can get this agreed to, you can proceed. If you set this scenario up as a given and then cannot get permission, you've shot yourself in the foot!

We use the example of your manager, but it could in fact be anyone relevant to the question raised by the client. For example, if a client looking to buy software from you wants to know its compatibility with her existing system, you may need to check with a technician. Thus you would set up the sale with the prospect by saying, 'If I can get assurance that the two software programs will work together, then are you prepared to go ahead with the purchase?' You set up the call with a technician to confirm the issue at the relevant time and seal the order. (You know from pre-visit research what potential scenarios you might come up against. Prepare for these so that you have a technician at hand.)

Ultimately you use the higher authority to confirm that the prospect's special request is in fact allowable. And by making it allowable, the prospect is positioned so that she can now only agree to the sale. If the request obviously is something trivial, the prospect will expect you to know the answer. You'll lose favour if you appear to be less than competent.

You can also use the testimonials of satisfied or prominent clients as a higher authority. Instead of setting up your manager or your technician to answer a crucial question on the telephone, you set up the chance to call an influential client and allow her to be the authority. To set up such a scenario, you might say, 'If I can arrange for you to speak with one of our existing clients who experienced the same doubts and apprehensions as you and can maybe see it from your perspective, would that be helpful?' Refusing this call would be unreasonable if she is at all serious, so the answer will always be a yes. You then make the call that you already set up before your sales visit.

Overcoming Your Prospect's Stalls and Fears

When you're closing sales, you may encounter situations in which your prospects stall for time or hide behind a wall of fear. So in the following sections, we show you exactly how you can help the prospect work through that fear so that she has no more objections or concerns – and you can close the sale.

> ## Close with empathy
>
> *Empathy* is understanding another person's feelings, thoughts, and motives, and is vital in the world of selling. When you have empathy for your prospect, you put yourself in her shoes. You know and feel what your prospect is feeling – which means you know exactly how to proceed based on the information the prospect has given you.
>
> Until you develop empathy for your customers, you probably won't make it in selling. Your prospects need to sense that you understand and care about helping them solve their problems, not think that you're just out looking for a sale. As a professional salesperson, you must truly believe that you can satisfy the prospect's needs. You must see the benefits, features, and limitations of your product or service from your prospect's view; you must weigh things on the prospect's scale of values, not your own; and you must realise what is important to the prospect.

If you frequently come up against these forms of resistance, you need to be rehearsed at dealing with them and pull them out of the prospect early in the conversation. If they're common and to be expected, then you need to strategically raise the point for discussion early, preferably using a story to illustrate the scenario and defuse the objection before it becomes a sticking point. Actually the prospect isn't voicing a real objection – one that means she cannot go ahead – she's just expressing a fear response to help her not buy now. You need her to buy now as this is the time when her emotions and involvement are highest and so you must develop ways to overcome these fear responses and push ahead for a successful sales conclusion.

Using a simple pros and cons approach

This decision-making strategy – in which you make a list of the positives and negatives surrounding a choice – has been used by great leaders for centuries to help negotiate treaties and international deals, and it can be used just as effectively in any sales environment. Indeed, whenever you have to make a decision yourself you weigh up the pros and cons, you look at all of the points in favour and all of the points against, and you make an informed, balanced choice. Thus using this simple approach with a prospect feels natural and reasonable, and consequently can be very successful.

Here's an example of a situation in which a salesperson uses this approach with Kevin and Karen Smith in a car showroom:

> SALESPERSON: Do you think that the new family saloon is the right vehicle for your everyday life and can you see that this is a very special offer price?

KEVIN [hesitant, non-committal]: Well, you know it is a great car but I'm really not sure. I don't know that I'm ready to make a decision on this right now.

The salesperson has asked a lot of questions up to this point, and now she's ready to put the answers to work for her in order to close the sale. She can see that Kevin and Karen really don't want to make the final decision. They're impressed with the car but something is holding them back and they're trying to avoid committing to the purchase. In other words, they are behaving like typical buyers. This is a perfect opportunity for the pros and cons decision-making process.

SALESPERSON [calm, determined to help Kevin and Karen to make the decision they want to make, to help them make the best decision for them]: Could it possibly be, Karen and Kevin, that the problem is that you haven't had a chance to weigh up the facts involved?

KEVIN [nodding, open to reason]: Yeah, I don't think we've really sat down and talked about what is best for us at this time.

SALESPERSON: Well, a decision is only right when you have made a balanced choice and considered all of the pros and cons, don't you agree?

KAREN [seeing the wisdom of the salesperson's reasoning]: Yes, I think that's probably true.

SALESPERSON [reflective and sincere]: Clients often find making a choice challenging as it is something they don't do every day. What I have found to be genuinely helpful is simply making a list of all the good and bad points on a piece of paper and then looking at them to see which side wins. Would it be okay with you if we tried it now just to get a feel for the facts influencing your decision?

The important thing here is to keep the conversation flowing. After you master this strategy, you'll know how to weave this story into any conversation.

SALESPERSON: If a decision is the right thing to do, we want to be sure to go ahead with it. If it is wrong, we want to be sure to avoid it. So why don't we very quickly try to pull apart the choices and see what's best for you?

KEVIN AND KAREN [as one voice]: Okay, yeah, let's do that.

SALESPERSON: Great. So let's get a piece of paper and make some notes. The reasons in favour of the new vehicle go on one side, and all those against go on the other side. Then you can add up the columns and the right decision should be clear. We have time, don't we? It'll take us just a couple of minutes.

KEVIN: Yeah, okay.

The salesperson has a long list of things Kevin and Karen like about the car because she's made notes on every positive comment they've made since they walked into the showroom. If Kevin and Karen run out of positives off the tops of their heads, the salesperson can remind them of those on her list.

When you make note of each item, do it with a tick. But don't write down their actual reasons. You're just tracking how many there are now. If you start writing each one out, this strategy takes longer and the prospects start weighing each reason against the others.

SALESPERSON [waits a beat for Kevin's agreement, then draws a line down the centre of the page she holds in front of her]: Okay, let's start it off here. Let's think of the reasons in favour of the decision. You agree that the car has the right specifications: it's the right size, right engine, right interior specifications. You feel that you'd enjoy driving it around?

KAREN: Yes.

SALESPERSON: And we've already established that, with the right financing, you can actually afford to buy the car because in fact it will only be a little more than your existing payments?

KEVIN AND KAREN [as one voice]: Right.

SALESPERSON: You said that you wanted to have a family-sized car that was not expensive to insure or run, with low service and petrol costs that don't create an extra burden that hadn't been accounted for?

KEVIN AND KAREN [as one voice]: Absolutely.

SALESPERSON: Okay, and we talked about the second-hand value of this model in a couple of years' time. Remember we recognised that you obviously aren't going to keep this car forever and you'll need a good price when you trade it in.

KAREN: [looking at the salesperson, but seeing the future]: Yeah, because in just a few years' time our oldest child will have left home and the youngest will probably have a separate life and not be coming out with us very often.

SALESPERSON: And above all else, you drove it and it felt really easy and comfortable to drive and park. Remember how it felt right to both of you?

KAREN: Yes, it really is a lovely car.

SALESPERSON [counting the positives]: Okay, well let's see; that's five major pluses. Can you think of any others?

KEVIN: Well, I must admit that because I tend to drive a lot more than Karen I really do need something more comfortable because that old car of ours is a bit of a bone-shaker.

SALESPERSON: All right. We'll put that down.

KEVIN: And because it's old now, the chances are it will start breaking down and costing us lots of money.

SALESPERSON: Okay. We'll put that down, too.

KAREN: And to be fair, I really like the safety angle in this new model because these days the roads are a nightmare, and I'd probably feel a lot happier having a newer, safer vehicle.

SALESPERSON: Great. Is there anything else you can think of?

Set a goal for between six and eight items on the plus side. If you haven't reached eight at this point, refer to your notes and remind your prospects of other items to add to this column. When your goal of eight reasons for the decision has been reached, continue:

SALESPERSON [objective, fair]: Now, how many reasons can you think of that might say to you it isn't a good idea?

KEVIN [with a heavy sigh]: Well, let's see. The money! It is a little more than we planned to spend.

SALESPERSON: Okay, what else?

KEVIN: We were really interested in finding a car but probably had thought that we might be able to hang on for another few months. I guess the timing isn't quite what we felt was right and possibly we aren't ready.

SALESPERSON: Those are both valid points, Kevin. Can you come up with any others?

A pause follows, and Karen and Kevin aren't coming up with any more concerns. They've just told the salesperson, bottom line, exactly what will keep them from owning this particular car. She doesn't even have to answer those objections at this point, because what she's looking for is a clear desire on the part of Kevin and Karen to own this particular car. When that decision is made, she'll work on the financial details of how they can own this vehicle, so she says:

SALESPERSON: All right. Why don't we just add these up?

She shows them the list and together they count aloud. Afterwards, she announces the results: 8 pros, 2 cons.

SALESPERSON: Karen, Kevin, don't you think the answer is rather obvious?

Expect to wait through a long silence after you pose this question. The key here is to shut your mouth and not do or say anything that takes away from your request for a decision. Your prospects will do one of three things:

- ✔ They will try to stall, put off making the decision by asking for more time or asking a question to change the subject.

- ✔ They will decide to go ahead.

- ✔ They will give you an objection.

In this situation, a silence pervades the room for some time while Kevin and Karen think their decision over. Finally, Kevin replies:

> KEVIN: I'll tell you something. We're the kind of people who really need to think it over.

He's stalling, which can be frustrating. Fortunately, Kevin is providing the best stall, because you can pretty easily get around it. The 'time to think it over' just means they need to come to terms with spending the money. Except for rare occasions when the customer doesn't like the product and hasn't told you the truth, a stall is about the money! When you're faced with a stall like this, consider using the story in the next section to move past it.

Getting past a vague stall to a concrete final objection

So how do you handle a situation in which the prospect absolutely insists on thinking it over? Continuing the story from the preceding section, where Kevin and Karen are thinking about investing in a new car, here's how the salesperson proceeds:

> SALESPERSON: That's fine, Kevin. Obviously, you wouldn't take the time to think it over unless you were seriously interested, would you?
>
> KEVIN [reassuring, but committed to the stall]: Oh, we're interested. We just really need to think about this before we decide.
>
> SALESPERSON [trying to keep communication open]: Just to clarify my thinking, what is it about the deal that you want to think over? You mentioned that the timing might not be right – tell me your thoughts on the timing.

Kevin and Karen answered in favour of every benefit and that they like the arrangement except for the money issue and the timing. In this case the money and the timing mean the timing of the money! The deal is to be financed in some way, so they may be worried about their creditworthiness for a loan or their overall monthly budget.

> SALESPERSON: Well, could it be the financing or the timing of the payments?
>
> KAREN [as though offered a life raft]: Well, actually we also have a payment each month for a new three-piece suite that still has six payments to run, and to be truthful, this new car payment was really not planned until we finished paying for the sofa.

Now the salesperson has a concrete idea of what specifically is the hurdle between herself and the close. In this scenario, it now is really easy to close the sale and reach agreement. All the salesperson has to do is say something like the following:

> SALESPERSON: So, Kevin and Karen, what you're saying to me is pretty understandable. There isn't a lot of money to go around and frankly you have to budget carefully. Can I just clarify that what you're saying is that the payments for the car are affordable and that you want to buy this car, it's just that the payments for the sofa don't allow for both. You can pay for the car when the sofa payments finish?
>
> KEVIN AND KAREN [relieved and grateful for the understanding]: Yes.

As the salesperson, you then simply allow them to have the 'pay nothing for six months' option that you always had as a variable in the finance package. Remember that you deliberately do not say yes to a question and deliberately do not tell all that you know. Holding something back allows you to get agreement on the car purchase 'except for the payments' and now you can remove that objection and secure a deal – a deal, incidentally, that Kevin and Karen will be extremely relieved and pleased to make! You've now done your job, made some money, and genuinely helped out the clients!

Always remember that the 'I want to think it over' line is a stall. You use it yourself when you're on the customer side of a selling situation, so why shouldn't you expect to hear it from others when you're doing the persuading? Don't give up or convey the impression that they are wasting your time. Just keep cool and smoothly come at the decision from another angle – so that everyone wins.

Responding to 'it costs too much'

When you isolate a money objection as the obstacle to final agreement, the following technique is ideal. This tactic helps both you and the customer see the big pound signs she's afraid of in much smaller, easier-to-handle numbers.

To show you this technique at work, here are Karen and Kevin in the car showroom again:

> KAREN: I just feel that this car costs too much.
>
> SALESPERSON [ever in search of specific obstacles to yes]: Yep! Tell me about it! Doesn't everything these days? Out of interest, when you say 'too much' how much too much do you feel it is?

Salespeople tend to look at the total investment when they hear 'it costs too much', but this tendency usually spells trouble. Instead of addressing the total cost, go for the *difference*. If your prospect plans to spend £20,000 for a car, and the car she's looking at is £22,000, the problem isn't £22,000 but £2,000.

> KAREN: We really wanted to spend around £18,000, and I don't feel that we can go as high as £21,000.
>
> SALESPERSON: So, Karen and Kevin, what we're really talking about is £3,000, aren't we?
>
> KEVIN: £3,000. Yes, I guess that's correct. It's about £3,000 more than we wanted to spend.

Now the salesperson has got Kevin and Karen to admit that the real problem they're having is over £3,000. And she's ready to move to the story in the following section, where she shows them just how little money that really is.

Reducing an expense to the ridiculous

When you know exactly what amount of money your prospects are concerned about, you can work with them to help them see how they can handle the amount and have what they really want – the product or service – at the same time. All you have to do is address the new issue of the difference. Here are Kevin and Karen again, in the car showroom:

> SALESPERSON [asking what Karen already knows]: Karen, would I be right in saying that this new car would be an ideal purchase for your family and you'd be very proud and happy owners if the payments were all right for you?
>
> KAREN: Probably. I think it would be a great car – ideal in many ways.
>
> SALESPERSON: Okay, so let's just say that you're going to keep this car for about four years – would you say that's about right?
>
> KEVIN AND KAREN: Four or five years – yeah, that'd be about right.
>
> SALESPERSON: Okay, so let's divide that £3,000 by five years, okay? That's about £600 per year.
>
> KEVIN: Yes.
>
> SALESPERSON: Okay, so then divide the £600 yearly cost by the 50 weeks of the year that you are going to be driving it – and we get just £12 a week. Or less than £2 a day! A couple of pounds to have safety, comfort, reliability, economy, and the wonderful feeling of owning that gorgeous car instead of getting back into that old one – for just a couple of quid! Be honest, just one breakdown or engine problem with your old car and you'll see nearly all of that difference eaten up.

The salesperson has just succeeded in getting Kevin and Karen to see that they're really upset over just a couple of pounds. Pretty ridiculous, isn't it?

Use a calculator when calculating

Champion salespeople always do their calculations with a calculator when selling.No matter how confident you are in your mathematical abilities, always use a calculator. Yes, it is right to know your formulas and figures so that you can quickly provide any numerical information that your prospect may request, but do not do all of your workings out in your head even if you're able to.

A prospect who sees you punch numbers into your calculator – or one who helps you by doing it herself – probably won't question the figures. But if you start furiously scratching numbers on paper with a pen, the prospect gets uncomfortable sitting and watching you. Even worse, if you rattle figures off the top of your head, your prospect may doubt that they're valid and question *your* validity. Instead of paying attention to your presentation, she'll be looking over your shoulder to double-check your sums.

Indeed, not using a calculator could raise doubts about your mathematical abilities. If the prospect finds maths as challenging as sky diving, she'll assume you to be much the same. You don't need the prospect even slightly distracted. Keep all workings out visible, and involve the client so that she remains focused upon the purchase at hand.

Making the indirect comparison

An indirect comparison is a simple and natural way of reducing a price difference to a small amount the customer spends daily on trivial or unnecessary purchases.

When you make an indirect comparison, you help your prospect rationalise having the product, service, or idea you're offering simply by sacrificing, for now, some small luxury that she would certainly give up in order to have a much larger gain. You're simply saying indirectly, 'All you have to do is give up a little of those things to have what we're talking about.'

The salesperson working to get Kevin and Karen a new car applies this strategy to their objection that the car costs £3,000 too much, which was reduced to £12 a week in the preceding section:

> SALESPERSON [giving them something to compare it to]: Kevin, do you and your family buy lemonade and crisps?
>
> KEVIN: Well, yes we do – maybe a couple of bottles of pop and a large pack of crisps per week.
>
> SALESPERSON: Okay. How much do these items cost nowadays?
>
> KAREN: Around £2 for a bottle of pop and probably £4 or so for a large multi-pack of crisps.
>
> SALESPERSON: Yep, so you can easily spend nearly £10 on junk food that probably isn't that important in the grand scheme of things and that your kids wouldn't miss if it meant having a brilliant new car to drive to school

in! Besides the health benefits, do you really think you should let a few bags of crisps and bottles of pop keep you from having a fabulous, safe, and reliable new car?

KEVIN: When you look at it that way, I guess it's a bit silly. It's not actually so much money these days is it?

SALESPERSON: Okay then, so let's get the new car sorted and begin planning who will get to drive it first. By the way, would you prefer to have it delivered or are you happy to collect it?

Obviously we use a scenario as an example, but the pattern is really very simple.

Telling a story

Storytelling is perhaps the most powerful of techniques. We most definitely recommend that you become proficient at storytelling and have a repertoire of great stories that illustrate nearly every potential selling situation. You can then use these tales as appropriate in your sales process.

A well-crafted story relays a tale of how a couple or business similar to your prospect was in a similar situation, found a way out, and successfully became an owner of your offering. After all, what better way to ease your prospect's fears than a story of another person who had all the same concerns and indecisions, but who still decided to buy and now is glad she did? Here's an example of a story you can relate to your clients, based on their fears and hesitations:

Jill, I know you're hesitant about the financial commitment involved in buying a new data management system for your growing business and I fully appreciate why. You know we had a situation recently with a client of ours – Bilby Technical Supplies – struggling to get all of their client data into a manageable system. They'd discovered, like you, that as a company grows and adds more staff, without a specifically designed data management system to organise contacts, details get lost and clients get upset. They couldn't really see that they were regularly losing business in this way. They agreed in theory that a client data management system was a necessity but couldn't really visualise the difference the introduction of our product might make and could only see the investment as a cost.

Well, to cut a long story short, Jill, they took the plunge and committed to letting us help them. It actually wasn't as large a requirement as yours, but we found that when the system was installed and people used it properly they saw a 12 per cent increase in sales in the first six months! Messages weren't getting missed, clients were being followed up, and fewer mistakes occurred, all of which led to more add-on sales that they weren't previously getting! The improvement really was fantastic – as we thought it might be – but it needed a small leap of faith and a little trust before Bill at Bilby Supplies could see the benefits.

My thought, Jill, is very simple: your business is actually an even larger data user, and I promise the benefits will be more visible more quickly. I'd love to see you as happy as Bill is now, so shall we get this sorted? The sooner we get going on it together the sooner you'll see the returns Bill has achieved. Would 12 per cent growth be something you'd like to see?

By ending on a rhetorical question, you assume the answer is 'Yes, I want the growth', and thus she needs to proceed with an order for your data system.

Make notes about the stories you have to tell about your other satisfied clients, and then use these stories when new prospects experience the same situation, as will inevitably happen. Storytelling really is an excellent and powerful way of binding prospects and winning sales.

Creating an edge over their competitors for them

If you're faced with a prospect – especially in a business-to-business environment – who doesn't want to make a decision about your product, service, or idea, you can tell a competitive-edge story to help her along. These stories don't need to be elaborate, and they're not meant to talk your prospects into anything they don't want or need. The stories just remind prospects that they have competitors. They plant a small fear in the prospects that if they don't buy your offering someone else will, and if it actually does what you say it does, then their competitors will use it and gain advantage. And running a business is hard enough without knowingly giving the competitors a winning edge!

A little competitive-edge story like this, for example, works well:

Mrs Brown, do other people also sell what you sell, roughly speaking? Oh, yes I thought so. Our new business phone rates could probably save you several thousand pounds each year – money you could reinvest in out-marketing your rivals. Mrs Brown, would you like to have that competitive edge? Or more importantly, how would you feel if your competitors had it instead?

Prospects are just like anyone else: They need help making decisions. How many things have you been talked into owning that you really didn't want? Probably not very many. Few people get talked into buying something they don't really want. On the other hand, you probably own lots of things that in the first instance you were prepared to not buy or not buy at the time. But you were talked into, nudged gently, or persuaded into buying, and now you are extremely glad you were. Selling to someone isn't a crime.

Is closing good for your customer?

Are closing questions, assumptive statements, and sales-time stories in the best interests of your customers? Is it right to use techniques to gently persuade and encourage prospects to buy instead of just walking away and leaving the decision with them?

Based on experience, the answer is an unequivocal 'Yes'. The two of us have done a lot of selling, and we both always take customers' interests to heart. We know that they'll get the truth from us, as well as great service. But we can't guarantee them truth in selling and excellent service if they go somewhere else.

All along, from early days in selling to today, we've tried to help every consumer have a positive image of the sales industry. We knew that positive image would be there if we gave our customers professional service, and we've always provided it. That's why we worked harder than many associates to consummate sales that were in the best interests of our customers. Obviously we didn't sell them anything they didn't want. However, if all the details were right, we would do everything we could to help our customers get over the hills of fear and procrastination.

If you properly qualify people, you'll know whether they truly have a need or desire for your product or service. If their lives will be better because they own your offering, you can do your best to persuade them into having it. In fact, we'll go one step further: If you believe that what you have is the best, that what you have will help them, and that others do not have such high standards and will not serve the prospects as well as you could, then you have an absolute duty to make sure they purchase from you. It is your job to help them avoid dealing with someone who will sell them an inferior offering or leave them without the enhancements you know you can give them.

Drawing on your own experience, have you appreciated the professionals who have helped you make buying decisions? Have you been happy enough to recommend those people to others? Of course you have! We all have. To become a champion salesperson, set a goal to become someone people will not hesitate to recommend, someone people seek out as an expert in your field. And then everyone – you and your customer – wins.

Problems arise when unscrupulous salespeople lie about what a product is and what it will do. Through deceit, these salespeople violate the buyer's trust and the buyer ends up owning something other than what she thought she was getting. Such salespeople let greed get in the way of their service to customers. Such an approach to selling is the direct opposite of the kind of selling we advocate. *Do not lie – ever!* Stick to the absolute truth and you will always be rewarded. If you put customer service ahead of money, you will *always* come out on top.

Chapter 13

Referrals: The Best Way to Grow Your Business

*F*or many seasoned salespeople, referrals are a major source of new business. Clients who contact you on an existing client's recommendation are usually more inclined than cold-call clients to own your product, service, or idea. Why? Because they already have a positive feeling about you and your offering – and the source of their positive feeling is someone they already know and trust. These *pre-qualified leads* are usually a dead cert inasmuch as the mutual contact you share probably has told the person he referred to you everything about your offering, even the price, and the potential client is still calling you to come round and see him. What they're saying is, 'Come round and I want to buy the same as my friend'.

Pre-qualified referrals, according to some studies, show a 60 per cent closing rate. Compare that impressive figure to a closing rate of 10 per cent with non-qualified non-referrals, and you can see just how much harder you have to work on cold calls. Don't get left out in the cold. When you discover how to be successful at getting referral business, giving all those choice customers to your competitors just doesn't make sense.

Salespeople universally agree that referrals are easier to convince than non-referrals. However, many in selling believe that 'everyone gets referrals' yet at the same time often admit that they 'get the odd one' or 'wouldn't mind having more'. They recognise both the desire for and the lack of referrals and yet don't actively do anything to get more!

Some salespeople think controlling referral business is impossible, so they refuse to give referral methods much attention. Such salespeople take the attitude that attaining referrals is just luck and maintain a 'sometimes-it-happens-and-sometimes-it-doesn't' approach. Don't buy into such thinking for a second. Referrals can be driven, and they aren't just random results. *Professional* salespeople consistently benefit from referral business – so consistently, in fact, that they blow apart the luck theory every day.

Effective ways to benefit from referral business are what this chapter is all about. Here we provide you with a proven, highly effective referral system that can help you produce a much greater number of leads. The system may not work 100 per cent of the time, but even if it works only 50 per cent of the time, it will generate many more selling situations with clients who look forward to finding out about you and your offering.

Never take a referral for granted. As with any other sales technique, method isn't the only factor to consider when trying to get referrals. Salespeople must show referrals the same positive attitude, the same high energy level, the same respectful manner, and the same quality presentation that they show to cold calls. Referrals are only *partially* sold on you or your product – but crucially, they're willing to give you the chance to convince them of how they'll benefit from your offering.

Be warned, though – you can still mess up a referral! If you bowl in to a presentation all arrogant and selfish and pay little or no attention to the person behind the sale or the concerns that he has as an individual, you'll destroy your credibility and lose a source of further referrals as well as the current appointment.

When you're successful and apply the principles advocated in this chapter, referrals just keep on coming. Before you know it, you'll create an endless chain of happily involved clients who want to do whatever they can to contribute to your success.

Where and When Referrals Arise

With qualified referrals having proven successful, you cannot afford to not know how to identify and obtain such a superb source of business and thus to produce a substantial increase in your sales. If you're in a role labelled 'selling', you must drive towards a system that encourages referrals.

You may promote referrals that aren't directly useful to you and what you sell. In conversation with a client or prospect of yours, the business need of another supplier comes up in conversation, and so you have a potential referral situation that isn't for you. You can then pass those referrals on to your suppliers and colleagues. The recipients of these referrals are then inclined to do the same for you. Thus you receive referrals from other suppliers not only your own clients.

One way or the other, then, whether as a source of prospects for your own business or as general public relations, referrals play a key part in your success in sales. Take advantage of every opportunity that presents itself for both receiving referrals and passing them on.

Where you get referrals

Referrals are like flies – always buzzing around you. But unless you swallow one just as you're about to proclaim your undying devotion to a cause, you don't always notice them. You need to be like flypaper and catch all referrals that fly by without them ending up as extra meat portions in your staple diet!

From family and friends

Perhaps the easiest and most accessible referrals are those provided by your family and friends. Now, if you sell rectal thermometers, referrals from close family members may be few and far between! However, family and friends do have all sorts of weird and varied conversations – just because you're not privy to them doesn't mean they don't happen – so make sure that they know exactly what you do. They might not see how they could ever get referrals for you but at least if they fully understand what you do, if and when someone announces that he works in a similar field they can pass on your details.

Through networking

Networking at business conferences, clubs, professional organisations, and religious gatherings is a way to increase your number of referrals. Loads of organised network groups operate within the UK business community and are an excellent place to generate referral business (we discuss networking briefly in Chapter 7).

Networking, though, isn't limited to organised groups and official business communities. Your network is, in fact, all the people you touch and know. Getting referrals can be as simple as mentioning to others what you do or relaying something exciting that happened during your busy week of selling. When you're excited, other people will be too. People are attracted to energetic conversation and happy dispositions – so be a people magnet.

If you're having a particularly great week, share it with the world. Let them enjoy your success! Don't brag – just allow yourself to be exuberant about your accomplishments. Your exuberance will be contagious. Many people enjoy the good news of others and will be genuinely happy to hear that you're really flying high. They'll also remember what you told them well enough to pass on to their contacts, and thus become a great source of referrals. Even if your week has been particularly trying or difficult, ask for the advice of the people you respect. You can use these conversations as a way of getting others interested in your business offerings, too. The next time they see you, they'll want to hear your appreciation of the positive effects their advice had for you.

So what have you done? Through your willingness to share your concerns and victories, you've involved others in your career: Other people now have a vested interest in your future success.

From happy customers

Unfortunately, people remember bad stuff and spread conversation and rumour about mistakes almost ten times more often than they do about good stuff. Ensuring that your sales and service are beyond reproach is thus imperative. Slip up just once, even just a little bit, and visiting your clients and their associates becomes awkward where it was once comfortable. Depending upon the level of error, it is entirely possible that you avoid old clients altogether if a bad reputation precedes you. Honesty and integrity therefore must be first and foremost in your mind if you intend to succeed in business and in life.

Avoid promising the moon and stars within a two-day delivery window unless you can also conjure up spells like Merlin. Getting carried away and telling your client what he wants to hear even when you know your information is inaccurate is all too easy. In the long run, not only will you lose the disillusioned client, but you can also kiss goodbye to all the wonderful referral opportunities he could have steered your way. So, as a good omen for referrals and good practice for business generally, keep your sales pitch straight!

The best time to obtain referrals is when you've just wrapped up the actual sale with the prospect. At this moment, the client is on an emotional high and feeling really good about the whole deal that you have done for him and excited at the pending delivery or start date. Now is the time to strike. If you don't ask for the names and contact information of other people he knows who could benefit from your offering, now when your current client is at his hottest, you really are doing yourself out of a huge chunk of income.

Consider also the psychology of the new client. He's excited or relieved or feeling some emotion related to his purchase, and in this state of raised emotion he actually wants to shout about it. He's buzzing with news so let him stand on his soapbox and tell his world how great his future looks now that you've introduced him to the greatest widget this side of Oz. He wants to shout and you want to let him. Don't cheat your customers out of all their fun by not giving them the referral tools they need to help others help you.

From other salespeople in your field

Thinking of other salespeople in the same or related fields as your enemies is neither necessary nor productive. Believe it or not, thinking of them as a possible source for referral business is much more profitable. For example, if you're in the advertising sales game and you meet a sales representative who is extremely successful selling printing and marketing materials such as flyers that a company can distribute to promote itself, when you think about it your clients buying adverts and his clients buying printed materials have the same aim – to spread their name around. Therefore if you help each other, perhaps even swapping contact details after you sell to a client, then the client of yours is likely to be grateful and you probably get a number of equally warm prospects handed over in return from the printed materials chap.

If your relationship with other salespeople is based on mutual respect, you'll find other salespeople sending clients your way whether you have a formal arrangement to do so or not. Perhaps another salesperson's company is smaller than yours and prefers to handle smaller-sized clients. Bingo! He sends the big clients to you. Or maybe a contact insists on having a feature that your competitor's product doesn't have – and another prospective client is passed over to you (and of course if you can develop this type of arrangement you either reciprocate or you express your gratitude in another previously agreed way to keep the flow flowing).

Of course, returning the favour is only common courtesy. Salespeople at car dealerships or insurance agencies often recommend another salesperson who is better suited to meet a particular customer's needs. After all, if a prospect isn't going to buy from you, you may as well help both a friend in the trade and the prospect by pointing them in a safe direction rather than simply saying goodbye. These people are professionals who have the needs of the client at heart and know they would do him a disservice by handling him ineffectively. They also know the value of giving good service to their fellow salespeople.

Through public-speaking engagements or teaching appointments

Public-speaking engagements and teaching appointments are great opportunities for referral business, especially if you're the professional chosen to give the presentation. When this happens, you're automatically considered the expert in your field. But to really earn the reputation you've been awarded, you'd better be prepared and handle your engagement well. Compare your performance to giving your best sales presentation to an audience of 50 or more potential clients simultaneously. Pretty important, isn't it?

Participate in large public-speaking forums only if you know you can carry it off effectively. Too many people get carried away with the moment of stardom and forget that they're there to build their business, not to audition as a replacement for Jonathan Ross. Prepare well and take some advice. You can find many public speaking tips on the Internet and in books, including *Public Speaking For Dummies* by Malcolm Kushner (Wiley).

At many conferences audience members are asked to fill out a form containing all of their details and encouraged to add comments about what they're looking for in the way of potential partner or supplier assistance. Of course, a description of what they do, who they are looking for as clients, and identification information helps enormously – you can go up to them and collar them in the seminar venue! The forms are then displayed prominently on the back wall for the duration of the conference and everyone and anyone can look for what matches their needs and also identify the person rather than just take away details. Try the same thing whenever you attend a function, if the organisers also like the idea – maybe you'll even get a bonus or some Brownie points. The net result is that everybody who attends succeeds in walking away with genuinely well-targeted contacts and the feeling that it was a superbly helpful event. Maybe you'll be booked for the following year!

When you get referrals

You get referrals when you ask for them. The situation really is that simple, yet you'd be surprised how many salespeople feel awkward asking for referrals. How do such salespeople solve the problem of their awkwardness? They avoid the referral part of the selling situation altogether and in the process cost themselves and their companies a lot of money and lost sales.

Some salespeople try to get referrals by asking their clients, 'Can you think of anyone else who may be interested?' In response, the clients can think of no one who may benefit from the offering and in consequence the salespeople conclude that asking for referral business didn't really work for them.

In reality, it wasn't impossible for these two groups of salespeople to get referrals, it was just impossible to get referrals *using the methods they were using*. Instead of analysing their methods and trying something different, they stopped asking for referrals altogether.

So when do you get referrals? You prepare to get referrals the moment you make contact with someone or even from the moment you mentally plan to meet the person. From the first words he utters, be looking for areas in which you can help the client isolate names and faces that he can give you later (the names, that is, not the faces). Listening well is crucial here – often a rare skill in salespeople! If you truly listen to the prospect, you'll hear all sorts of clues and indicators as to how you can best give and receive referrals.

Good referral business comes from customers with whom you have a good relationship. This situation doesn't necessarily mean that they own your offering. For example, you may have built a good relationship with a past or potential customer who for some reason is unable to own your product at this time. If you've kept in close contact and done a good job in building rapport with the customer, though, he's more than likely willing to steer you towards a business associate who can benefit from your product or service. All you have to do is ask.

Although any time is a good time to get referrals, some specific times provide a better chance than most: just after you've successfully closed a sale and the customer is excited about owning your offering; and the first time he experiences your product or service and is thankful for and satisfied with the result. At either of these two moments, the client is usually more than happy to give you referrals – names of other people who need what the client now owns – because enthusiasm is high and resistance is low.

Don't just plunge in and say, 'Do you know anyone else who might want my product?' If you ask in this way, your client probably won't be able to come up with a name. He's too distracted by his new purchase. You have to *prepare* him in the art of giving good referrals.

Five Simple Steps to Getting Referrals

Gaining a list of referrals isn't that difficult if you do it properly. The following sections describe five critical steps to ensure that when you ask for referrals, you don't simply hear, 'I can't think of anyone now, let me get back to you.'

Each step is outlined in detail, so that you can make this referral system an integral part of your successful selling plan.

Step 1: Time it right and make sure the referrer is sold on you

Getting referrals is all about timing. You won't get much mileage out of asking for referrals when the person you're talking to isn't sold on you or your product yet. Focus on the timing of when you ask.

It isn't critical that the person actually owns your offering, he just has to be 'sold' on you. If he cannot purchase for the time being, he can still be a realistic and effective referral generator if he's enthusiastic about you and what you offer. How will you know this? When will he be 'sold' on you? Look for signs that clearly indicate it. Perhaps he's really interested in you and your hobby that you've been discussing with him and he suggests that you share social time together along those lines. Or you might hear him invite you to a function that's clearly not a specific requirement but is an offer of friendship. The meeting shifts and takes on a more friendly air.

Step 2: Prepare the client

Second to timing is setting up the question. You have to help a client focus before he can think effectively for you. You won't get much response if the client isn't emotionally hot for what you've done for him. He needs to be excited, enthusiastic, and positively buzzing about the fabulous thingamajig he's just bought off you. He needs to be *emotionally* linked to the positive benefits of ownership. You can influence him while he's in this emotional state.

Setting up the scene in this way is vitally important if you want to optimise the situation. Get him to be truly thankful for owning your offering and consciously aware of the positives.

Step 3: Avoid asking 'Who do you know?'

You must ask this question in the correct way. What you say profoundly influences its effectiveness. The question style is worthy of your attention. No doubt you've been asked 'Can I help you?' in a shop. What did you say in return? You probably said, 'No, I'm just looking, thank you'. Not exactly an effective question, is it? In much the same ineffective way, asking 'Do you know anyone who might be interested in what I'm offering?' usually draws an equally blank response along the lines of 'I'll have a think and get back to you'.

You need to ask for referrals in the correct way, by engaging the client and keeping him in a positive emotional mood. A question along the lines of the following is our suggestion: 'John, I can see that you feel exactly as I do about your wonderful new luxury bathroom installation. Who else do you care about that I can help out and share this wonderful experience with?'

You use a twofold approach here. First, you use words that tell his brain to access feelings – feelings drive the human action triggers and are more powerful than thoughts. Second, you ask him whom he cares about. This tactic is powerful because it keeps him in a feeling zone (caring) and it isn't simply asking him whom he knows. Thus he links the feeling to his emotional connections and remembers that he has a chance to help someone he knows and likes to experience the joy he's feeling.

This technique taps into a different level of brain engagement and produces the desired results thick and fast.

Step 4: Direct him with a glance

The fourth step is equally as subtle and powerful as the previous three. You look directly at where the customer stores the information you need as you're asking for referrals. So, in a business sales environment, you look the client you just completed a sale with in the eye and, when he's 'locked on' and you're in mid-sentence, you deliberately look at his computer as you say, 'Who else do you care about that can I share the benefits of this offering with?' His brain will subconsciously get the message and realise that the answer to the question lies within the data stored and he'll be subconsciously programmed to answer. He will in fact – almost on autopilot – open up the PC! In a home environment, the data will probably be stored either in his computer or in his address book sitting beside the telephone. If he looks at either of these, you'll have access to his data and he will have no excuse to not give you names.

When you ask for referrals, you have to give your client a group of faces to focus on. Centring on one or two faces is impossible when his thoughts are full of his new possession – so your job is to get him focused again.

Step 5: Make it personal and get his permission

The fifth and final step is simple. As you see names on the computer screen, simply say, 'Tell me about them'. The client is programmed to answer this harmless question and names will start to flow. After telling you all about each person, he may even tell you who are the most likely referrals.

You then ask your client if he minds you mentioning his name to the people he's referred. The value of referrals lies here – the personal connection – so you must ask for this endorsement.

How to Set Appointments with Referrals

When you call someone and you already have contact with a close personal friend or respected business associate, you have common ground. You also have the benefit of knowing some pertinent information that may be relevant to getting the appointment.

Before you call such a referral, review the information you wrote in your notes, which as a professional you made when you were with the client or immediately after you left the client who referred him. You can then decide how to set the stage for this selling situation. You probably know enough about the prospective customer to ask just a few additional questions to get him involved and interested in your offering.

When you call, clearly introduce yourself and then immediately explain that you're calling because of a link to his friend or business associate. Establishing this connection is vital because it allows you the opportunity to go a little further based upon the credibility that your new client might have in the eyes of this referred prospect. Pause after your introduction, though, to check that you've chosen a convenient time to call. You could annoy the prospect, who may then express his annoyance to the client who referred him, if you continue when it isn't convenient.

If the new prospect says that it's okay to continue, then you quickly explain that you had a wonderful opportunity to get to know his friend and help him out with the installation of a new multi-screen home cinema. In the course of conversation, the client friend mentioned that the new prospect had also chatted about having a home cinema. You're simply calling because the mutual friend suggested you do so, and in view of the connection you're more than happy to pop round, whenever it is convenient, to let your new prospect know a little bit more about the home cinema range you offer – the one his friend just bought.

This gentle approach is amazingly powerful, especially the last element, because even if the new prospect isn't that hot to purchase he'll probably be hot to find out what his friend bought! Once you make that home visit, you have a chance to reel him in with your superb sales skills.

SALESPERSON: Hello, James, my name's Alan and I work at B & B Entertainment Specialists. I just helped Bill Robinson get his dream home cinema installation and I promised him I'd call you and let you know about the special offer we have this week. He just bought a beautiful high-definition installation but he mentioned in passing that you and he often spend time together and that it is something you have both talked about.

REFERRAL: Well, I'm not really ready to buy yet. I've just been looking around.

SALESPERSON: Obviously, I appreciate that James. I just really called today to suggest that as Bill and you are friends, I could just pop round and show you a little more about how it might work in your home and, of course, show you how it has been installed for Bill. Is it convenient for you at a weekend or is the evening better?

REFERRAL: Well, I suppose it is something that I might be interested in at some future date, but it would have to be an evening.

SALESPERSON: Okay, no problem. Shall I call at the beginning of next week or would you prefer perhaps a Thursday or Friday evening?

REFERRAL: No, not Friday, that's my wind-down night. Maybe Wednesday is better. Can we make it late Wednesday evening, to give me time to get some dinner after work?

SALESPERSON: Actually, James, I have a call to make in your area at 6.30 p.m. How about I call after that, as I'm close by? Say about 8 p.m.?

REFERRAL: Actually 8 p.m. would be perfect. Thanks.

SALESPERSON: Great, I'll see you then. I look forward to meeting you.

Trying for referral appointments every time

Just as you won't get a sale every time, you won't get a referral appointment every time. But always *try* to get referrals, even when you don't persuade or convince the prospect to get involved with your product or service. Now may not be the right time for that prospect, but that doesn't mean that he doesn't know anyone else who may be ripe for getting involved with the product, service, or idea you represent. If you've done a good job and sold yourself, then you stand a great chance of getting good referral leads.

An appointment with a referral requires more time and persistent follow-up because people who are referred to you don't have a relationship with you. You need to build that relationship by keeping your face and name in their minds at all times.

Granted, staying on top of those referrals isn't the easiest thing to do when you're busy trying to service old clients and contact leads you've received from other sources. Often, the ability to get the referral appointment depends on the success of your follow-up programme – if you

use one at all. We strongly recommend that you use a data management system for precisely this reason (see Chapter 6). Going through all the work to get referrals, only to lose them because you lack an organised follow-up system is disheartening.

In Chapter 14, we show you how getting referrals and making appointments are closely linked with practising proper and creative follow-up methods. When you follow up on those who offered the referrals, they're happy to refer you again when the situation arises. When you follow up on the referrals themselves, you give yourself greater opportunities to increase your profitability. How? By improving your closing rates through cultivating an effective referral business.

You may not get an appointment with every referral and you may not close every referral that you get to visit, but then you don't need to in order for referrals to become a highly productive way for you to find new business. Selling is a numbers game. Everyone you meet is likely to know someone else who may benefit from your product or service.

Not only did this salesperson use the qualifying questions from his referral notes, but he further qualified James by asking more questions. He was more likely to get the appointment because James knew that Bill had purchased a similar installation and perhaps had similar financial concerns – and he knew that the salesperson was able to work out a way for Bill to own his dream setup, so is already subconsciously aware that it might be possible for him.

What do you think the chances would have been of getting the appointment if the salesperson had been making a random cold call? You're right – they fall in the slim-to-none category. A referred name, however, made the idea of such a large purchase seem less threatening, and made James's fantasy about owning a home cinema seem perfectly acceptable.

Part IV
Growing Your Business

'My friends on the dock helped me
with the slogan.'

In this part . . .

When you're comfortable with the selling cycle, you can turn your attention to expanding your business so you can help even more clients with your product or service. In this part, you'll find information on staying in touch with your clients so you can best serve their needs. You'll also discover how to put the Internet to work for you to generate even more sales. Finally, you'll get some great tips on managing your time, so you're available to do what really matters – keeping the balance between your work and home life.

Chapter 14

Following Up and Keeping in Touch

*P*ractising consistent and persistent follow-up is proven to be one of the most important factors in successful selling. So developing an organised, systematic approach to follow-up, while individualising your chosen methods with your own creative flair, works to your advantage. Follow-up not only applies to existing clients but also applies to *all* contacts that you've interacted with. Following up is about maintaining contact in order to develop the relationship and make purchasing from you conducive.

In today's market, more and more professional salespeople are practising aggressive, thorough follow-up methods that even a few years ago would have been considered unnecessary. The reason for this development is simple: today's business environment is so dramatically changed that without being persistent and visible you'll be forgotten about and lost.

Whereas only a few years ago the potential purchaser had only a few choices for any given need, today buyers have hundreds of options. Buyers have a bewildering number of choices and, as a seller, you face a huge challenge in being the one chosen. This overload of options is often referred to as *clutter factor* inasmuch as the purchaser is bombarded with so many adverts and messages that she just switches off until she has an immediate need and then she hunts around for someone to fill the need. To make your offering the one she chooses, you need to maintain 'front of mind' awareness and you can do this only with regular and interesting follow-up.

Consequently, you need to make follow-up an important part of your regular selling routine. In this chapter, we let you know with whom you should follow up and when. We also fill you in on the importance of sending thank-you notes and show you how to get the best results from your follow-ups.

Knowing When (and with Whom) to Follow Up

The kind of follow-up you do depends on the kind of person you're following up with. The groups of people below are the foundation of your business, and keeping in touch with them will build your future:

- **Referral contacts:** Asking for referrals if you don't follow up with the referrals you get is pointless. Referrals are a great source of business. Studies show that experienced salespeople spend half as much time selling to a referred, qualified lead as they spend selling to a non-referred, non-qualified lead – with a much higher closing rate.

  A referral is not a guaranteed sale. But contacting a referral is definitely easier than starting from scratch.

- **Current clients who are happily involved with your product or service:** You need to contact these people as part of the professional service you provide to them in appreciation of their continued loyalty. They need to feel that you value them or else you may well lose them. Indeed many of them are probably happy with what you're supplying, but they may also be ready for an add-on sale or an upgrade, so following up is a very good source of sales.

- **Difficult-to-reach prospective clients:** Some prospects who are clearly identified on your target list are hard to reach, so you need to follow up with them several times in order to finally get an appointment.

  The hard-to-reach ones are hard to reach for everybody else too, so your persistence probably will pay dividends when you finally get through.

- **Network contacts who may be effective introducers:** Often people you've met who are not on your target prospect list accurately read your follow-up as non-threatening because you have nothing that you can sell them. They see your constant communication and visits as a sign of a genuine relationship – and thus can help you by feeding you leads and recommendations.

Even the briefest contact or smallest sale can lead to a whole list of potential referrals for new business.

So how well do prospects respond to follow-up?

The way your prospects respond to your follow-up depends entirely on the effectiveness and efficiency of the method you use and the content of the message. If you use follow-up with flair, and imagination is evident in the content of the message, you can expect a higher percentage of responses from your prospects. Of course, the response you get also depends on whether you've chosen prospects who can benefit from owning your product or service – your targeting.

Don't get discouraged if some prospects don't respond at all. Sometimes, no matter how good your follow-up, you get a blank response that makes you think that you've got a contagious disease and are dealing with Martians while speaking Armenian. However, if you consistently get more rebuffs than Buffy the Vampire Slayer, possibly your message and targeting have room for improvement.

Knowing which methods work best for you and sorting out which types of clients respond to one method of follow-up as opposed to another takes time. So be patient. Don't give up if, after your first few attempts at follow-up, you get disappointing results. Instead, keep seeking ways to improve your follow-up programme. Contact other professional salespeople who are willing to listen, look at your follow-up, and offer advice. Good follow-up techniques can sometimes take as long to master as good selling techniques. This skill doesn't happen overnight.

Recognising How to Follow Up

If you want your customers to remember you and your offering, you need to offer them a memorable experience. If you see follow-up as boring, tedious repetition, you can expect your clients to feel the same way: bored and tired of your constant contacts.

You must *create* a need in your customers or prospects. And that need is directly proportionate to the enthusiasm and creativity you put into your follow-up programme. So make sure that your methods of follow-up – and the messages you give through them – add up to a rewarding and memorable experience for your customers.

Many salespeople complain that they do the follow-up but get nothing from it. But, often their follow-up is simply a repetition of the first message. For example, they sent a message asking, 'Would you like to buy our fantastic widgets?' and the subsequent messages all asked the same question with no further information. Unsurprisingly, therefore, the resulting response from clients was lousy. The next sections look at how you can vastly improve on that technique.

Paying attention to what your customers want

To adopt effective methods of follow-up, you need to know the concerns that customers have about service and follow-up, and you need a good handle on the challenges that your clients and prospects regularly face. You can only serve your clients well when you know what they want.

The list here offers common customer concerns about the selling and servicing of their accounts:

✔ Receiving a call that a salesperson promised to make

✔ Knowing contact numbers and the best available times to keep in touch with the sales and service people

✔ Having the ability to talk to somebody in authority

✔ Knowing that the salesperson and the salesperson's company appreciate their business

✔ Spending minimal time on hold in order to speak to a real person

✔ Being kept informed of ways to keep costs down and productivity up

✔ Being informed promptly of potential challenges and getting any problems resolved quickly

✔ Receiving acknowledgement of recognised challenges and accepting responsibility for errors

✔ Being addressed politely and receiving personal attention

✔ Being given realistic and honest information about delivery or problem-solving issues

By making follow-up and service a regular part of your day, you can efficiently address all these customer concerns and maintain an edge over your competitors, who may not be as determined to follow up as you are. When you provide excellent service and follow up with your customers and prospects, you earn the reward of serving the lion's share of all the clients who need your offering.

Phone

Telephone follow-up is perhaps the most common, least expensive, and most difficult method of follow-up to turn into a memorable experience. Why? Just look at all the ways your customers can miss you. People can avoid your calls by using screening devices such as answering machines, secretaries, or voice mail. If your phone calls are being screened, you have to get creative to instil enough curiosity in the people you're trying to reach to make them want to talk to you. Even if the people you're calling aren't trying to avoid you, they may be very busy and what you're offering may not be the most important thing in their day – even though you may view it differently.

Reaching someone by telephone can be difficult if you aren't creative in your efforts. For example, when you try to reach that high-powered executive on the phone, you probably have to go through a company receptionist, a private secretary, and sometimes even a business partner before you get to the decision-maker. (At this juncture, we refer you back to Chapter 8 for tips on how to get to the decision-maker.) The biggest frustration however comes when, at the end of running this gauntlet, you discover that you've gone through it all just so the decision-maker can advise you to leave a message on her voice mail. You've done all of that battling through for almost nothing! If you aren't prepared with a creative and tempting message, how often do you think the important decision-makers will return your call, which lines up with the dozens of other sales calls they receive on a daily basis? If you said, 'Not often', you're right. Give your follow-up your own little flair to maximise its value.

To make your phone calls memorable, prepare a message that will get the person's attention and stimulate her curiosity. The people at the top are always looking for ways to improve profitability and productivity to carve out a greater percentage of market share. If you believe that your offering can help the person you're trying to reach, give her a teaser in the message that will make her want to put your name at the top of her call-back list. A message such as this one, for example, helps you cut through the clutter and connect you with the people in charge:

> I'm sorry you missed my call, but I may still be able to help you in your business challenge. I know I can show you a way to increase your productivity while lowering your company's costs in both labour and promotions. Please, look out for the information package that I'll send to you in tomorrow's post, and I'll call again next week to discuss how you and your company will benefit from our new offer. My name is Jennie and you can reach me on the following mobile number if you'd like to discover the secret to winning the promotional challenge sooner than next week. I look forward to speaking with you!

One short phone message such as this accomplishes several objectives:

- ✔ **It stimulates the customer's interest by teasing her with possibilities of how to do her job more efficiently.**

- ✔ **It tells the executive that you can provide individual as well as company benefits.** Unfortunately, no matter how loyal someone is to a company mission, the first person she really cares about is *herself*! Thus appealing to that interest and implying that *her* role will be easier, *her* stresses reduced, and *her* career enhanced through this smart decision makes sense. Mentioning or even highlighting the benefits to the individual is a superb habit to get into, whether your offer of individual benefits occurs during follow-up or you incorporate it right into the fabric of your presentation. Stroke the ego of a high-powered executive and show her how she'll look good to the corporate elite, and she'll be that much more willing to own your offering.

✔ **It gives the customer a time frame within which to call if she wants to hear more.** Obviously in today's almost hectic executive schedule, expecting someone to jump when it suits you is unrealistic. However, you can subtly imply that *you* are prepared to jump should she need you. If she happens to have a challenge in the area where you represent a solution, then she'll remember your message and call you. If the customer is too busy (or has not been tempted enough) to return your call, you've at least given yourself the opportunity to contact her via direct mail or e-mail. And guess what follows the mailing? Yes, another phone call!

Direct mail

Direct mail is a common method of follow-up, but your mailings don't have to be common. Personalise your follow-up to make it memorable for the person you're contacting.

For example, you may want to include special offers with your mailings. *Special offers* are offerings that benefit customers when they respond to a mailing. They may include a special promotional discount on your offering or a coupon to use the services included in your mailed package. Such offers should be unique to that particular mailer or at least to new prospects or the target group. Sometimes a mailing is nothing other than a special offer promotion and when this is the case, the follow-up's only purpose is to build goodwill with your prospects and encourage them to take advantage of the offer.

If you use this method of follow-up, let the customer know in your mailing that you'll call her in a few days for her feedback. Your notice about the upcoming call gives you *another* opening to contact her with effective follow-up. All of these contacts build up a mental record of recognition in the prospect's mind, which is critical if you want to win her over in the face of modern 'clutter'.

Another personal touch you can give to direct mailings is to include helpful guides or tips – sheets or booklets that can (and should) appear to be neutral unbiased helpful notes conveying the impression that you're genuinely interested in the prospect's well-being. You can also send interest items, such as a press release relating to your client's field of expertise. This type of incidental mailer is very powerful because it implies that you really are thinking of the client – otherwise you wouldn't have cut out the news story and posted it. This approach can only be used for a specific mailer; it cannot be a mass mailer. Knowing that you're thinking of her carries huge weight for the client.

The more spontaneous your mailings are, the more effective they will be. Instead of having your secretary type a formal covering letter, just jot a little handwritten note and attach it to the mailed material. Your note can be as simple as a few lines to let her know that you were thinking about her. Don't forget to include your business card with the note and maybe a little teaser about what's new with your product or service to get her to call. This approach takes a lot more time – but pays off.

E-mail

E-mail is a wonderful tool to use for follow-up, if your client accesses her e-mails regularly. For those clients who do, you can send a note with an attached URL (Web site address) of an article or piece of information that the client may find useful in her business, in much the same way as you might include a newspaper cutting. At the very least, send an article or link that relates to her hobby. If the article is a long one, summarise in your message why you thought she'd find it interesting. Doing so shows you thought enough to actually read the article yourself, which is impressive.

Also, whenever a new development occurs in your industry or within your company that may impact this particular client, drop her an e-mail about it. Keeping clients informed is always a good move.

Keep your e-mail messages to clients brief and to the point, and they'll be much appreciated.

Including in the e-mail an offer to serve the client's needs should a question arise is also a good move. Always, always keep yourself open to hearing from your clients.

Crafting Your Message

Success in sales means being creative about keeping in touch with current or potential buyers. These sections inspire you to make your mark in the most effective way possible.

Vary the theme

As a sales professional you need to avoid insulting the intelligence of the prospect by continually re-sending the same message. For example, if you're in the bag business with a major product line in travel bags and a customer purchased a travel bag from you, sending frequent messages to this client about travel bags is a waste of time and money. Sending frequent messages needs a bit more attention in order for it to become effective. Simply communicating with the same message eventually annoys the customer who's already purchased the travel bag; she removes herself from your mail list and you then lose her altogether. Sadly many businesses do use this approach in the belief that because they are sending regular mail, they are following a correct principle and should succeed. Well, the principle is correct – unfortunately the execution isn't.

Crafting a series of separate messages all talking about a different product and highlighting further advantages of your range of products or services is a better approach. For example, the first message might be about a rucksack range for hiking. The second, a month later, might be highlighting a suitcase range that the prospect may need in preparation for summer holidays. The third, another month later, might be about the range of executive cases and how they enhance the image of the person carrying them. Next might be a message showcasing the benefits of storage compartments and illustrating your new 'storage space saver' range of compartment-type bags, which are incredibly handy for reorganising loft space, garage space, and so on.

Whatever you send needs to offer separate interest and contain information that is informative and interesting if the prospect has a need for that item, and if she doesn't, it reminds her who you are and imprints a memory tag that says you're there to help and have a range of useful solutions.

The skill in this approach lies in the crafting of the variety of styles and the showcasing of the range of offerings. When used properly, a series of sequential mailings can be a very successful part of your follow-up.

Make it visual

Although a letter to say 'hello and nice to meet you' is acceptable and correct, to send plain letters as the only element of your follow-up is generally less than effective. Actually the best way to structure a follow-up programme is to use all of the media mentioned in the preceding sections.

When sending e-mail or hard copy mail, make the piece visually striking as well as having it carry a well-crafted message. Your mailing doesn't have to be in full colour and expensively produced but it can easily include some colour elements and be artistically laid out – for example, with shaded paragraphs and boxed highlighted areas, much as this book is laid out. It can also include graphs or illustrations, which are known to be powerful attention-getters in a world where mailers are often scanned then disposed of. When scanning, people look at pictures, assuming that a picture will tell a more complete and instant story. So to ensure maximum impact and response to your mailing, try to make the visual content as structured as your follow-up process itself. Choose images and colours to increase the attraction and impact of your message.

TIP

Network to find more ways to follow up

Top-producing salespeople have found ways to follow up that are both effective and creative. Asking your competitors for their methods of follow-up probably won't be effective. But other salespeople in your company may be doing creative things that they would be more than willing to share with you.

At your next sales meeting, make a point of discussing different methods of follow-up. This approach is called *networking*, even though you're doing it at home within your own ranks of salespeople. Before you toss all those collected business cards from all those business meetings into the bin or tuck them away in a top drawer so that you'll never see them again, take the time to go through the cards and write a note about how much you enjoyed the person's input or conversation at the business meeting. If you've been thorough enough to jot down a word or two on the back of each card to remind you of your conversation, you'll have something specific to address when you do your networking follow-up. Better still, use a contact management system such as Goldmine or Act to enter the contact details from all these business cards and store your comments as notes. You'll be surprised at how many people respond in a highly positive way to this type of follow-up — the type that includes a reminder of the conversation that you had with them when you met. Many even go out of their way to contact you with future needs!

If you follow up shortly after you attend the business breakfast or networking event, you can more easily recall what everybody said. Keep a copy of your correspondence attached to the prospect's card so you can remember her when she calls.

Make it targeted

Although you already did some targeting in the qualification stage of your sales activity, following up demands that you target the information still further. The client or prospect may be in the right target sector but already have and use some of the products you sell, and if you constantly send messages about things that aren't relevant, you risk annoying her. Your follow-up messages need to show that you're aware of products your client already owns to let her know that you care about her as an individual and she isn't just another one of the masses you're trying to sell to.

Thus when preparing a follow-up make sure that your contact data includes information on the targeted product or service that you've determined may suit her and what she already has. By including this information, you'll increase the percentage of the messages read and as a direct result the percentages of responses and sales.

Remembering the Importance of Thank-You Notes

Everybody likes to be appreciated. So use your follow-up system to let your customers know that you appreciate their business and all the referrals they've sent your way. This approach is called *warm-and-fuzzy follow-up*, and it comes in a form that should become a permanent part of your sales repertoire as soon as possible. So what form should this take? The deceptively modest thank-you note.

The following list makes it easy for you to get started with the thank-you note habit. It offers ten instances in which thank-you notes are appropriate, followed by examples of wordings you can use for the occasion:

- **For telephone contact:** 'Thank you for talking to me on the telephone. In today's business world, time is precious. You can rest assured that I will always respect the time you invest as we discuss the possibility of a mutually beneficial business opportunity.'

- **For in-person contact:** 'Thank you for taking time to meet me. It was a pleasure meeting you, and I'm thankful for the time we shared. We have been fortunate to serve many happy clients, and I hope to someday be able to serve you. If you have any questions, please don't hesitate to call.'

- **After a demonstration or presentation:** 'Thank you for giving me the opportunity to demonstrate our product and discuss the potential association for the mutual benefit of our firms. We believe that quality, blended with excellent service, is the foundation for a successful business.'

- **After a purchase:** 'Thank you for giving me the opportunity to offer you our finest service. We are confident that you will be happy with this investment towards future growth. My goal now is to offer excellent follow-up service so that you will have no reservation about referring to me others with similar needs.'

- **For a referral:** 'Thank you for your kind referral. You can rest assured that anyone you refer to me will receive the highest possible professional service and courtesy.'

- **After a final refusal:** 'Thank you for taking the time to consider letting me serve you. I sincerely regret that your immediate plans do not include making the investment at this time. However, if you need further information or have any questions, please feel free to call. I'll keep you posted on new developments and changes that may benefit you in the future.'

- **After a prospect buys from someone else:** 'Thank you for taking the time to analyse my services. I regret being unable at this time to help you appreciate the benefits that we can provide. We keep constantly informed of new developments and changes in our industry, though, so I will keep in touch with you in the hope that, in the years ahead, we will be able to do business together.'

ANECDOTE

Ben's Tenerife thank-you lesson

Ben learned the value and power of thank-you notes early in his sales life. When he was working in Tenerife, the company had a policy of sending a thank-you to every client who purchased – as a company choice, not that of the representative. While many moaned at the rigidity of this follow-up requirement, a little communication a few days after the sale prevented a lot of cancellations, and always caught those who were suffering from 'buyer's remorse' in time to re-spark a conversation and remedy anything that was causing them to wobble in their decision.

Since his return to the UK, Ben has made it a policy to thank those he meets simply for their time regardless of whether the result was a sale or not. This approach costs very little. Because people were giving up something so very precious (their time), Ben felt he owed them a thank-you whenever they created a gap in their hectic schedule to meet him.

✔ **After a prospect buys from someone else but offers you referrals:** 'Thank you for your gracious offer to give me referrals. As we discussed, I am enclosing three of my business cards, and I thank you in advance for placing them in the hands of three of your friends, acquaintances, or relatives whom I might serve. I will keep in touch and be willing to render my services as needed.'

✔ **To anyone who supplies you or gives you a service:** 'Thank you for your continued and professional service. It is gratifying to meet someone dedicated to doing a good job. I sincerely appreciate your efforts and thank you for serving me so well. If my company or I can serve you in any way, please do not hesitate to call.'

✔ **On an anniversary:** 'With warm regards, I send this note to say hello and, again, thank you for your patronage. We are continually changing and improving our products and service. If you'd like an update on our latest advancements, please give me a call.'

As you can see, you have many reasons to say, 'Thank you'. A thank-you note or two to the right person at the right time can go a long way towards building your success. For example, suppose receptionists or assistants who think they don't get enough recognition *do* get recognition from you. They'll remember you and feel good about you. In turn, they'll be more receptive to your calls and questions.

REMEMBER

You can never go wrong by thanking someone.

As an indication of how well this technique can serve a business, Ben has found that adopting this idea has literally changed relationships from 'potentially good' to 'very good indeed' over the course of a couple of meetings. The impact of showing appreciation is considerable – doing so can literally open doors to agreements that you previously only dreamed about. Figure 14-1 shows an example of a Thank You card. Add a sincere and genuine handwritten comment each time to get noticed – this has so much more impact than a pre-written or mass-produced card message.

Figure 14-1:
Show appreciation by sending a Thank You card.

Do you say 'thank you' or send a gift?

If someone has gone *way* out of her way to help you, and if you think she deserves a little gift or an extra-special thank you, then by all means send that person a thank-you note and a little gift straight away. You don't send a thank-you note *every* time someone does something for you – you do it at those times when you know someone has put a lot of her effort, time, and energy into something for you. If a customer likes classical music, consider sending her tickets to a symphony performance. You may want to send film premiere tickets or gift vouchers to secretaries or assistants. You can thank clients with a round of golf at their favourite course, or give a secretary and her guest a gift certificate for lunch to show your gratitude for her extra effort in arranging the appointment that you worked on for a month. Loads of opportunities exist in which to show your gratitude if you're creative and stop to think for a moment – and this stopping to think adds even more value, as you tailor each one for its recipient.

In circumstances where you've been helped tremendously over and above the line of duty, a thank-you gift may be appropriate. In general, a sincere thank-you card will make you stand out above your peers and competitors.

Maximising Results from Your Follow-Ups

Maximising results is a great goal to focus on in handling any contact, not just a follow-up. To do so requires efficiency, a well-laid plan, and good records. In this section, we cover just those aspects of follow-up so you can get the best results from your efforts.

Imposing order

Follow-up sounds so simple when somebody advises you to send a letter or to just pick up the phone and make a call, but establishing an effective follow-up system involves much more than that.

An effective follow-up plan requires you to master and implement the Rule of Six, a rule of selling that can increase your sales volume many times over: In order to make the sale, you should contact prospects six times within a twelve-month period.

Think of all the contacts and prospects you have – and those who you're bound to meet in your next active year out there covering the ground in your area –

and multiply that number by six. When you look at your client base that way, you can easily see how some salespeople get overwhelmed by follow-up. For that reason you need to employ a contact management system to do the work for you.

Especially if you're new to sales and unable to hire someone to take care of your follow-ups, then using an electronic system is vital. You need to design your follow-up and prepare the messages in advance before adding them to the system as template letters or e-mails.

In order for your follow-up to be effective, and because it's a constant in the selling process, you must also organise your follow-up time and programme activity so that the task gets done without blocking out the other millions of jobs that need doing!

In today's world of high-tech equipment, the most efficient way of keeping all your follow-up is on a sales force automation software program designed to store the maximum amount of information in the minimum amount of space. Doing so allows you to use the diary function in the organising program to schedule the follow-up activity into your daily planner so that it doesn't get missed. For example, if you know in advance that you're going to a business network meeting, then you know also that the follow-up letters should go out the next day. You can then slot time in your diary the morning after at the same time as you slot in the network meeting itself. If you already use one of these services, invest some time in learning how to maximise the 'alarm' or 'reminder' features. If you don't already use one, be certain these features are easy to manage in any program you choose. (Check out Chapter 6 for more information on putting technology to work for you.)

Whichever way you choose to organise your time and the follow-up information you collect, your method should enable you to systematically and periodically keep in touch with all your contacts.

As you schedule your follow-up time, keep your customers informed of the best times to contact you. Be sure that you are accessible at the times you tell them to call. Just by being there, you eliminate telephone ping-pong or the nagging fear that the call you've waited for all week will come when you're out on an appointment.

Let your customers know your work schedule (as much as possible), and they'll appreciate being able to reach you when you say you'll be available. Keeping to your stated office hours is just another way to let your clients see how efficiently you run your business and, likewise, how efficiently you would (or do) service their needs.

Gauging your nuisance quotient

Whether you get a chance to talk in some detail about your offering or whether prospects remain contacts not clients, they all need a follow-up communication. The trick is making that communication happen without becoming a nuisance.

With those who become clients, service is key and you can't serve them if they don't make a connection with you – although it won't surprise you to realise that responsibility for making the move lies with you. You want to stay in touch fairly often, depending upon the product or service they acquired. For example, if they're purchasing office consumables from you, you may need to be in touch weekly, but if the purchase was a full installation of an air-conditioning system, you may only need to be in touch once every month or so after you have signed off the system as delivered and correct.

You will soon learn how to assess the optimum frequency for follow-up, bearing in mind that every client has individual needs. Some respond to a frequent call or visit and others will be annoyed by the same frequency. The easiest way to gauge a client's follow-up requirement is simply to ask. However, don't just ask, 'How often shall I contact you', because invariably you'll receive a 'Don't call us; we'll call you' response. Instead, use this approach: 'With your permission, I'd like to follow up with you in about 30 days just to see how well the product is meeting your needs and find out if you have any questions. Would that be fine with you?' She may suggest you call sooner or that she'll be fine for at least 30 days. You can gauge your nuisance factor based on her response.

If people are contacts but nothing more at this stage, you'll want to keep your name in their minds without bombarding them with junk mail or nuisance calls. Gauging the right frequency for these contacts is pretty much impossible. The prospects will either delete or unsubscribe if you're sending an e-mail or simply throw the hard copy mail in the bin. The fact is you have to chip away at them slowly and not expect to win them all. As a good guide, though, a monthly call is suggested if you class a prospect as having high potential.

One of the most important and obvious snippets of sales wisdom is this: avoid harassing your customer. Sometimes knowing when keeping in touch with your client has crossed the line to downright bothering her is difficult, but you defeat the entire purpose of follow-up if you fail to recognise the signs of annoyance a customer is sending your way. A customer hanging up on you is a pretty good sign that you've failed to recognise her annoyance, but hopefully the situation won't get that far!

Be sensitive to your clients' needs. Don't call a client at lunchtime or at the very end of the day and expect a long, drawn-out conversation with her undivided attention. Also avoid physically popping in and expecting to chat every time you're passing, unless you have called and checked that she has five minutes to spare. Consider how you'd feel if you were very busy and someone persistently called and acted in this way.

Keep your follow-up short and sweet and do it at times most convenient for your prospects' schedules. Interruptions are sometimes unavoidable, but when too many occur, give your customers the opportunity to get back to you at a time better suited to their busy schedules.

If, after all the follow-up, you still get a no from a client, leave the contact or meeting on a positive note. If you know that her answer was not based on your poor performance, you may still be able to get a referral from her or do future business with her when her situation changes.

Be polite! Find out when she expects her situation to change and ask her permission to call back again. She may be receptive to hearing what you have to say a few short months down the road when she *is* ready to own your offering. If you leave her with a positive feeling and continue to build rapport through constant and persistent follow-up, the only thing stopping her from owning your offering is time and that, too, will pass.

If your customer admits that she has bought from your competitor, don't you think you need to discover why she chose your competitor over you? If this situation arises, don't get angry with your prospective customer. Instead, make her feel important by asking her if you can take up just a few more moments of her time to hear her reasons for choosing to do business with someone else. You may even seek advice on how you can improve your sales skills or your product or service.

If you've invested a lot of time in a customer who has decided not to take you up on your offering and has instead gone with someone else, she may feel obliged to meet you. These meetings can be the best learning experiences you have. Not only will you find out what you may need to improve, but you will gain new insight into your competitor's offering or into what your competitor says about you and your company. Think of these times as invaluable opportunities to become a better salesperson. And don't forget to take this opportunity to follow up with a thank-you note to the customer for her advice.

If you're diligent in following up with customers who choose not to own your offering, you may just draw them away from your competitor the next time they have a need to buy. By keeping in touch with them even better than the salesperson with whom they chose to do business, you make the customers wish that they'd done business with you. Let them see how your organisation cares for their well-being through your effective follow-up – and when they need a new-and-improved version of what they now own, they'll probably think of you first.

Being disappointed and letting your clients know you're sorry not to have the opportunity to do business with them is okay. Do *not* let them see you sulking, being moody, and acting like a spoilt child who hasn't got her own way. Don't phone them and ask if the product they bought elsewhere has gone wrong yet either. While you may be hopeful, letting them know you're secretly praying for them to suffer isn't professional! Keep in touch by all means, as nothing is for ever in this world, and a change of circumstance or personnel can easily create an opening to let you back in. Remain just as consistent and persistent in the service you provide and one day your diligence will pay off.

Keeping track of your successes

As you're developing your sales skills and your sales career, keeping a record of everything you learn is a great idea. You can include how you learned what not to do as well as how to do it well, preparation techniques, after-sales service calls, and so on. Be sure to keep thorough notes on all your follow-ups and the success you have with your current follow-up methods. When you do something great that gets an excellent response, write it down in a *success journal* (a place where you can keep track of everything that has worked for you, follow-up or otherwise). Be specific and detailed, and describe the selling situation in which you implemented the successful follow-up method. The more information you record, the more likely you are to repeat the experience in the future.

When customers tell you what you need to work on, put those comments into your success journal, too.

If you take all this time to write down what you do well, in addition to what you need to improve on, you should also take the time to review your journal periodically and evaluate whatever changes you make.

You may need to solicit the help of another professional salesperson in your office to hold you accountable for making the changes you know you need to make and to help you implement such changes. A good manager is a friend who wants what is best for you as well as the sales figures, so having her on your side to nudge you along is a real blessing. When your manager sees you settling back and relaxing, she should have your permission to give you a gentle wake-up call, a reminder of what you said you wanted to do to improve your sales results.

Be a fanatic about follow-up! Even if you haven't found the most creative or memorable way to follow up, practising follow-up with zeal is better than doing nothing at all. Allow yourself a few mistakes and plenty of time to organise and maintain your chosen follow-up schedule. Expect *gradual* increases in the number of times you get a 'Yes'. Be diligent about follow-up with your prospects, your customers, and yourself. And above all, think of follow-up as your way to travel the path of sales success.

Chapter 15

Using the Internet to Make More Sales

. . . .

In This Chapter

▶ Researching your client's business online

▶ Presenting to your clients across the country with web-casting

▶ Being there for your clients, no matter what technologies you use

. . . .

*T*he Internet is a fantastic tool for preparing and making sales. This excellent resource allows you to take advantage of technology that may otherwise be beyond your means. Think about the time, effort, and financial means it would require for you to have access to the most up-to-date information on any potential client if it weren't for the Internet. We strongly suggest that you quickly adopt the Internet as your new best friend and like all great friends become inseparable.

Positive Impact from Cyberspace!

Countless surveys show that people are embracing the Internet as a living and working best friend at an extraordinary rate. Currently in the UK approximately three million homes have a broadband Internet connection and rare is the business without broadband. Indeed the speed and quality of connections are expanding so that almost everybody that wants it has access to high-quality Web provision and can look at or download music, film, and pictures whenever they so choose. Never before has accessing information, educating, and communicating all at the same time been easier.

The Internet is an empowering tool that allows you to stay one step ahead of your competition and find out about a client's potential need sooner than ever. Having access to the Internet resembles having a reference library at your fingertips. In years gone by encyclopaedias were seen as 'all-singing, all-dancing' comprehensive reference points and veritable fountains of knowledge. The Internet makes a complete set of encyclopaedias fade into pale comparison and allows for access in a minuscule fraction of the time it takes to find the correct volume and then heave it down from the shelf! It is so comprehensive that you can look up nearly every topic, company, or product you can think of. And the best part is that you'll usually find more than one source of information, so you can make sure that what you're getting is accurate.

Having said that you can find absolutely anything out via the Web, bear in mind that not all sources are completely genuine or truthful. If the information was posted by a corporation or reputable organisation, you can usually trust it as valid and current. But if you're not familiar with the source of the information, be aware that it may not be the most reliable. Wise businesses and organisations post prominently the date the site was last revised, so you know how current it is.

Better than the newspaper

On the Internet, you can read all the latest news releases for your industry on a proliferation of sites. The industry you're in probably has an official site linked to the official governing body or association and doubtless at least two or three others that are reporting in a similar field. By correctly using good search engines such as Google or Yahoo! you can pretty much find whatever you want in an hour or two. If the information is important to your selling career, take advantage of the latest news. It just might be the specific talking point of the next prospect you're going to visit, or the rapport-building topic that creates a bond with that person – it may be the best hour you've ever invested.

For information specific to client companies, visit their Web sites instead of waiting for the newspapers or trade magazines to pick up their news releases and print them. You'll also find news releases linked to the stock page for publicly held companies, because they want their latest good news to boost the public's confidence in their stock.

Many of the most popular newspapers and magazines have online content that is searchable, so you don't even have to flip pages to find what you're looking for. You simply type a word or phrase related to your area of interest in their Search box and let it take you directly to that article.

Better than word of mouth

You can experience for yourself how your competition handles client concerns by submitting a request for information on your competitor's Web site. Look for something under the heading 'Customer Service', 'Technical Support', or 'Contact Us'. (Do the same with your own site every now and then to be sure your service is better than your competition's.)

You can also review Web sites to find out how your product ranks compared to the competition. Then you can pass that information on to your prospects.

Showing your prospects that you're on top of things helps them to recognise your high level of competence, thus inspiring trust in your advice.

As a matter of principle and a 'must do' discipline, take at least 15 to 30 minutes every morning to review the Web sites of the companies you're going to call on that day. Don't look merely for news items, although obviously they can be supremely useful, but take a close look at what you can deduce about how the company does business.

For example, say you're selling a high-end service and are proud that you're amongst the most expensive, as you feel this differentiates you from the 'cowboys' and that people respect and admire the prestige of dealing with you. Then you look at a client's Web site and clearly see that they have a culture of 'cheap', that they're proud to be 'lowest priced', and that they almost scorn high prices as a 'rip-off'. In this case, you need to look really hard at what you can learn about the business's market positioning to see if any way exists at all for you to justify how expensive your offering is in their eyes. You may have to look for an urgent situation where their buying need is greater than a cost-focused buying process. In this case, you resolve their pain and sell without a cost comparison. On the other hand, you may find out that your client takes the opposite view; their Web site has text explaining that they're not cheap and they're proud to be exclusive and top of the range. You can then develop a level of rapport and mutual appreciation long before you get to the pricing.

Looking at Web sites of companies before you go visiting them gives you conversation, news, and massive clues as to how to 'pull their strings' and make a sale happen. Clearly demonstrating that you've done research immediately increases your chances of a sale because many of your potential competitors won't have bothered. Your knowledge of the prospect company wins you Brownie points and respect – both of which help you get a deal.

Better than guesswork

The Internet allows you and your company to capture very specific information on customer needs and respond to them effectively. It can allow your clients to receive answers to their concerns faster than ever before, which increases their confidence in you and your company's ability to serve.

As an example, if you purchase a particular book at Amazon.co.uk, you'll find a list of other books purchased by the people who purchased the one you just did. In other words, Amazon is pointing you to other sources of similar information. If you want, they'll even send you e-mail updates when new books are scheduled for release by the same author or in the same genre. They understand the old qualifier that, based on your past purchases, you're likely to make a similar choice in the future.

Using your systems to avoid personal burnout

Using current technology, you could easily be available to your clients 24 hours a day, 7 days a week, 365 days a year. Isn't that great? You can live your life entirely for your clients. Unfortunately, many salespeople try to do this and they lose in the long run. Why? Because they lose their personal relationships and, even worse, they often lose their health. Always remember that your family and friends or support systems come first.

Top people in the field of selling manage their lives to balance business and personal issues. In order to do this, yet maintain a high level of service to your clients, you have to put in place systems to ensure that everything goes as smoothly as possible all the time.

Your task is to develop systems that manage and systems that report. Then, when you have

a system that records what has happened, who ordered what, when they want delivery, and so on, you don't have to remember everything in your head. And the single biggest cause of stress is trying 'not to forget' everything that needs to be done. So stop! Don't even try to remember it all. You put into place a great system and then a discipline that says you enter information as soon as anything has happened, and then use technology to keep everyone informed. You aren't allowing technology to trap you but you *can* allow it to do what it was created for – to release you. Remember, computer systems and programs were invented as 'labour-saving' and 'time-saving' . . . so use *them* instead of you!

Why is customer information so important? Well today the consumer is much less tolerant of poor service. People are conditioned to move on to another supplier if they feel that service and response are slow or second-rate. Purchasers are choosy and better educated. Thus, as a salesperson, you must be absolutely aware that your prospect is in fact a choosy, possibly impatient consumer. You cannot afford to get your information wrong because customers will go elsewhere to shop.

You must use the Internet to capture information to ensure that your next marketing message, your next special offer, your next bonus promotion, and your next product launch are all in tune with what your current client or marketplace expects. As a salesperson, if your company collects such in-depth information, gain as much access to it as possible and use it whenever you're talking to clients. In addition, take a shared responsibility for relaying back to the company any information you glean as to the habits and preferences of your clients. The more you know about all of your clients, the better you can handle each one's individual needs.

If your clients don't make purchases online, this technology may not be for you, however if you discount the Internet as a source of sales, you're sentencing your company and your future to oblivion. If you aren't currently attracting sales from the Internet you're missing out on a whole section of the market. Nothing in today's marketplace isn't at least sourced from the Internet first – even if the actual purchase transaction is still done in the conventional face-to-face way. And the consumer or purchaser of tomorrow is a young and Web-wise student of today, so if you don't want your business to die within five years, you need to embrace this new wave of Internet-savvy purchasers now.

Using the Internet to Your Advantage

Selling is all about servicing your clients' needs, and the Internet doesn't change that. But the Internet *does* allow you to help your clients in new and exciting ways, whether they're next door or on the other side of the world. The following sections offer some suggestions for ways to put the Internet to work for you in your daily selling life.

Prospecting online

The Internet can be a great source for finding potential clients. It can be a two-way street – clients or prospects can find you if you have a clearly defined and well-structured Web site, and you can research and find those you want to sell to.

Whatever you sell, sit and think for a few moments to identify an 'ideal' client or prospect profile – the type of purchaser you'd like to sell to if you had the choice. If you're in the business-to-business (B2B) environment, that is, you sell to other companies rather than individual consumers, you may evaluate according to size of business, where they're located, how many they employ, and so on. If you're selling in the business-to-consumer (B2C) environment, your identifiers might be where they live by postcode, what leisure clubs they belong to or frequent, or who they are linked to in terms of associations or groups. All of this information can be located by whizzing your mouse around – a lot warmer and cheaper than driving your car!

You can also find people through online phone and e-mail directories. Good sources of directory information include `www.Yell.com`, and many other directories, such as Thomson and The Phone Book, now offer a Web-based listing, which you can search through just as easily as being registered on it.

For more specific information you can buy data from many list brokers – just look in your local area directory or in an online directory. Hundreds of companies sell data (mail lists, company details, and so on), and you choose what you want to target and they send you a list of those fitting the chosen categories. Buying information really is simple and many companies base whole prospecting campaigns on such data.

You can also use the Internet to get back in touch with former classmates, who may be potential prospects for you today. You can visit sites such as Friends Reunited (`www.friendsreunited.com`), for example, where old school and college friends can list their current contact information by the name of the school and the year they left. Whatever school you attended you enter the year you left school and you're linked with former schoolmates. You may also be able to locate them via a class listing on your college or university's Web site.

If you belong to an organisation related to your industry, it may have a Web site listing the other members and how to contact them. Other members may be a big help in reaching decision-makers who may be excellent prospects.

Whenever you're looking for something from other people – introductions for example – offering to give to the other person first (before asking for something from him) makes for good networking. Sometimes, all you need do is ask, 'What can I do for you?' The other person will often feel obliged to make the same offer and you get what you wanted in the first place.

The Internet cannot replace a warm-blooded sales professional for creating long-term, caring relationships. So even if you gain most of your clients via the Web, if you really want to *keep* their business, you need to provide them with a warm body to contact if they have questions or concerns.

Presenting and selling online

Ideally, your company's Web site presents your message effectively and therefore creates enough trust that potential clients who view or read about your product or service choose to get happily involved – maybe even placing an online order. Selling online is how hundreds of small companies have become very, very profitable.

Not only does your online presence need to present the image and message that you desire, but the living, breathing people who actually fulfil the orders need to do what your site promises. Keep in mind the old selling adage to 'under-promise and over-deliver' in order to please your clients.

Be careful regarding how much dazzle and showmanship you put into your Web presentations. Being 'flash' isn't always the best; indeed, jazzed-up Web sites aren't always enjoyed by the target audience or the search engines that help them find the sites. Plus, not everyone has a broadband computer connection at the maximum speed, so develop your presentation to dazzle the low-end connections or you'll lose them to frustration.

Keep your words to a minimum, use contrasting colours and easy-to-read fonts, and don't clutter the screen with images. For more information on the look and feel of your Web site, pick up a copy of *Digital Marketing For Dummies* (Wiley).

Presenting from afar

If you can't be with your prospect, but he needs information immediately, you can get it to him via your Web site. Know your Web site inside out, so that you can direct your prospect to the relevant pages. For example, your instructions to your client may be as follows:

> Start with our home page at www.mycompanyhomepage.com. Then go to www.mycompany.co.uk/theparticularproductyouare interestedin. Here, you can see a photo of the item and read a description of what it will do for you. Next go to www.mycompany.co.uk/ testimonialfortheparticularproductyouareinterestedin. Here, you'll see how much others have enjoyed and benefited from owning the product. You may want to follow that by going to www.mycompany. co.uk/howtoordertheparticularproductyouareinterestedin. Here, you can place an order and receive a confirmation-of-delivery date.

If you have to work with clients via your Web site, *always* telephone them first to talk through what exactly they're looking for and where it can be found. Then *always* follow up your instructions with a personal phone call to answer any questions they may have about ownership, delivery, installation, and so on after they've viewed your site. You can also recommend that they download a free brochure or report from the site; that way you can be certain that they did in fact visit your site and that they have some specific information to hand. Your job then is to fill in the blanks, answer all the questions they may still have, and push on for the order.

For more sophisticated products or services, or when a more in-depth online presentation is needed, you can also take advantage of the latest video-streaming technology and include a sales presentation on your Web site. All prospective clients can then benefit from your sales pitch wherever they are and at any time of the day or night.

The Internet also allows you to invite prospects and clients to Web-based seminars and press conferences. You can also use interactive technology such as multi-person teleconferencing. As a top sales professional you need to utilise all available avenues because if you don't, your competitor will.

Telemarketing with the best of them

If you do a lot of long-distance selling or if you're in telephone sales (where you rarely meet your client in person), you can use your Web site to enhance the prospective client's satisfaction. How? By directing him through the site while you're on the phone with him. Walking through the site together is the next best thing to sitting at a table with your prospect and demonstrating your product or brochures. You may use the same links you describe in an e-mail inviting him to look by himself, or you can follow an entirely different path, dictated by his questions and concerns. To telemarket well, you must know what's on your site and what may be missing so that you never get caught off guard by a client's question.

Never direct a client to an area of the site that you haven't been to recently. The site may have changed and you could appear incompetent.

Staying in touch with your clients

The Internet also provides an ideal way of staying connected with your clients, building long-term relationships, and inspiring loyalty. Sounds like a lot of reward from just a few keystrokes, doesn't it?

If John Brown plc is your largest client and he loves fishing, spend some time seeking out new Web sites on fishing and pass those URLs along to him – just to let him know you're thinking about him and want him to enjoy his hobbies. Why? When John enjoys his hobbies, he's happy. And if he's happy because of something you did for him, he'll want to stay connected to you.

If you find an article online about a client's particular industry or his competition, you could print it out and send it to him with a short note. Or you could just send an e-mail with the link attached.

If you're dealing with much larger publicly floated companies, make a habit of watching the share price to see how the company is faring. If your client's company shares have a great day, send a congratulatory note. How will you know about that great day? Check the company's listing on the stock exchange. Doing so is very easy: simply log on to any share index Web site or even a newspaper such as the *Financial Times* (www.ft.com) and you'll find the relevant stock market information displayed.

Avoiding techno-burnout

The best thing about having all this technology to help you take care of business is the 'Off' setting. Take advantage of that button in order to rest and recreate. If you don't take care of yourself, you won't be able to do a good job of taking care of anyone else. Champion salespeople know when to forward everything to someone else and let that person take care of it.

Although most salespeople like to think of themselves as being indispensable – and they actually may be the only people in the world who can serve their clients best – everyone requires balance. In order to achieve and maintain balance,

you need to determine how many of the 86,400 seconds of your day you'll devote to clients, how many to your personal development, how many to your loved ones, and so on.

Don't become so much of a techie that you lose sight of what's really important – the service you provide to your clients and the personal relationships that fulfil your life. Your computer, mobile phone, and hand-held PC won't show up at your funeral, so don't allow them to take over your life. They're just tools for you to master in order to live your life to the fullest.

Chapter 16

Managing Your Time for Optimum Effect

· ·

· ·

Time is your most valuable resource, and until you realise that, you'll always be wondering where all your time goes. Don't worry, though. You're not alone. Everyone is searching for more time. We haven't met many business owners or sales executives who don't complain about the time pressures and the never-ending jobs still on the 'to do' list. Indeed because the challenge is so common, the value of time has increased dramatically in recent years.

So why has time's stock risen so high? Because of an adaptation of the law of supply and demand: The busier you become, the more time you need. Ask a dozen people to name one thing that would make their lives easier, and the overwhelming response is more time. When you have more time to do the things you *need* to do, you can usually generate more income to do the things you *want* to do. We love the way Zig Ziglar (author of *Success For Dummies*, Wiley) puts it when he says, 'When you do what you need to do when you need to do it, you will soon have the time to do what you want to do when you want to do it.'

In this chapter, we give you some great tips for staying on top of your time, so that you have more time to do the things you *want* to do instead of only being able to do the things you *need* to do.

For more great tips on managing time, turn to *Time Management For Dummies* (Wiley).

Investing Your Time Instead of Spending It

Average salespeople often spend their time foolishly doing unproductive 'busywork' – and then they wonder where their day went, why they accomplished so little, and why they never seem to have time for the fun stuff they'd really like to do or enough money to buy the lifestyle they wish for. The key word in that sentence is *spend*: they *spent* their time instead of *investing* it. And doing so makes all the difference.

The words *spending* and *investing* connote very different ideas. When you spend money, you probably think of the loss of that money rather than the benefits you'll enjoy from whatever it was you spent your money on. On the other hand, the word *invest* signifies a payment from which you will derive a return; you don't focus on the momentary loss of money, but rather on the gain of the product or service that you will receive. Similarly, when you spend your time instead of investing it, you focus on lost time rather than on personal gain.

If you've never put a monetary value on your time before, do it now. To determine what your time is worth, take your hourly rate and follow this simple equation:

$$\frac{\text{Gross Income}}{\text{Total Annual Working Hours}} = \text{Hourly Rate}$$

To see the value of this equation, suppose that your annual income is £30,000 and you work 40 hours a week for 48 weeks a year (allowing 4 weeks off for holidays). That means that the value of each hour in your working week is £15. In straight-commission sales, if you spend just one hour each day of each working week on unproductive activity, you spend about £3,750 a year on nothing. And that's exactly what you have to show for your wasted time, too – nothing. When you choose not to manage your time, you may end up wasting 12 per cent of your annual income or more. And this amount doesn't even account for all the future business you lost because you spent time instead of investing it. If you're a regular, full-time employee, that £3,750 is money your employer may as well burn for all the productivity they get for it.

In sales or persuasion situations, you often don't see immediate financial pay-off from the time you invest. The final transaction commonly occurs weeks, and in some cases months, after the actual investment of time. During the period between the invested time and seeing the financial reward, you can sometimes lose sight of your goals and even begin to doubt if you are doing the right thing or that you are in fact any good at doing what you do – but that situation's quite normal in selling! Don't worry. Just keep focusing on the pay-off time. Sales cycles are always a challenge because you don't know if you've done enough for the decision and process period. Indeed, the longer the period between selling and pay-off, the harder it is to stay focused and keep investing your time wisely. When you invest time in the people you're trying to persuade, thinking of the returns on your investment is normal. We don't know of any new salesperson who doesn't take out her calculator and figure the percentage she gets on a sale as soon as she's out of sight of the client. After all, helping others is a career choice that pays very well when done correctly.

Managing yourself to get a handle on your time

Time management is really all about managing yourself. Can you stop time or even slow it down? Can you negotiate with time? Of course not. If you've worked out how, then you should be writing a book instead of reading one. No one has more time to invest than you do and you don't have any more time than anyone else, yet some people succeed more often than others, and they do it without controlling time. They do it by disciplining themselves to make the most of every minute.

If people such as Edward Jenner, Mahatma Ghandi, Marie Curie, and Louis Pasteur can change the way we live and change the ways of the world for future generations and they only had 24 hours in a day the same as we do, then complaining about not having enough time is rather pathetic. Great things can still be achieved – if you are disciplined and manage yourself.

For example, if you have a healthy dose of road time in your selling life, you can choose to use that time to listen to motivational or educational tapes or CDs. In doing so, you turn your required expenditures of time into investments in your professional education.

Clustering your appointments is another way to manage your time when travelling. By organising

your presentations or customer service appointments by geographical area, you can save a lot of travel time – and if you live in a city or town, you're saving time sitting in traffic as well. If your travel time is primarily within major cities, schedule it so that you don't get stuck in rush-hour traffic. Taking side streets and back roads may lead you to new opportunities if you keep your eyes open and remain aware of your surroundings.

If you can't locate contact information for all your clients within a matter of minutes, consider using contact management software. With today's technology, the only reason a client's or prospective client's information won't be at your fingertips is because you didn't invest time in learning and using a good system. Entering the information only takes a few minutes, and then you have it forever.

If you think that people who practise time-management strategies are fanatical workaholics who leave no time for personal relaxation, you're mistaken. Just the opposite is the case. In operating more efficiently, they create *more* time for personal endeavours. Invest time in planning your time, and you'll think of dozens of ways to manage yourself more efficiently.

Beware of Fluffy Time!

We need to warn you about a killer disease infecting almost every business start-up, small business, and salesperson alike. This insidious disease creeps in and slowly suffocates you without you really noticing. Worse, it even makes you feel like it doesn't exist and gradually poisons you to death. Beware of fluffy time disease!

What does the fluffy time disease look like? Well, it starts with a salesperson getting ready to launch her new venture. She thinks of all the things that have to be done, such as logo design, stationery print, and office establishment, then getting furniture for the office and buying computers and phones, and so on. She's busy focusing on what's called *creation of product*. Then she refines the creation of product. Then she does some more planning and some talking and some meetings with people who might be helpful/useful one day. And then an awareness of needing income creeps in and provides a gentle push into creating some enquiries, but that needs adverts, so that needs planning and design, so that consumes more time.

Do you see the picture gradually unfolding? You always have an abundance of stuff to do and your 'to do' list can never be completed. Somewhere among the action, though, has to be income generation. You have to go and sell something! Fluffy time is consumed every day with everything that is seemingly needed but really is not. Fluffy time is those phone calls, or those moments (that become hours) when you're planning (thinking or daydreaming?). And those days when you plan to leave the house at 9 a.m. but actually do so after 10; when you mean to be really proactive until you open your e-mail box and are consumed for three hours dealing with replies and following links in the name of finding out; when you decide to make some phone calls to generate leads but don't really know who to phone so sit and make a target list that takes three hours because the data is all over the place.

Now, we could go on! But can you see what happens? Fluffy time is spent, lost, and wasted and you can never get it back. It consumes your most precious resource, it eats away at your life, it devours and drains your energy, and eventually it leaves you washed up and with nothing to really show for it. General lack of organisation means you lose time instead of use time, and it kills sales activity stone dead. Be extremely careful not to let fluffy time happen to you.

We pass on some important ideas that prevent time from being fluffed away if you stick with them and help keep you focused. For your survival and ongoing success in this wonderful field of selling, you need to ward off signs of this disease in the early stages, which means using a data management system and a diary.

Using a diary within your content management system is key. Make sure that all your time is planned and all of your activities on your 'to do' list are diarised in time slots. Create a discipline and get used to sticking to it and you'll find it easier to avoid losing time.

Making Time to Plan Time

People who don't practise effective time management often complain that they don't have time to plan their time. But if you don't make time for planning and self-improvement, you may as well plan to earn the same income that you earn today for the rest of your life. By taking the time to plan, you save as much as 20 to 30 times the amount of time that you expend in the planning process.

When you plan your time, divide the tasks on your 'to do' list into an order of importance. You can try the following method. First, divide tasks into *urgent* or *important* activities.

Urgent tasks are those you must do immediately, for example a deadline to meet a publisher, or a presentation to complete before a sales meeting tomorrow.

Important tasks are those that need doing but that you can do next week or even later in the month, for example get your car serviced or visit the gym. Next comes *secondary activities* – activities that you want to do and plan to do but that are actually more 'wish list' than 'to do' list. Examples include sorting out the stock cupboard or learning to use a new gadget such as a Web cam so that you can send video e-mail.

- ✔ **Urgent activities:** These are the tasks you must complete today.
- ✔ **Important activities**: These tasks are ones that are close to immediate, but not quite. You probably need to complete them this week instead of today, for example.
- ✔ **Secondary activities:** These tasks don't need to be completed by a specific deadline. You can work them in when you have a spare moment.

In the following sections, we go into more depth on each of these three categories.

Undertaking urgent activities

Urgent activities are *only* those activities that you must complete today. If you clutter your mind with things that should be secondary activities (the things you don't have to do today), you can end up neglecting your immediate activities or not giving them the full, focused attention they require.

Ask yourself these questions to determine the immediacy of your activities and prioritise them by either the amount of relief you'll feel in getting them done or the amount of goodwill or income they'll generate:

- ✔ If I can achieve only three or four activities today, which ones should they be? What if I can only accomplish one?
- ✔ Which activities will yield the most immediate rewards?
- ✔ Which activities will complicate my day tomorrow if I do not accomplish them today?
- ✔ Which of these activities can I delegate to someone else in order to leave myself more time to generate more business or enhance my personal relationships?
- ✔ Which activities, if I postpone them, will damage my relationships with others?

Have your urgent activities in front of you at all times. If you can't see what you need to accomplish today because you've buried your urgent activities under other less important work, those activities can get lost in the shuffle and you can lose sight of your goals.

Enter your immediate activities into your computer or handheld planner and set them so that you're reminded about them automatically. If the task is a large one, break it down into smaller pieces so you can accomplish those pieces and get them off that screen. Accomplishing those smaller pieces of the project leaves you with a very satisfying feeling – and when you're feeling good, you're more productive.

Sorting important activities

Identifying your important group of activities is usually easier than identifying urgent ones. Some important activities may be almost-but-not-quite urgent, so put them at the top of your important activity list. As you do for immediate activities, prioritise your important list so you finish what's most important first.

Important activities may include meeting your sales manager to review your targets and to ask for help and clarification on whom best to talk to in a particular client's organisation, for example. Clarifying these details and meeting your manager are both important, but schedule them into a non-prime selling slot and with plenty of time before actually visiting the client in question.

Staying on top of your paperwork

If you dread doing paperwork, don't leave it for the end of the day if you can help it. By paperwork, we also include computer-generated reports or online reports that your company may require. If something unexpected comes up, you won't get to your reports, and the next day you'll just have twice as much to do. This build-up, in turn, causes you even more anxiety because now you *really* have a big task ahead of you.

Do your paperwork in the first hour of each day, if at all possible, when you're fresh. When you've finished it, you're free to concentrate on the more productive parts of your day. Hopefully, as a professional salesperson, your first hour of the day is before the rest of the pack start work. Don't start your day at, say, 9.15 a.m. if everyone else is in and buzzing by 9 a.m. – especially your prospects and your clients. You need standard office hours to optimise your selling potential. Paperwork is very important but it can be done in non-selling or less optimum selling time, for example before 9 a.m., during lunch hours, or after 4.30 p.m. when getting hold of the people you need to talk to is harder.

Other important activities may be to meet a potential contact who could be a great source of referrals. Developing good relationships with these types of people is important but recognise that selling is about selling – not just looking like a salesperson. Thus you need to put selling and results first. So meet a source of referrals if they can produce immediate potential clients that might, say, be sold to over this next month or quarter, but make the meeting happen when you have a sales call already in the area.

Put any paperwork related to those secondary activities in a desk drawer, a letter tray that you can move to your desk, or better still actually file it there and then and remember that everything you need is correctly filed in the correct place ready for when you want it. Don't let yourself get preoccupied with piles of paperwork. Paperwork overload causes stress and confuses you about what really needs immediate attention.

Paperwork traps people into a belief that it must be dealt with, so they often look at it and then put it on another pile to be sorted out later. Often the paperwork then doesn't get dealt with until a lot later, and is quite possibly found to be out of date. Putting paper on another pile for the future and not getting around to it shows that you didn't actually miss it. You didn't do it and didn't lose out, so why not just throw it away in the first place? You need to develop your decision muscle. Make a habit of asking questions such as 'Do I need this now?' If the answer isn't a resounding 'Yes', then throw the piece of paper away. You'll eventually realise that your procrastination and poor decision strength only smother you with work and stress. Be ruthless and learn to throw papers away. 'Touch it once' is the motto. Pick up paperwork only once. Decide its importance and deal with it by passing it on or filing it. Don't read it and put it in a pile to be looked at again later.

Deciding on secondary activities

Identifying which tasks fall into the secondary category is difficult: You may think everything needs your attention (if it didn't, it wouldn't come your way, right?). But such thinking simply isn't true. Other people pass many unimportant activities to you to take care of – activities that have a funny habit of working themselves out if you just give them a little time. By putting those activities in your secondary category, you may be able to avoid spending time on these chores when you need to be investing time in your immediate activities.

Secondary activities are *relatively* unimportant activities. For example, think about the number of times an associate has come to you for help with a problem, only to reveal that it wasn't your assistance she wanted after all? She just wanted you to take on the problem as yours. What begins as a favour thus ends up being a real chore. Her worries become your worries – and she's off having a relaxed two-hour lunch, knowing you'll take care of it. Or, secondary activity might be where you're planning a sales launch or marketing event such as a mini-exhibition or party and you get yourself dragged into planning the room layout or organising the catering. Doing so really isn't your job and doesn't need your valuable selling time.

We're not suggesting that you never help an associate, but we are cautioning you about taking on work that should be someone else's responsibility. If you help an associate, make sure that you get compensated, either financially or by an exchange of help with one of your projects. And always get *your* work done first. Establish reasonable rules with your peers about work-related assistance. Doing so helps prevent hard feelings later. Remember, you are there to push your sales career forward and while you must be a team player, you also must survive and flourish to make yourself happy. And if you don't sell enough and wish to blame all of these other interferences for your poor performance, then we hope you sound silly even to yourself. If anything gets in the way of your selling, you're allowing it to!

Making time for unplanned happenings

Planning your time efficiently can prevent some emergencies from happening in the first place, but always have an alternative approach to your most important activities just in case an emergency arises. Planning ahead and being prepared will keep you from panicking and completely trashing your schedule, and that of others, when emergencies do arise.

If you have children, you know that occasionally they're ill or get hurt, or they forget to tell you about vital events that you need to attend. If you have a whole day of report writing to get done and school phones asking you to collect your child, do you have a back-up person, such as a grandparent, who's willing to care for her? If not, organise it now. Save all your report data onto a portable memory stick so that you can grab your laptop and your daily planner, and head for the door at a moment's notice. Or e-mail your files to yourself at home so they can be waiting for you when you arrive.

Technology being what it is, don't count on every e-mail being *where* it should be *when* it should be 100 per cent of the time. Transferring your files to a portable memory stick is a good idea.

Have back-up plans in place for transportation as well. If your car breaks down, does a colleague live nearby who can give you a lift in? Or if you're on a bus route, do you have a schedule handy? Do you have a taxi company's number in your address book? Better yet, do you have a few vital numbers stored in your mobile phone so that if a situation arises, wherever you are you can contact the right people? Preventing emergencies from happening isn't always possible, but you can be less of a victim and be organised so that the event passes without major fall-out.

Saving client phone numbers or important contact numbers 'just in case' is a great habit to develop and is why many salespeople carry mobile devices that can store hundreds or thousands of contact numbers as opposed to just a hundred or so in a more basic phone. You never know when you're going to need them. Just remember to always turn the phone off when you're doing something really important or when etiquette requires.

Accounting for Your Time

Just as you separate work tasks into three categories, you need to separate your life time zones into three areas in order to effectively organise yourself. You need to

- ✔ Investigate your yesterday.
- ✔ Analyse your today.
- ✔ Discover your tomorrow.

In the following sections, we show you how to do it.

Investigating your past

Start by taking some time to write down what you do with each of the 168 hours in your typical week. If you're like many self-management beginners, you probably have some seriously time-wasting habits, but you can easily eliminate those habits when you become aware of them. Try to be as honest and thorough as possible.

Keep a daily record of your typical routine for seven days. Print out on separate sheets of A4 paper a daily planner from your Microsoft Outlook diary or similar. We mention Outlook because frankly we live in a Microsoft-dominated world and most people use it, but it could be the diary in another program – just choose a day per page view.

The record sheets will help you establish an accurate record of everything you actually do – including the habits you may need to change. The best way to keep such a log is to jot down the time you spend moving through your daily routine: Three hours running errands, five minutes looking for a purchase agreement, half a day scouring around for a misplaced phone message, ten minutes trying to get refocused after an interruption, and so on. After completing this time log for seven days, you'll be amazed at how much time you cannot account for and how much time you waste on relatively unimportant activities. This is the fluffy time we talked about earlier in the chapter, and seeing it visually can be a frightening exercise! In fact, you'll probably feel so guilty after only one day that you'll be tempted to fill in the blanks. You'll look at it and say, 'I know I've done more than that!' but truthfully you will have recorded what you've done, and either you haven't done much or you haven't done much of any great worth.

Get tough with yourself. Do this audit for seven days. After you complete each daily sheet, tally your total hours spent on each kind of activity. Keep all your sheets and evaluate them at the end of the week. Above all, be honest when you record the time you spend on each activity. If you cheat, you're cheating yourself.

Analysing your today

If you use the word *productivity* when you refer to time planning, time planning won't be such a mystery to you.

People frequently say that they just can't plan their time or that they just can't seem to keep up with everything they need to do. The answer to their time management problems is to do the most productive thing possible at every given moment.

We both have been teaching and helping people improve their sales activity over many years, but the concept of being productive at every moment is so simple that many people don't understand it. So, no matter what you're doing, ask yourself, 'Is this the most productive thing I can do at this time?' Doing so makes you focus upon results, and productivity equals results achieved – and in selling, that is pretty much your top priority. You need to do a few simple things to answer that question:

✔ Keep a list of important tasks.

✔ Keep an appointment calendar.

✔ Know what your time is worth.

To increase your productivity, you must learn – by doing the most productive thing at each moment – how to increase the value of each hour. If doing so sounds simple, that's because it *is*. You increase the value of each hour by constantly asking yourself that same question: 'Is what I'm doing right now the most productive thing I can do?'

Some salespeople spend all their time getting organised and getting ready for persuasion situations that never come about. To them, getting organised itself has become the game. Sometimes people overvalue the organising stage because they're afraid of facing rejection or failure, so they hide from seeing the public. In some cases the salesperson makes organisation a focus because she lives in a misconception that you can't take action until everything is perfect. But that situation's a recipe for disaster, as we live in a very imperfect world. In most cases, though, salespeople who make organising the end rather than the means just don't appreciate the difference between productivity and organisation. To many salespeople, time planning revolves around just buying a time-planning device, program, or binder and filling in the squares. Of course, those tasks are necessary. But they're just a small part of a very big picture. Time planning actually starts with goals because setting goals is the only way you can tell what the most productive tasks are at any given moment.

When you're planning for the coming day, ask yourself the following questions:

✔ Did I accomplish all my high-priority items today?

✔ Did I reach or surpass my goals for today?

✔ Did I invest as much time in persuading others as I had planned?

✔ Did I contact every prospect that I put on my list for today? If not, why not? What prevented me from getting to that prospect?

✔ How much time did I spend prospecting for new clients?

✔ How much time did I waste chatting with colleagues or clients?

✔ What is the most productive thing I did today?

✔ What is the least productive thing I did today?

- Of the things I consider a waste of time, could I have avoided or eliminated any of them?

- How much time did I spend doing something that will profit me? Can I devote more time to that activity tomorrow?

- Was today a productive day for me? Was it productive for my company?

- Did I take care of all the paperwork I needed to take care of today?

- How many of today's activities have helped me achieve my goals?

- How much time did I allot to my family today? Did I spend this time with them? Was it quality time, or was I just in the same place at the same time?

- What can I do to improve the quality of the time I devote to my family?

- Did I plan for, and take some time to work on, my emotional or physical health?

- If I could live today over again, what would I change?

- What did I do today that I feel really good about?

- Did I send thank-you notes to the people I dealt with today?

- What or who wasted the greatest amount of my time?

The answers to these questions will help you see what you're doing right and let you know what you can improve upon tomorrow.

Discovering your tomorrow

Assume that your goals and priorities are in line (and turn to Chapter 18 if they're not). You know what you want and how you want to get there. Your goals are all in writing and your priorities are set. Start your daily time planning at night before you go to bed. Go through your time planner and lay out the day to come. Get a handle on your top six priorities, as well as whom you'll see or call, for the next day. Then add any personal areas you also need to cover the next day. Writing down or entering the next day's top six priorities shouldn't take more than 10 to 15 minutes. When you've mapped out the next day, forget it and go to bed.

We suggest doing next day's planning last thing at night because it helps you sleep better. Restless sleep is caused by the stress resulting from trying to remember everything you need to remember for the next day. Thus writing it all down just before you retire for the night lets the brain relax and switch off safe in the knowledge that it cannot forget because you've already sorted it.

At the beginning of the day you've just mapped out, the most productive thing possible may be a 20-minute workout at 6.00 a.m., or breakfast with your family, or working in the garden, or any of a thousand other things that may be important to you and your goals and priorities. You have many choices throughout your day. Only *you* know if what you're doing is the most productive thing in relation to the goals you want to achieve.

People grow up being told what to do for the first 20 or so years of their lives – at home, at school, and sometimes even at work. So the fact that some people lack a certain amount of self-discipline when they go into a career such as selling, which leaves people almost entirely to their own resources, isn't surprising. We'd like to have a pound for every time we've heard a salesperson say, 'I went into sales so I could be my own boss', or 'I went into sales so no one would tell me what to do', or 'I went into sales for more free time'. All those reasons are great. But the people who hold those reasons had better develop a strong degree of self-discipline for doing what needs to be done. If they don't, they'll soon be back in a job where someone's telling them what to do because being their own boss is the weak link and their productivity slumps.

To get started with an effective time-management method, don't try to plan for every minute of the day. Being inaccurate is too easy when you forecast time for task completion. Instead, start by planning just 75 per cent of your total work time. That way, you allow for interruptions, delays, and unexpected emergencies. As your work planning improves, you can increase to planning 90 per cent of your day. But never plan for 100 per cent – if you do, you won't leave room for the unexpected, and you'll just frustrate yourself when you can't accomplish your designated goals.

Remain flexible. Not much is black and white in the world of selling; many areas of grey exist. By staying flexible, you can maintain your equilibrium and move on to greater things. Don't lock yourself into a time-management programme so rigid that you don't have time for anything else.

Winners always plan their time. To increase your productivity and your income, you must plan your time like a professional. Professional salespeople are very conscious of the value of their customers' time, as well as their own. All sales professionals must make daily decisions on priorities. Some are major, some are minor – but all are factors in the management of time. Every professional salesperson needs a systematic approach to setting priorities.

Over the years, we've noticed that successful people who run large companies and build fortunes don't spend much more time working than anyone else. The difference is that they get more productivity out of each hour of every day. They don't try to do too much at once and, because they don't, they are more productive at accomplishing the day's most important goals.

Achieving balance

Take a look at five areas of your life: Family, health, finances, hobbies, and your spirit. Why focus on so many areas outside of your career? Because when you're turned on, motivated, and feeling good, you persuade better. If you let yourself become just a sales machine with no time for anything else, you burn out. You also probably create problems in your personal relationships. And your health may suffer. Besides all that, you have no fun, you start feeling sorry for yourself, and your career goes down the drain.

Sometimes meeting your spouse for lunch and thanking him or her for supporting your goals and putting up with your long hours, or seeing your child in a school event and enjoying his or her childhood, or going for a walk, breathing in nature, and recharging your soul, is the most productive thing to do.

To be successful, you need to be a finely tuned machine that can function over the long haul and face deadlines, rejection, the public, and your competition. You also must be able to meet your company's expectations and all the other demands put on you as a professional salesperson and problem solver. Keep yourself tuned and in balance – physically and psychologically. And remember that balance starts with goals and productivity.

Knowing When and Where to Plan

If you want to manage your time wisely, you need a planning device of some sort. Whether you prefer the pen-and-paper route or the high-tech one, find an option that works well for you. Use contact management software that includes a calendar section so you have both your contact information and meeting schedule all in one place. Many of these programs will even flag you if you try to enter a meeting that conflicts with another event you already have scheduled, which can help you save face with clients instead of having to call them to reschedule. Some contact management software is even available online so you don't have to be concerned about your laptop crashing and losing all your valuable information. Others are customised to the specific needs of salespeople with forms for travel itineraries, charting activity and productivity, meeting notes, expense reports, and so on. Take some time to find one you think you'll be comfortable using. If you're not comfortable with it, you don't use it and you defeat your purpose of planning. (Turn to Chapter 6 for more information on contact management software.)

Set aside 15 minutes every morning – at your desk or with your briefcase or laptop (wherever you keep all your pertinent information) – to do your planning. Take a few moments to review all unfinished business and plan how and when you'll get it done. Write down everything you want to accomplish during the day or during the coming month. Be realistic and be very specific. Include any family or social events that you're committed to attend. Then add any important dates: Family, friend, and client birthdays; your wedding anniversary, if it's this month; your child's school play; your spouse's company night out. Then note all the company meetings you must attend for the month. Add any projects you're working on, their estimated completion dates, and reminders to follow up on them. If you're working on a large project, break it down into smaller pieces that you can accomplish each week. Taking large projects a week at a time helps you see your progress, and the one big project then doesn't seem so oppressive.

In daily time planning, keep track of *all* activities *as you go*. Don't wait until 4.00 p.m. to try to remember what you did at 9.30 a.m. Be truthful. Don't play around with numbers or fake anything just so you can check it off. And don't overwhelm yourself with writing down every detail of your working day. You're not trying to write a book. Just note the key events and any information you simply wouldn't want to forget.

Do your planning where you conduct your business. If you wait until you get home, you won't have that phone number or other detail you need to record and you'll only half-plan. If doing so means you sit in your car to plan, so be it – you're just joining the rest of us in sales where the car doubles as a second home! You may need triggers to remember everything you need to plan and those triggers are most available to you at your place of business.

Organising Your Work Space

Disorganised office space is the most common cause of wasted time and lost income. Believe it or not, clearing your desk also helps to clear your mind. When your mind is clear, you're more able to focus on one task at a time. And all you can accomplish is one thing at a time, anyway, so why try to do more. So where do you start? Try the tips in the following sections.

Keep only immediate activities on your desk

Keep everything but your most pressing tasks out of sight. And keep everything you need for accomplishing the immediate tasks somewhere nearby (in a place you'll remember), so you don't waste time running here and there looking for what you need. Develop two simple habits:

> ✔ Touch a paper once, dealing with it or throwing it away.
>
> ✔ File everything that you need but don't need now in a proper filing system.

These two simple habits can save you much time and effort.

Take charge of your time

If you suffer innumerable interruptions, close your door. If you don't have a door, try earplugs or a headset attached to an MP3 player to isolate yourself. Maybe your company will allow you to put a sign on your door saying something along the lines of: 'Unless you are a client with a large need, or have a fantastic lead for me, please let me do what I need to do to find those people.' As a last resort, consider posting a snarling Doberman near your desk!

Develop your ability to focus on your work. Let your colleagues or family know that sometimes they simply cannot interrupt you. Don't answer your telephone – let voice mail be your receptionist for a while.

Make yourself less accessible. If you need to, set up a specific time of day for your associates to freely walk into your office; make all other times off limits. If an associate drops by at a bad time, don't be afraid to look at your watch and say, 'I'd love to catch up with you, but let's do it at 3.00.' If what she has to tell you is important enough, she'll be happy to schedule the time. If it's not that important, she'll beg off, and you'll have saved yourself from spending time listening to her.

And if interruptions from team members are an issue, we strongly recommend that you read a terrific book called *The One Minute Manager Meets the Monkey* by Ken Blanchard, published by HarperCollins Business.

Handle phone calls wisely

If the phone is not a necessary tool of your immediate business, learn to ignore it or turn off the ring tone, or tell your colleagues that you are not in and will not be accepting calls.

Do *not* be ruled by the phone. Unless you are expecting an urgent call, turn it off and come back to messages. You won't lose out but will gain from your own feelings of self-satisfaction and accomplishment when you've successfully done lots of jobs because you stole an hour or two from a hectic day.

Also make sure that when you're actually using the phone, your conversation is relevant to the tasks ahead. If you have to take a call, manage the content of the call. Keep it on track for your business. When the other party gets off the subject, or when the other party stays on the subject but is long-winded, try these techniques:

- ✔ **If you initiate the call, tell the person, 'I have three things to cover with you'.** If she starts to get sidetracked, you have the right to bring her back to one of your three topics.

- ✔ **If the other party initiates the call and you don't have a lot of time to give her, let her know her call is important, but that you were just heading out the door.** She doesn't need to know it was to get a glass of water. Get the basic information she needs to tell you and make an appointment to call her back if a call back is really necessary. Unless you're dealing with an irate customer whose assembly line has completely stopped because of your equipment, most people will be willing to accept a call back. If they can't wait, it's an emergency and you'll have to handle it on the spot.

- ✔ **Call a known long-winded person just before lunchtime or just before she goes home for the day.** If doing so isn't possible, start your call by saying, 'I'm really pressed for time, but I just wanted to let you know something' or 'I'm on my way to an appointment, but I wanted to touch base with you'.

If you don't take control in these situations, you'll forever be at the mercy of others. And they will hardly ever have your best interest in mind. They aren't deliberately unhelpful; they just don't see your situation as you do.

Avoiding the Most Common Time Traps

You probably know some people who've raised time wasting to an art form. They've mastered the ability to fall into every time trap they encounter. Not surprisingly, these aren't the people who get things done, help the most people, or earn the biggest incomes in selling. If you want to get more 'Yes' responses in your life, knowing and avoiding the following common time traps is a great place to start.

Avoid 'I can't find it' waste

A sure way to waste valuable time is to keep looking for something you desperately need because you were careless when you put it away. Looking for lost items is the single biggest time waster for everyone. How many hours have you wasted looking for the scrap of paper you wrote an important phone number on or for the folder with all the referrals that your new client gave you? How about your sunglasses or your car keys? Those few minutes here and there can really add up, so designate a specific place for every item you use regularly, and then make sure you always use it. If you always hang your keys on a hook by the door or always file client information in the correct place, you won't spend precious time searching for them.

Avoid duplicating tasks

Because of the demands salespeople place on themselves, they tend to rush through their paperwork and their planning of presentations without carefully checking or rechecking details. Get out of that habit immediately. An old saying goes, 'If a job's worth doing, it's worth doing well'. Why do something half-heartedly and less than correctly if it only means that you duplicate your input time when you have to redo it correctly? Consider how much less time you need to do something right the first time than you need if you have to go back and do it again. Don't risk angering others with costly delays or mistakes caused by carelessly written paperwork. Champions double-check everything for accuracy and clarity.

Avoid indecision

Procrastination can kill your career and most people procrastinate because of fear. They fear doing it wrong, so instead they do nothing. The trouble with doing nothing, though, is this: doing nothing can only *produce* nothing. Mistakes can and will happen. Champions accept their mistakes and learn from their experiences. Better to act and learn than to not act.

If a client phones to report a problem with the product or service she acquired from a salesperson, what do most salespeople do? They avoid talking to the client and make excuses for being unavailable. They put off the challenge until tomorrow. By then, though, when they do call to apologise and solve the problem, the client may be furious and vow never to do business with the salesperson's company again. So the salesperson has to work doubly hard and spend even more time with the client, just to defuse her anger.

Always call an angry client immediately. The longer you wait, the more the anger grows. In short, the longer you take to deal with a situation, the worse it is when you finally do.

Avoid the telephone trap

The telephone can be your greatest ally or your greatest enemy, especially when it comes to time management. Here are some ideas to help you deal with wasted time on the phone:

- **Control incoming calls.** If you can, divert calls to an answering service or a receptionist, especially during peak work times.

- **Set aside specific time each day to make phone calls.**

- **Set a time limit for your calls.**

- **Write down your objective for each phone call and focus on it.**

- **Have all your materials and information within reach before you pick up the phone.**

- **Encourage e-mail whenever possible.** That way a person can give you all relevant details and you can reply without making five attempts and just missing each other. Plus, you can communicate with her without her being around, at a time that suits you, such as later in the evening.

- **Find polite but effective exit lines to help you get off the phone without interrupting the other person or abruptly ending the conversation.** For example, try saying, 'Barbara, just one more thing before I have to press on.' Such a statement lets the person know that you're coming to the end of the call.

- **Invest in a high-quality headset.** If you spend lots of time on the phone, or if you're in telemarketing, a headset allows you to use both hands to attend to other things while you're on the phone.

If you think of the phone as a business tool, not unlike your computer, mobile phone, and calculator, you'll be able to form new habits for using it that will keep you out of this common time trap.

Avoid meetings that leach time

Attending too many non-productive meetings can be a major time waster. Often meetings are held about meetings! Unfortunately many meetings are unplanned, unstructured, and poorly disciplined so that they bleed away precious time. Our suggestion is to avoid them whenever possible and make them tightly planned when they must happen. Create an agenda and limit input to concise business information rather than personal battles and opinions.

As a sales manager and leader you of course need meetings to keep your team inspired and informed, but hold these meetings at sensible intervals – weekly or monthly – with a planned duration of one hour. Hold them early in the morning so that plenty of the selling day is left, and tightly manage and design them, preparing content ahead of time. Make the delegates aware that it's a business meeting, not an extended coffee break.

A great technique Ben learnt from Stelios Haji-Ioannou, creator of easyJet, is to hold stand-up meetings in corridors instead of sit-down meetings in luxury board rooms.

Another great idea is to hide away from those who might suck away your time and avoid meetings almost altogether. The topic of discussion can usually be written down and faxed or e-mailed to you. If you prevent the meeting and ask merely for the topic to be explained to you via e-mail, you may find you can answer in just a few moments instead of consuming an hour or two, plus travel time, to bash out the same topic and reach the same conclusion. And avoid giving out drinks in meetings – if people aren't offered a pleasant cup of coffee they have less desire to stay around!

We do, however, still encourage meetings with a potential client or an existing client if the subject matter is sales-focused and enhancing to the relationship. The meeting must still be structured, not waffle-driven, and it needs to be managed in a precise time frame, thus creating a professional image. When done well, a meeting can be productive, rather than damaging and time-consuming.

Avoid the long lunch

As with the phone, when you're out for lunch with clients, you need to develop ways to let them know that you've finished your business for today and must move on. For example, when you sit down for lunch at noon with a notorious afternoon waster, you can say something such as, 'This slot works out great. I don't have another commitment until 1.30, so we have plenty of time to talk.' If you know the lunch meeting is likely to drag, don't put yourself in that position in the first place – take control and make the meeting somewhere else at another time.

Avoid a negative energy drain

Negative thoughts that produce negative talk are another big waste of time for salespeople. If you dwell on life's negatives, what do you think you can accomplish? We're positive that you'll accomplish very little. Push negative thoughts from your mind. No one who was a negative thinker ever became a success in selling. Besides, if you dwell upon bad stuff you'll feel pretty lousy after a while and hardly be energised to go out and sell record-breaking amounts and earn top commissions!

Instead of focusing on things you don't like, think about the positive things you can do. And do whatever you can to mix with and associate with positive thinkers, as their positive energy will rub off on you. Associating with positive people may be just the tonic when you're a bit low. (Everyone feels a little down sometimes, but don't dwell on it. When you feel like this, make a focused effort to do something or call someone to take your mind off the negatives.)

Avoid wasting driving time

Most people in professional selling spend a lot of time in their cars driving from appointment to appointment. The average salesperson drives 25,000 miles a year doing the job. Depending on the varying traffic disaster zones and the usual hassles you expect with higher mileage, this can account for up to 15 or 20 hours each week you spend in the car. At almost four hours a day, driving uses a lot of precious time. So what can you do with it?

Well, if you compare these hours with time spent at a college learning an extra skill, which might mean two evenings a week over a year, then you're spending twice that in your car. So, why not learn something? An abundance of superb audio programmes exists, especially about sales development, motivation, financial management, and personal development, available on CD. These programmes represent a positive use of your car time. You could even learn a language!

So choose something to try because you really feel great about yourself and arrive in a far better mindset when you do – and that helps win business, so you can't fail.

Avoid lost appointments

It never ceases to amaze us that so much time is lost when appointments are cancelled or the person isn't there when you arrive to see her – because the appointment wasn't cancelled and the prospect didn't realise or forgot. Whatever the cause, the time is now dead – and you can't afford dead time.

Say 'No' more often!

Many of us just can't say no when people want a piece of our time. But saying no to someone, and getting the job done, is better than saying yes and not getting the job done. Sometimes you're not even the most capable person to do the job.

Professionals recognise their limitations. And when they bump into their limitations, they delegate requests for work that's outside their scope to colleagues who are more capable and more likely to complete the job efficiently. If you explain, with warmth and care, the fact that others are better suited to getting the job done properly, the people who ask you for favours will appreciate your honesty and your ability to refer them to someone trustworthy to do the job.

As you become more successful, your time becomes more valuable, making it all the more important for you to learn when (and how) to say no.

Why do salespeople fail to confirm appointments? The old standby: fear. Some salespeople fear that, if they call, the person may say, 'I'm too busy now'. Such salespeople would rather drive all the way to a customer's office and have the receptionist tell them that the customer's been called out of town for the day. Isn't hearing the truth better than wasting much more time in a false illusion? Hear the truth, erase a non-interested prospect, and clear the way to go and earn some money from a client who is keen!

A quick phone call before you leave not only can save you valuable selling time; it also tells the prospect that you're a professional with something valuable to say. If you handle it properly, your brief call to confirm may keep your appointment from being the one that gets cancelled if your customer needs to change her decision-making schedule. When you call to confirm an appointment, do it this way:

> Hi, Jane. Just a quick call. I shall be with you at 2 p.m. as arranged but just to let you know I have some very interesting material that I have uncovered whilst preparing for this meeting that I shall share with you. A quick question – is there likely to be a parking space in your car park or is it best to find a place to park before coming across to you?

Never say, 'I'm just calling to confirm, is it still convenient?' This line simply invites a 'No'. Better to assume the meeting and switch focus onto something such as parking or where to meet if not her office. Of course, if she really doesn't want to meet or something has genuinely come up, then this is the chance for her to cancel, but you'd rather hear it now than drive there and find out later. And another benefit: even if the decision-maker does have to cancel, you have her on the phone to immediately schedule another appointment. If for some reason you can't get to the person you have the appointment with, tell the person taking the message that you're on your way and you'll be on time. Ask the person who takes the message to pass it on to the customer you're meeting.

Always take the time to confirm your appointments. The time you save frees you up to prospect for new business or to take care of something else on your list.

Being Selfish Is Okay Sometimes!

Always allot part of your day to working with people, supporting your colleagues, or helping to solve the variety of challenges that a working week presents to you, but also allow yourself some solo time, both at work and in your personal life. *Solo time* is time for whatever you need to do. It can be your time for emotional and physical health in your private life, as well as your most productive work time.

During your solo work time, if someone asks, 'Do you have a minute?' just answer, 'Not right now. Can it wait until this afternoon?' By that time, most people who were looking for your help will have solved the problem themselves, or they'll have realised that their problem wasn't all that important anyway.

Here are some tips for handling interruptions to your solo time:

- ✔ **Rearrange your office so that your desk is out of the line of sight of people who walk down the corridor.** If people don't see you, they're less likely to stop by to chat.

- ✔ **Remove extra chairs from your office.** Position any necessary chairs as far away from your desk as possible. This way, people won't be tempted to sit down for long periods of time.

- ✔ **Place a large clock where you and any visitors can see it clearly.** A clock will help you and your visitors keep track of how much of your time they're taking up.

- ✔ **Don't look up when someone walks into your office.** This habit is hard to get into, but if you appear to be extremely busy and the potential interruption is nothing serious, most people will simply walk away. This advice may sound cold, but if you can't get your work done, your inefficiency will cause your customers to receive less service, and you to earn a lower income.

Staying in touch with customers without losing time

Following up on clients and prospects is always a challenge to your time resources (Chapter 14 has more on doing follow-up). In the past few years, many new time-saving products have enabled salespeople to become more and more efficient. Back in our early selling careers, computers were in their early days and laptops and handheld portable devices were mere dreams, so the challenge to stay organised and time-efficient meant adherence to stronger disciplines. Now the high-tech revolution has accelerated the pace of all aspects of our lives and the ease of information storage and access is changing how you can be. And, especially for salespeople, those changes are for the better.

If you haven't already got a good one, invest in a smart mobile phone that stores hundreds of contact details and includes a diary planner and reminder function. Everyone in outside sales can benefit greatly from this important time-saver. A phone such as this more than pays for itself in the greater income you will earn because of the improved service you can give your customers. With a smart mobile phone or PDA, your office is always with you and you can always be reached if a customer has a problem or if a prospect you've been working with calls to say that she's ready to do business with you.

Use proper business etiquette in relation to your mobile phone. Never leave it turned on during a presentation unless both you and the customer are waiting for an important call about that particular meeting. If your phone rings in the middle of the presentation and you stop to take the call, you in effect tell that person that she isn't as important as whoever is calling. And that's not the message you want to communicate. The same advice is also true for pagers; set them on vibrate or turn them off when you're with a prospect.

To get started on minimising interruptions, keep an interruption log just for one day. In it, record the following:

- ✔ Who interrupted you
- ✔ What time they came and left
- ✔ How much time you wasted
- ✔ What you can do about it

If the same person is interrupting you all the time or the same type of challenge is continually presenting itself, taking a bit of time to train that person or to institute a new procedure can save you a lot of time in the long run.

When an occasional crisis comes up, deal with it quickly, and then go straight back to your original schedule. You don't have to become antisocial around the office, but you may be surprised at how much more efficient you can be when you start taking back stray minutes here and there. Time flies – and you never hear the rustle of its gossamer wings.

Part V
You Can't Win Them All

In this part . . .

Rejection is a part of life, and it's certainly a part of selling. So in this part we help you handle the knock-backs you're bound to face and show you how each one actually means more success for you. We also help you focus on your long-term goals so that the daily setbacks of selling won't get you down.

Chapter 17

Staying Positive

. . . .

In This Chapter

▶ Using the values that motivate you to make more sales

▶ Avoiding situations that make you want to stay in bed

▶ Persevering through rejection until you succeed

. . . .

*E*veryone has experienced rejection. And you will, too. You cannot avoid rejection, but you can plan and discover how to minimise its impact. In this selling game, what separates you from all those who let themselves get sidetracked by rejection is your attitude towards it.

As you gain more experience in the game of selling to, persuading, or convincing others, you also create a protective shell that shields you from the cheap shots and hurtful jibes of rejection. If you don't expose yourself and get hit and hurt by some of those rejection shots, you never discover how to protect yourself. You take rejection personally, and you may end up depressing yourself right out of the business altogether.

In this chapter, we focus on how to overcome such feelings. We cover what motivates people and what you can do to increase your own levels of enthusiasm in your selling career and beyond.

Promoting an Enthusiastic Attitude

So what's the best weapon to use when fighting those feelings of inadequacy created by temporary failure and rejection? *Enthusiasm!* That one little word, a word you've heard so many times, can make the difference between being a highly successful champion in sales and an ineffective struggler. If you just go through the motions of selling but do so with little or no enthusiasm for the job, your results on payday are terribly disappointing. Your income in selling is in direct proportion to the amount of service you give others. Little service equals little income. Lots of service equals lots of income. And, you won't have much success in serving others unless you're enthusiastic about what you do.

Clients have as much enthusiasm for getting involved with you as you have for getting them involved, so if you aren't enthusiastic about every selling contact you make, you may as well save yourself and your prospects the time and trouble of showing up at all. You can be just as productive staying home in your pyjamas and slippers.

Dwindling enthusiasm isn't the only concern of professional salespeople, but it leads to many more difficulties that may short-circuit your career. Often other factors lurk just below the surface but when your enthusiasm is high, you can overcome and work around much that you couldn't otherwise. When your enthusiasm dies, other challenging issues seep through and are evident as negative and depressive actions.

To see what makes enthusiasm such a rare commodity in many sales situations, you need to examine where enthusiasm comes from and why it so easily gives up the ghost to depression and inactivity.

If people knew the secret of why enthusiasm wanes and depression creeps through the back door, they'd easily see the enemy approach and prepare for its descent on their livelihoods. Most people don't consciously allow enthusiasm to fade; instead, it slowly, insidiously creeps away like erosion of a sandy cliff and you don't notice its absence until it's almost gone. The hard part about battling the depression you experience because of failure and rejection is that it sneaks in disguised as a friend because well-meaning friends and associates lavish you with sympathy and attention. The attention itself can be welcome and addictive. The 'cushion' that attention from others gives becomes a warm, soft embrace – inadvertently the depression feeling actually brings about a good feeling. This is a dangerous cycle that you need to guard against.

Finding Out What Motivates You

Maintaining enthusiasm for your selling role is directly linked with the conscious or unconscious motivation that was your driving force in the first place. So the question to answer is, why do you do what you do?

Philosophers, psychologists, and psychiatrists have had a field day with that question for centuries. And they've come up with a short list of the most common reasons people give for doing whatever they do. Review the following sections so you can determine what *your* primary motivator is and then use that knowledge to spur yourself on to even greater success.

Money

Many professional salespeople admit to being motivated to sell because they enjoy lighting up the faces of the people they help to benefit from their offering. Few but the candid and outspoken, however, say that money motivates them to sell.

Give yourself permission right now to admit that money is a big motivator. Being money-conscious is perfectly acceptable as long as the method you use to generate and earn that money is honest and the offering provides good service, quality, and value and is in the client's interests. Charging a fair market price and even a little more if your offering is genuinely of better class is perfectly acceptable, but talking it up when it honestly isn't that good underneath is taking advantage of the prospect's naivety, and that road eventually leads to failure.

You can be money-motivated and make a lot of money from your selling; just ensure that the prospects get value and you remain motivated to carry on because their feedback as thankful and happy clients keeps you going.

Money can be one of your motivators, or even your primary motivator, but it cannot be the be-all and end-all of your sales transactions. Many top producers look at the amount of money they make as a reflection of the excellent service and high sales standards they develop over the years in their industries. When champion salespeople notice a decline in income, they look to improve service and product knowledge instead of wasting time being depressed about how a drop in income could have happened to them.

Security

Many people say they work to create security. But what exactly does that statement mean? Security is a false motivator, because no guarantees exist in life, much less in sales. Security isn't actually possible. In fact, you are only as secure as your ability to handle insecurity.

Especially in today's changing economy, security in employment is rare.

Security lies within. No matter who you are, what you've achieved, or where you've risen to, you've experienced fear and want somewhere along the way. Fear and want can be read as insecurity – but they can also be driving, creative, and positive forces that motivate you to achieve. So the state of being free of these feelings isn't what contributes to security, but rather how you interpret and deal with them as they confront you.

The key to getting what you want may be the ability to give up what you have. If you're determined that you'll never take a chance to further your career, then you may as well get out of sales right now, because taking risks is what selling is all about. In selling you soon find out that security and complacency are actually enemies to high achievement and increased performance. Indeed any sales manager worth his crust will keep you pushed to the limit and feeling on edge because that is precisely the best way to operate a successful sales team. When you can appreciate this state of affairs, your sales career will really take off. If you can't get used to this pressure and long for the stability and comfort that you have become accustomed to, resign yourself to the knowledge that you can never go much further up the ladder of success.

Most famous and powerful people who have acquired a great deal of security or money have also lost as much (if not more) than they've made. What sets these people apart is that they were willing to take the chance in order to become all that they could be, whereas the average worker isn't willing to take the necessary risks. A winner always looks at what can still be made instead of looking back and lamenting what was lost. The saying that you don't appreciate the highs unless you've lived through a few lows can be a welcome reminder. You get little or no sense of achievement when your road to success is 'safe'. The pressure and risk-taking are what set you apart from the rest – where you win, and others won't even play. The challenges and uncertainty are what makes your success ultimately worthwhile.

Great salespeople are willing to give up what they have for what they can attain. So can you. Be a risk taker. You may wonder how you'll ever find security if you're constantly taking risks. With whatever semblance of security you achieve, though, comes the knowledge that you create your own destiny. Your success and security are determined primarily by your ability to overcome the setbacks that your career in sales hands you. And in sales you have plenty of time to test your ability to be a risk-taker.

Achievement

Everyone wants to achieve something. Some people strive only for modest goals, while others shoot for the moon, but all are ready to achieve. Few people wander aimlessly through life without, at the very least, the desire to achieve the basic needs of food and shelter. Indeed, everyone feels the same desire to improve his life. Those who lose that desire have experienced people or circumstances that squashed their spirit and buried the desire.

All people believe that they should get what they deserve, and unfortunately many of them feel they're deserving of greatness, whether they work for it or not. In those moments when you're brutally honest with yourself, you probably realise that you usually get what you deserve. The question is: What could you get if you really pushed for it? What *could* you deserve?

Achievement isn't always measured monetarily. Instead, you can measure it by the influence and power you wield or by the humanitarian efforts you give to those in need. To you, achievement may be seeing your children go through the best schooling and become supremely rounded and well-balanced adults bringing up a happy and united family. Or achievement to you may be rising from the lowest ranks to owning the business and helping others who strive to climb through after you. Or it may be sharing your wealth by funding facilities for your community or releasing yourself so that you can really contribute instead of being tied to a desk.

Achievement can be many things to many people. Whatever it means for you, appreciate that achievement is often a great motivator.

Recognition

For most people, the need for recognition begins in childhood. When you were 5 or 6 years old, you probably stood on your head, played dressing-up, or did other clever little-kid things that adults thought were adorable, just so that you'd get attention. In later school years, you may have focused on academic prowess or have striven for supremacy in sport. But everyone can remember pushing for a chance of being recognised for his achievement. People have an in-built, subconscious need for recognition and appreciation. Only if you believe that 'no matter how hard you try, it still won't be enough' is this need not evident, but even then, you probably feel that you would like the recognition if only you felt you could achieve it. Recognition is a prime motivator.

Not only do people have a need for recognition, but they also like to be the ones to do the recognising. Look at much of the media today and its massive focus on celebrity. Whether the recognition is negative or positive, the results are similar. In recent years television has delivered a proliferation of shows that provide millions with the hope of a few minutes of fame and recognition. As Andy Warhol suggested, everyone wants his 15 minutes of fame.

Recognition is a tricky business, but it can motivate you nonetheless!

Acceptance from others

Relying on acceptance from others for motivation can be a dangerous thing. The day you rise above the masses as a top producer is the same day that the masses that you've been associated with turn against you. When you were with them, they were encouraging because they felt you were one of them, but when you make it, they no longer experience that empathy and try to pull you back down again. 'It's lonely at the top' is an experience shared by many.

When was the last time you heard people say or do things to bring a person down who is already in the dumps? That situation just doesn't happen. The commonly held belief is that you 'don't kick someone when he's down'. You generally try to build up someone who needs help and encourage him to succeed – just until they rise above you! Acceptance can soon turn into jealousy and many former peers become jealous and bitter when your efforts see you rise above them. Indeed your peers will often try to prevent your rise with subtle comments such as 'Oh, that won't work!' or, 'Well, that may have worked for them, but do you really believe that you can carry it off?'

Surround yourself with positive people who will support you in your efforts towards building a successful career. Adjust your peer group. Begin mixing with those who strive for success rather than those who accept the status quo. Make it your mission to keep company with people who have similar goals and desires to yours. Share leisure time with ambitious people instead of those who cocoon themselves and blame everyone and everything as reasons why they haven't had a chance. Acceptance from a peer group that doesn't see where you want to go is non-acceptance. Instead push for acceptance from those who you aspire to be. Mix and communicate with those who have surpassed where you are now and are still driven upwards.

Self-acceptance

When you accept yourself and are happy with the person you are, you experience a freedom you never thought possible. You are free to do things your own way or not to do them at all; to enjoy life and all the wonders it has to offer. You are also free of the damaging effects of rejection and failure. Self-acceptance, however, doesn't work as a motivator in isolation:

- ✔ You cannot get recognition if there's no achievement to recognise.
- ✔ You cannot attempt the things you want to achieve without first having a sense of security in your ability to do so.
- ✔ You cannot earn money without giving service. In fact, in sales, money is a reflection of the amount of service you give.

Most people measure their success by how much money they have, so self-acceptance goes hand in hand with the amount of money they accumulate. But you cannot measure yourself only in monetary terms. Money is a good thing, but it must not be totally consuming and the only measure for your self-acceptance. Indeed true self-acceptance releases you from the need to measure yourself with money, as you become happy with yourself as a person whatever level of cash or notoriety you achieve. When you truly accept yourself, you can do what you *want* to do and not what you think you *should* do. Life is much sweeter when you accept yourself and amazingly wonderful things and people will gravitate towards you.

All people are interrelated. You're not developing a career alone, so what you do or don't do may profoundly affect many others in your sphere of influence. Keep that in mind the next time you're tempted to do something you instinctively know is not right. 'What goes around, comes around' may well be true. If what you do today isn't in another's best interest, then rethink before you act. Whichever way you look at it, you are not alone in this universe and the ripple effect is alive and well, especially in the sales industry.

Knowing What Discourages You

If motivators are what make people move forward towards successful sales careers and de-motivators cause them to stop dead in their tracks or even go backwards, why doesn't everyone just do the things that motivate them? Believe it or not, the reason is that the average human being is more de-motivated than motivated. Negativity resembles gravity – a powerful force that can hold you back and requires tremendous effort to overcome.

The eternal conflict between motivators and de-motivators

Motivators and de-motivators are powerful opposing forces that work to contradict themselves in your selling situations. If you're unable to maintain a high level of enthusiasm, you de-motivate and enter your danger zone. When you are in this place, one of two things happens: either you become withdrawn or you become hostile. Neither is pleasant and both can create a downward spiral.

On the other hand, when you're motivated, happily striving for security, recognition, and the other feelings that motivate you forward, you're more likely to be in your comfort zone and encouraged to keep performing, reaching ever-higher levels of achievement. You are on an upward spiral.

As a paradox, the fear of a negative may be the motivation that creates momentum. Indeed, a vision of that negative may be what keeps you going. 'Bad stuff' can actually be good! Thus you face the eternal challenge to find a motivator that suits you and lasts.

As a rule of thumb, you can assume that when all is going well you're more motivated and when it starts to go wrong you lose heart and become de-motivated.

Turning negative situations into positive ones is what makes selling so exciting. Entering the office of a hostile or withdrawn executive and leaving him an hour later with a smile on his face and a positive attitude with which to face the rest of the day is really a kick. What an experience!

Just as you need to know what motivates you to succeed, you also need to recognise the danger signals that can bring your career to a halt. The following sections outline four of the most powerful de-motivators that stop people achieving.

Loss of security

A big de-motivator for many people is the fear of losing their security – financially or otherwise. But when you begin a career in sales, or when you take your career up a notch, you often have to spend money to make money or step back a level in immediate income to enjoy greater returns further down the line.

If you fear losing, then you're simply focusing on the wrong angle. Try asking yourself this question: 'Does what I do contribute to the value of the company I serve? Am I a cost or a profit centre?' If you're meeting your sales targets, then you should always be a profit to your company, and rarely does a company deliberately cut its profits! If you can sell, the last thing you need ever worry about is job security. Even if the current employer loses his head and asks you to leave, your talents are in demand in the marketplace! Loss of security *is* a de-motivator, but never a reality for a professional salesperson.

Accept that your selling career won't always be plain sailing and that you'll experience tough times as well as good ones. Overall, you have a skill that is much needed. Never dwell on loss; always remind yourself of the gain. Push yourself to be a profit centre and banish job insecurity forever.

Self-doubt

Self-doubt is a big de-motivator in selling. On the day you told them you were going into sales some of your family members probably said: 'What? Are you crazy?' or 'Selling – it's feast or famine!' Indeed Ben's mum said, 'It'll be all right until you get a proper job'! These sorts of comments can be massively motivational! To all of those who ever doubted us, we offer a resounding 'thank you' because you motivated us to prove you wrong! And if that worked for us, then it can work for you. Let self-doubt be a fuel for a fire to blast you forward. Set yourself the challenge of 'proving' what you can do and 'proving' the doubting voice wrong in the process.

Most beginners in sales busy themselves with the unnecessary question of 'What did I do wrong?' when their attempts at selling fail. The difference between champions and novices is that champions ask themselves a different question: 'What did I do *right*?' When you examine what was right about the sale or even about a non-sale, you can repeat what was right, gradually eliminate the wrong bits, and then succeed most of the time.

When you get a little experience under your belt you soon realise that self-doubt is a waste of time. Besides, how can you doubt that you can do it when you've done it before! If you couldn't do it, you would never have done it.

The champion in sales considers this important lesson: The only way you ever learn what to do right in selling is by doing it wrong, keeping your enthusiasm, figuring out what to do, and overcoming that pain. The only way to overcome self-doubts is to face them head on and then push yourself by doing the exact opposite of what they make you feel like doing. Kill the self-doubt dead. Simultaneously establish strong success habits – such as constantly looking to improve your sales skills, getting used to post-sales analyses from a constructive, 'recapture the positive' perspective, and keeping good notes for yourself – and you'll shake off moments of doubt and make it through to the winner's circle.

Fear of failure

A great many people are so afraid of failing that they just quit trying. They discover a sure-fire way never to experience failure – never attempt anything in the first place! Of course, you won't experience any successes, either, so you throw out the baby with the bathwater if you let this de-motivator get the better of you. You will never *not* close the sale if you never meet the client.

Instead, live by this principle: Do what you fear the most, and you control your fear.

If you're afraid of one of the required aspects of selling, such as phoning for appointments, you need to overcome it if you truly want to succeed in sales. Almost anything you do that you once feared doing turns out to be much easier to do than you thought. The process gets easier each time you make yourself do it until, one day, you forget how badly you feared it only a few months before. (Did you follow that?) Make that phone call despite the fear until it becomes a well-practised, familiar action that holds no fear because you're already familiar with the outcome.

Fear of failure is only possible when you see a chance to fail. If you view failure only as another way not to do it – as a learning and thus positive step – you'll never see failure and never be afraid. The only time you can ever actually fail is when you stop trying.

Control your fears, and you'll receive such gratification that soon you'll burn with anticipation to do what you once dreaded. Bungee jumping, anyone?

Change

Change is a fierce opponent of progress. You've probably heard statements such as: 'We've always done it this way', 'You'll get used to it – it's just our way of doing things', and 'We prefer to stay with the standard procedure'. These statements are not accurate, though. People don't really want to stay in old ways – unless you meet someone who still uses papyrus, doesn't drive a car, and lives in a cave! Any other human on the planet who has a mobile phone, a computer, and a car can safely be said to in fact like 'new ways'. By mouthing platitudes, people are trying to tell you that they don't like change if the change process makes them feel uncomfortable and inadequate for a time. When they're completely hooked on the perceived new benefits, the pain of change moves aside and the anticipated pleasure of the new way takes hold. This process works in the same way for a progressive salesperson, too.

If you ever feel a fear of change – about a new sales process, a new product or department, or a new company – remind yourself of all the 'new' things in your life and how much better life is with them than it was before you had them. Then fast-forward your new position to that future state and keep focused on that time. The present soon fades and the pain of change is gone.

For example, you'd probably love a change that funnelled all of your future clients and hot prospects through the front door and directly to your desk – though that scenario isn't very likely! More likely is that the lead flow dries up a little and you have to go out and find your own prospects. Now that's a change that may induce fear. But play a future vision that shows that all new sales are a lot stronger because you find them yourself and thus your cancellation rate is a lot lower, the sale value is higher, and you earn more money and get loads more referrals. Your own generation of leads leaves you with a virtually unique ability, word gets out, and you're in such high demand you get offers and promotions coming your way. Your future now actually looks so much better and wealthier all because you learned to find your own leads for a short space of time! You see, change isn't so frightening when you look at it the right way.

Doing what you don't want to do is what you're paid the most to do. You really have to *want* to change. Being satisfied with yourself today is still crucial, but if you want more tomorrow, you must be willing to put up with the pain of change. According to Dr Maxwell Maltz, former plastic surgeon and developer of psycho-cybernetics, change takes 21 days to effect. So you need about 21 days of concentrating and studying the material in this book for this material to become a part of you. Don't fear change, welcome it and all that it can bring.

The champion salesperson's anti-failure formula

What's one of the first words your mother and father taught you when you were a baby? 'No'. Ah, those were the days, weren't they? And why do you suppose 'no' was the first word you learned? Because your parents wanted to protect you from painful experiences.

But all you knew as a child was that 'no' kept you from getting what you wanted. So, as you grew older and kept hearing 'no', you didn't give up quite as easily as when you were a baby. You caught on to this persuasion stuff early on when you realised that 'no' doesn't necessarily mean 'No! Absolutely not! Never! No way!' and you tried to cajole your parents to see things differently – even if it involved holding your breath and turning several lovely shades of blue.

The same thing happens in your selling career. When you begin in sales and you hear 'No', you think that's the end of the discussion. Some beginning salespeople even relate stories of how they never got completely through their prepared presentation because the moment the client said 'No' they slid out the door quicker than a speeding bullet.

As they matured in sales, though, their stories changed. 'No' took on different meanings. 'No' came to mean many things besides a plain-old, final, everyday 'No'. These salespeople began to realise that 'No' could mean, 'Slow down', 'Explain that part a little more', 'You haven't presented the feature I'm most interested in yet', 'You need to ask more questions about my likes and dislikes', or, 'I don't want to part with that much money right now'. These salespeople realised as one of their first steps towards professionalism that they could overcome *all* those things and win the day instead of having to slip out the back door with their tails tucked between their legs.

To help keep new salespeople sane and motivated to stick it out, we recommend looking at the process in a slightly different way. Imagine that for every sale you receive £500, and when you look back over the last few weeks you sat in front of 20 people and sold your offering to four of them. What that really means is you've earned £2,000 (4 × £500) and spoken with 20 people. In other words, you earned £100 for each and every person you spoke to whether he bought or not. Every non-sale was in fact a step nearer to a sale and still meant that you earned your money. In selling you earn your money for staying the course, not for quitting. You earn even when you don't sell provided you keep on trying.

Keep measuring your performance but appreciate that you *earn* every time you present. If you concentrate on that fact, you can see every 'No' as a money-maker instead of criticising yourself. Rather than getting angry or feeling as though you've wasted an hour of your day, think of a 'No' as being handed £100 and moving you one step closer to your goal.

Or look at that scenario another way: If you work with a prospect who has said 'No' many times, but you persist in your attempts for a 'Yes', then you may sit through 200 to 300 pounds' worth of 'No's over a course of several visits, but when it results in a sale you've in fact earned that commission from all of those visits, not just from the last one.

Overcoming Failure

As a salesperson (especially if you're new to sales) you'll experience non-success (another word for failure) at least once or twice a day. How you handle that experience determines how far and how fast you'll go on this sales journey. In the following sections, we recommend five strategies for overcoming failure – specific attitudes to adopt to help you look at failure in a new light.

View failure as a learning experience

When you demonstrate your product to a disinterested party, when you are rejected by a prospect, or when you thought you had your offering sold and the transaction falls through, you can react in one of two ways: You can get angry and be unproductive, or you can investigate the reasons for the temporary failure. We recommend the second of these two options, because when you discover what went wrong, you can prevent those pitfalls from happening again.

Look at the tremendous negatives Thomas Edison overcame when he invented the light bulb. Edison performed over 1,000 failed experiments before he succeeded. But because of his persistence, today we have the light bulb, an invention that has changed our quality of life. Can you imagine receiving a big fat 'No' to what you want to achieve more than 1,000 times – and still persisting? What fortitude! The priceless part of the story of the light bulb, though, is Edison's comments in response to questions about how he felt after experiencing all that failure: 'I did not fail a thousand times. I only learned a thousand ways that it wouldn't work.' You see? Your sense of success or failure depends on the way you look at things.

Think of failure as necessary negative feedback

Negative feedback is really just the information you need to change direction. What a delightful way to look at rejection! When a client never gives you any negative feedback and loves everything presented in your offering yet still decides not to own it, you have nowhere to turn. But when a client tells you what he doesn't like, you have a place to start.

Negative feedback is in fact positive if you view it as steering hints to keep you on track to your future success. If you view this feedback as hurtful and feel that you aren't good enough, you are missing the point. Feedback provides you with the reason why a prospect didn't buy. And if that person is a pretty similar type of person in a pretty similar type of role as your next chosen targets, then possibly your other targets may feel the same way in reaction to being presented with the same selling process. Thus feedback from the one who didn't buy can actually steer you to a whole series of future sales. Take negative feedback on board as a positive pointer not a damning report on you as a person and respond accordingly rather than inwardly self-destructing.

If you take negatives personally, not only will you not reach your destination, but others around you will be caught in your fall-out. You wouldn't like it if another person in your sales team dumped a whole load of negativity on you, so don't take criticism the wrong way and then offload it on others around you. Thank the person who gave you the feedback and then share it with others to help them too. That's what a winner does.

Allow failure to develop your sense of humour

Can you remember having an absolutely disastrous meeting with a prospect? At the time, you wanted to crawl in a hole and never see daylight again. But what did you find yourself doing about two weeks down the road? Sure enough, after a little time to heal, you told the story to your peers, embellishing it to provide special effects, and everyone – including you – had a good laugh.

When you're dealing with failure, you have to learn to laugh sooner. Laughter is a powerful tool in healing hurt feelings and wounded pride. When you share your humorous stories with other salespeople, you'll probably find out that similar things have happened to them. As a result you can release the pressure you put upon yourself to be the best performer and realise that everyone makes a mess of things now and then, even those who succeed the most. The way in which you get back up and fight another day is what makes a winner.

Look at failure as an opportunity

What happens when you do everything you were supposed to do and the client *still* doesn't decide to own your offering? What has he given you? He's given you an opportunity to practise and perfect your selling skills. Are you really any worse off? No. You probably had the chance to enhance your people skills, made a few new contacts who might recommend you even if they didn't buy, and laid the ground for a potential future sale when and if his circumstances change. Meeting with a non-buying prospect is never a waste of time, merely a non-sale.

Winning words

To keep your spirits up when things are down, take a moment to read an excellent verse that Ben discovered many years ago as a rookie and glued in the front of his sales manual. He's kept it close ever since and shared it with hundreds of students as he shares it with you now:

Life's battles don't always go
to the stronger or faster man
Sooner or later the man who wins
is the man who thinks he can

Selling is all about belief. If you fall, get up and try again. You aren't doing anything any other successful person hasn't done. Look upon temporary failure as a refining process like the smelting process for pure metals. When a metal is stressed, heated, and pushed to beyond boiling point, the impurities are sent to the surface. When those impurities are scraped away the remaining metal is much purer – 24 carat indeed. So, too, with you – the hard times and the knock-backs are merely refining moments that make you even better and more precious.

View failure as the game you must play to win

Selling is a percentage game – a game of numbers. The person who sees more people and faces more rejection also makes more money. So, even if you haven't gambled before, you begin to do just that when you get into the game of sales. With every 'No' you hear, you're one step closer to hearing a 'Yes'.

In life, what counts is not the number of times you fail, but the number of times you succeed. And selling is no different.

Chapter 18

Setting Goals to Stay Focused

· ·

In This Chapter

▶ Achieving balance in the goals you set

▶ Following through with your goals

▶ Keeping motivated for fresh goals after you've achieved a few

· ·

Success isn't something you can have a half-hearted 'it would be nice but I'm not that bothered' attitude towards. In order to achieve success, you must want it badly enough to push for it. You *must* focus. Whatever your own goal is, you have to commit to getting it. Don't be fooled into believing some people are lucky; those who achieve the most, burn with a *have to* not a *want to*.

If you have no concrete goals and you feel that you've been succeeding already, just think of how much *more* success you would enjoy if you set your sights more firmly on specific aims. If you had a definite path, a specific time frame in which you expected to reach your destination, and a very clear and identifiable end destination, how much more could you be enjoying? Your success in selling is directly linked to your ability to clearly establish and then stick with your pre-set goals. The sooner you map a course of success, the more likely you are to reach what you want.

You *may* well achieve some level of success without planning too far into your future and without setting many clear goals. However, most professionals who fail to set goals reach a 'peak' in their selling skills and lack either the motivation or the direction to go beyond it. This is not *the* peak of attainable success; it is merely their peak because they are not equipped to go higher. What they don't know – and what you *should* know – is that goals give you three distinct benefits that help you succeed:

✔ Goals keep you on track.

✔ Goals let you know when and what to celebrate.

✔ Goals give you a focused plan to sell by.

And, if nothing else, goals raise the bar and show others around you the level to aim for if they're to keep up with your standards of selling. In this chapter, we give you the information you need to make goal-setting a part of your daily life.

Setting Realistic and Effective Goals

When you first considered a career in sales, you probably had some vague notions of success in mind. For many the initial mental picture is one of being a rep with a pretty cushioned lifestyle, swanning around in a suit, driving a fancy car, and not really working, just talking to people all day! If only that image were the whole truth. You have broad expectations and ideas; our job is to refine them and make them clear and achievable.

You must make your goal or target real. You need to turn vague notions into specific, vivid pictures to keep you on track during difficult patches when you feel like throwing it all in.

When you're setting goals, give yourself the time and privacy you need in order to think about what would make you happy and motivate you to keep going when it gets a little tough. Your goals need to be big enough and inspirational enough to carry you forward. They should even be fun to think of, so don't make your goal-setting session so difficult that you end up setting no goals at all, fearing that the goals you set will be wrong. So what if they are? Are the goals police going to come to your front door and ask to do an audit of them? Probably not. Goals are maps or destination choices – and sometimes both destinations and roads you take to get there change. Maps include unfinished roads or roads that you need to detour around while improvement is under way. The road map you create for yourself is no different.

When you're in the beginning stages of goal setting, you need to remember two things:

- ✔ **The goal must aim for more than you've already achieved but be believable.** Don't set a goal that you don't think you can reach. The trick to setting goals is to make them high enough to push you to higher levels of performance, yet reasonable enough so that you can envision reaching them. If you set goals you don't think you can reach, you probably won't pay the price to reach them when the going gets tough.

- ✔ **The goal must be something that *you* personally really desire.** Having a goal that others prescribe, such as being wealthy, is tempting, but perhaps you're less motivated by money than by family closeness. Your goals must be *your* vivid and 'real' picture.

You're in more control of yourself than you are of exterior circumstances, so losing out on a desired goal when it was beyond your control from the start can be negative and counterproductive.

By setting your own personal goals you become more motivated than perhaps in previous stages in life when goals were set but not really pushed for (such as New Year's resolutions). Big-picture goals break down into daily goals too – these could even be productivity-based, concentrating on achieving your passion step by step. Remember, productivity precedes production, so if you set production goals you're more likely to hit other goals. Actively pursue your productivity goals and increased production will result. For example, you're productive if you make 20 phone calls today. Even if you only spoke with three people, you've been productive. You're productive if you mailed information and thank-you notes to those three people, even if you didn't generate a sale from those contacts – yet. Productivity is seed planting – plant enough seeds in the right ground and surely one day you'll reap a bumper harvest.

Keeping these two rules of goal setting in mind will help you create and stay committed to what is important in your life.

Breaking Down Your Goals into Smaller Pieces

A journey of a thousand miles starts with a single step. So don't worry or focus on the whole journey; instead pay attention to a small, easily attainable first step, and then keep taking steps and eventually you'll reach your end goal. So, when you're setting goals, always begin with long-term ones and work backwards to medium-range and short-term ones. Work backwards to set a small one-step task. This process is also often referred to as 'chunking it down'. You can deal with bite-size chunks and stay motivated.

Long-term goals

Long-term goals should be 20-year projections. Granted, if you're 75, your 20-year goal may be just to plant both feet on the ground each morning. No matter how young or old you are, picturing what you want your life to be like 20 years from today is difficult. But set goals anyway – keeping in mind that they may change along the way.

You may want to consider many areas when you set your long-term goals, but for the purposes of a selling career, we focus on personal accomplishments, asset accumulation, and net worth.

When you set long-term goals, be specific. Instead of saying, 'In 20 years, I want to live in a large house and be financially independent', say something like the following:

> By this date in 20 years, I want to live in a large beachfront house on the shores of the Mediterranean, with beautiful gardens, a swimming pool, and garage that houses my Range Rover, Porsche, and motorbikes. I will own this house mortgage-free and I shall enjoy the freedom that healthy savings of £500,000 invested in various bank accounts allows. I shall also have a beautiful country property back in England with landscaped gardens and roses growing over the front door.

Get the picture? Your long-range goals don't have to be this grand, but they do need to be this *specific*. And they must be something that excites you, so dream in full colour and dream big!

Medium-range goals

When you finish setting your long-term goals, cut them in half and set medium-range goals for about ten years down the road. Compare your 10-year goals to your 20-year goals, and then determine what you must do to make those goals a reality. Then, divide your 10-year goals into 5-year goals. Your medium-range goals are your largest and perhaps fuzziest area, the goals you'll probably have to adjust the most frequently.

These goals are the stepping stones and signposts. All sorts of variables will apply, but as 'all roads lead to Rome', don't worry so much about the route, just have several markers along the way to make sure you're still heading in roughly the right direction.

Short-term goals

Surprise, surprise, your short-term goals demand most of your attention. For best results with short-term goals, never set them for any longer than 90 days. Short-term goals for anything longer than 90 days aren't immediate enough to create a sense of urgency. Immediately after you set short-term goals, you need to start taking steps to reach them. That way, they take root as real, not-to-be-denied entities in your mind – not tomorrow, not next week, but as soon as you make them. Your 90-day goals should then be broken down into 60-day goals, 30-day goals, and eventually, the steps you can put in your planner to take today to achieve them.

For example, if one of your short-term goals is to buy a new BMW, then go down and order one that you can pick up in 90 days. That action will light a fire under you, don't you think? Ordering that car now will get you sweating about making enough money to cover the payments – and will certainly make it a reality!

Balancing your goals with the help of your family

The work/life balance is currently a hot issue, and rightly so. Setting personal as well as career goals is important in order to keep your life well balanced. If all your goals are related to business, you'll have trouble taking time out for family and friends because you'll always be pushing towards the next career goal.

Although we encourage you to pursue your business goals with fervour, we also encourage you *not* to pursue them at the expense of family, friends, or time out for yourself. If you do, you risk becoming so single-minded that you eliminate the human qualities you need in order to succeed in sales. Nobody wants to do business with someone who's too busy to understand and care about her needs. Indeed this behaviour is often correctly interpreted as selfishness and indifference by a client or prospective purchaser. Hence, balancing career goals with personal goals gives you a life both in and after your business day.

As a way to make sure that your goals are well balanced, let your family help you set them. If you do, they're more likely to understand when, say, you have to spend a late night working or invest in a two-day training seminar. Your family will be more willing to share in your sacrifices if you let them share in the celebration of achieving your goals as well.

Another benefit of involving the entire family is that they hold you accountable for your part of the goal and will do what it takes to motivate you. Have you ever thought that sleeping an extra few hours is just what you needed, only to have your partner encourage you to get up and get busy earning your share of that holiday that you both set as a mutual short-term goal? You knew you should get up, but your immediate desire for sleep clouded your judgement. How do you think you'd feel, and what message would you send to your partner, by showing him or her that sleeping is more important to you than working to achieve shared goals?

Remember that your family and friends are your true support system. Indeed life without them, even when you achieve all of the material trappings that your success attains, is empty, sad, and lonely. You need a family to help you perform at a higher level, so share your goals, your successes, and even your failures with them. When you make a sale, schedule a big appointment, or give a poor presentation, give someone you care about a call and share the moment. *She* then knows that you're thinking of her and that she is important to you (that you're not consumed with just your success or failure) and *you* feel a whole lot better for sharing with her.

If you feel too pressured to take that kind of action, then learn a little more about how you're driven. Some people can take big audacious steps and use them to spur themselves forward; others are frightened by big immediate things and this fear holds them back, so taking smaller steps is more appropriate for them. But when you understand what drives you, you take a step that slightly pushes you out of your comfort zone without frightening you rigid! Knowing how you motivate yourself can be a massive contributor to your future achievements.

Putting Your Goals in Writing

When you've set your goals, you need to make your final commitment to them by putting them in writing. You can draw pictures or cut out photos of the things you want to attain – you can even commit yourself by signing a contract. These next sections tell you how to make your goals more real by writing them down.

Making use of the supreme attraction system

The day you write down your goals is the day you commit yourself to reaching them. Until they're in writing, they're merely wishes and dreams. After you write them down, your mind starts seeking out whatever it takes to make those goals a reality.

Putting your goals in writing is the *single, most vital step* in goal setting. Writing down your goals makes them something you can latch onto.

Writing down your goals helps you make use of the *supreme attraction system*, as Ben calls it. For maximum effect, don't just write your goals, make a pictorial storyboard as a future image of your planned life – an image or vision board. This supreme attraction system keeps you focused and driven. Place this vision board somewhere you will see it every day as you get up and as you go to bed. Make it in-your-face and it will permeate your mind. And then your mind will help you to attain your vision on a subconscious level by attracting things into your life.

By making your goals a written and tangible plan, you also give yourself a constant task list. And when you focus on a 'one step at a time' approach as you tackle the list, you slowly but surely tick off the achievements. You will be visibly on your way, and that in turn becomes a huge motivator.

The harder you work towards a goal, the sweeter the taste of success. Don't think for a second that your road to success won't be painful at times. If you don't experience at least a little bit of stretching to achieve your goals, you probably haven't set them high enough to challenge you. And if your goals *aren't* high enough, then they may be holding you back, making you content to reach levels that are no big deal for you. So when the road gets rocky, dig in your heels and let nothing distract you from your goals. Be aware, though, that giving up immediate gratification or postponing what would satisfy you today just for a promise of greater things down the road isn't natural. In today's instant-gratification society, long-term gains are difficult to cling to. But don't sell yourself short by settling for what you know will bring you only temporary satisfaction. Don't be like all of the rest – be outstanding. If you settle for less than your goals, that's exactly what you end up with – less.

If you're determined and enthusiastic about your goals, you won't settle or waver. Your resolve helps you keep a vivid picture in your mind of what you want to happen and how you will make it happen. If your imagination isn't vivid enough, cut out pictures or write detailed descriptions of your goals so that you can refer to them when you get distracted. The more reminders you force yourself to bump into, the more determined you are – and the more determined you are, the more goals you will achieve.

Take all of your goals extremely seriously, no matter how small. Reward and congratulate yourself for starting the habit of planning your life. You'll reap unbelievable rewards.

If you want a better, bigger, brighter future, you must do something different to achieve it. If you want your life to change, *you* have to change it or you'll stay pretty much the same as you are now. So set some goals that whip you up and get your life into gear. All you have to do is make the effort. You can change and become or do anything you want.

Follow these four steps to reaching your goals:

1. **Set goals that really inspire you.**
2. **Vividly imagine your goals and create a clear picture of them in your mind.**
3. **Make your goals real – use images and write them down**.
4. **Commit to your goals sincerely and completely.**

If you do all four of these things, and if you review your goals daily, you soon find yourself making great headway towards achieving them. You're focused both consciously and subconsciously on seeking out the means to your chosen end.

The Law of Attraction

Most people have experienced the phenomenon of fulfilled expectations, but they tend to shrug these off as coincidences instead of planned, envisioned events.

The Law of Attraction states otherwise:

When you think something will happen, and you feel strongly about it, focus upon it, and believe it to be possible, you will bring about its happening.

This idea is probably where the phrase 'mind over matter' came from. The Law of Attraction works with simple things, as well as with matters as complicated as achieving your 20-year goals.

For example, have you ever thought about someone just before she phones you? Or opened your mouth to say something to your partner who actually says the same thing to you before you speak? Well, these events may well occur as a result of the power of the universe and the Law of Attraction – what you focus upon, you experience.

People who always focus on illness and debt experience poor health and poor finances. Here is a real example of this phenomenon: A good friend of Ben's was prone to adopting a negative mental attitude, and Ben constantly told him that he had to change his mindset and stop talking about how he was always short of cash. Indeed Ben told him straight to stop attracting negatives and said he wouldn't visit him, and so give him the chance to attract negatives towards Ben himself, unless he changed his focus and conversation. Ben did stop visiting and calling, but the friend made a point of meeting up some six months later. The change was quite noticeable. Over the months, every time he'd started expressing negative thoughts he'd made a concerted effort to stop them and strange events had happened – including the arrival into his life of a very positive woman friend who refused to look at what was missing and insisted on helping him count his blessings. Guess what? Two years later his business is doing incredibly well. Why the sudden turnaround after 14 years of struggle? We assure you it wasn't coincidence. He literally attracted into his life, with a little help and nudging, the good fortune he desired.

You can do the same. The Law of Attraction sets no boundaries. It doesn't judge goals as worthy or unworthy, it merely provides for those who call upon it in the right way.

You really can have everything you desire. If it is physically available for someone else, then no earthly reason exists why it isn't available for you. You may have to work a little smarter, learn a little more, or even mix with different people. You may well have to take a little responsibility for achieving instead of merely wishing and being lazy, but if you do so anything can be yours.

So be your own fortune-teller. Predict your own success by making your goals happen. The more you believe in your own success, the more you will do to turn your goals into realities. Success is no accident! You plan it, you work on it, you monitor it, and you adjust it to enable yourself to enjoy a productive and prosperous life. People may look at the success you've spent years accomplishing and see you as an overnight wonder. They may even try to tell you how lucky you are to have the things you have. Well, we say you create your own luck. You control your own destiny. Lady Luck has little to do with your success, and she shouldn't get the credit for your achievements.

Creating leverage to achieve your goal

Most people don't achieve their goals because they haven't shared them with anyone and thus don't fear the embarrassment of failure. People need to experience pain to achieve their goals and are more prone to act when they hurt than when they just want more. The common tendency is to want more, but when getting more becomes really tough, most people slacken off and tell themselves, 'Oh well, it's not that bad'. So, pain is a necessary motivator.

First, you need to create a lever to propel you forward. Use a pull – much more money to spend, or greater prestige amongst peers, and so on. These pull points are very strong and effective but in themselves are rarely enough.

Then you add push leverage. Here, you make public – and loudly so – the goal and tell everyone to help you, police you, and ridicule you if you don't achieve it! (Well okay, maybe you don't tell them to ridicule you. But you won't need that anyway because the embarrassment of not achieving a goal you loudly proclaimed will be enough.)

To guarantee you will reach a goal, give yourself pain and leverage – and embarrassment is pretty effective if you've allowed yourself to brag a lot in the first instance about where you're going to be in a year or two!

In addition to a verbal declaration, and to help make it more public, you can make a physical agreement to achieve – a contract – with a neighbour or an associate, someone you know but aren't over friendly with. A partner or spouse is no good as he or she believes your excuses and loves you anyway. You need to fear the pain of being disowned! The sidebar 'Signing a Goal Contract' has a sample contract.

This is a strange idea, perhaps, but it works because you're trained not to break contracts. When your goal becomes something real, public, and signed it becomes binding, and mentally it carries more weight. Put the declaration and contract together and you have a very public announcement of what you intend to achieve coupled with a notice to all that you must achieve it as it's contractually binding. The pain or penalty of not doing so is hideous embarrassment and never being able to appear in public again! Is that motivator strong enough?

Treat your contract seriously and abide by terms and conditions such as the ones we suggest here:

1. Any goal ever included in this contract, no matter how small, must be treated with great respect, because the achievement of goals builds character and self-image.
2. This contract must be completed in full, with start and completion dates, and including a witness to the statements and intentions declared.

Signing a Goal Contract

For a bit of light-hearted but helpful fun you can use this contract to make a deal with yourself and a partner. By making a 'contract' you give yourself a piece of paper that you can stick in a prominent place on your wall so that it serves as a daily reminder, helping you to have supreme focus and to stick to the disciplines. Signing the contract in itself could be the very action that ensures you get your goals.

Date: _____ 20_____

Name: _____

The undersigned proposes to make available all resources, to learn any and all relevant skills, and perform all labour necessary to complete the following goal:

_____
_____
_____
_____

I hereby swear to start today to reach out and do more with my life and achieve the greatness that I know lies within me, which is waiting to be brought out.

From this day forward, I will not deny myself any longer. Today is the day when I finally get the courage and strength to do what I know I must do and stop taking the easy way out. I will pay the price that is necessary to reach this goal because I know the pain of not fulfilling myself is greater than the pain of doing any job, no matter how hard the job may be.

I understand that I will reach my life's plan by reaching one goal at a time, each smaller goal putting me one step closer to my greater future. I understand that each contract I fulfil always puts me one step closer to what I want out of life, and I will not have to settle for what others give me or for just earning a living. I have the power to change my life.

_____   _____
Signature   Signature of referee

As I endorse this contract, I understand that my future is in my hands only and I can look to no one else for its fulfilment.

Acceptance

Upon the completion of this goal, I will allow myself to be congratulated for proving that I can do anything that I want and be anything that I want. I also acknowledge that I can get anything I want as long as I know what it is and I am specific in my requests when calling into effect the Law of Attraction.

I have taken one more step towards being the person I dream of. I may take pride in knowing that I have the commitment and courage to plan and reach a goal.

I am now one step closer to my major goal as I fully appreciate that major goals are just a string of successfully attained smaller goals that combine to become the full path.

_____   _____

Signature   Signature of referee

Date Fulfilled: _____ 20_____

3. The goal must be precise and explicit. It must paint a very clear picture of what you want and when you want it.

4. This contract must be read out loud in front of the mirror every day, and read with great conviction so as to embed the goals into your subconscious mind.

5. When a goal is reached, the contract must be signed and the words 'This contract fulfilled' written in large red letters across it. All fulfilled contracts must be saved and kept in order by date completed, so that a pattern of growth remains on record.

6. You must remember that you can be as great as anyone, but that you must be disciplined and maintain a plan to achieve your goals. Each goal in your plan, no matter how small, must become part of the larger plan; when it does, it may then help you to turn your beautiful dreams into a fantastic, rewarding life.

7. Be very aware of some potential for conflict when setting goals and make certain a goal is correctly thought through before adding contractual weight behind it. Do not make conflicting goals, such as 'I will spend more time at home' and 'I will double my sales' because they may not work together and may cause frustration in your life.

8. Your goals must entice you so intensely that they ignite your soul and make you burn with enthusiasm.

9. You cannot reach a destination if you don't know how to get there. Each goal becomes a stopping point or starting point on the road map of your life, which in turn becomes the blueprint for your every success. You must have a blueprint if you desire to enhance your life.

Planning What to Do When You Achieve Your Goals

The funny thing about achieving your goals is that, as you get close to doing so and look back, the struggle to achieve them doesn't seem as difficult as you'd originally thought. Indeed by the time you reach or almost reach a pre-set goal, you've probably mentally moved much further ahead, and the goal you set no longer feels much of a goal! It feels easily achieved and pretty normal.

Everyone has a tendency to remember only the good bits, even though they probably experienced many noteworthy struggles and hard times on the road to achieving most goals. Time has a way of softening the edges of the tough times, thankfully. For example, think back now to what you were doing five years ago. Now think forward five years. Which seems longer? You tend not to feel a day older but you know you're in fact years older. You look back and it seems like yesterday, but look forward and it seems much more distant.

Undoubtedly, when you get in the habit of setting goals, you find yourself looking and jumping ahead towards the next set of goals before you close on those you're about to achieve – which is a good thing to do. Keeping yourself fresh and driven is better than having no ambition or desires to look forward to. But remember that you need to give a little mental focus to the now. You need goals that drive you forward but you must not be consumed with the future to the extent that you miss life as it passes you by. Success is in the journey, not the arrival. You need to have a work/life balance and enjoy some of the achievements as they come your way. For example, if you set yourself a goal a few years ago to earn another few thousand pounds and thus afford a new car and a special holiday, make sure you celebrate your achievement and enjoy the rewards when they arrive. Pushing yourself past these achieve-ments and not even stopping to say well done and thank you to yourself just because you've already mentally moved on to the next goal would be wrong.

When you achieve your goals you must celebrate your success. When you celebrate, keep these suggestions in mind:

- ✔ **Include in your celebration everyone you involved in the setting and accomplishing of your goals.** They were there with you in the beginning, and they'll be eager to rejoice with you in your successes.

- ✔ **Celebrate in proportion to your achievement.** For example, don't reward yourself with a luxury holiday just for calling a hundred people in one month. A hundred calls in a month is part of your job, and you know it. You must reward yourself a little, though, so perhaps book a night out for you and your partner or get a new addition for your wardrobe.

- ✔ **Allow yourself a temporary slowdown after you achieve a difficult goal.** Indulging the natural tendency for a slowdown is okay, but don't allow the easing-off period to run for too long. The longer you remain inactive, the harder it is to get revved up again, and you may well find that maintaining the rhythm is actually more enjoyable than stopping and starting. After you celebrate, start working on the new goals you set for yourself.

Keeping records of all your successes is a good idea, too. Just having a record in a book, or a file of your achievements can in itself be a motivator as you look back and admire how far you have come. Keep a scrapbook of notable sales orders or promotion notices and include wage slips that track your income growth over the years.

And when you set the next goal, push yourself just a touch more. Always stretch yourself; that's what keeps you growing in sales. Better to stretch yourself a little too far and not quite reach your goal than not to be stretched at all. Even if you don't reach the too-ambitious goal, you'll have come a long way forward and you'll know it. Besides, if everything's too easy, you get bored and then selling stops being a hobby and looks more and more like a job.

The harder the goal is to achieve, the more value you find in its achievement. And don't wait until you close on one goal before you set your next one.

Part VI
The Part of Tens

'... and the beautiful princess kissed the
frog and, hey presto, the frog turned into
a handsome salesman.'

In this part . . .

These short chapters are packed with quick ideas about selling and persuading that you can read any time you have a few minutes. Here you'll find information on the most common sales mistakes (so you can be sure to avoid them), the characteristics of professional persuaders, and ways to master the art of selling. We also give you some fantastic Web sites to turn to for even more information.

Chapter 19

The Ten Biggest Sales Mistakes

In This Chapter

▶ Avoiding the mistakes of those who've gone before you

▶ Learning from those mistakes

*E*veryone makes mistakes in life. And you can *expect* to make some when you're trying something new. In this chapter, we share with you the ten most common mistakes others who have gone before you (including us!) have made, so that the start of your journey may be a bit more successful.

Misunderstanding Selling

In most cases, the only contact a business has with the outside world is through its salespeople – and the only reason to have salespeople is for them to sell the company's product or service. Selling is done through the gathering and sharing of information via professional skills and business interactions. The interactions help create the environment and the skills help the prospective client make decisions that move him to making the final ownership decision.

This observation may seem a little basic, but if you walked into most small businesses in the UK today you'd probably find it almost impossible to get someone to describe with any accuracy the style and aim of a sales strategy and very few people indeed would understand the importance of correctly analysing the numbers and what measurements are required. Dangerously true is that often they'd even have trouble describing their ideal customer to you.

You can't know too much about why customers do and don't buy your product or service – and gaining that knowledge is a *primary function* of selling.

Professional sales training doesn't involve tips for becoming pushy or aggressive. A sales trainer who teaches persuaders to become pushy and aggressive is incompetent. Professional salespeople or persuaders are low-key, service-orientated relationship-builders. Especially in today's world, you need to recognise that knowledge and trust override the jazzy, flashy, shallow sales approach. Selling is helping people buy, not forcing them to. Do *not* fall into the trap of getting pushy or stronger – instead, go away and get better.

Expecting Things to Improve by Themselves

Having incompetent or untrained people serving customers is bad business. Business is *all* about selling and maintaining clients or else there simply isn't any money circulating to pay for all of the other roles within the company. But effective selling needs working on; it doesn't just happen by itself. You must apply *effort* to selling and then look after those that you've sold to or you're literally throwing away the money spent in other areas of the company. The same goes for individuals. If you aren't satisfied with your personal success rate or conversion rate on sales calls, you *can* improve. To realise that you have room for improvement and then *not* take any active steps to correct the situation is simply foolish.

Refined sales skills aren't a gift of birth. They are learned skills that anyone can perfect with a little study and work. Start watching others in persuasion situations wherever you go. (Remember, selling is simply persuading others to see it your way, but persuading sounds better than selling!) Ask yourself why some persuaders are good and why some are bad. As with most things, seeing what's wrong is a lot easier than noticing exactly what makes it all seamless when it's right, but keep a keen eye on persuasion situations all around you and watch and learn. When salespeople are well trained and highly skilled, things seem to move forward so smoothly that spotting the sale happening is almost impossible. You may tend to think of these people as naturals and often feel that the sale wasn't a sale because the person wanted to buy! Well, of course he did – but that state of mind was cleverly engineered! Even when a salesperson is naturally comfortable talking with others, the actual skill of persuading must be learned, just as the ins and outs of the product or service must be learned in order to succeed.

Talking Too Much and Not Listening Enough

Most people think that in order to persuade, you have to be a good talker. A typical good talker thinks that if he tells the customer enough about the product, he'll automatically buy. But the truth is just the opposite. The myth about salespeople is perpetuated with phrases such as 'the gift of the gab' or 'kissed the Blarney Stone', implying that success is a result of what is said. Well it is, but only *after* the skill of listening. You have two ears and one mouth – use them in that ratio!

A good salesperson is just like a great detective: He asks questions, takes notes, listens intently to the customer's spoken words, and observes his body language.

In most cases, people who want to talk too much want to control the conversation and are more likely to be aggressive and pushy. Professional sales training involves more questioning and intense listening techniques than it does speaking skills. Knowing the proper questions to ask, not just talking, leads to closing a sale. A salesperson who's been trained to ask questions *leads* the buyer down the path to the sale. He doesn't *push* him down that path.

When you're talking, you're only finding out what you already know.

Using Words That Kill Sales

In any presentation you make, your words paint a picture. And a few wrong word pictures can ruin the entire portrait you're trying to paint.

How many presentations do you suppose are made daily throughout the world in an effort to win approval but don't succeed just because of the sales-killing pictures that the presenter's words paint? For example, a salesperson may create an image of ownership of a period property to a young couple, then raise doubts and concerns by saying something about how home-ownership helps develop do-it-yourself skills. The young couple may have no do-it-yourself skills and now fear expenses of upkeep for the property. Or, the mistake may be as simple as using the internal language or jargon that you're so used to, forgetting that the prospect doesn't understand it. A salesperson talked to Ben about car purchases and was very efficient at *telling* all that he knew after 18 years in the game, expounding on 'peppercorn rentals' and 'balloon payments' – but he didn't get an order! By using the wrong words, salespeople create negative pictures in the minds of the people they strive to serve – giving them more reasons not to go ahead than to get involved.

Not Knowing When to Close the Sale

Most customers who leave a place of business without owning a product or service are shrugged off by untrained salespeople as being 'just lookers' or 'be-backs' or any number of other euphemisms that hide the basic fact that the salesperson didn't manage to sell to them. A professional salesperson, however, prefers to see such customers as what they really are: lost sales.

Basic rules state that you won't get a sale unless you actually ask for the order! If you don't ask, you don't get. Learn to recognise the *buying signs*, such as when the prospects are asking more questions or using language that shows an attitude of ownership, such as, 'Yes, that Van Gogh original certainly will enhance our living room.' A key word to look for from the customer is *will* as opposed to something more hesitant such as *might* or *would.* A client or prospect asking, 'Will it allow me to do 10,000 miles between servicing?' shows he's mentally assuming ownership and playing through ownership situations, which is hugely indicative of his mindset. Buying signs also include asking for more details, wanting to see the instructions for how to operate your product, and asking financing questions. The prospect may ask questions that refer to delivery, such as 'Is it in stock?' or 'Is there a delivery charge?' When you see such signs you *must* ask for the order and close the sale.

Not Knowing How to Close the Sale

In many cases, all you have to do to close the sale is ask. So often you hear the prospective purchaser asking something like, 'Do you have it in red?', to which the reply is 'Yes, we have several red ones in stock.' Such a reply is one of the worst in a professional selling role. The purchaser now has nothing to make him decide today and will probably walk away muttering, 'Okay, I'll come back tomorrow.' He won't and you have lost your commission.

A professional salesperson considers all of the buying thought processes and asks something like:

- ✔ 'If I can get a red one for you, do you want to take it with you today, or shall I have it delivered?'
- ✔ 'I'll check for you. By the way, would you like it gift-wrapped or is it okay just as it's packaged?'

Ask a question that moves the prospect into a position of having to make an ownership decision. Always confirm that if you can give him what he asks for, he's asking because he wants to buy it.

Showing a Lack of Sincerity

If you're trying to persuade someone else to adopt your point of view, to own your product, or to start an account with your service, you must first get him to see that you're talking with him for his benefit, not yours.

You have to get the 'commission vision' out of your eyes. Never let greed get in your way of doing what's right. If you don't sincerely believe that what you have to offer is good for the other party, yet you still try to convince him to own, one of two things will happen:

- ✔ He'll recognise your insincerity, not get involved with you, and tell at least a dozen other people how terrible his experience with you was, thus ruining your reputation.

- ✔ If you do persuade him, and if what you're selling is *not* good for him, you're nothing more than a con artist and he'll take every measure possible to see that you're punished for being one and again spread the word to everyone that what you're selling is a waste of money.

First and foremost when you're professionally selling or persuading others must be your sincere desire to serve others and help them get involved in something that's truly beneficial for them. Regardless of the stereotypical image of salespeople, you will never win long term if you sell anybody anything that isn't right for him. Honesty and integrity are the key elements to every successful selling career.

Not Paying Enough Attention to Details

'Little things go a long way', we are told, and 'The devil is in the detail'. Why? Well, a person's mindset is revealed by little things and how you think eventually shows up as what results you achieve. When you 'wing' it on your presentation, skim over details, and ignore important cues from others, you also skim over big potential wins for yourself and line yourself up for small returns and struggles. Lost or misplaced orders, letters with typing errors, and missed appointments or delivery dates all ruin your credibility with your prospects. They detract from the high level of competence professionals strive so hard to display and if your clients don't have the impression that you're the best, most professional choice for them, they'll find someone who they feel is – maybe even someone else in your own office. Ooh, that would hurt, wouldn't it?

Letting Yourself Slump

If you could chart your daily activities, productivity, and winning presentations on a graph, what would it look like? Are you a hare in the first week of every month and a tortoise in the last? Most people have patterns to their selling cycles and efforts. Having slower periods and better times isn't unnatural, but keep track of your styles and rhythms and learn to look for signals that indicate a slowdown. If you watch your cycles carefully, you'll see a slump coming long before it hits and be able to adjust your behaviour to even out your successes. Getting out of a slump takes a lot out of you, both mentally and physically. Why put yourself through hard times when you can keep on an even keel instead?

Failing to Keep in Touch

Most people who switch from your product, service, or idea to another do so because they are feeling less important. Maybe you've forgotten to call them for a while and someone else – possibly a competitor – is paying them more attention. Someone else is keeping in contact on a regular basis while you have taken them for granted. Someone else is making them feel important and you're not.

When all it takes is a few contacts by phone or mail to keep people doing business with you, why would you ever get so lazy as to let them go?

People feel left behind, which leads to feeling unnoticed and uncared for, when you don't communicate frequently. And when they feel like that, they'll easily be won over if someone else pays them attention.

All you need to do is schedule two or three quick phone calls to say, 'David, this is Tom from ABC Company. I'm just calling to see if you're still enjoying the new furniture you had from us a month or so ago. Is it still making working at your computer more comfortable? I hope it is! I don't want to keep you but I'm just checking that you really are happy with your choice and that it's all that we both thought it would be. Thank you once again for your business. Look after yourself.' These words take about 12 seconds to say. And isn't a 12-second investment worth it if it keeps a customer?

Chapter 20

Ten Ways to Improve Your Selling

In This Chapter

▶ Recognising the little things you can do to make a big difference in your sales

▶ Putting your clients first

*W*hen you attain a certain level of professionalism, you find that you're selling more. This increase in sales is a culmination of a lot of things: Your prospecting is a lot more refined in that you find the best people to sell to, you qualify those people as potential customers quickly and smoothly, you make more appointments with better people giving you more opportunities to sell, you present in a people-friendly manner, you recognise buying signs along the way, and, most importantly, you enjoy all of it. You're well on your way to having what we talked about in Chapter 3 at the beginning of this journey together – a 'hobby' that's a career, and the next stage is simply just to make it more fun! Here's how you get started on your rise to that fun level of professionalism.

Be Prepared

Preparation is absolutely paramount. Preparation is what separates the wheat from the chaff and the winners from the also-rans. Thus you need to prepare yourself both mentally and physically for the challenge of persuading others. Dress appropriately. Give yourself an attitude check. Clear your mind of everything except what you need to think about for the presentation. Prepare the route to the premises, prepare the agenda for the discussion, review any notes or information that may be vital within a few hours of meeting with your prospects and make sure you're there on time. Doing your homework will help you pass the test every time. The chapters in Part II help you prepare.

Make a Good First Impression

You won't hear many winning stories about people who overcame bad first impressions to go on to land a major account or persuade an important person to their way of thinking. Going in confidently and handling the initial rapport-setting stage properly goes a long way towards winning. Remember, first impressions last. Tips for making a good one are in Chapter 2.

Get Your Targeting and Qualification Spot On

By asking a few simple questions when calling to make appointments, you can determine quickly if the person you're meeting is right for your offering. By doing this, you maximise your efforts by delivering presentations only with someone who is seriously a purchaser not just casually interested. You haven't got time to waste on tyre-kickers, those who give the impression and pretence that they're in the market but in truth haven't a hope. Only meet those people who are in a position to buy and who express a genuine interest. Chapter 7 covers productive prospecting.

Give Every Presentation 110 Per Cent

Never sell a prospect short. In doing so, you show a lack of respect towards her, which will eventually become clear and when it does, you'll probably lose whatever you gained. Don't take shortcuts – we guarantee that when you slack off it will be with a client who you misjudged and then lose. No one is good enough to know exactly how serious a potential client is or how much in a position to buy she may or may not be, so until you perfect the art of mind reading, do yourself and the prospect the honour of a full-blown presentation. You'll never be worse off and you sometimes can turn it around and come out with a great big order, and those are the *supremely* satisfying ones!

By making every presentation seem like the most important thing in your life at that moment, you show the decision-makers that you're sincere about their needs and that they're important to you. Generally, people will be whatever you expect them to be, so expect your prospects to be vital to your overall success in life, and treat them with the proper amount of respect. Turn to Chapter 10 for tips on presenting well.

Address Objections Completely

If and when your prospect voices a concern about something, don't ever glide over it. Let the concern stop you momentarily. Think about what was said and what you may have said or done to trigger the comment. Then carefully and thoughtfully address the concern: 'What I understand from your comment, Mrs Newman, is that you're concerned about the size of the boot in your new car – is that correct?' If it is, you'd better find out what Mrs Newman expects to put into it. And if the issue's critical to the sale, find the right car for her based on the boot or luggage-carrying size.

Remember that raising a concern or an objection shows that the prospect's thinking enough about the ownership of your offering to come up with a sensible comment. If you overcome that comment, you can be sure that her thinking seriously about your offering is likely to lead to a sale. So welcome objections, and turn to Chapter 11 for more advice on how to handle them.

Confirm Everything

Miscommunication costs people lots of money, time, and effort every year. Missed appointments, wrong information sent, or phone calls not made can destroy in minutes what may have taken months to build. Selling relies upon a lot of trust being placed by the purchaser in the seller and her organisation. The act of buying implies that a responsibility exists to 'look after' the buyer once the initial sale is completed. If slips-ups happen prior to completion of the sale, it sends fear signals to the purchaser that you're also going to let her down once she is the owner of your offering, and that can mean big trouble. Lack of attention to details, wrong orders, and wrong people handling important tasks all take their toll. Taking just a few seconds to confirm (and reconfirm) everything along the way will bring you more success.

Ask for the Decision

You have nothing to lose by asking a prospect for a decision. If she's not ready to make a decision, and that's what you find out by asking, great, but if she *is* ready and you don't ask, you lose everything. If you truly believe in the good of what you're doing, you should have no problem asking the other party to commit her time, effort, or money to your cause or for your product or service.

If she's not ready, she has reasons why she isn't ready. By asking for these reasons you can then clarify that they are the only reasons and proceed to address them, and make a sale happen. Asking in the first place shows you how to proceed to get the sale.

Hesitation is an indication of doubt and when you're in the persuader's seat, you should never be the one having doubts.

More sales are lost than you could possibly count just because the salesperson in question sat there hearing positive noises and didn't ask for the flipping order! The buying psychology rarely, if ever, leads the purchaser to actually lean forward and say, 'Can I have one, please?' If she's nodding and agreeing, she's saying 'Yes' in all but the words. *Your job* is to lean forward and ask a closing question, and it can be as simple as, 'So, can I have your order then, please?' Chapter 12 has more on closing the sale.

Use Testimonials and Case Studies for New Products

Very few people want to be guinea pigs. They don't want to be the first to try something out. Most people want to know that others have preceded them and that the product or service is a proven entity – new to them is not the same as new, full stop. New, full stop could mean that the product will break down on them, won't do all that it's supposed to do, and may create loads of trouble. 'New' and 'First' strike fear into many people and stir negative emotions about purchasing. Your job is to create positive emotions about purchasing, which you do by using client testimonials and case studies in abundance.

By sharing experiences you've had with others just like your prospects – others who bought your product, use your service, or are committed to the same project – you give them permission to be like those others and invest in what you're selling. They can recognise the landscape and understand that they're not going into uncharted waters. Overcoming their fears will take you far in convincing or persuading people; especially if you can use examples of people they know.

Work at It Constantly

The most successful people in the world rarely take time off from what they do that makes them successful. We're not suggesting that you become a workaholic, but you can certainly think about new strategies, new ideas, and new people to contact even when you're lying on a beach in the Bahamas for a well-deserved rest. You must switch off occasionally, but if you allow your mind to wander when you are completely away from work, very often you come up with amazing clear strategies and ideas.

Living and breathing what you believe in the most will draw the best new ideas to you. You'll constantly have your success antenna up and tuning in to the best information for you. Indeed, we heartily recommend having more time off and allowing these brainwaves to flood across more frequently . . . they're often excellent and make you more money than slogging away for that day off might have.

Practise What You Preach

If you believe in what you're doing, you must *personally* be a part of it. If you're selling Fords, don't be seen driving a Vauxhall. If you sell home-security systems, you'd better have one in your home. If you market freelance graphic design, your business cards had better be creative. People definitely are not stupid. Even if they don't say so, they're watching with both eyes firmly open to see if you are practising what you preach. Prospects look and sometimes ask – and they can tell if you are lying, too!

Do as you would advise your prospects to do, and then sing with even more conviction as to the merits of what you offer – doing so will help you get hundreds of sales.

Chapter 21

Ten Ways to Become a Master Practitioner

In This Chapter

▶ Taking your selling skills up a notch

▶ Committing yourself to continual improvement

*I*f all you want to do is discover how the masters of sales accomplish what they accomplish, or to admire the top professionals for their incredible achievements, you could do that by reading this book. But if you want to achieve that master's status in sales yourself, then you have to do more than just read this book. *Selling For Dummies* is a reference tool for people like you – people who want to discover the basic techniques of sales and establish a strong foundation of good habits on which to build great careers, but don't think of it as a passport to a privileged future and an automatic entry into a hall of fame winners' circle. You need to consistently re-read the book and then apply the ideas and refine your techniques – so don't save *Selling For Dummies* a space on the top shelf of your bookcase with all the other dust collectors. Keep it within easy reach so that when you need to refer back to one of its pearls of wisdom for encouragement, you won't have far to go.

In this chapter, you have ten choice bits of selling wisdom to return to over the years. Use this chapter as your road map to becoming a master practitioner of the art of selling, as your ten easy steps to becoming a champion in all your future selling situations.

Adopt an Attitude of Discovery

Before you enter into any new experience, make sure you bring an attitude of positive anticipation and enthusiasm. What you gain from this book will be directly proportionate to the time you spend studying and practising the techniques and suggestions offered in its pages. The contents come alive only when you apply them and learn from them. As a result of what you learn, your income will grow alongside the maturity of your knowledge in sales.

If you want to be a master of persuasion and selling, keep in mind that all masters were excellent students first. If you really wish to learn and are supremely committed to the task, then you might also spend a few minutes discovering how *you* learn or remember things. The human brain is a better-known entity these days and scientific evidence now exists explaining how best to absorb information. Without going into an in-depth conversation about neuro-linguistic programming (NLP) here and now (though if you're interested, we can recommend *Neuro-Linguistic Programming For Dummies* by Romilla Ready and Kate Burton (Wiley)), we can point out that such things as making up rhymes or songs, repetition, and writing things out are all incredibly powerful memory and study aides. Try adding movements or actions or sounds, and have fun. Remember that humans learn most rapidly between birth and 3 years of age, and a lot of that was fun-based repetition learning, so no magic is involved in NLP; it's merely an appreciation of differing methods.

In addition to that general advice, we offer three specific hints to make your experience more productive:

- **Discover your best learning environment.** Figure out where and how you can most effectively focus on learning. For some, sitting in the living room with the family as they watch football may be the appropriate place, while others require silence and isolation to best comprehend what they read. Whatever your personal needs, if you plan to study, memorise, and adopt the sales techniques in this book, you need to make the most of the time you set aside for that purpose.

- **Study at a pace that fits you.** Some people learn better when they read little bits of information and give themselves a chance to internalise what they've learned. Others like to take big clumps of information at one sitting so they can see the bigger picture and understand the full concept of what is being presented.

- **Limit your interruptions.** Set up a regular time to study, and let your family and friends know that you'll be unavailable during this time. Let your answering machine screen your calls and turn off your mobile phone. If your concentration skills are anywhere near average, you need 8 to 10 minutes after being interrupted to regain the concentration level you were at before the interruption. Getting 30 minutes of uninterrupted reading and studying is better than patching together four or five interrupted periods to equal an hour of study time. If you can't hide out for a long period of time, cut your time or break it into two sessions in order to maximise your learning.

By analysing your optimum learning patterns and working with them, your attitude about the material being studied will be positive. You'll be more relaxed and definitely learn at a faster pace.

Have Realistic Expectations

Reading this book and continuing to study sales can help you use common sales techniques in unique ways. But recognise that more than one way of selling exists! Don't feel lousy if you don't quite remember the same sequence of questions or don't mimic exactly the conversation style suggested in this book. Instead, add to the structure a unique part of you – and the result will be even richer. We're not trying to turn out uniform little sales clones by having everyone who reads this book say the same words and practise the same methods at the expense of their own individuality.

If you take from this book ideas you hadn't thought of before and combine them with the sales experience you already have, you'll lend to the selling situation a flavour that's all your own. But you need to *adapt* some of this material in order to create a genuine presentation and communicate naturally with the customer. Make the material your own. Use the ingredients as a base and bake your own cake.

Be patient with yourself. Don't expect to be a winner 100 per cent of the time. On the other hand, be honest with yourself and recognise times when inadequate knowledge or an inaccurate application of new selling techniques has kept you from giving your best performance.

Know your limitations, but don't be bound by them. Do what you know you should do, do it the best way you know how, and stay on the lookout for ways to improve your selling skills.

Keep an Open Mind and Welcome Change

Wanting to shrink back into your old ways when things get tough is only natural, especially if you experienced some success through your old methods. Nobody ever said that change would be easy. Think what those poor little caterpillars have to go through to become butterflies. The truth is that many people have a resistance to change and fear the unknown, so you're the same as everyone else. The difference you want to add is that you can *Feel The Fear and Do It Anyway*, as the wonderful book by Susan Jeffers (Random House) says. What stands winners apart from the rest is that they don't let fear hold them back.

If you have a difficult time with change, adopting some of the techniques in this book will require a supreme effort on your part. Most of the time, changing your old selling habits is harder than trying new ones.

To better accommodate change, select only a few things to alter at first. No matter how much you need to work on, you're likely to be too distracted and fragmented if you try to change everything at once. Changing all your selling skills at once is like going on a diet, setting out to become super-fit, and giving up smoking, all at the same time. Not an easy thing to do. For best results, choose two things to change that can significantly increase your sales. Work on those aspects of your performance until they become normal parts of your routine. When that happens, choose two more new selling skills to practise or change.

During this period of change or improvement, you're likely to go through the normal feelings of anxiety and confusion. Sometimes your presentation may be awkward or rough around the edges. Just think of yourself as a diamond in the rough – as soon as you get some polish and put yourself in the proper setting, you can outshine them all.

As these new ideas become more natural to use and as the process of selling becomes second nature, then your selling practices naturally spread to become a part of you as a person – you'll always be talking in such a manner of optimism and questioning. Please note that your family may need to adjust to the new you! They're comfortable and familiar with the old you and as your wings spread and your head rises to look for bigger and better outcomes, some of your close friends and family members will notice and even possibly ridicule you. But hang in there. When you've cracked your new approach they'll be supremely proud of your achievements – and willing to help you spend the rewards!

If you remain open-minded and flexible, you can welcome the changes necessary for a successful career in sales.

Rehearse, Perform, and Critique Your New Skills

After you internalise and absorb some of your new selling techniques, you need to practise them. At first, go over them by yourself until you feel confident enough to practise them in front of your family, friends, or peers who can give you some important pointers.

Ben vividly remembers repeating over and over again a scripted sales presentation many years ago. Okay, scripted isn't how we recommend that you do it today, but rehearsing how to get across your points is always good. And if you have to wear out that bedroom carpet and stare endlessly into the mirror to get it right, then that's what you have to do. Then aim for a dry run – not a live client audience but an audience nonetheless – to get some feedback.

If you get advice from people you respect, listen! On the other hand, if you get unsolicited advice from people you don't respect, don't let them share in your learning experience: Their responses may damage your delicate psyche. Your confidence is tender and fragile at the beginning, so be careful about who you perform in front of.

Performing new selling skills and concepts in front of strangers may be scary but don't beat yourself up. Give yourself permission to be a novice, but be sure to follow the novice rules:

- ✔ Give yourself many, many opportunities to perfect your new selling techniques.

- ✔ When you look back, feed the positive – celebrate all the things you did right.

- ✔ Hold on to your novice enthusiasm even when you become a polished sales professional.

The client or prospect doesn't know what you were supposed to say, so he doesn't know you got it wrong. A mistake matters not! Critique your performance of your new skills with an honest but fair eye. You can judge yourself only after you've performed your new skills for an extended period of time and can see measurable increases in your sales. If you have a sales manager, this person is your obvious first port of call for support and critical feedback. The ratio of closed sales to total sales is a key benchmark for seeing how much you improve. The scenario might be that in the beginning you visit 20 people to get a sale and then after a month you visit only 8 people to get a sale, and so on. Seeing positive results gives you something tangible to encourage a continued pattern of improvement.

If a specific stumbling block keeps inhibiting your sales growth, ask another sales professional you respect for some advice. Sometimes taking such a person along on a presentation or recording a meeting and critiquing it together can be a big help. In fact, you may be surprised to review a recorded presentation and discover all the things you could have done differently. Critiquing a recorded presentation gives you some distance from the excitement and anxiety of the initial meeting and allows you to look at your performance more objectively. You'll be amazed at how many things you don't remember and how many things you'd have sworn you never did, and some of it will make you cringe, but deconstructing your performance in this way can be constructive fun. Go on – try it!

Personalise Your New Sales Skills

No magic wand can help you memorise concepts and specific words; you just need to repeat them until you have them 'parrot fashion'. But do *not* memorise whole passages! The idea is to learn a structure and add your own detail and personality – use a tried-and-tested skeleton but add your flesh. Just learning the basic structure means you won't be panicky and stressed about what you might forget.

Just memorising phrases and then shutting off your personality and resorting to a robot imitation whenever you get desperate is the worst thing you can do. Always remember to be genuine and personable as you sell. Being yourself is almost impossible to do if you haven't made the concepts you've learned uniquely yours by wrapping them in your own words and actions. The last thing you want your clients to feel is that they're being given a scripted presentation.

Be Disciplined

If you crave the financial and personal freedom that a successful sales career can provide, you have to be willing to go the extra mile. If that means working on a Friday night when all your friends are at an office party, then so be it. If that means getting up hours earlier each morning until you master your new skills, then that's what you must do. If that means no more two-hour lunches or lazy afternoons for a while, then make the sacrifice.

Be a self-disciplined self-starter, and eventually you'll reap rewards.

Failing to *continue* to push is one of the major pitfalls of great success in a short period of time. Too many people want victories without battles. Too many want a quick fix with no pain and then want to rest on their laurels when they know they're good. Slowing down after achieving success quickly is a dangerous mistake. The fact that you've tasted some success doesn't mean that you can stop. Your success may have been justly deserved but nothing is a permanent right. If your new-found success slows down, the slippery slope down is a lot faster than the climb back up.

Stay on your feet and run the race to the finish. Don't allow yourself the luxury of self-doubts or overconfidence – they're production killers. The real trick is to remain balanced during your successes. Don't let increased sales go to your head or repeated rejection beat you down. Although it can be almost impossible at times, always strive to keep your activities and attitudes balanced.

Evaluate the Results

Accurately evaluating the results you're getting with your new-found selling skills is difficult if you don't know what your sales results were before you changed. Sure, you'll have an idea about how things are going, but often you can't trust these feelings. For example, when you're fed up, you tend to feel that everything is going wrong and that you're completely useless – even though it isn't true. During such times, your successes diminish, and you can easily feed the negative feeling until it grows into an unconquerable monster. On the other hand, on days when you're overly optimistic and possibly even cocky, you may conveniently blame a screwed up presentation on the customer and fail to take the necessary steps for self-improvement.

When you evaluate the results of your efforts, avoid comparing your progress to someone else's. Even if the salesperson has received the same training and has read the same books as you, everyone learns differently. Some learn more quickly than others yet can't retain the information for long. Others learn slowly and give the appearance of having fallen behind, when actually they've internalised the information and will receive longer-lasting rewards for their efforts. Some are more suited to certain marketplaces and some are less suited to some products or services. Failing to fly as a massive success in selling kitchen appliances doesn't mean that you cannot sell but possibly that selling travel is more your thing.

Keep a Sales Diary

In the early days of your selling career keeping a *sales diary* to monitor your performance can be extremely helpful. Either in paper format with a simple A4 pad or electronic format with a PDA, or computer, writing a page of notes to report back to yourself what you remember saying, in what order, what response you got, and how you handled the sale is an excellent idea. Your report may never be comprehensive to the word but it can be a great tool for discovering patterns of success. By recording specific instances and details of when you successfully used new selling techniques, you not only immediately reinforce the benefits to your career, but, more importantly, when you need encouragement you can review your journal and relive a positive selling experience. You'll be surprised at what a great motivational tool a sales diary can be.

When you review your sales diary, compare what you did right in a given situation to what you did when you did not get the sale. When you make such a comparison, the reasons for not getting the sale become obvious to you. By comparing an unsuccessful experience to a successful one, you see what you left out or skimmed over and why you failed to convince the customer of the benefits of your offering.

If you can master being honest with yourself – not beating yourself up when you don't make a sale and not 'bigging' yourself up when you do make one – you can create a really useful feedback tool. When you've concentrated on this sales diary for a year or so you'll have a very good grounding and can be excused if you don't continue it, but, like many of us old pros, you may want to carry it on as a sort of war story book!

Think about all your 'If onlys', envision yourself as that master of sales, and then act on your visions. 'If only' is a game of recognising areas that need improvement and then improving them. After you recognise those areas, you need to take action and turn your 'If only' into 'Because I':

> 'If only I had asked more questions' becomes 'Because I asked more questions, I closed the sale.'

> 'If only I had been able to overcome the client's objections with more skill' becomes 'Because I successfully overcame the client's objections, he was able to benefit by owning my offering.'

Don't keep your sales diary just to look at and feel regret over the 'If onlys'. Stop longing for perfection. This game is designed to keep you on your toes – like golf! You'll never master the 'If onlys' totally – something or someone will always bring you back down once in a while!

By monitoring and adjusting your new selling skills, you continue to increase your sales ratios. Be diligent and persistent in your self-evaluation, though. Don't just look at your sales once a year and make bold promises about how you'll do things differently at some unspecified future date. Be meticulous in your search for excellence and be *specific* in your plans for improvement.

How effective can a statement such as 'Next year I want to do a bigger volume of business' really be? A specific goal is much clearer and more productive: 'Beginning on 1 January, I will spend two hours more a day prospecting and increase my face-to-face selling by 20 per cent. In the process, I will increase my sales volume by 5 per cent.' This revised statement gives you a more distinct monthly, weekly, and daily activity schedule to follow in order for you to improve.

Learn from Every Selling Situation

You may be surprised at how many unexpected selling situations you notice when you keep your eyes and ears open. You can soon see in almost every situation an opportunity for someone to sell. Not only do you become alert to the selling situation, but you also start to critique the selling skills used in situations that surround you on a daily basis. When you witness a good job of selling, make a note of it in your diary. When a polished professional sells you something, jot down the superior job he did in selling to you. Make specific notes of things that especially impressed or influenced you.

To observe all this selling going on around you, you have to stop, listen, and take time to reflect on the situation. If you are not directly involved in the sale, being an observer is, of course, easier. Not being involved gives you the distance to recognise some of the familiar selling techniques being used. But that distance also enables you to observe the expressions and actions of the other party as a result of these selling techniques.

You may see a salesperson use a common technique with a personal twist and realise that the strategy you previously thought wouldn't work for you most certainly can if you give it an individual tweak. Creativity is the name of the game in many selling situations. Don't let yourself become trapped into one single mode of thinking or one way of looking at things. If you can be flexible, almost anything is possible.

If you're a person who learns by experience, isn't it better to learn from others' mistakes than from your own? Their loss becomes your gain. Remember, the experience you observe doesn't always have to be positive in order to have a positive effect on your selling career. Sometimes the negative lessons have a stronger impact than those that appear smooth and effortless.

Make a Commitment

Think of every technique you read in this book as one link in the chain of your success in sales. If you can identify a weakness, then you may need to review a chapter or two to build, say, your presentation or prospecting skills. If you don't go back and make the weak link stronger, your career chain will never stand the strain of pulling you up to top producer status.

When you find yourself in the fortunate position of top dog, champion salesperson, you'll probably get asked to teach some of what you know to others. The class you teach can be a training session for newcomers to your office; or a back-to-basics programme for seasoned salespeople who've allowed their focus to blur; or it can be as simple as letting your children know what gets results and what doesn't.

If you don't already know it, you re-learn one *big* lesson every time you teach: When you teach, you learn. By teaching your techniques to others, you clarify your own skills and reinforce your knowledge of what makes an effective salesperson. You also remind yourself of things that you used to do as habits and that were partly responsible for your success and that now you've stopped doing. Teachers are students, too. If you can remain flexible, the opportunity to learn in diverse situations will constantly present itself and you'll be there to learn from the experience.

This business of getting what you want cannot be a totally selfish act, though. Your selling success increases at a significant pace when your commitment to serve your clients and satisfy their needs is number one on your list. Even though you want to make more profit and more sales, remember that you're most able to accomplish these goals only when you put your customers first.

When your clients know that you're concerned not just with winning a commission cheque, but that you're putting their needs before your own, they'll forgive some awkwardness or lack of product knowledge. When they know your integrity and honesty, most customers go the extra mile with you to make your meetings mutually beneficial.

People are the key to your sales success. 'The Customer is King', posters always used to say. The client is the focus, not you. Always, always remember you are there for him, not for you. Treat customers with great sensitivity and unflagging respect. Remember this fundamental principle and, before you know it, all the techniques you've mastered will naturally improve your ability to sell with the best of the best.

Chapter 22

Ten Characteristics of Winners

● ●

In This Chapter

▶ Modelling yourself on the best of the best

▶ Fine-tuning your skills to become a champion

● ●

*I*n analysing people who are most successful at persuading or convincing others to buy their products, or services, we've found ten characteristics that appear to be common among them. These winners are winning for a reason. Read through this list and see how many apply to you now. If you don't find these characteristics in your current repertoire, work hard to develop them.

A Burning Desire to Prove Something to Someone

A professional persuader has a strong reason for wanting to succeed.

Ben's story: If I'm honest about *my* core driving situation – about what motivated me in the early days – I can tell you that it was a burning desire to prove to someone that I was worthy. I'm simplifying as an adult the many mixed and confused emotions that were ingrained as a child, but I always felt that coming from a cash-strapped family, with one pair of 'best' trousers in my wardrobe and no pocket money, that I was viewed by my peers as inferior – a view that I substantiated and proved right with my youthful anger directed into being a 'troublemaker'. But the indelible stain was one of needing to prove that I was actually better, and that desire to raise myself pushed me beyond just earning a comfortable income even when I was doing well. I am not alone. Very often that burning desire to prove something to someone is what identifies a top persuader.

An Interest in Others

Professional persuaders are truly interested in other people and in making those people's lives better. They know how to draw others out and make them feel important, and how to get to know their prospects well enough to determine how they can help. While initially success is perhaps attributed to an interest in self, in most cases the interest in self eases and is replaced by interest in others. As the desire to prove yourself fades, the desire to give back and contribute grows.

Confidence and Strength

Professional persuaders radiate confidence and strength in the way they walk and talk and in their overall presence. An 'air' exists about them that other people sense. Their confidence is demonstrated by their good posture and their care and attention to grooming. They wear their clothing well. They use positive body language to emphasise their competence and they've learned to cope with situations better than many around them.

A Force Field of Energy

Winners generally are full of life. A professional salesperson who is used to succeeding is also usually full of energy. And years of selling experience proves to us that people are drawn to that energy on a subconscious level. It appeals to a security and protection instinct, and those who are winners ooze vitality. If you desire to be a winner, work on your energy levels and maintain your genuine 'buzz' (as opposed to one that's caffeine-induced!).

A Focus on Goals

Professional persuaders set themselves clear and precise written goals. They know exactly what they're striving for and when they expect to accomplish it. A winner knows that the route might be twisting but is never fazed or deflected from pushing forward, even if forward only means looking ahead as far as the end of the current month and hitting the sales target. She remains focused on doing what is productive today and is able to prioritise activity so that little or nothing gets in the way of her principal objective – not even leisure time.

An Ability to Stick to Daily Plans

Having set goals for what they want to accomplish, professional persuaders are able each day to plan their time most effectively to take steps towards achieving those goals. The ability to stick to their goals is made possible because of this commitment to managing their time effectively. They rely on proven systems for planning their time and have discovered effective time-management strategies.

Enthusiasm through Difficult Situations

Professional persuaders know the past can't be changed and the future can't be controlled, so they live for the present, striving to make each day one of accomplishment and fulfilment. They don't have a 'devil may care' attitude towards tomorrow, but more an awareness that worrying about what is beyond controlling is a pointless exercise. Much better to enthusiastically focus on what you *can* control and make it happen to the absolute best of your ability.

A Positive Attitude

Maintaining a positive mental attitude is vital. A positive mindset isn't a reliance upon willing away the weeds to make the garden neat without effort, it is the steadfast ability to see the good even when certain issues could be better. Professional persuaders avoid jealousy, gossip, anger, or negative thinking. Winners stay strong when others are tempted to slate a colleague or deride another's character. Staying positive means not even entering into negative conversations – 'if you've nothing good to say, say nothing' applies as these people guard their energy with a positive outlook.

An Understanding That People Come Before Money

Professional persuaders love people and use money instead of loving money and using people. They understand the old adages that you have to spend money to make money and that persuasion is a people business. And they invest wisely in things for the good of the people they serve.

An Investment in Learning

Professional persuaders are lifelong learners. Congratulations! We know you have this trait simply because you're reading this page. Many people allow the sentence 'you learn something new every day' to trip off their tongues but never deliberately try learning anything after they leave school and get their first job. To most ordinary people with ordinary lives and ordinary bank balances, active learning is interpreted as more work, and their inherent lazy nature keeps them in an ordinary comfortable life. Winners are eager to learn, push themselves, and work their minds because they appreciate that all worthwhile rewards and goals have to be worked for. They also realise what too many lazy people fail to see: learning actually is tremendously enjoyable. Professional persuaders recognise this fact and have learned to love learning. So, set a goal to be a lifelong learner, and you never have a dull moment. In addition, you achieve tremendous success in whatever you set your mind to studying!

Chapter 23

Top Ten Tips for Sales Success

*I*f you read much of the preceding pages, you have much to absorb and embrace. But if you have to choose just ten points out of the thoughts and contents throughout the book, choose the ten we digest here.

Start with Preparation and Planning

It goes without saying that proper preparation is paramount to winning a sales challenge, but probably best to say it anyway! Not preparing for any eventuality, not knowing answers, and not checking your equipment before presentations are the behaviour of amateurs. Plan your telephone call, sales meeting, questions, and strategy. Prepare for all eventualities and prepare to be challenged, even when you're hoping for a smoother ride. Prepare for the unexpected and still plan to win.

Your happiness is the most important thing to you. Success can make you happy and content – so planning and preparing for it is crucial. Don't be sloppy, don't try to wing it, and don't be casual about outcomes. Sooner or later the real results show the level of dedication and commitment you apply. People who don't plan properly and get by without being properly prepared do so only for so long. Take control and make sure you plan and prepare properly every time.

Focus on Your Goals

If you don't know where you're going, how will you know when you get there? Goals are paramount to success. Winners don't win by accident; they see success in their mind's eye and they imagine the glory of coming home with an order in the bag and a lead in the team.

In selling, you have plenty of down moments, and if you don't have a huge drive to achieve your goal, you don't succeed. Know what you want and keep it in the front of your mind.

Selling is a fabulous career and a game of great fun but you still need determination and focus to get to the top.

Embrace Punctuality

To a great many people, your being late for a sales appointment or not calling when you said you would or not returning a sales proposal by a specified date is a sign that you don't really have them as your number one priority.

Of course when you're selling, you have lots of clients to handle and many want proposals and calls and you're hard pressed to please them all, so our simple advice is to make fewer promises that are time-relevant. Be conscious that you'll face time pressures and tell the prospect that you'll get the job done but be loose on the specifics or you'll run into trouble. If you promise a definite time in any situation, stick to it or expect to lose the prospect's respect and confidence – and the sale.

Punctuality may seem an insignificant issue, but failing to do something or to be somewhere when you said you would indicates to the buyer that you're prepared to let him down. Such behaviour raises doubts that you'll meet promised delivery dates or make agreed back-up services available or provide requested information. Being late says you care more about you than him. Late says trouble. So be punctual; doing so pays off in the end.

Develop People Skills

In some people's eyes, selling is a career in which you have a selfish and even arrogant attitude. In truth, the real key to winning the selling race is winning with people. Each and every potential client is a person first. He thinks and intellectualises and presents all sorts of body language clues and personality traits but essentially he is a person with feelings and instincts that mostly override his conscious thoughts and steer him towards a choice.

Do you avoid buying from someone you don't like? When you're making a purchase decision, are you aware of instinctive feelings about someone or something? The answer, of course, is yes. The person whom you're trying to convert to your way of thinking about the proposed purchase also has these feelings. He's influenced by his emotional contact with you. Use your people skills to create feelings of warmth and liking in everybody you meet.

Just as every prospective buyer is a person first, remember that you're a person first and a salesperson second.

Consider the Other Person's Perspective

Beware the level of self-focus that destroys the prospect and consumes the seller with bitterness, leaving a trail of frustration and anguish after every sales interaction. Remember that the interaction isn't about *you*! Put the customer first. The prospect's interests are more important than yours. If you get that approach right, you still serve your interests as the sales will happen and you'll achieve the sales targets you hoped for. But focusing on your benefits not your client's is a sure-fire way to shoot yourself in the foot.

In a strange but true paradox, often the more you care about your needs, the less they'll be served, and vice versa – the more you care about the needs of others, the better yours will be looked after. Especially when selling, you must empathise with your prospect and focus upon how best your offering will serve his needs. Whatever happens, never sell something to anyone when you do not genuinely believe that doing so is in his best interests. If you're ever asked to sell in this way to earn a commission, seek employment elsewhere.

Think about how your customer may be feeling – apprehensive about the expense involved or the performance of what you are selling; concerned with juggling his financial obligations, or okaying the purchase with colleagues. All these very real concerns may be swimming through your prospect's mind, so focus on him and not on yourself. Apart from the commissions and glory for you when you make more sales than anyone else, you can also enjoy the sheer pleasure on the face of the prospect who buys happily and thanks you profusely for helping him make the right decision.

Selling is simply the best career ever: You help others fulfil their needs and get paid lots of lovely commission and bonus money in the process! Put others first and come first yourself.

Stop Talking and Listen

Listening to your prospect sounds so easy! Many salespeople, however, are concentrating so much on what they have to say, how they need to say it, and when they can say a little bit more that they miss the point of buying interest. Being quiet isn't easy. You like to tell how good your service or product is, what exactly you or it can do, and just how much better you are than others doing the same thing!

You need to stop talking and let your customer talk instead. Why? Because if you let him talk, he will be like you and talk too much. And when he does so, he'll tell you everything you need to sell to him. Just let him chatter away.

If you're gabbing away nineteen to the dozen, you're too busy to listen to what your client just said or notice that he's looking at his watch as if to say, 'You're boring me!'

Selling is more about listening to a customer's needs and answering them than it is about telling. Indeed, we're made with two ears and one mouth. If the client just said, 'Can I have one in this specification by Monday the 14th?' you may only need to respond 'Yes' and walk away with the order. So don't rabbit on about the 56 benefits and the 100 reasons why your offering is superior. This information isn't relevant!

Say less and earn more.

Ask More Questions

Too many salespeople are surprisingly weak at asking questions. You need to think of non-work-related questions so that you can become a skilled people person. Devise a bank of questions that involve a personal interaction, not just a simple answer. Use these questions to uncover the emotions involved in the selling cycle, such as fear of not getting the right product or fear of poor image when choosing the wrong provider or product supply.

And don't forget you also still need to ask the direct questions that relate to how the prospect perceives your offering alongside his need. Asking what he wants, why he wants it, and other direct questions is pretty basic (although you'd be surprised by how many people don't even ask these questions) – but paramount is asking for the order. Many salespeople just explain the product and the benefits and wait for the client to say, 'Okay, I'll have it!'. This scenario doesn't happen; you have to ask.

Take Your Time

Salespeople the world over are seen as a threat to the poor purchasing partner in any transaction as the seller is perceived as a marauding pirate rampaging through the wallet of the enquiring party. So the defence mechanisms invented by these poor innocent buying types now include a repertoire of excuses designed to put off the marauders. Not having time is a favourite excuse.

A fundamental flaw in thinking when selling is to believe that your time must match or become the client's, that because he said he has an hour, he means only one hour and therefore you have to sell your product or service in the hour! *Wrong!* First, he isn't going to kick you out if he's genuinely interested after one hour, and even if he does he'll want you back to complete the process. Remain professional and take your time.

Limiting a sales appointment time is a defence mechanism that has proven to work with many salespeople. When hearing that time is limited, some salespeople give up almost before they get started and shorten the presentation, leaving the buyer less pressured and unarmed with the facts he needs, such as price. In fact, setting a time limit is a comfort thing. The buyer realises that he might become more comfortable with the idea of buying the longer you are with him and thus as he's trying hard at this stage not to buy, he's programmed to get you out of there before he warms to you and gives in.

Also, people do not like to spend money quickly! Money takes too long to earn and is in limited supply, so what you have you spend slowly and carefully. For many people, one hour isn't enough to spend larger sums of money.

The time taken to sell your product is, of course, relative to the cost, but ultimately people buy from people, so the time taken for human interaction and for personalities to gel is what decides the sale. Slow down, allow for a relaxing of the buying fears and a warming of the personalities, and you'll make more sales. Do *not* listen when a prospect offers a time constraint as a reason for you to hurry up. Trying to shorten or condense your presentation will hold you back. You won't be seen in any better light and you aren't going to be in with a chance to make a sale. Keep to your normal pattern – you need time to gel. Give your presentation your best effort or don't do it at all.

Stay Strong!

Fear of failure is one of the biggest areas of weakness for many salespeople. This fear leads to crazy reactions in the middle of a selling situation that destroy much of the good work already done. Salespeople are prone to becoming weak!

For example, they might feel that the customer is looking at competitors and making comparisons across the offerings. The prospect may mention and even clearly state that he's looking at competitors' wares, but rarely does a prospect mention that he didn't like anything else that he'd seen – and this is just as likely as that he liked the other offerings more than yours. Usually a competitor that is both better *and* cheaper doesn't exist.

At times, though, an advanced stage of paranoia and competitor fear creeps in, swamps the rational mind, and releases a crazed psychotic! Believing that the prospect is about to choose a competitor and favour a cheaper offering, the seller sweeps down from his higher-than-thou perch and offers an amazing reduced price and series of giveaways to sweep the purchaser off his business feet and ensure that the order is safely in the bag as he swaggers home full of pride at a job well done. Or he might experience a resistance when asking for an order and immediately offer further benefits when the prospect was merely pausing and the added inducements weren't needed. A moment of weakness can mean a lost commission and make the swagger home seriously unwarranted – the job was definitely not well done!

Becoming weak kills profits and doesn't get more sales. On the contrary, you can win more sales at a better margin when you project the professional commitment that strength portrays in a selling situation.

Make Them Yearn

Some people won't want to make a decision to buy an offering simply because they feel they can make the decision at any time. And this may be true, unless you're working on a special offer or limited quantity of product.

As a child, if you knew you were good at a sport, but someone said you weren't good enough for the team, you probably wanted to be on the team more than ever. No one wants to be thought of as not good enough for something. By subtly implying that you have to see if your prospect qualifies before he can own the product, he may try awfully hard to get it. This tactic works especially well on products that involve financing or insurance (which may require the client to meet a certain health standard). If customers want your product, they can have it. Your job is to make them want it *more* by making it difficult to obtain. You can use a pricing strategy, a discounting strategy, or a timing and availability strategy, but however you do it, keep your offering just out of reach.

Everyone wants what they can't have; this has been human nature since Adam bit into the apple. If something is out of reach, it has more appeal. So stop making your product or service so freely available!

Chapter 24

Ten of the Best Web Sites for Sales Professionals

In This Chapter

▶ Knowing where to turn for the latest and greatest sales information online

▶ Researching your choices for software systems that streamline performance

▶ Finding great forums and idea centres to keep you ahead of the pack

*W*e hope this book gives you all you need for success in selling. However, we can't resist sharing our favourite Web sites here to further inspire you. If you've been online for a while, you may have already found the benefits offered by these businesses. If not, check them out and consider adding them to your Favourites list in your Web browser.

The Business Booster

www.thebusinessbooster.co.uk

If we don't believe that our own sites are helpful to salespeople, we shouldn't be writing this book.

Ben's programme, The Business Booster, is a highly energised and supremely effective two-day event that will transform your sales and business experience. The material is also available in CD or book format to keep you buzzing. You can join our community and receive newsletters and even get hold of Ben personally if you so desire. Links also exist to our other sites that hold a mass of resource and live event information. How do you learn best: through CD, printed book, online training, live seminar, or video? Ben has them all.

Tom Hopkins International at www.tomhopkins.com is another must-visit site. Visit the site now for free newsletters packed with tips and inspiration for sales champions.

ABC Training and Development

www.abctd.co.uk

If you're looking for sales support or a connection with more sales professionals, this site is a superb doorway for you to visit regularly. The content is ever evolving but always dedicated to the mission of making training and development available for people in a selling and business situation. Books, videos, and network contacts are all actively promoted. The site is a usable and valuable resource.

Modern Selling

www.modernselling.com

This Web site is an excellent resource for anyone in selling. It is fresh, informative, and easy to use. You can read articles on people's experiences and views in the world of selling and you can also plan your year to include attending many of the seminars or speaking events highlighted. As with some other sites many of the leaders are available via forums and any and all of the contributors are willing to pass on advice if you have a specific challenge. The features cover lots of helpful topics, the people featured are at the top of the game, and you can subscribe to a community newsletter for free. Get on, get in, and enjoy!

Toastmasters International

www.toastmasters.co.uk

Whether you're a professional, student, stay-at-home parent, or retiree, Toastmasters is the best way to improve your communication skills – and you don't need to be classed as a professional speaker to join. Toastmasters can help you lose the fear of public speaking and gain skills that will help you be more successful in whatever path you choose. You'll be a better listener. You'll easily lead teams and conduct meetings. You'll comfortably give and receive constructive evaluation. You already have some or all of these skills, but through Toastmasters, you enhance them.

They have regular meetings in a town near you where you can meet up with loads of great connections – what are you waiting for?

The Professional Speakers Association (www.professionalspeakers. org) also offers assistance in improving your public speaking.

Resource Development International

www.rdi.co.uk

This site is where to go if you need education relevant to the corporate world. The site offers a host of great courses and a variety of training choices to suit all budgets, needs, and environments. Your company may want to consider customising some of the courses to your particular needs. This company is a terrific source of reference on the best sales and management information available today.

The Sales Board

www.thesalesboard.com

This American site is well put together, with an excellent list of courses that you can download and embrace to make your performance rocket. Explore the site and take the bits that fit where you are and what you're selling. You can find useful technique appraisals that you can compare to your role and how you sell or approach a prospect. The content depth is worthy of digging through; the site has everything from prospecting ideas to closing techniques.

Goldmine

www.goldmine.co.uk or **www.frontrange.co.uk**

We've banged the drum pretty much all of the way through this book to the tune of 'get a good contact management system to drive your career forward'. Goldmine (and its sister site Front Range) is the best in our humble opinion for value and performance. Now, your employer may have other options and ideas, but if they haven't, you absolutely *must* get hold of this and take charge of your life. The product is easy to learn and the support and back-up through a range of dealerships is superb. Don't ever be wanting for the lack of contact details again.

Sandler Sales Institute

www.sandler.com

This Web site is another American-based resource, but it's franchised throughout the UK. To find a franchise, go to the main Web site and search country options. Essentially this is an introduction site that also provides some useful taster guides. The site has a long list of UK agents and Ben recommends them because he's had the pleasure of working alongside the Birmingham-based agent and knows that the training is excellent and will be very useful to add to your skill base. Ultimately, 'there is nothing new under the sun' as the Good Book tells us but this Web site offers a different slant and is well worth investing in if you really want to improve your performance.

Peter Thomson International

www.peterthomson.com

Peter is probably the most established name in the UK for growing businesses and people and has been at the forefront of sales development for over 20 years. Ben has had the good fortune to meet him on several occasions and has learned a huge amount from him. Peter's personal impact has been massive. We wholeheartedly encourage you to join in his community and get hold of his books and tapes – you'll only do yourself a disservice if you don't.

Anthony Robbins

www.tonyrobbins.com

The path of career success needs more than just a focus upon selling. Such success depends on a balance and a wholesome approach to mankind and the greater scheme of things. We cannot give you any greater advice than to investigate all that Tony Robbins does. He has helped change the lives of literally millions of people globally in the last 20 years through his championing of personal development. We all have challenges and belief systems and these are hugely influential in the performance of our careers and family life. Working through everything that Tony Robbins has produced will launch you to even greater heights. Make doing so a priority: Get his books and CD programmes, and attend a live event if you can. You can actually achieve anything you set your heart on!

Index

FOR DUMMIES®

Do Anything. Just Add Dummies

PROPERTY

UK editions

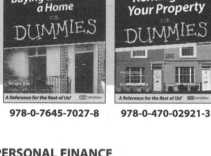

978-0-7645-7027-8   **978-0-470-02921-3**   **978-0-7645-7047-6**

PERSONAL FINANCE

978-0-7645-7023-0   **978-0-470-51510-5**   **978-0-470-05815-2**

BUSINESS

978-0-7645-7018-6   **978-0-7645-7056-8**   **978-0-7645-7026-1**

Answering Tough Interview
Questions For Dummies
(978-0-470-01903-0)

Arthritis For Dummies
(978-0-470-02582-6)

Being the Best Man
For Dummies
(978-0-470-02657-1)

British History
For Dummies
(978-0-470-03536-8)

Building Self Confidence
For Dummies
(978-0-470-01669-5)

Buying a Home on a Budget
For Dummies
(978-0-7645-7035-3)

Children's Health
For Dummies
(978-0-470-02735-6)

Cognitive Behavioural Therapy
For Dummies
(978-0-470-01838-5)

Cricket For Dummies
(978-0-470-03454-5)

CVs For Dummies
(978-0-7645-7017-9)

Detox For Dummies
(978-0-470-01908-5)

Diabetes For Dummies
(978-0-470-05810-7)

Divorce For Dummies
(978-0-7645-7030-8)

DJing For Dummies
(978-0-470-03275-6)

eBay.co.uk For Dummies
(978-0-7645-7059-9)

English Grammar For Dummies
(978-0-470-05752-0)

Gardening For Dummies
(978-0-470-01843-9)

Genealogy Online
For Dummies
(978-0-7645-7061-2)

Green Living For Dummies
(978-0-470-06038-4)

Hypnotherapy For Dummies
(978-0-470-01930-6)

Life Coaching For Dummies
(978-0-470-03135-3)

Neuro-linguistic Programming
For Dummies
(978-0-7645-7028-5)

Nutrition For Dummies
(978-0-7645-7058-2)

Parenting For Dummies
(978-0-470-02714-1)

Pregnancy For Dummies
(978-0-7645-7042-1)

Rugby Union For Dummies
(978-0-470-03537-5)

Self Build and Renovation For
Dummies
(978-0-470-02586-4)

Starting a Business on
eBay.co.uk For Dummies
(978-0-470-02666-3)

Starting and Running an Online
Business For Dummies
(978-0-470-05768-1)

The GL Diet For Dummies
(978-0-470-02753-0)

The Romans For Dummies
(978-0-470-03077-6)

Thyroid For Dummies
(978-0-470-03172-8)

UK Law and Your Rights
For Dummies
(978-0-470-02796-7)

Writing a Novel and Getting
Published For Dummies
(978-0-470-05910-4)

FOR DUMMIES®

Do Anything. Just Add Dummies

HOBBIES

Poker FOR DUMMIES — A Reference for the Rest of Us!
978-0-7645-5232-8

Sewing FOR DUMMIES — A Reference for the Rest of Us!
978-0-7645-6847-3

Drawing FOR DUMMIES — A Reference for the Rest of Us!
978-0-7645-5476-6

Also available:

Art For Dummies (978-0-7645-5104-8)

Aromatherapy For Dummies (978-0-7645-5171-0)

Bridge For Dummies (978-0-471-92426-5)

Card Games For Dummies (978-0-7645-9910-1)

Chess For Dummies (978-0-7645-8404-6)

Improving Your Memory For Dummies (978-0-7645-5435-3)

Massage For Dummies (978-0-7645-5172-7)

Meditation For Dummies (978-0-471-77774-8)

Photography For Dummies (978-0-7645-4116-2)

Quilting For Dummies (978-0-7645-9799-2)

EDUCATION

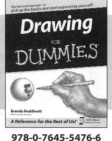

Cooking Basics FOR DUMMIES — A Reference for the Rest of Us!
978-0-7645-7206-7

The Koran FOR DUMMIES — A Reference for the Rest of Us!
978-0-7645-5581-7

Anatomy & Physiology FOR DUMMIES — A Reference for the Rest of Us!
978-0-7645-5422-3

Also available:

Algebra For Dummies (978-0-7645-5325-7)

Algebra II For Dummies (978-0-471-77581-2)

Astronomy For Dummies (978-0-7645-8465-7)

Buddhism For Dummies (978-0-7645-5359-2)

Calculus For Dummies (978-0-7645-2498-1)

Forensics For Dummies (978-0-7645-5580-0)

Islam For Dummies (978-0-7645-5503-9)

Philosophy For Dummies (978-0-7645-5153-6)

Religion For Dummies (978-0-7645-5264-9)

Trigonometry For Dummies (978-0-7645-6903-6)

PETS

Puppies FOR DUMMIES — A Reference for the Rest of Us!
978-0-470-03717-1

Dog Training FOR DUMMIES — A Reference for the Rest of Us!
978-0-7645-8418-3

Cats FOR DUMMIES — A Reference for the Rest of Us!
978-0-7645-5275-5

Also available:

Labrador Retrievers For Dummies (978-0-7645-5281-6)

Aquariums For Dummies (978-0-7645-5156-7)

Birds For Dummies (978-0-7645-5139-0)

Dogs For Dummies (978-0-7645-5274-8)

Ferrets For Dummies (978-0-7645-5259-5)

Golden Retrievers For Dummies (978-0-7645-5267-0)

Horses For Dummies (978-0-7645-9797-8)

Jack Russell Terriers For Dummies (978-0-7645-5268-7)

Puppies Raising & Training Diary For Dummies (978-0-7645-0876-9)

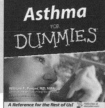

FOR DUMMIES®

INTERNET

The Internet FOR DUMMIES
978-0-470-12174-0

Search Engine Optimization FOR DUMMIES
978-0-471-97998-2

Creating Web Pages FOR DUMMIES
978-0-470-08030-6

Also available:

Building a Web Site For Dummies, 2nd Edition
(978-0-7645-7144-2)

Blogging For Dummies
(978-0-471-77084-8)

eBay.co.uk For Dummies
(978-0-7645-7059-9)

Web Analysis For Dummies
(978-0-470-09824-0)

Web Design For Dummies, 2nd Edition
(978-0-471-78117-2)

Creating Web Pages All-in-One Desk Reference For Dummies, 3rd Edition
(978-0-470-09629-1)

DIGITAL MEDIA

Digital Photography FOR DUMMIES
978-0-7645-9802-9

iPod & iTunes FOR DUMMIES
978-0-470-04894-8

Digital SLR Cameras & Photography FOR DUMMIES
978-0-7645-9803-6

Also available:

Photoshop CS3 For Dummies
(978-0-470-11193-2)

Podcasting For Dummies
(978-0-471-74898-4)

Digital Photography All-In-One Desk Reference For Dummies
(978-0-470-03743-0)

Digital Photo Projects For Dummies
(978-0-470-12101-6)

BlackBerry For Dummies
(978-0-471-75741-2)

Zune For Dummies
(978-0-470-12045-3)

COMPUTER BASICS

PCs FOR DUMMIES
978-0-7645-8958-4

Laptops FOR DUMMIES
978-0-470-05432-1

Windows Vista FOR DUMMIES
978-0-471-75421-3

Also available:

Macs For Dummies, 9th Edition
(978-0-470-04849-8)

Windows Vista All-in-One Desk Reference For Dummies
(978-0-471-74941-7)

Office 2007 All-in-One Desk Reference For Dummies
(978-0-471-78279-7)

Windows XP For Dummies, 2nd Edition
(978-0-7645-7326-2)

PCs All-in-One Desk Reference For Dummies, 3rd Edition
(978-0-471-77082-4)

Upgrading & Fixing PCs For Dummies, 7th Edition
(978-0-470-12102-3)